CONNAÎTRE SACRAL OLO

THE MEANING OF **A METAPHORICAL LIFE COMPANION: THE CENSORED EDITION**

in Periculus AudAx

Collaborated by

Enthusiast i. P. audAx, Transformed i.P. audAx, and God

authorHOUSE®

AuthorHouse™
1663 Liberty Drive
Bloomington, IN 47403
www.authorhouse.com
Phone: 1 (800) 839-8640

Published by AuthorHouse   12/05/2018

ISBN: 978-1-5462-6612-9 (sc)
ISBN: 978-1-5462-6611-2 (e)

Th is book is printed on acid-free paper.

"Dedication

I dedicate this book to [the following people:]

- [T]he married marrieds and the single singles.

- [T]he man with whom I was able to release some pent up puberty energy without having intercourse.

- [...] [T]he first man I ever had sex with[1].

---

[1] Older i.P. audAx:

- The father of my future children.

- The Artist Formerly Known as Prince, for reconciling sex with religion.

- Aleister Crowley, the man who popularized thelemic sex magick.

- The man with whom I shared a past life with as a soldier fighting for the same cause.

- One of my [former] female penpals.

- I also dedicate this to Skitter, the main character in the written comic serial, *Worm*, with whom I share many similarities: lost a mother, bullied in high school, had an ability I struggled to control, did all the wrong things for the right reasons (such as using people as a means to an end), took care of my people but found heroism awkward, got around by foot or flight, and had to leave my friends behind to affect many more lives.

- Lastly, this book is dedicated to The One Who Taught with the Pen.

Warning:

This is not for the

faint of heart.

Table of Contents

Excerpts from The Introduction of The Meaning of a Metaphorical Life

Definitions[2]

There are two sets of definitions in this book: society's definitions and my definitions. To understand myself better I noticed the importance of creating my own definitions so that I could make better sense of life. Life could almost be figured out if we knew the definitions of certain terms. I grew up as Protestant [sic] and I noticed that The Bible uses certain terms continually but never gives a definition for them. Since we all grow up learning different definitions of the same terms [sic] it gives much room for translation. *The Bible* is customized to us, Protestants say. But that sure makes understanding the Bible confusing. We can only infer the definition of a term by the context of the term, but a term that is praised in *The Bible* can be despised in society and vice versa. After some thought, I realized that pride, for instance, is not necessarily a "bad" thing and humble is not always godinterm[3], though they are portrayed as such in *The Bible*, and the reason for that is because the definitions [sic] dictionaries give are not the definitions used in *The Bible*. I will explain at the end of the book what I think my definitions for terms should be according to the life I have lived. You may need to reference it while you read[4].

---

[2] Acronyms:

AIDS=Acquired immune deficiency syndrome

BV=Bacterial vaginosis

[The] H=Herpes

HIV=Human immunodeficiency virus

[The Big] O=Orgasm

STD=Sexually transmitted disease

T=Testosterone

VD=Venereal disease

[3] *See* Appendix A: New Terms

[4] *See* Appendix A: New Terms

1

Why You Should Read This Book

One learns through experience. I will become your experience. I know that some people will never do the things that I have done. Some people will forever be denied access to what I have access to understanding and will have access to what I do not understand. This is why this book is so large and with so much information. What is a book that excels even the Bible? You. Due to geographical differences, I cannot provide you the love you need and cannot provide a listening ear; I cannot hold your hand and look into your eyes, but I am trying to give you the next best thing. I can only hope that this is not a futile effort, that my life has not been wasted on deaf ears or blind eyes. If nothing else, *I just want you to know that I exist.*

Gail Godwin: About This Book[5]

All of this book is based on focus free [sic], or stream of consciousness, notes taken from age twelve to twenty-one (or more specifically, the end of college), with the exception of some transitional sentences. I have used other material before age twelve that were not notes. All dialogue has been accurately recorded since it was recorded the day of the event soon after I heard the dialogue. I took very accurate notes. I am glad that it is in my adolescence that I have written so many notes because it prompts my memory to remind me how life was when I was younger. The notes I took varied in size of font, in medium, and in writing utensils[6]. Most notes ran together so I had to decipher from context where an idea would end. The notes I had from senior year of high school until senior year of college filled seven Amazon.com boxes, not to mention random notes I typed and saved on computer. I also included diary entries from childhood that only filled a box or two. I began typing my notes into a computer in the beginning of my junior year of college. I felt that I had stabilized enough by then to handle the emotions that stirred in me in high school[7].

---

[5] Older i.P. audAx: Regarding the footnotes, I am the sponsor of my own 17-year-old self.

[6] Older i.P. audAx: This is the first book that is a giant quotation, as the technology had not been previously available (e.g., the ability to mark up a portable document file) nor used for this purpose. It is the first autobiography with alteration of proper names beyond the people's names, extensive quotations, a list of neologisms, self-made poetry, and references to websites that gives credit to God as the author. It is the first autobiography with extensive use of Microslop's and Page's reference capabilities: an index, MLA-formatted bibliography, cross-references, and footnotes. The encyclopedia-like quality makes it accessible for a history or psychology course, rather than just a literature course. Also, the headings in themselves stimulate cognitions and curiosity.

[7] Older i.P. audAx: In reference to the section, New Old, I felt that enough time had passed by 2018 to see everything that happened previous to 2016 more clearly.

Some days I would do nothing all day, but type, even when it hurt my wrists. I edited by cutting out unnecessary and redundant diary entries[8]. I have tried to keep the notes exactly as I have written them.

---

[8] Older I.P. Audax: And changing names for privacy (not just names of people). Since this is an interactive book (meaning the references can be googled), I have replaced as many proper nouns as possible, including school names, screen names, restaurant names, and store names with names that did not previously exist in the context of this book. (As far as the reader is concerned, I lived in a generic suburban town near the nation's capital.) I have treated this entire book as a quote. I used "[sic]" to indicate a grammatical error, but in New Olo I did not add "[…]" to indicate omitted text. [However, in Old Olo I did.]

Note: Before I turned it into an uneditable PDF, I made a few global changes that affected the grammar of some sentences. If I found those, I returned them to their original state, before the global changes.

Old Olo: Ages 16-21[9]

Preface[10]

Read this book as a learner of wisdom, not as an immature, horny being[11].

P.S. Any believer in the book Olo shall be called an Oloian.

Introduction to Olo (No Shame)[12]

It is apparent that the most pressing concerns all have to do with sex and the only way to get us out of our hole[13] is to learn about sex. I have seen many people stricken with guilt over sexual pleasures [sic] and this guilt would destroy their entire life[14]. I bring this book to show how one can enjoy sexual pleasures with a full set of ethical codes differing from the present society's set of ethical codes. I plan to release those with higher-than-average sex drives from condemnation to hell (unless they have stygiophilia or pecattiphilia and actually get off on the idea). I have noticed in my lifetime the trend of people immersed in the sexual lifestyle to either go insane and commit suicide or become reinstated into the "normal" way of life, neither of which I think are good[15]. All of this is due to the mindset that what they are doing is sinful.

Even if my philosophy concerning sex is completely "incorrect," I still believe that of all times it is quite imperative that someone at least tries to reconcile Christianity with the growing

---

[9] Older i.P. audAx: Written from.

[10] Nothing has been fictionalized, but names have been changed to protect individuals.

[11] But if you must, you must.

[12] Disclaimer: These are my heterodox opinions.

[13] Older i.P. audAx: No pun intended.

[14] Older i.P. audAx: And make them quite unpleasant to deal with.

[15] Older i.P. audAx: Meaning neither of these require a great deal of critical thinking.

sexuality prevalent in society[16]. This is because the woes of our country at the present have to do mostly with sex [...] [Also,] the churches are mostly so weak and political[17] that they are [sometimes] helpless to help the causes out there: wimmin's[18] rights, homosexual rights, children out of wedlock, interracial marriage, and a whole slew of others[19]. Due to this conflict of sexual topics [sic] so many people have been turning away from God or else have turned toward God without understanding a thing about Him. [...] Sex is one of those subjects that the more my generation understands [sic] the least they understand because it has become for them like an abused substance. This section is written especially for the people who think sex is simple and is just an act of putting a penis in a vagina. There are certain ways to learn in this world. The best way is usually experience, but if one is weak in guts [sic] the second best way is through vicarious living[20]. I sought to discover the inner workings of the world through sex [sic] and I bring you what I have learned. I have nothing to hide about myself. I have all the reason to share. How many people do you know will have sex for the "good of humankind"?[21]

Marriage[22]

No matter what lies you are told [sic] a bad sex life can possibly destroy a marriage. Life is made up of relationships [sic] and the relationship many people give the most attention to is their romantic relationship. There is nothing more damaging to a romantic relationship than ignorance about sex. And yet, even though you might see it everywhere in the media, it is still not discussed as a serious political topic[23]. When people say they talk about sex [sic] it is more often in the form

---

[16] Older i.P. audAx: Something a lot of people conveniently ignore is that Islam came from Christianity and Christianity came from the Jewish religion. Jews are comfortable with their sexuality and the sexuality of others in ways that one would be hard-pressed to find in the other two. In terms of sexuality alone, Christianity has seemed to become less and less freeing and more and more suppressive. Isn't it interesting how the truth sets you free?

[17] Older i.P. audAx: In essence, creating secular Christian churches by putting pressure on religious leaders.

[18] See Appendix A: New Terms

[19] Older i.P. audAx: Like natural family planning.

[20] Older i.P. audAx: It might even turn you on if you have vicarphilia, arousal from others' sexual experiences.

[21] Older i.P. audAx: The reason why Jesus is so against passing judgment is because there is nothing more debilitating to our freedom than worrying about what people think. The irony here is that to free others from worry about what people think, I had to worry about what people thought [meaning I needed a tendency toward sexual compulsion] just to have experience that could allow me to help others eradicate such worry from themselves.

[22] See New Olo for more discussion about marriage.

[23] And even when it is, the actual mechanics are not discussed.

of flirtation or openness, but it is still not used to increase working knowledge. Besides in the media, why does no one ever talk about sex frankly?

The happier people can joke about sex; the unhappy people think that to talk about it is so horrible[24]. My argument for sex: I have heard that guys mostly think about sex more than anything else collectively and if God created men first as God's likeness[25] then what does that say about God? Wimmin were created for their companionship. In the happiest marriages [sic] the spouses remain sexually active.

The happier people are the ones who believe God created sex (well, he did, for reproduction). The unhappy ones are the ones who give up sex with disgust and believe the Devil created it. Sex is like anything that is godinterm[26]. It is wonderful until you abuse it and do not know how to use it, as long as we do not use it as a weapon to hurt anyone. If humans seek happiness, as Aristotle said, then why should they not love sex? I know happiness is the way to go, for all these rules that God created are for our benefit so that we can be truly happy. It is so sad that many people do not understand this. Maybe it is godinterm that I was born with superpower hormones (a large clitoris[27]) and was born into an environment that gave me a godinterm moral education. Due to my upbringing, I can look at sex in a logical perspective. I am sure that sex is godinterm. I have seen so much unhappiness from the denial of this fact.

Many people see marriage as a happy ending, but is it really or is it just a prerequisite to being parents, whether good or abusive? Love does not conquer everything[28].

Revolution

Humans are the only creatures that are called ["]perverted["]. But do you know what I think is very perverse? Attempting to hinder what is natural: stifling the human ["]need[".] Sex was born with womyn[29]. [W]ell, even before that. Why deny the most human need that has always been since the beginning of creation? Have you yet realized that there is no amendment stating thou shalt not pleasure thyself with sex or thou shalt not use your sex to make money? It may be a rule somewhere, but the 10 Commandments[30] are rules overriding any other rule and nowhere in

---

[24] Older i.P. audAx: including people who used to love it.

[25] Older i.P. audAx: or "in God's image" or "in God's imagination."

[26] *See* Appendix A: New Terms

[27] Older i.P. audAx: This would turn on someone who has macrogenitalism, arousal from large genitals.

[28] Older i.P. audAx: It is not the be all and end all, but it is the motivation and the reason. Once the motivation is lost, it's all lost.

[29] *See* Appendix A: New Terms

[30] Older i.P. audAx: or Commitments

the 10 Commandments does it say thou shalt not enjoy sex. I despise it when people look down on those who drink and party and have a fun time[31]. They say "but they are really not happy" or that they are "fake." I understand that they say that because that is all they see, such as when [someone] only sees Onyxes[32] that act dumb and so forth. But what about the exceptions?

I am an obvious exception, but let us take someone else as an example. She is similar to me and her name is pronounced Lay-luh[33]. She is the one [womyn[34]] who is definitely not a poseur. She is an intelligent, non-monogamous married hippy who does not drink and has her own philosophy on life that she lives. Now I think that she is terrific for being true, but I still have problems with people like her too. It is much better to build a life philosophy and be true to that life philosophy but how is that going to change the world? She gifts herself as any horny girl would, the way I do at times. That is not going to change the opinion of those who look down on the sexual community. Revolutions have not occurred because someone chose a unique life philosophy and stuck to it (because really everyone should do that).

Revolutions occurred when that [womyn[35]] with the unique lifestyle publicized it in a way that made people think: they wrote, they made speeches; they were vocal. The reason why the sex community is being infiltrated with as many fakes as the preppy community is being infiltrated with fakes is because no one stood up and said "This is what we believe in, why we believe in it, and why we should continue to live our lives this way." People who choose to be in the sexually active community just do it because it "feels good" or because they prefer it to other options.

Sex Education

"I insist that my daughters be aware of the value of their bodies. I emphasize
the sublime significance of the sexual act, an expression of love. The existence
of means of contraception must not lead to an unhindered release of desires and
instincts. It is through his self-control, his ability to reason, to choose, his power
of attachment, that the individual distinguishes himself from the animal.
Each woman makes of her life what she wants. A profligate life for a
woman is incompatible with morality. What does one gain from pleasures?
Early ageing, debasement, no doubt about it, I further stressed.

---

[31] Older i.P. audAx: Such as people who look down on xSFP types in the Myers-Briggs Type Indicator (MBTI).

[32] See Appendix A: New Terms.

[33] Older i.P. audAx: Layla Hill.

[34] See Appendix A: New Terms.

[35] See Appendix A: New Terms.

> My words fell uneasily on my female audience. Of us all, I was the most vulnerable.
> For the trio's faces registered no surprise. My chopped sentences aroused no special
> interest. I had the impression that I was saying the obvious." (Ba, 1981, p. 89)

I think in a way it is a shame that people do not discuss sex enough other than to preach abstinence (encrasty) or to show pictures of nude wimmin[36]. A bad sex life can be damaging to a relationship. Many men have come out of having sex saying that it is really not that much of a deal and some wimmin[37] have come out preferring to refrain from sex[38]. Many have come out seeing sex as merely sinful and unenjoyable. Sex is like anything else, it can become boring and tiring if just performed without passion. I think that people should learn sex is just as any other thing in this universe. [W]hy should it be considered as something so different? There are the inexperienced and the professional. There are always techniques to be learned and the more years [of] experience [sic] the more knowledgeable you are. It is a field people can find pleasure in like a hobby (a thing to escape from the world) and people should learn to research and study sex as any academic subject, a humanitarian [subject] and not [a] medical subject. The group of people who wants their listeners and followers to be ignorant is the group of people who wants power. Have you not noticed that the dictionary is practically void of thousands of sexually related terms?

Why Sex as a Mission?

> "We have a popular culture that celebrates superficial sexual gratification and
> demonizes it at the same time, dangling before your basic everyday sexual being ideals
> of sexuality that are hopelessly unachievable and, oddly, shameful at the same time
> [...] Perhaps the commercial sex-fest and the punitive public policies that regulate and
> prescribe sexuality are not so contradictory after all. Both negate human sexuality, and
> remove it from its complex intersection in pleasure and responsibility. Both use sex
> for other ends—the marketplace for upping sales and reinforcing consumption, and
> public policy for creating classes of deserving and undeserving." (Peters, 2004)

---

[36] See Appendix A: New Terms.

[37] See Appendix A: New Terms.

[38] Older i.P. audAx: I think it's a shame that there is a stigma for female sexual compulsives because I believe that at least 50% of American females could benefit from recovery from compulsive sexual avoidance, also known as "acting in."

Reason 1: To Find The Truth (Unknown Variable[39]) To Life

I believe that out of all the animals [sic] God chose to bless us with amazing sex. We certainly have better sex than animals because we have opposing thumbs. And if God chose to bless us with amazing sex then why did we choose to desecrate it? If mating were such an evil thing [sic] then God would not have given the birds song. I was convinced that if I knew the truth behind sex that I would know the truth about the world. Since my theory is that if you understand sex you would understand life [sic] that would mean, though it is controversial and dangerous if one gets too involved, that it is necessary for someone to study it[40].

Reason 2: To Heal the Wounded[41]

I have found within the Goth culture[42] and also the sexually active community lots of feelings of guilt or the belief that they truly are going to hell (this could be due to the fact of many of them being disowned by their parents), but having seen that their true selves are not evil [sic] I have felt it to be my mission to release them of this guilty feeling.[43] I also wanted to bring information to the adolescents who are just discovering sex. Not only is the mind of an adolescent maturing from child to adult, but they are also learning about their own sexuality because [sic] since no one talks about it much (at least when I grew up[44]), they learn about sex and are conditioned by the media and their peers, who are also misinformed.

Reason 3: To Live According to My Wilderness[45]

People might wonder why I did not just come out and admit my true wilderness to my parents. I will tell you. It was not just being bi that stressed me; it was being bi, Goth, and frankly obsessed with sex, and all this after being considered a goody-two-shoes[46]. It is relatively easy to say "Mom.

---

[39] See Appendix A: New Terms.

[40] Older i.P. audAx: and in different time periods.

[41] Older i.P. audAx: Nowadays, my reason is also to let someone else take the reins. I get tired of being the only person people can talk to about their fetishes. By the third time, my compassion has worn off, and I no longer want to be an unpaid counselor.

[42] Older i.P. audAx: Did I forget to mention that I'm a Christian Goth? Perhaps you didn't read my other book. This book is intricately connected with *The Meaning of a Metaphorical Life*.

[43] Older i.P. audAx: My primary audience would be intellectual Christian Americans who struggle with feelings of sexual guilt or who judge others for their use of sex.

[44] Older i.P. audAx: and especially previously.

[45] *See* Appendix A: New Terms.

[46] Older i.P. audAx: ...who toed the line out of instinct and fear.

Dad. I am gay," but it is something entirely different to say "Mom. Dad. God has given me a calling toward sex. Sex is a huge part of who I am [sic] and you will never know me because I do not feel comfortable talking about sex with you." And it is not just the fact that my vocation—my calling—is sex that bothers me, but the fact that honesty has been drilled into me as such a large part of my upbringing and to be forced to hide myself tore me to pieces.

Reason 4: To Love

There is no other way to truly make someone happy [than] to become that person's lover. For some [sic] no other happiness can top that.

Reason 5: To Uncover the Truth of the Past

There was some truth to the chant "Make love not war," for there is always much truth to find in events that are on such a large scale [sic] and I was determined to figure out what that truth was. The mission of the hippies and other teenage generations of the past were not over, their voice was only quieted.

"Reconciliation"

I was able to reconcile
my sexuality
with morality
because I was
consistent and
true.

I've had to reconcile—
I've had to reconcile
My lifestyle
To God.

Connections to God

"A righteous man regardeth the life of the beast: but the
tender mercies of the wicked are cruel."
—Proverbs 12:10 KJV

"Let your speech always be gracious, seasoned with salt, so that
you may know how you ought to answer each person."
—Colossians 4:6 ESV

Sex and God

I feel most comfortable with people who can talk seriously about both sex and God, but sometimes I question how far they have delved into the topic in order to reconcile the two as I have done. God is love[47]; love is God. Love is sexual. God is sexual. "But," you object, "the Ultimate Force that we call God is impersonal, and does not experience sexual desires or passions." Indeed! Then, may I inquire, my friend, [from] whence you received your own sexual desires? Do you suppose, for one moment, that there is any attribute of your being that is not an inherency of the First Cause? Is there, indeed, anything in all of this universe, even your own capacity for personal liking for a given man or woman, that can be conceived of as not inherent in the First Cause? Therefore, the First Cause, the Ultimate Force, impersonal though it may be, must be inherently capable of sexual feeling and of personal attraction to any given creature. The Ultimate Force of the universe must, of necessity, be both masculine and feminine in its inherencies. As masculine essence, it should be thought of as entering through the man's organ during the sexual embrace, giving pleasure and receiving pleasure from the wife [or womyn]. As feminine essence, it should be thought of as residing within the wife's [or womyn's] body (the temple of the Holy Spirit) at the vagina and uterus, riding the man's organ, giving pleasure and receiving pleasure therefrom. Thus, the experience is shared with God in every possible way, and is sanctified and glorified.

Androgyny

I bet there is not a single man who has not wondered if Jesus was gay, for as God's only son he must have been required to be androgynous as God is androgynous. Androgyny in many cultures is represented as holy, take e.g. [for example], the Mona Lisa (derived from Amon L'isa or Amon Isis)[48].

Sex in Heaven

Sex in heaven is not for baby making or marriage. If those two purposes for sex are taken away, then sex is just love, right? And this is how those two terms connect. Promiscuity in heaven is a virtue. [...]

---

[47] Older i.P. audAx: We are love. I recommend reading anything by Osho.

[48] Older i.P. audAx: Amon is male and Isis is female.

AudAx

It is true for me that I detest earthly things and long always for the heavens. I know that I do not fit into this world, but that is godinterm[49] because those who do fit in will not reach heaven, for they love the world too much.

I am a little too enthusiastic about sex [sic] and people just plain do not understand. When I have sex with people who do not go to college I am treated like a whore. When I have sex with people who are in college, or at least people who have only had sex once or twice before, they are more polite… some more than others. But instead of treating me like a whore they just keep their opinions to themselves and internally disagree with my lifestyle. If I ever set up shop I will make men sign a form beforehand stating two things: That they are free of sexually transmitted diseases and [that they] will treat me with respect. Funny thing, even though sex[50] does not satisfy, it is the next best thing to intellectual pursuits[51].

So I know that my place is not on earth. If I ever decide to quit sex it will be because I have found it is hard to be selfless[52] when you are sexually active, not because I will find it to be an evil sport.

Jainism and Opus Dei: Abstinence[53], Asceticism, [Aphallatia, and Asynodia[54]]

> "It hangs deep in his robes, a delicate
> clapper at the center of a bell.
> It moves when he moves, a ghostly fish in a
> halo of silver seaweed, the hair
> swaying in the dark and the heat—and at night
> while his eyes sleep, it stands up
> in praise of God."
> —Sharon Olds, "The Pope's Penis"

> "Now concerning the things whereof ye wrote unto me:
> It is good for a man not to touch a woman.

---

[49] *See* Appendix A: New Terms.

[50] Older i.P. audAx: …by itself, depending on the definition of it.

[51] Older i.P. audAx: That is why I prefer to combine the two.

[52] Older i.P. audAx: This begs the question of "Is it good to be selfless?" In the age of codependency and the awareness of Objectivism, this can be up for debate.

[53] Older i.P. audAx: I wouldn't recommend abstinence for someone who has issues with premature ejaculation. "[A]bstinence hampers control." (Zilbergeld, 1992)

[54] Older i.P. audAx: Asynodia is celibacy due to impotence (astyphia), which doesn't make sense to me. If I were a man and I were impotent, that would be like a green light to have more sex.

Nevertheless, to avoid fornication[55], let every man have his own wife, and
let every woman have her own husband." –1 Corinthians 7:1-2 KJV[56]

"These are the bodies that hold the brains we're supposed to shut off all day at work, the
same bodies that aren't important enough to heal. These are the bodies that come with
the genitalia that we should be so protective of? I really don't understand the logic.
You can't tell us that our brains and labor and emotions are worth next to nothing
and then expect us to get all full of intrinsic worth when it comes to our genitals."
–Hand to Mouth (Tirado, 2014, p. 100)

"such a beautiful
day
and I'm not
fornicating."
--Adília Lopes

The only reasons I see to be celibate are fear of pregnancy[57], sexually transmitted, diseases [sic] and boredom of sex, but not because sex is "evil."[58] There will always be some males and females who are completely not interested in sex and their lives will be perfectly fine [sic] and they will remain perfectly well adjusted. But why would God give us all these gifts of feeling if He did not expect us to use them?

I prefer abstinence to celibacy because abstinence is without sex but celibacy is without sex and masturbation[59].

---

[55] Whenever the Bible has been translated to say "fornication," the literal translation was actually "intimate immorality," but on the list of intimate immorality practices in Leviticus 18, fornication was absent unless the true definition of fornication is "extramarital sex that willfully and maliciously *interferes with marriage relations*" [emphasis added] as opposed to "premarital sex." Most of the intimate immorality practices dealt with incest, which is in no way related to fornication as premarital sex but related in every way to sex that would interfere with marriage relations.

[56] Older i.P. audAx: Um…translator? How does marriage prevent fornication if fornication is sex that interferes with marriage? This is worded to make it sound like premarital sex. How can one understand this without knowing the definition of "fornication"?

[57] Older i.P. audAx: "Having a baby is expensive only if you want it to be." –Hand to Mouth (Tirado 100)

[58] Older i.P. audAx: My paternal grandmother had two sons during a five-year marriage to an alcoholic. After the divorce, when men would ask her out she would get on her knees and pray to God that she would never be tempted to go back into a romantic relationship. And for 64 years until the day she died, she never was again. The closest thing she ever got was her collection of romance novels.

[59] Older i.P. audAx: This is why the new term"incel," an abbreviation for "involuntary celibate," really makes no sense at all.

AudAx

Celibacy is not The Unknown Variable[60]. It only leads to pedophilia or "perverted" daydreams (not saying there is anything wrong with that[61] in general, just saying that it may not be what one desires since one is striving for celibacy after all).

Unlike what most people believe, celibacy has never been in the Bible and Jesus never commented on it. The only reason there is celibacy in Catholicism was so that no heirs could inherit property and all the property would go back to the church[62]. Also, if celibate priests questioned the church they would have no family to support them financially. The only reason for celibacy is for political control and financial reasons[63].

However, I do have to give celibacy some credit: BV prevention[64]. There are just too many things that can go wrong in the nether regions and only a [small] percentage is STD-related.

My favorite version of safe sex is writing sexy notes to prisoners[65]. It's like online dating, except better. They are more desperate because they have fewer prospects and more careful as a result. Even an unlikely match can be a temporary match made in heaven (prior to release). The world only sees Hyde in them, but in them I see Jekyll, unless proven otherwise.

Prayer and Meditation

"Raymond explained to me the scientific concept of brain activity producing electrical discharges with different frequencies, classified as beta, alpha, theta, and delta. [...] Alpha is the creative realm. Many times a day, a man unconsciously enters alpha during moments of intuition, inspiration, or while having a daydream. There is also alpha sleep or REM (rapid eye movement) sleep, during that most remembered dreams occur. Theta is deep sleep with little or no dream activity—the level for trance and hypnotic states. I had heard of yoga masters who consciously go into theta with meditation. [...]

The Rutgers experiment made sense. The minute I threw the switch on my vibrator, my brain waves registered alpha, and they stayed there throughout the entire masturbation

---

[60] *See* Appendix A: New Terms.

[61] Older i.P. audAx: Perversion.

[62] Older i.P. audAx: Catholics forced people into making the church their sole beneficiary.

[63] Older i.P. audAx: The Catholic church would have you believe that there is celibacy because Jesus was celibate, but the Gospel of Jesus's Wife turns the tables on that one.

[64] Older i.P. audAx: Actually, I had BV when I was celibate, so that debunks that myth. For more conversation on celibacy, see New Olo.

[65] Older i.P. audAx: I still write letters to prisoners, but now I have clear boundaries, and none of the letters are sexy.

sequence except just before the medium orgasm and again before the Big O they missed recording. At those points, my brain waves dipped down into theta. I was using a deeper dimension of my mind for experiencing pleasure. My brain was having a quick, deep, restful sleep, while my body was moving, heart pumping, blood flowing, and muscles flexing all the way through orgasm. This had all taken place in a waking state.

The EEG data confirmed that masturbation was indeed a delightful form of meditation!

What confuses me is that I know people say prayers before they go to bed and people have sex before they go to bed. So when does one say prayers? Before, during, after, or not at all? Is it not strange to say prayers in conjunction with having sex?[66]

Symbolism

"'Hold on! He thinks a cathedral's entrance represents a woman's…'
The examiner nodded. 'Complete with receding labial ridges and a nice
little cinquefoil clitoris above the doorway.'" (Brown, 2003, p. 326)

"The blade and chalice.
Fused as one.
The Star of David… the perfect union of male and female… Solomon's
Seal… marking the Holy of Holies, where the male and female deities—
Yahweh and Shekinah—were thought to dwell." (Brown, 2003, p. 446)

[Most esoteric and Kabbalic symbolism involves the union of male and female, such as the union of night and day, Nuit and Hadit.]

---

[66] Unless sex is prayer in itself.

Virgins[67]

"Some guys have all the luck
[...]
Some guys get all the breaks
[...]
My arms are empty
[...]
It seem so unfair when there's love everywhere
But there's none for me
Someone to take on a walk by the lake
Lord let it be I
[...]
I got no one"
—J. Fortgang, "Some Guys Have All The Luck"

After a while, for some, a virgin to a sex enthusiast goes from being a pain in the neck to a rare delicacy[68].

---

[67] "In my world, you don't score any points by claiming you're a virgin." (Ellis, 2014) (I cannot find the page number because book loan ended.)

"Now concerning virgins I have no commandment of the Lord: yet I give my
judgment, as one that hath obtained mercy of the Lord to be faithful.
I suppose therefore that this is good for the present distress, I say, that it is good for a man so to be.
Art thou bound unto a wife? seek not to be loosed. Art thou loosed from a wife? seek not a wife.
But and if thou marry, thou hast not sinned; and if a virgin marry, she hath not
sinned. Nevertheless such shall have trouble in the flesh: but I spare you.
[...]
But if any man think that he behaveth himself uncomely toward his virgin, if she pass the flower
of her age, and need so require, let him do what he will, he sinneth not: let them marry.
Nevertheless he that standeth stedfast in his heart, having no necessity, but hath power over
his own will, and hath so decreed in his heart that he will keep his virgin, doeth well.
So then he that giveth her in marriage doeth well; but he that giveth her not in marriage doeth better."
—1 Corinthians 7:25-28; 1 Corinthians 7: 36-38 KJV

[68] Older i.P. audAx: Virgins are attractive to sexual compulsives because after enough sexual encounters, the risk of STDs increases. Sex with a virgin reduces risk to the sexual compulsive. However, it increases risk to the virgin.

Flirty Fishing[69]: Sex and the Christian Missionary[70]

The reason I use[71] to justify my nonmonogamy is flirty fishing. Though I do not introduce my lovers to God, because it is not [always] the right time, I have planted a seed, and that seed is the memory of me, so that when the time comes I can introduce all my past lovers to God at the same time[72]. I find that whenever I try something that I have consciously avoided before [sic] I find that my life is better for having been enlightened. And thus the world shall come to know that being enlightened makes their life better and thus the enlightened should try to devirginize the world[73].

Someone who desires to devirginize a girl is much like a Christian missionary. Both have remembered a life without sex or God, and both find that life miserable in comparison with their present life. Both have found something so wonderful that it must be shared. Both want to feel the memory of what it was like for them to come to God or to come into adulthood. Devirginizing someone is like converting someone to Christianity and both are accomplished by determined missionaries (whose determination at times frightens off the potential convert). The idea of dating a "bad boy" in order to tame him[74] is much like what motivates missionaries to convert people. People like the rush they get from seeing strong reactions. Some people like to frighten, some people like to annoy, some people like to inflame, and some people like to excite. This is all the same feeling that one gets as a missionary. Your entire purpose is to lead others into a new universe. Your entire purpose is to frighten, annoy, inflame, and excite, for only when emotions are [at] their highest [sic] will it be possible for God to enter their hearts. I get the same feeling being a missionary as I do when I fall in love. I think about the other person non-stop and I get excited and anxious.

I have great capability of inflicting wounds, for I have the attitude that it is far better to incite intense, unpleasant emotions than to incite no emotion at all.

---

[69] Older i.P. audAx: The name of a 1960s Christian missionary style.

[70] Older i.P. audAx: Sometimes, the stranger one's life is, the greater the desire to lead a "normal" life. What most people do not understand about the missionary mentality is that missionaries do not sacrifice. When I "sacrifice" my life by giving you a part of me, I sacrifice nothing at all for it is merely fulfillment of my purpose.

[71] Older i.P. audAx: This was unsustainable.

[72] Older i.P. audAx: When they read this book, it will be the right time.

[73] Older i.P. audAx: This would have to succeed Ascension for it to be understood for what it is.

[74] Older i.P. audAx: Attraction to bad boys is called sclerophilia and is very common. I have it, and yet people think I need help to get rid of it despite how common it is. Apparently, even normal people are crazy. For more information on this, see Love Addiction in New Olo.

AudAx

One nice thing about writing about sex is that it causes what all writers desire their reading to cause: a response. Writing about sex is the one thing that is guaranteed to elicit a physical response, usually in the form of someone jerking off. I am aware of my capability of inflicting psychological damage, but I have learned to live with it[75].

Be careful about trying to corrupt or enlighten someone. You should only go on with it if you are determined, but then you will be considered a rapist or fanatic [sic] and no one wants to have those labels on their hands. If you want someone to be "corrupted" or "enlightened," you must let them come to you and even at that you must give them all the pros and cons, tell them that you made a choice but that person does not have to, and give that person time to think it over only if e[76] sounded absolutely positive the first time, otherwise wait.

Remember that not everyone wants to be corrupted or enlightened and those who do want it already are corrupted or enlightened in their heart. I suppose that you can say the same thing for any non-sexual subject concerning someone being corrupted or enlightened but who is possibly not ready to be corrupted or enlightened. It is all about timing.

[Meandering down a different path, my Dad] is very assertive and unafraid of conflict, which is godinterm[77] for his position as a boss. He tells me that he too used to feel guilt when he played his role and wanted people to like him, but it is detrimental for a boss to be nonassertive like everyone else. His reasoning for confronting people assertively is that there will be positive results—that whoever is being reprimanded will hopefully see it as constructive criticism and with that knowledge might change and improve themselves.

I have similar reasoning for devirginizing people. I too hope that it will have a positive effect—[sic] meaning that in a life based on learning, that they will learn to think more seriously about life and love and will learn to evaluate their own feelings on the subject. This is how I feel no guilt about devirginizing, though I never have actually devirginized anyone[78].

My Experiences With Virgins

I know virgins because the main group of people I hang out with are girls who are not very interested in romance in the slightest andor[79] have not been in a romantic relationship[.] [They]

---

[75] Older i.P. audAx: Now when I read this I think of premenstrual dysphoric disorder (PMDD).

[76] *See* Appendix A: New Terms.

[77] *See* Appendix A: New Terms.

[78] Older i.P. audAx: Even to this day, over a decade later, even though I've come close.

[79] *See* Appendix A: New Terms.

get quite annoyed at the mushy sweetness that drips from the mouths of those who are in a relationship and they say that it makes those people stupid[80].

I intimidate virgin boys, [sic] they tend to focus their attentions on someone as innocent as them. A virgin certainly cannot understand the life of a sex hobbyist, but they can certainly understand related ideas such as the idea of getting used to something, the idea of cravings, and the idea of relationships[81].

The Loss of Virginity

> "Whatsoever thing from without entereth into the man, it cannot
> defile him; because it entereth not into his heart."
> –Mark 7:18-19 KJV

Though this scripture concerns food it can also prove how loss of virginity[82] does not make one impure. Physical things do not make one impure, only things concerning the soul. As for the soul, we are all impure for we all sin[83], but Jesus can make us pure again if we die and are reborn in Him.

The [Religious] Praise of Virgins[84]

As for some, strict Christians believe that virginity is better than marriage and a godinterm[85] marriage without divorce is better than a bad one with divorce. They think that way it is easier to be strong and to keep godinterm morals without being influenced into a bad route. But, of course virginity is still bad if you cannot survive on your own with strong morals. ([B]efore knowing that something is better than an alternative, you must know why.)

---

[80] Older i.P. audAx: It reminds me of how I used to make fun of girls who liked pink when I was a kid.

[81] Older i.P. audAx: I am thankful for confirmation bias because even when I came on to a virgin, he completely forgot the whole experience.

[82] The real reason why you should save yourself for someone you love is because once someone has sex with you, they will never leave you alone. They will blow up both your phone and Facebook wall.

[83] Supposedly.

[84] Older i.P. audAx: The church's argument for virginity is that the body is a temple. If I had a temple, I would want active followers who spread the Good Word. Firing someone upon the discovery of nude photographs is temple shaming. It promotes the idea that body temples cannot be beautiful and youthful and that men can only worship at dilapidated temples lacking a janitor and groundskeeper.

[85] *See* Appendix A: New Terms.

The Fearful [Peer-Pressured] Virgins

Frankly, I get annoyed with the fearful virgins[86]. They are the type who believes what they are told to believe without questioning. They are the type to dehumanize the other person, to ignore the fact that if a person has a crush on them that there is something beautiful in that, and to disregard the possibility that the other person might be lacking savoir-faire[87]. I see these people as close-minded and sexually repressed.

Romantic Attitude [Virgins]

Love to a virgin is so pure and untarnished. Virgins are romantics. A virgin gets so excited about any show of romantic interest. Virgins do not like to be touched by anyone except for who they have a crush on. If someone besides their crush touches them, then they think hardly anything of it and believe it is merely a platonic touch[88]. Virgins prefer cuddling to in-your-face sex. A virgin would most likely prefer spooning, which is really just cuddling. Voyeurism might also be something a virgin would prefer[89].

Virgins are still stuck in what I would call middle school stage (see the related episode of *Fresh Off the Boat*, the TV show): For example, Matthew Hays thought we had dated when I didn't realize we did.

Even though I may joke about "corrupting" virgins I would rather not purposefully change their romantic ideals and the respect they give to a girl; the time they think about only one girl is so beautiful. When one has had sex so many times and has gone through so many boyfriends in such a short time something is somehow lost. Inexperience has a sort of beauty to it. The inexperienced have so many rules, or believe that there are so many rules, about how to behave and so many rules about reading body language to tell them when to move on to the next step[90]. For someone like me, I just go as far as I am able until the other person tells me to slow down. It

---

[86] Older i.P. audAx: Not to be confused with other types.

[87] Savoir-faire means know-how[.]

[88] Older i.P. audAx: Or they might go the other direction and avoid all touch in general, acting as their own correctional officer.

[89] Older i.P. audAx: which means a person can be a sexual compulsive even if e has never had sex. The intent of using myself as the control (not the best control) in my science experiment may have been similar to the intent of Gerald Foos, the subject of Netflix movie, *Voyeur*, about a man who spied on guests of the Manor Motel House in Aurora, Colorado. He said, "I know a lot about life. Probably more than anybody that there is. [...] If you get to my age and you don't know anything, then your life has been a waste." (Walker)

[90] Older i.P. audAx: Which makes me wonder how much experience the "gurus" have anyways, with their instructional booklets.

is nothing to me to have sex on the first date[91] and to sleep with that person as long as I am able as if we were already married. There are no rules when non-monogamy has become a way of life[92].

The Sex Drive of a Virgin

The virgin will NOT imagine having sex unless they explicitly see people having sex. It is a misconception to think that sex is an inborn thing among males or females. I myself did not imagine having sex when I was younger, nor did my peers, unless they had chanced upon porn[93].

The problem with Victorian society was exactly that no one talked about sex and the wedding night was absolutely horrifying to young virgins (a Doris Day movie is a perfect example of this[94]). As with anything, knowledge will bring happiness much better than ignorance ever could[95].

A Virgin Devirginized

Virgins, once devirginized, should experiment, because it is only through experimentation that you find out what you like. If you do not experiment, then you shall[96] have sex in only the missionary position without ever knowing how much better sex can be. I have been able to introduce people to many new types of sex. New ways of having sex are like food. Sometimes people make judgments on a food before ever trying it, but once they have tried it they may end up loving it more than any other food[97].

---

[91] Older i.P. audAx: I would say that's different though for online dating, because for me to have sex with someone there has to be rapport, and I have rarely found that with online dating.

[92] Older i.P. audAx: Wow! That sentence is embarrassing in hindsight. *See* How to Tell if a Sex Enthusiast is Ethical in The Sex Scene.

[93] Older i.P. audAx: Which, according to my dad, was not available in the '50s, and society was, according to him, better for it. I do agree with him that today's society is more morally corrupt than it was in the '50s, but not in terms of sexuality, but in terms of the use of credit cards.

[94] Older i.P. audAx: As is my mom's experience.

[95] Older i.P. audAx: Ignorance is not bliss. Not. Not. Not. A problem with virgins is lack of experience. Everyone knows that it takes a team to move a project forward and that talking to more experienced people makes a product better. However, sex is one of the few fields in which there is little to no collaboration. Even anything that appears to be collaboration is labeled a disgrace, hedonistic, sinful, and so on. Then in the same breath, those very labelers complain about their sex life. Puh-leeze!

[96] Older i.P. audAx: Will.

[97] Older i.P. audAx: "Don't knock it 'til you've tried it." —Well-known idiom from an anonymous source

AudAx

A Non-Virgin with a Virgin Sex Drive

People I have met who are or are not a virgin and have a low sex drive nonetheless tend to come from families that have run into trouble with the law or have run into trouble from unplanned pregnancies or STDs. These are the type that I normally steer clear of, not because they annoy me, but because I respect them.

Love and Sex

If most devirginized males fall in love with the first person to have sex with them [sic] then sex and love must be greatly intertwined, right? The idea that the first time a male has sex they usually fall in love with the person who devirginized them seems terribly incongruous to the idea of males who are stereotypically known to objectify wimmin[98]. I do not really blame the chauvinists actually. I think that it is a natural defense mechanism. Men are told to be tough and macho. They are not supposed to fall head over heels in love. If the first person they fall in love with is the person who devirginized them, then it is quite likely that this is not true love[99] and therefore they will eventually get their hearts broken. Sex is a very powerful feeling and sometimes I get the feeling that men feel it more powerfully than wimmin perhaps. If that is so, then it is very difficult to have sex and not become emotionally involved. But I want to make clear that sex does not overpower emotions, love overpowers emotions. When one gets confused for the other it is more difficult to get satisfaction when one is taken without the other. Men then get it in their minds that if they go the opposite route of what they had originally, then they will not be affected by the emotions, so that is when they start objectifying.

In love each persons [sic] thinks often of the other and wants to please the other. In sex one gets pleasure from knowing that they are pleasing the other. Love is patient. Sex is not. It is not common for both parties to be in the mood for sex at the same time. Sometimes it takes cajoling[100] and sometimes one party cannot be cajoled. Love, on the other hand, is mutual more often. Infatuation is like worrying, [sic] reality sure is a disappointment in comparison with what is possible with the imagination. Disappointment here does not necessarily mean a negative disappointment[101].

I believe that all love in any form is sexual, but sex is not love. E.g., there's not much difference between the love of a couple and the love of best friends[102]. What is easier to imagine: Spending

---

[98] *See* Appendix A: New Terms.

[99] Older i.P. audAx: With quotes.

[100] Older i.P. audAx: and, unfortunately, coercing.

[101] Older i.P. audAx: More like a surprise.

[102] Older i.P. audAx: As couples should be best friends.

a lifetime with a sexcrazed [sic] lover or spending a lifetime with a friend? The message the action of sex conveys is either "my mind and soul love you as well as my body" or "only my body loves you."

Sex and love tie in so well together because sex is love, just a particular type of love: bodily love. Sex is neither ultimately godinterm[103] nor bad. It is a tool that can do great godinterm if put in the right hands and great harm if in the wrong hands. Sex is only as godinterm as it is believed to be. It IS possible for love to blossom out of a purely sexual relationship and it is possible to destroy a wonderful relationship through the power of sex. Sex has the possibility of getting awfully boring awfully fast and love is the only way to keep the flame alight.

The Word "Love"[104]

Sociolinguistics

> "Why should the English taxonomy of emotions be a better guide to emotional universals than that embodied in some other language?" (Wierzbicka, 1997, p. 9)

Before discussion on the word "love" [sic] a thing or two must be said for language across cultures. "In spite of the fact that language acts as a socializing and uniformizing force, it is at the same time the most potent single known factor for the growth of individuality" (Sapir, 1970, p. 19). This can mean that language unites those in the same culture and is the force that makes each culture unique. It is naïve to assume that a word such as love, one of the "basics of human nature"[105], [sic] is exactly the same in every culture. Every word similar to "love" in one language may differ greatly in meaning from our actual Anglo perspective on that word. Not only does the meaning differ, but the frequency of similar words may differ as well, which says something about the importance of that word in a language. For example, "the Hanunóo language of the Philippines has ninety different words for rice" (qtd. in Wierzbicka 10). [One assumes t]hat shows the difference of importance rice has in the Hanunóo culture and the American culture.

---

[103] *See* Appendix A: New Terms.

[104] Older i.P. audAx: One can tell the level of soul growth one has had by how they define love.

As for "love," saying, "I love you" cannot both be a stage that happens fairly early in relationship, before cohabitation or a marriage proposal, and something reserved for "The One." And when people disagree on this matter, it is unlikely to come to a resolution in which both stay in the relationship.

[105] Older i.P. audAx: According to Kabbalah, a true relationship requires a sincere desire to transform our nature.

AudAx

By assuming a gloss[106] means the same thing as the original Standard American English (SAE) word is a huge mistake.

Love in Romanized Languages

Noun:

Romance Languages

French (m): amour

Italian: affetto, amore, passione

Latin: amor, amare

Portuguese: amor

Spanish: amor, amar

Asian (Altaic)

Chinese: ài

Japanese: ai

Korean: ae

Germanic Languages

English: love

German: die Liebe

Dutch: liefde

Verb:

Romance Languages

French: d'aimer

---

[106] Older i.P. audAx: Summary of the meaning of a word.

Italian: amare, piacere, voler bene a

Latin: amati

Portuguese: amar

Spanish: encantar, amor or carino

Asian (Altaic)

Japanese: ai

Germanic Languages

Dutch: aan liefde

English: to love

German: lieben

As one can see here, all romance words [nouns] seem to have evolved from the Latin word "amor" or "amare." The Japanese language, though not a romance language, also seems to have evolved from that word. This makes sense because the Japanese language is similar to SAE in that its influences are everywhere. As for the Germanic languages they all seem to have generally evolved from the German word "die Liebe".

Foreign Counterparts

A common way of saying "I love you" roughly translates to "I like you" in Japanese ("suki" as a non-conjugated [sic] verb) and French ("aime" first person singular conjugation of verb). The Japanese [and Arabs] have many more ways of saying "I love you" than American speakers do[107].

Here are different ways to say "I love you" in Japanese:

- Kimi o ai shiteru (used mostly by males)
- Aishiteru Chuu shiteyo [sic]
- Ora omee no koto ga suki da
- Suitonnen
- Sukiyanen

---

[107] Older i.P. audAx: What is the importance of this? I might just mean these languages have more levels of formality.

- Sukiyo

- Watashi wa anata ga suki desu

- Watashi wa anata wo aishite imasu

- Watakushi-wa anata-wo ai shimasu

- Suki desu (used at 1st time, like for a start, when you are not yet real lovers)

- Ini wa aishite

Arabic ways of saying "I love you":

- Ana Behibak (to a male)

- Ana Behibek (to a female) Ib'n hebbak.

- Ana Ba-heb-baknhebuk Ohiboke - male to female

- Ohiboka - female to male

- Ohibokoma - male or female to two males or two females

- Nohiboke - more than one male or female to female

- Nohiboka - more than one male or female to male

- Nohibokoma - more than one male or female to two males or two females

- Nohibokom - more than one male or female to more than two males

- Nohibokon -more than one male or female. to more than two females

- Bahibak - female to male

- Bahibik   - male to female

- Benhibak - more than one male or female to male

- Benhibik - more than one male or female to female

- Benhibkom - more than one male or female to more than one male

Evolution of the "Friend" in the English Language[108]

In order to help explain the difference between "love" in SAE and its gloss in other languages [sic] the word "friend" will be briefly analyzed. This is being done since these words are closely related. While the word for "friend" has evolved other the years, so has the accompanying word

---

[108] In 2016, during the time I started my recovery journey, friendships were difficult for me because they require a change of perspective. I have had a challenging time convincing people that I am a whole person whose activities are not confined to one group of people. People want to see me as a girlfriend, freelancer, teacher, or mentor, but not as a friend, which I find to be the more valuable occupation.

"love" evolved with it. The most noticeable change in the word "friend" over the years can "be crudely described in various ways as 'devaluation,' 'broadening of scope,' shift from 'vertical' ('in-depth') to 'horizontal,' from 'exclusive' to 'inclusive,' and so on" (Wierzbicka 36). In Old or Middle English one could only have one or, sometimes two, permanent relationships described by the word "friend". [sic] In SAE this term applies more broadly and can be used to label ten, twenty, forty temporary relationships. "'Friends' in the older sense of the word were expected to be loved, whereas 'friends' in the modern sense are expected to be liked" (Wierzbicka 40) [109]. A reason for this may have been that there is much more travel than there used to be, so that it is necessary to leave friends behind and "make new friends" (also a relatively new expression). The more frequent the travel, the less the possibility of creating permanent relationships, so the term has come to be applied much more loosely as something temporary. "A man who had moved sixteen times in twenty-two years of marriage contended he had at least acquired 'a few close, lasting friends at every stop" (qtd. in Wierzbicka 36). Such a statement would never have been possible to make in Old or Middle English. Due to this change, adjectives are needed to explain what "friend" means in different contexts. "The most common collocations with the word friend included *faithful friend*, *steadfast friend*, and *old friend*" (Wierzbicka 38). We have even included new expressions in the SAE vocabulary to follow this change of broadening scope such as "circle of friends" and "a friend of mine". Note that it seems much better to refer to those who aren't very close as "a _ of mine", but to do the same for someone who is close seems like an insult:

A colleague of mine

A student of mine

A fan of mine

Vs.

A brother of mine

A son of mine

A husband of mine

Not only has the term broadened but its expectations have changed as well. "A desire to do good things for one's friends was (it seems) expected to be a permanent feature of the relationship and not something restricted to times of adversity. But this is not the case with the modern

---

[109] Older i.P. audAx: This could also explain why "love" in some languages roughly translates to "like." This conversation could also easily become a conversation about "friends with benefits," which is the intersection of friends and "lovers." The word "friend" comes from "freond," "vriend," and "freund," the latter two meaning boyfriend. "Vriend" relates to "vrijen," which means to make love. So surely the concept of "friends with benefits" is not a new one.

concept of 'friend'.... Rather, friends are now expected to do things WITH us – and not so much 'good things' as 'fun things'" (Wierzbicka 40)[110]. Also, the past usage of the word in Old and Middle English used expressions such as "choosing a friend" which is no longer so commonly employed[111]. This change of the term "friend" is extremely related with the word "love".

Often when discussing romantic love [sic] one is always seeking "the One" who is given all the qualities of a "true friend". One is only expected to have, of course, one true "love" [sic]. We still "choose" who we want to marry. We are expected to do "good things" for our love, not only in times of adversity. Our love, of course, expects to be loved and not just liked. One cannot leave their true "love" behind due to travel and make new "loves". [sic] There is no such thing as a "circle of loves" and no one refers to their love as "a love of mine".

Etymology

The American-Heritage Dictionary states that the word "love" came from "leubh" [112] to care, desire; love whose derivatives include *livelong, belief,* and *libido*. This dictionary states that "leubh" came from [the following:]

[*=Suffix form]

leubh-o-. *lief; leman, livelong,* from Old English

lof, dear, beloved, from Germanic

leubaz. O-grade form [of] *loubh-*.

[Derivatives of leubh:]

1a. *leave,* from Old English *laf,* permission (< "pleasure, approval");

- [1]b. *furlough,* from Middle Dutch *verlof,* leave, permission (*ver-,* intensive prefix, from Germanic **fer-;* see per1);

---

[110] Older i.P. audAx: I had a friend like this. These are not the kind of friends I'd make a beneficiary.

[111] Older i.P. audAx: This is the difference between my generation and my dad's generation. He chose his friends, and my friends just "happened."

[112] Older i.P. audAx: Most English dictionaries say that love evolved from "lufu," but I think that love in the Germanic languages came from "leubh," which evolved from "lufu." I've also heard that "love" comes from "lubha," which is Sanskrit for "greed." In any case, the similarities should be taken into account.

- [1]c. *belief*, from Old English *gelafa*, belief, faith, from Germanic **galaub* (**ga-*, intensive prefix).

- [1]a–c all from Germanic **laub*.

2. *believe*, from Old English *gelfan*, *belfan*, to believe, trust (*be-*, about), from Germanic **galaubjan*, "to hold dear," esteem, trust (**ga-*, intensive prefix). Zero-grade form **lubh-*.

- **lubh--*. *love*, from Old English

- *lufu*, love, from Germanic

- **lub*. 2. Suffixed (stative) form

- **lubh--*. *quodlibet*, from Latin *libre*, to be dear, be pleasing.

3. *libido*, from Latin *libd*, pleasure, desire. Before the year 900 [sic] Random House Webster's College Dictionary states that the Middle English "lov(i)en" came from: Old English [--]

- *lufian* Old High German

- *lubon* Old Norse

- *lofa* to love; akin to Latin

- *libere* to be pleasing

Before the 12th [sic] century Merriam-Webster's Dictionary states that the word came from: Middle English, from Old English *lufu;* akin to Old High German

- *luba* love, from Old English

- *leof* dear, from Latin

- *lubere*, *libere* to please

Lexicon

Noun Definition

[Underlines added for emphasis:]

American-Heritage Dictionary (The American Heritage Dictionary, 1992):

1. A deep, tender, ineffable feeling of affection and solicitude toward a person, such as that arising from kinship, recognition of attractive qualities, or a sense of underlying oneness. A

feeling of intense desire and attraction toward a person with whom one is disposed to make a pair; the emotion of <u>sex</u> and romance.

a.   <u>Sexual</u> passion.

b.   <u>Sexual</u> intercourse[113].

c.   A love affair[114]. An intense emotional attachment, as for a pet or treasured object. A person who is the object of deep or intense affection or attraction; beloved. Often used as a term of endearment. An expression of one's affection: *Send him my love.*

2.

a.   A strong predilection or enthusiasm[115]: *a love of language.*

b.   The object of such an enthusiasm: *The outdoors is her greatest love. Mythology* Eros or Cupid. *Christianity* Charity.

Random House Webster's College Dictionary's Definition (Random House, 1997)*:*

- A profoundly tender, passionate affection for another person esp. when based on <u>sexual</u> attraction

- A feeling of warm personal attachment or deep affection

- A person toward whom love is felt[116]

- A love affair

- <u>Sexual</u> activity

- A personification of <u>sexual</u> affection, as Eros or Cupid

- Affectionate concern for the well-being of others; love of one's neighbor

- A strong predilection, enthusiasm, or liking: a love of books

- The object of such liking or enthusiasm: The theater was her great love

- The benevolent affection of God for His creatures, or the reverent affection due from them to God

---

[113] Older i.P. audAx: The dictionary's willingness to say that sex is love has been duly noted. Everyone thinks that the dictionary is this great authority on everything, yet turn around and say that love is not sex even though our own English dictionaries say it is. How confusing that must be to a foreigner (*gaijin*)!

[114] Older i.P. audAx: Note that love affairs, not marriage, are connected to the word "love."

[115] Older i.P. audAx: Note that there is a fine line between compulsion/obsession and love.

[116] Older i.P. audAx: I thought you weren't supposed to define a word with that word.

Merriam-Webster's Dictionary's Definition (Webster, Inc., 2005)*:* a: strong affection for another arising out of kinship or personal ties <maternal *love* for a child>

> (2): attraction based on sexual desire : affection and tenderness felt by lovers

> (3): affection based on admiration, benevolence, or common interests <*love* for his old schoolmates>

b: an assurance of love <give her my *love*> warm attachment, enthusiasm, or devotion <*love* of the sea> the object of attachment, devotion, or admiration <baseball was his first *love*>

> (1): a beloved person : DARLING -- often used as a term of endearment

> (2): *British* -- used as an informal term of address unselfish loyal and benevolent concern for the good of another: as (1): the fatherly concern of God for humankind (2): brotherly concern for others b : a person's adoration of God a god or personification of love

Transitive Verb Definition

[Underlines added for emphasis:]

American-Heritage Dictionary (The American Heritage Dictionary, 1992): To have a deep, tender, ineffable feeling of affection and solicitude toward (a person): *We love our parents. I love my friends.* To have a feeling of intense desire and attraction toward (a person). To have an intense emotional attachment to: *loves his house.*

a. To embrace or caress.

b. To have <u>sexual</u> intercourse with.

To like or desire enthusiastically: *loves swimming. Theology* To have charity for. To thrive on; need: *The cactus loves hot, dry air.*

Random House Webster's College Dictionary's Definition (Random House, 1997): To have love or affection for

- To have a strong liking for: to love music
- To need or require: Plants love sunlight
- To embrace and kiss as a lover
- To have <u>sexual</u> intercourse with

AudAx

Merriam-Webster's Dictionary's Definition (Webster, Inc., 2005): to hold dear: CHERISH to feel a lover's passion, devotion, or tenderness for

b (1) : CARESS

(2) : to fondle amorously

(3) : to <u>copulate</u> with to like or desire actively : take pleasure in <*loved* to play the violin> to thrive in <the rose *loves* sunlight>

Intransitive Verb Definition

The American-Heritage Dictionary describes the intransitive verb of "love" defined as [the following]: To experience deep affection or intense desire for another.

Synonyms

American-Heritage Dictionary (The American Heritage Dictionary, 1992) Synonyms: affection, devotion, fondness, infatuation

These nouns denote feelings of warm personal attachment or strong attraction to another person. *Affection* is a less ardent and more unvarying feeling of tender regard: *parental affection*. Devotion is earnest, affectionate dedication and implies selflessness: *teachers admired for their devotion to children*. *Fondness* is strong liking or affection: *a fondness for small animals*. Infatuation is foolish or extravagant attraction, often of short duration: *lovers blinded to their differences by their mutual infatuation*.

Merriam-Webster's Thesaurus (Belanger, 2005): affection, attachment, devotion, fondness, amorousness, amour, passion, adore, delight (in), heat up, adore, affection, worship

Conjugation of the Word "Love"

The SAE conjugation is far more simplified than the Latin conjugation from which other romance languages evolved.

SAE Conjugation

[	sing.	plural]
1st	love	love
2nd	love	love
3rd	loves	love

Latin Conjugation

	sing.	plural]
[		
1st	amo	amamus
2nd	amas	amatis
3rd	amat	amant

Poetic Language: Metaphors and Idioms

"Contrary to the elitist scientist views—poetic language is a major aspect, function, dimension, and potential of all natural language" (Dil & Friedrich, 1979, p. 441).

"Many individuals in most if not all societies would probably agree that the meanings most particular and sensitive to the culture are located in the relatively poetic levels of language use: magic, myth, religion, ritual, and of course all the folk genres of literature" (Dil & Friedrich, 1979, p. 479).

Metaphors[117]

Love is war[118][.]

Love is a hunt[.]

Love is a game[.]

Love is a journey[.]

Love is insanity[.]

Love is the sweet and the sour[119][.]

---

[117] Older i.P. audAx: As Anna from *Frozen* famously put it, "love is an open door" (written by Kristen Anderson-Lopez).

[118] Older i.P. audAx: Or, as Pat Benatar would say, "love is a battlefield."

[119] Older i.P. audAx:

"Love is how you feel about yourself when you're with that person. It goes beyond personality" –Dad

"Love is like a rollercoaster" –Red Hot Chili Peppers, "Love Rollercoaster"

"The definition which the Scripture gives us of love is this: 'Love is the bond of perfection' [in 1 Corinthians 13:1-13]" —A Model of Christian Charity (Winthrop)

Idioms

Random House Webster's College Dictionary: In love (with) infused with or feeling deep affection or passion (for); enamored (of) *Make love* a) to have <u>sexual</u> relations b)to [sic] neck; pet c)to court; woo

American-Heritage Dictionary: for love Out of compassion; with no thought for a reward: *She volunteers at the hospital for love. for love or money* Under any circumstances. Usually used in negative sentences: *I would not do that for love or money. for the love of* For the sake of; in consideration for: *did it all for the love of praise. in love*

1. Deeply or passionately enamored: *a young couple in love.*

2. Highly or immoderately fond: *in love with Japanese painting; in love with the sound of her own voice. no love lost* No affection; animosity: *There's no love lost between them.*

Sex and Linguistics

Our language[120] has many problems pertaining to sexual topics:

- The problem with [the] word evolution: youths will find it difficult to separate the happy meaning of gay from the homosexual meaning of gay, prostrate from prostate, organism from orgasm, etc.

- The Americans lack a certain beneficial understanding of the term "sex." They usually associate it with the act of sex or occasionally the gender of a person, but not all the other spiritual connotations contained within the topic of sex[121].

- Our language is lacking in that it does not use a gendered article. Perhaps the introduction of gendered articles will make the concept of "sex" more food for thought (haha! Like that will ever happen). But problems arise from the lack of gendered articles too[122]. I have a qualm with the German use of the neutral article as a brainwashing technique. Mark Twain once remarked, "In German, a young lady has no sex, but a turnip has." I can only take a guess as to why this ridiculousness is so. Is it to imply the purity of a girl? Does anyone besides me see anything wrong with this?

---

[120] Older i.P. audAx: In case this gets translated, the original book was written in SAE, Standard American English.

[121] Older i.P. audAx: See Mr. 3000, starring Bernie Mac.

[122] Older i.P. audAx: In this sentence, I meant neutral articles. No, not periodicals, more like determiners.

- I am one of those odd geeks that find it fun to read a dictionary. I have on many occasions found the lack of terms common in my everyday vocabulary, all related to sex[123].

Bonobo: Not a Sin

"And you can just make believe
When it comes down to makin love
I'll satisfy your every need
And every fantasy you think up
CHORUS:
So when you need a little peace of mind
Come on over boy, anytime
I'll keep you happy and so satisfied
In my house, in my house"
—Mary Jane Girls, "In My House"

Me: "All tension is sexual tension."

Faye ["Coraline"] Viola: "I agree."

Bonobos

"Zoo observations suggest, on the average, that every male, female and child bonobo engages
in some form of heterosexual, homosexual or self-sexual activity every 1 ½ hours. [...]
But it's not the frequency that seems to startle people, Bell says;
it's the too-human-for-comfort mode of the behavior.
For example, the frontal orientation of the bonobo's genitalia makes it one
of only a handful of animals able to copulate face-to-face. [...]
When females embrace -- which is often [...] – "it's called a GG rub," says
Bell. "Genital-to-genital stimulation. It's like, 'Hello, how are you? [...]'
[...]
And the bonobos—especially the males—seem to enjoy grossing them out. "They
like to put their butts up to the glass because it gets such a great reaction."
"When Lomako, a 13-year-old male, is in rare form, he masturbates.
Usually it's when he sees uniforms, when there are 30 Brownies or Girl
Scouts out front," says Bell with a sigh." (DeBartolo, 1998)

---

[123] Older i.P. audAx: Can the dictionary staff please hire a sexologist? Oh nevermind, I'll do it myself. Coming (not) soon.

AudAx

The bonobos are famous, not necessarily for their likeness to humans, but rather for their interesting sexual habits. They are one of the few species of primates that engage in sexual behavior all year long, even when the female is not in estrus[124]. They also seem to engage in homosexual behavior, both males and females, and have been observed engaging in what some people like to think of as oral sex. But Bonobos do not have to worry about consequences.

[Junior Year of High School:] William (Will) Wood

The following was recorded April 2000 and July 18, 2000:

Day 1

I met Will when I was sitting in the hallway between our school and the adult education center. (We usually ate outside but we could not that day or any following day because there was construction; a new building was to be made there.) Melissa (she had curly brown hair) knew him (she goes out with Cameron now). He introduced himself. He was acting silly and hopping around on the ground pretending to be a monkey. He was cute and funny and sexy [...].

Day 2

The second time that I met him I was bored of eating indoors[.]and decided to go see Rachel (pronounced Rah-shell) Billings who was going out with Jason Privateer[.] ([T]hat summer after school was out they had broken up and Jason wanted to go on a date with me but was too old for me, according to my folks, and I thought of him as just a friend[.]). [T]he only place outdoors where people could go to eat was a place that made me feel like a sheep because it was small and had a wire fence at the end so that no one could go anywhere. I hated it and tried to eat in the hallways outside the cafeterias but adults would always catch me and tell me "uh-uh" even though I always clean up after myself[.]

I asked how she was doing but realized that nothing interesting was going on over there. I noticed him [Will] look over a few times. He said later that he thought I looked like a nice girl. When I was going to leave, Billy [Will] was blocking the way so I asked to get passed [sic] and he introduced himself briefly as "Will or Billy, I go by either one. Some people call me god." We shook hands and looked at each other's eyes (time seemed a little slower that instant).

---

[124] Older i.P. audAx: "In heat," which is the opposite of dioestrum.

Day 3

I was eating lunch across from Mwana Aloogo. He saw me as his friends were going to get in line to buy a snack. I was chewing an apple when I noticed that he always slicks his hair.

"[H]ey haven't seen you in 1...2...3...4 days (counting on his fingers)." He came over and sat on the table left of me and introduced himself again. I felt his leather jacket and mentioned that I liked leather. [He responded:] ["]I like leather[.] You should see my leather underwear[.]" I blushed and smiled. [He said,] "Ah, there's a smile[.]" There was not much to discuss and his friends called to him so he left.

After the leather discussion I was walking down the hallway with [Jenna Pony] after lunch and asked her to point out who she thinks is "stalking her" that she is trying to avoid. She pointed out Will who she calls Billy. [I said,] "Him?! I was expecting someone different. Actually, I think he's kinda cute. If you don't want him you can give him to me."

Thursday

Thursday, William Wood saw me on that day wearing a witches hat and sexy black clothes (skirt, heels, slip, shiny black shirt) & [sic] asked what my boyfriend thought of what I was wearing. I said I didn't have a boyfriend. He asked if I want one[.] I said yes[.] [H]e asked if I wanted to go out[.] I said yes then asked if he asked me just to ask me or if he had anything planned[.] [H]e said just to ask me. We had fun joking around at lunch[.]

"You're taller than me[.]"

"Hey, yeah, I'm taller than you" (looking at the wall as he said it)

"You're talking to the wall[.] [T]he wall's taller than you[.]"

"Yeah" (looking up)

"You're taller than the stump over there and your backpack, so that must mean you have power over them, but sometimes smaller things have power over taller things[.]"

"Yeah, like you have a power over me." He gets [sic] on his leather jacket even though its [sic] hot outside.

"Aren't you hot? Why are you putting on that jacket?"

"I wanna make sure you don't run away[.]"

AudAx

"How's putting on your jacket gonna help?"

"If you start running, I won't have to take the time to put on my jacket so I can catch you faster."

"Hey, Mike" (talking to some guy I've never seen before)

"This is i.P., I want you to be nice to her or I'll come beat you up" (I'm laughing)...

We talk. [H]e asks how to act the first day (hug, handshake, whatever)[.] I don't know. So it's a little awkward saying goodbye. The next day he says I'm acting strange. He calls me 2 [sic] times a day over the weekend, [sic] we don't go anywhere. ([H]e has 2 parties. I have karate[.]) We start making sick jokes and telling each other our fantasies.

Phone Sex

One of the first questions he ever asked me [on the phone] was whether or not I masturbated, in which I answered in the affirmative. Then he flattered me by saying that my body was like Britney Spears, yeah right.

[Censored]

I guess the spin the bottle and um...other stuff Helped [sic] me learn. Next day I don't see him all day and when I come near where he should be his friend says "He's not here yet" then at the end of school his friend asks me if I've seen him but I haven't. He called me the second I got back from school, [...] and told me it was my poems that made him wanna kiss [me].

Afterwards

Since this was the same year as my rebirth[125] I felt terribly guilty about conducting phone sex with him, so much so that I could not help but tell my mother about it. She was terribly shocked, but she could handle it. Of course, my father never knew.

After the "Will" experience and after knowing what a nice, muscled hug is like, [the] body has become more important to me, not for looks, but for touch. I did not like Will's weak skin and weak grip. But the pressure against my pelvis and the wildly thrashing tongue was all that I felt, everywhere else I was numb, as if his hand never grazed there.

---

[125] Older i.P. audAx: See *The Meaning of a Metaphorical Life*.

What Else Happened During That Time

During the fling I found out that he was a freshman from Jenna Pony. Wow he acted mature for his age (sexually mature I mean). After the fling, […] I saw him […] the next day. I saw Jenna and sat down with her on the floor by her locker before school started. I said that it was over and that it was all a physical thing and nothing else[.] She told me how surprised she was to find out that we were quote unquote going out. She did not ever think that we would be interested in each other. She knew he had a reputation for being a player and a "stalker" but thought that when he went out with me he might have changed[126]. That afternoon when Jenna, Mwana, and I were staying after for chorus rehearsal we saw him in the hallway and he was all smiley, like nothing ever happened. Jenna whipped up her flirting magic and laid it on thick. She started to teasingly wimpish-like "beat" him up for something he did. Even I do not know for what (I guess for breaking up with me?) "Hey, what did I do?" Smile.

When Mwana and Jenna left I looked at him and said "Just friends." "Yeah I know we already discussed it." I tried to avoid the in-between-the-cafeteria place after that (next year I could not because the planetarium is right there where my astronomy class is)[.] I heard nothing about him until the trip to Boston with the chorus [class]. My "gang" (anyone who tagged along with Mwana, Jenna, and I) was hanging by a group of stores waiting near […] the place we were supposed to meet with the chorus group. Shelly [is] a hyper, talkative girl on my bus in eighth grade who suddenly started using bad language in freshman year of high school because I guess she thought it was cool "I never used to say it before but now I say it without even thinking about it." She […] offended Jenna once by loudly mentioning…(the rest of the notes are lost).

To me, everything in the world seemed sexual. Sexual situations in everyday life were [as follows]:

- anything emphasizing the difference between genders,
- anything that evokes passion,
- being in any relationship,
- buying a bed,
- exercise[127],
- holding hands,
- hugging or kissing anyone,
- lying down,
- physical check-ups (or in this case, anything medical),

---

[126] Older i.P. audAx: I wouldn't say that we were going out, but I wasn't going to tell her that.

[127] Older i.P. audAx: Sexercise is a physical exercise performed before or during sex. People have now discovered that a coregasm is real (an orgasm from core exercise).

- reading or seeing anything that tells a story (every story has love in it, even stories in art or music without lyrics), [or]

- sleepovers.

Other everyday things that could stimulate sexual thought were [the following:]

- being reminded of the difference between genders.

- doing anything physical,

- getting your hair fixed,

- having a friendly conversation with the opposite sex (or for that matter just seeing the opposite sex),

- jokes,

- seeing a shape that reminds you of something sexual,

- seeing anyone who has a very prevalent feature (you think about what you could do with that feature),

- seeing anyone who is attractive,

- seeing skin,

- something very disgusting,

- tensing and releasing to get rid of stress (tense-orgasm, release-after orgasm),

- terms in reference to sex (anything you relate to sex through personal situations (experiences)), [or]

- the dark.

Another sexual situation is seeing someone again whom you have not seen in a long time and whom you have missed very much (because the idea of love between the two is a topic raised in the mind that has not been raised much before), and also licking anything like a Popsicle [sic] or lollipop.

I have found out that I am extreme in matters dealing with sex. I began masturbating years before I became depressed. I do it daily. Whenever I had an orgasm when I was a teenager I would hear the ticking of a clock even if there were no clock or watch in sight. Very peculiar. Sex seems as ordinary now as sitting down with a newspaper and a cup of coffee. I really do find pleasure in sexual jokes[128]. The happiest days of my life, interestingly enough, were when I discussed sex. Because I had the freedom to do so!

---

[128] Older i.P. audAx: That's called moriaphilia, which is similar to phallolalia, arousal from talking about the penis.

A curiosity for me is: [W]hy are there so many strippers[129] and wimmin who love to get naked and yet the percentage of men to wimmin who masturbate is incomparably higher for men? I know my clit is much larger than for the average girl and yet I have draughts every now and then. Gosh! If I were male I would have already raped several different people of either gender due to my insatiable urges. Maybe that is why I am female. I consider myself much more informed than other girls my age. I am glad that there is this truth: The beautiful are not always the best at performing in bed (or elsewhere).

Freshman Year of College

Feeling so repressed in high school, the first thing I ever did when I went to college was to make it clear to my friends that I am a very sexual being. My friends EXPECTED me to make sex jokes. Perhaps I have become who I want to be. I am the comic relief of a comedy and the tragic hero of a tragedy. Comic relief on the surface; tragic hero underneath. I actually enjoy talking about sex. You can always flirt just by merely talking about it. As both my lovers and friends know, I am horny 24/7 and there is nowhere that I am more at peace than in the bedroom (or car or bathroom or table or…).

[Me]

"Why is there so much literature about prostitution?" –My notes from January 2001

"[R]eading & writing & [illegible] & nature & theatre are my drug. Sex is also my drug, my outlet, my escape from things I don't want to remember. [W]hy would someone so different as I am exist if not to be known or seen. [sic] We can only please ourselves so much by knowing that God sees us and we see us. But how are we supposed to add to the world or change the world? If you are different rejoice, you have a distinct (and different) plan ahead that not many or no one else has." –My notes from February 4, 2001

"I sat down on the warm toilet seat that reminded me of soft
flesh from a derrière" –My notes from 2001

"I'm a left-brainer wishing to be a right-brainer. If a person defines who you
are a bit by how you act and what you do then if you have an obsession you
become one and if the obsession is sinful then you become, really, anything
but holy, righteous, and good." –My notes from November 17, 2001

---

[129] Older i.P. audAx: Exotic dancers.

AudAx

Body Confidence[130]

I learned early on to love my weight. Why do men prefer voluptuous wimmin as opposed to skinny girls: Would you rather make love to a bucket of bolts or a bunch of pillows? Why do men prefer voluptuous wimmin as opposed to obese girls: Would you rather make love on a dirt hill or in quicksand?

My lips started looking larger to me in the mirror and it is then that I noticed why older prostitutes are depicted with long lips and hollow cheeks (at least in animé). It was the effect of sucking on a regular basis.

Control

I love non-monogamous sex because I crave control, a thing denied to me the first two decades of my life. If I am property, I would rather be common property so that no one single person has control over me[131].

If

If I were bad in bed, I'd have better relationships.

My Favourites in Sex

- My love of BDSM began as a combination of memories of my father yelling at me, the bullies picking on me, and the perverted enjoyment, or rather fascination that I had with ongoing internal pain from something like a physical illness.

- I consider myself to be an excellent dick sucker. I have been fixated on the oral stage of childhood development (a Freudian idea) up until the age of twenty[132] from biting my

---

[130] "When I've been with people who aren't good in bed the main thing I've noticed is how insecure they are." (Ellis, 2014) (I cannot find the page number because book loan ended.)

Older i.P. audAx: "Simmering should become a regular part of your life. People who consider themselves sexy and have good sex lives do it all the time." (Zilbergeld, 1992) (I cannot find the page number because book loan ended.)

[131] Older i.P. audAx: Yes, I meant that I wanted to be the town bike back then, but not anymore.

[132] Older i.P. audAx: And beyond.

nails. About Freud's theory of the childhood oral stage of development: the thumb really is like a penis (many men would agree with me)[133].

- I prefer playing with or fantasizing about playing with mens' penises the way that men fantasize about breasts, rather than actual intercourse. But if the intercourse is extremely godinterm[134] then it is even better then [sic] playing with private parts.

- I do not know if I am like a guy or if there are not enough wimmin who express this, but as a guy sometimes likes watching two lesbians go at it, I like watching two gay men (and I am not alone).

- I love leather, silk, and velvet, but I especially find leather to be my fave fetish, then silk, and I also like cotton balls.

My Observations About Genital Stimulation

In order of intensity:

- G-spot (deep sensation, sensation travels to stomach)
- Clitoris (sharp, cold, burning sensation)
- Shower head (intensity varies)
- Grinding (goal-oriented towards [sic] orgasm)

My Sexual Orientation

I think the reason that I am bisexual is because my father was often on work trips so I spent more intimate time with my mother as a young child. In my childhood I was boy crazy, but I think that is because I did not even consider lesbianism as something that was possible and[,] on some level[,] accepted in some part of society. If I had, then I might have been girl crazy too (I do not know). Even though I like girls, I guess I am partial to men because they do not show as many signs of the two things I detest more than any other: gossip & [sic] whining[135].

Never Bored

The fire in me never changes. After "conquests" I still have reason to smile all day beyond the point where my mouth hurts. Even if all it is is sexual I still want to sing songs of puppy love

---

[133] Older i.P. audAx: And the armpit is like the vagina.

[134] *See* Appendix A: New Terms.

[135] Older i.P. audAx: I'm about 66-75% straight and 33-40% gay.

AudAx

though I have already had many times to refine the way I show love and feel about love. I want to dance around my room as if it is prepubescent love, though the situation could be murky and clouded and feel bad, but so very "good." Elation always gets me, gets me bad, gets me "good."

"Alphabet"

It sounds odd but once I had a thought,

That I could feel every letter of the alphabet inside me:

A for anal,

B for blowjob,

C for cunnilingus,

D for doggy-style,

E for estrogen,

F for fetish,

G for grinding,

H for hair in the pubic region,

I for intercourse,

J for jelly,

K for KY jelly, to be specific,

L for lick,

M for mons pubis,

N for necking,

O for oral,

P for penis,

Q for queer,

R for rear view,

S for sex, of course,

T for testosterone,

U for U wanna get it on?

V for vagina,

W for wet,

X for excitement,

Y for you and me, and

Z for zygote.

"Being a Slut"

When I am feeling down

Flesh does not appeal,

Hugs are empty,

Kisses futile,

But thankfully I am an artist

And art gives me meaning.

"Cocktail"

Said after making safety precautions:

May I

AudAx

get high

off your cock

tail?

"Humanity's Dartboard"

They spat in my face

With cum,

Wounded and shackled.

They believed me to be somehow unhappy,

Somehow bound,

To the futility of the others in my species.

I took the lashes honorably—

Like being blamed for passing an STD,

Though no one was blamed for passing it to me—

And gave back continuously

Though I was deeply resented for perpetuating evil

When I did nothing of the sort.

If men lash out at those closest to them

Then I am glad to get the whippings.

Oh how they loved to call me a "bad girl."

Let me carry your burdens, the savior said,

And I like a donkey,

Treated like a piece of ass,

And ridiculed for bimboism—

An uncivilized female barbarism—

Gratefully received,

And never refused my station in life

After all the persuasion

Of the societal type,

And for the sake of not filling up hospitals –

Even though the comfort was tempting—

Because I knew that I was still a listening ear,

That I was still a companion of sorts,

That I was still a sounding board,

And the cum flew at me like darts.

"Secrets"

No one ever told me

that men do not read *Cosmopolitan*

and that every technique is all the same to them.

No one ever told me

that my vagina

would smell like the person I did last.

No one ever told me

that purity

was taught to Hitler.

AudAx

No one ever told me

that dicks

were beautiful with swirls and designs.

There are so many things unanswered

That do not have to be,

like things left out of the canon,

like African-American poetry.

"Vaginal Cum"

Wet as water

White as milk

Thick as egg yolks

Consistency like yogurt

Dries like Elmer's glue

Tastes like salty fish sticks[136]

Plentiful as a pint

Sophomore Year of College

6/7/[20]03

My closest lifelong friends have one thing in common and that is being a sex enthusiast[137].

---

[136] Older i.P. audAx: Well, not mine. I taste like a breakfast burrito.

[137] Older i.P. audAx: That makes it definitely odd that I was in the group of people that did not drink or have sex in college.

Sex is a natural part of my life now. It is a natural extension of myself. I am not myself if I cannot express my interest in sex. I feel so uncomfortable at home with my family. If you took sex out of the equation, then there would be no reason for me to dislike my parents. But sex rules my life[138]. Sex is so much a part of my life that my goals and dreams are influenced by it and especially my identity e.g. I want to die while having sex, I want a helicopter so that I can have partners in different states[139], and I am called to write this section[140], Olo. I am pansexual[141]. I have learned a lot from sex. Now that I have this love of sex, it is no wonder that I should be interested in e.e.cummings[142], my favourite sexual poet.

It is fun to see how many times one can go in one night. I have gone many times beyond the point of bleeding. For me, it is amazing how often I am horny and how frequently I masturbate per day. And in contrast, it is amazing how tired I get of having the act of sex per week. It is amazing how frequently I have orgasms on my own and how difficult it is to have them during sexual performance. It feels too much like an act. Sometimes I want sex less intensely because you cannot keep up a terrific intensity all the time, your muscles get weak at some point. Sometimes I will have the longest, greatest intensity sex but I do not have an orgasm, so because my muscles get weaker I will go for a less intense position.

Every now and then it is not that I get tired of sex, but that I get tired of what people see me as. Because I am a sex enthusiast, people do not expect me to get all serious and academic. But my second favourite[143] hobby is books and intellectual[144] pursuits. In high school I was known for the latter and not expected to enjoy sex, yet in college I am known for the former and not expected to enjoy intellectual conversations. I hate being put in a box. Just because I love sex and most things about sex I am not as single-minded as I lead people to believe. "69" is NOT my favourite number. "7" is actually my favourite number due to its holy qualities. I do NOT prefer Onyx men due to their dick size either[145].

From my experiences I have found that the best sex is of the playful type. This is why I consider it a hobby, though every now and then I do have need to turn it into something serious and religiously uplifting. I hate to be categorized, put in a box, because whenever I deviate from the box my acts are regarded with suspicion. If I for one moment say a perverse thought [sic] all the people who see me as a churchgoer are confused and whenever I say a Christian thought all the

---

[138] Older i.P. audAx: I don't like how that came out. Let me fix it: I am a sex goddess, and I rule sex.

[139] Older i.P. audAx: This no longer appeals to me.

[140] Older i.P. audAx: Obviously, I decided to make it into a separate book.

[141] Pansexual- exhibiting or implying many forms of sexual expression (Merriam-Webster, Incorporated).

[142] Older i.P. audAx: Haha, cum.

[143] Older i.P. audAx: Stylistic choice.

[144] Older i.P. audAx: Including spiritual.

[145] Older i.P. audAx: Which is a myth.

people who see me as perverse are confused. Since both are me [sic] I do not see a time when I can be my entire self and be completely happy (if that brings happiness). If I go one month without having sex with someone my boyfriend is shocked (See Sexual Compulsive Exes); if one year passes and I do have sex my parents are shocked[146].

Even though I have been a slut and seen the truth about how "all men are the same," I believe that that does NOT have to be a bad thing. I find being a sex hobbyist very rewarding. I also find it ethical because a true sex hobbyist rarely if ever discriminates, they are not looking for the most stunning beauties, they just wanna fuck and if they wind up with a stunning lovely then, hey, that's cool. The beautiful thing about sex and why I love it so much is the freedom. Always do we live in the bounds of society, fearing to say and do what we wish, fear to speak our thoughts. It is with sex that we are made free, in that [sic] we leave the safety net, the learning ground, of society. This is the time when no longer can society be much of an influence because everything now is purely you: what you like, not what society wants you to like[147], how you would instinctually act, not how society wants you to act. There is no better way to discover a person's individuality or lack thereof than in sex. When you have sex you say what you are thinking, you say what you want with an outrageous freedom and you do whatever you have fantasized, there are no constraints. You are free to expose yourself. You are free to live at the spur of the moment; you are free to give up yourself and your emotions to one person[148]. You are absolutely naked and there is no embarrassment. Everything that is exposed is perfectly private and away from society. And so I think it is a sin on the part of society to deny this human need to privacy and freedom.

The Emperor's New Clothes: Exhibitionism and Nudism[149]

"One day when I am putting Rebecca down for her nap, she suddenly focuses on my eye. Something inside me cringes, gets ready to try to protect myself. All children are cruel about physical differences, I know from experience, and that they don't always mean to be is another matter. I assume Rebecca will be the same. But no-o-o-o. She studies my face intently as we stand, her inside and me outside her crib. She even holds my face maternally between her dimpled little hands. Then, looking every bit as serious and lawyerlike as her father, she says, as if it may just possibly have slipped my attention: 'Mommy, there's a world in your eye.' (As in, 'Don't be alarmed, or do anything crazy.')

---

[146] Older i.P. audAx: Well, not anymore.

[147] Older i.P. audAx: I'd have to disagree with this statement. I was recently reading about how Hustler started the trend toward shaving pubes and how hair removal is a million-dollar industry. I think commercialism very much shapes all of our behaviors.

[148] Older i.P. audAx: Or more.

[149] Older i.P. audAx: The opposite of nudism is gynophobia, the fear of nudism. That probably occurs in men who are afraid of going to "sausage fests."

And then, gently, but with great interest: 'Mommy, where did you get that world in your eye?' For the most part, the pain left then…. Crying and laughing I ran to the bathroom, while Rebecca mumbled and sang herself off to sleep. Yes indeed, I realized, looking into the mirror. There was a world in my eye. And I saw that it was possible to love it: that in fact, for all it had taught me of shame and anger and inner vision, I did love it."
—Alice Walker, "Beauty: When the Other Dancer Is the Self"

It takes much time to get comfortable with your body. Parents, let your child see you naked (unless if you are the opposite sex, then only down to your underwear)[150]. This is so that they understand that it is not scandalous to feel godinterm about their body, or so that they will not be scarred for life the first time they see a naked body. Since most everyone looks relatively the same there should be no reason for feeling embarrassed about your body or someone else's.

One must address what the uninformed people may consider a deformity here. Let me make it clear that most wimmin's breasts are NOT even, most wimmin's vaginal lips are NOT even, and the size and shape of nipples varies widely. As there are such things as innies and outies concerning the belly button, the same is true of breast nipples. It is not a deformity. Sometimes comparison can be beneficial. Every [womyn] should see other wimmin's split beavers[151] to know that they are not odd or anything[152].

[If you are a womyn] look at yourself in a mirror sometime. First stand hunched over with your eyes to the ground then look up at yourself. Then stand straight with perfect posture and look at yourself. It is different. Just by changing posture it can change how you feel about yourself at that moment, how you make your first impression, the probability that someone might make you a symbol of confidence and maybe wisdom, and the probability someone could regard you as a distant role model. Those who seem sexually confident seem that they would appear confident for anything else that happened along the way. It is imperative whether wearing nice or bad clothes, but especially bad clothes [sic] to wear it with complete confidence.

---

[150] Older i.P. audAx: Unless sexual abuse runs in your family.

[151] Split beaver- when a woman holds her genitals open

[152] Older i.P. audAx: Also asses and urethras (yes, women have urethras!). These things can also be good to know from a medical standpoint.

[Gender][153]

Communication

I think that rape many times has to do with gender miscommunication. The womyn says that she was making no advances and yet the guy says that she was. I think many wimmin do not understand the way a guy's mind works and do not know what would come off as an advance. Likewise, many men do not understand wimmin and would not know what is not considered an advance.

As in general life, if wimmin become too accustomed to saying "yes," then their "no" will be ignored because in the land of free love it is more about bodily pleasure than love. This means that your true identity does not matter many times, only the sexual identity that you present.

The "evils" of sex do not come from sex itself, but from gender topics. The evils of sex concern themselves mainly with respect. Lack of respect anywhere, lack of understanding that all people are part god[154], results in evil[155]. All the problems with rape deal with lack of respect for a person as a person. All the problems of prostitution deal with the same topic of lack of respect for a person as a godly being, as does marital abuse. Do not blame sex[156], for sex is God's holy gift to us.

Satan[157] knows how to use conditioning to his advantage. He takes something pure and holy and puts a hideous mask on it. And then people will continually avoid any mention of that godinterm[158] and holy thing because all that they remember is a hideous mask.

Milkshake and Durian Fruit (Known by Gay Men as the Thing with Teeth)[159]

"you uterus

you have been patient

[...]

---

[153] Older i.P. audAx: See Epicene for more discussion on gender.

[154] Older i.P. audAx: or part of God

[155] Older i.P. audAx: In Kabbalah, not seeing one's divinity is called hatred, or is what hatred comes from.

[156] Older i.P. audAx: Or money. Or guns. Or anything else inanimate, tangible, and amoral.

[157] Older i.P. audAx: Also known as The Adversary, whose name comes from "satan," (sah-tahn) meaning ego.

[158] *See* Appendix A: New Terms

[159] Older i.P. audAx: The most important thing to know about gender is that wimmin tend to get hurt by it more than men, mentally, spiritually, and physically.

> while i have slippered into you
> my dead and living children
> [...]
> my bloody print
> my estrogen kitchen
> my black bag of desire"
> --Lucille Clifton (1936-2010), "poem to my uterus"

When Barbara Walters asked Debbie Reynolds (a famous actress) what was one thing she wished she knew then that she knows now, Debbie Reynolds replied that she wished she knew where her clit was. It may seem very strange to males that wimmin do not know how to stimulate themselves, many times do not know how to have an orgasm[160], and do not know where their clit is[161], but many of them do not. This might explain why sex is not as important to many wimmin as it is to men. Many males and wimmin themselves know very little about the sexual mechanics of the female body until they start having sex, but sometimes they still do not know much even then.

Another thing that men need to keep in mind about wimmin is mood. A woman will have sex if she is in the right mood. Wimmin are very in tune with how they are feeling at a particular moment. For many wimmin [sic] mood is what determines what we will wear the next day. Believe me, I know.

Different Approaches to Sex

Chauvinistic[162]- The chauvinists (mostly males) continue to have one-sided, unhealthy, gender-based relationships because they know no way else to act.[163]

Flirtatious- The flirts have the healthiest relationships because they encourage equal participation and healthy communication.

Obsessed- The obsessed have very unhealthy relationships and do not know how to love[164].

Orgasm-driven- The orgasm-driven are those who want immediate gratification.

---

[160] Older i.P. audAx: In Because I Said So, Diane Keaton's character asks her daughter what it's like to have an orgasm.

[161] Older i.P. audAx: Or their urethra for that matter.

[162] Older i.P. audAx: Not to be confused with misogynistic.

[163] Older i.P. audAx: The difference between a chauvinist and someone with sexually compulsive behavior is that a chauvinist has higher standards.

[164] Older i.P. audAx: And may not know how to be loved or feel loved.

AudAx

Routine- The routine people see sex as obligatory and therefore makes the activity seem quite boring.

Sex-Addict[165]- The sex-addict sees sex as a hobby or sport, so they are more prone to having one-night stands[166].

Timid- The timid sees sex as the most exciting since they are just learning about it. Generally, the quieter, less noticeable people seem to love sex the most.

Osculating

Kissing is seen as disgusting by many countries, but Americans have gotten quite used to it. The virgin kisser worries way too much about kissing. Has that person not ever kissed their family members? Lip-to-lip kissing is the simplest. French kissing, which is not actually French, is a little different[167]. The first time is always awkward and not always pleasant. But when you get used to kissing, small things like bad breath do not bother you as much. I have gotten used to morning breath many times.

Masturbation

"Do I wanna go out with a lion's roar?
huh, yea, I wanna go south n' get me some more
hey, they say that a stitch in time saves nine
they say I better stop—or I'll go blind
[…]
hey, hey—they say I better get a chaperone
because I can't stop messin' with the danger zone
No I won't worry, and I won't fret—
ain't no law against it yet—"
—Cyndi Lauper, "She-Bop"

"Let me go on
Big hands I know you're the one

---

[165] Older i.P. audAx: The correct term is "sexual compulsive."

[166] Older i.P. audAx: …or having xenophilia, arousal with strangers.

[167] Older i.P. audAx: True "French kissing" is one kiss on each cheek. It was certainly ironic that even though my mom taught French, where sex is never a scandal, we rarely discussed sex.

Body in beads
I stain my sheets
I don't even know why
My girlfriend she's at the end
She is starting to cry"
—Violent Femmes, "Blister in the Sun"

"Aside from its importance as a form of sexual self-help, the benefits of masturbation are many. Masturbation provides sexual satisfaction for people unable to find partners. It's a way for teenagers with irrepressible sex drives to have orgasms without the possibility of pregnancy or contracting sexually transmitted diseases. Masturbation also provides a sexual outlet for couples when they are separated, when one partner is ill, when one partner is not interested in sex, or when either partner cannot get enough stimulation to reach orgasm through sexual intercourse. Masturbation can also be done with a partner (or partners) as a valid alternative to intercourse; sharing masturbation is an important addition to the sexual repertoire of couples. Masturbating prior to partnersex is a way for men to eliminate sexual urgency and rushing. It also provides safe sexual satisfaction during the last stages of pregnancy, and can give relief from menstrual cramps. Masturbating to orgasm is relaxing and helps induce sleep[168]. Finally, and certainly a consideration these days, masturbation is the basic form of safe sex.

It's important to remember that there are all types of people who are not in a relationship—some out of choice, some because they're waiting for the right man to come along, and some because they lack confidence or have a physical disability.

Perhaps everyone is disabled in a way. I know I am, though not in a tangible sense. I remember being in a sexual education class in my church. We were asked about our opinions of masturbation. I did not know what it was at the time. Since then it has become like a best friend. Most all sexual partners I have had made regular use of masturbation, so therefore, masturbation is not just reserved for those who do not get laid. Masturbation is godinterm because you do not have to stifle your sexual energy to wait for someone to come along. You can please yourself and not have to bend to the sexual demands of others. Once, when I was a little too carried away with my hormones and not thinking straight I was given some advice. The advice I was given was to masturbate before getting in bed with someone. This eliminates the urgency and lack of judgment. Masturbation also teaches you more about yourself and is life not a grand love story about learning about yourself? Another thing about masturbation, after having been around the sex scene once or twice I have found that masturbation is mostly reserved for children [teens] going through puberty or people who are bored and doing it out of routine or for lack of nothing else to do.

---

[168] Older i.P. audAx: This was my preferred sleep aid, and it was free.

Nonmonogamy[169]

"Is this a lasting treasure
Or just a moment's pleasure?
Can I believe the magic of your sighs?
Will you still love me tomorrow?
Tonight with words unspoken
You say that I'm the only one
But will my heart be broken
When the night meets the morning sun?"
—The Shirelles, "Will You Still Love Me Tomorrow"

Pros

So that I do not hurt anyone's feelings I try to make it clear from the start that my hobby is sex and that I do not cheat for the reasons most other people cheat, a lack of judgment and lack of desire for the one to whom they should be true, but for the simple reason that I want to continue an interest of mine. Being honest makes everything hurt less and no one has to be left with a major life crisis. I also make it clear that I am not looking for "the One," not looking for marriage, and that also makes everything hurt less[170]. The most I have managed is four [boyfriends] at a time in my freshman and sophomore years of college[171]. Senior year I was so busy that I could only manage two. Here are the advantages to non-monogamy:

- I have no attachments to any one area so I can travel freely.

- It will not hurt as much if I never let them in close[172].

- I will stick to my philosophy.

- It can be undertaken in a relationship of complete trust. The most important elements in marriage, I think, are communication, trust, and lack of contempt. I think that the reason why most people end a relationship after one side cheated is because the trust factor is gone. Nonmonogamy cannot be undertaken when someone in the relationship exhibits jealousy[173].

---

[169] *See* Open Relationship/Open Marriage: Shared Infidelity in New Olo for further discussion.

[170] Older i.P. audAx: By changing my mind, as a woman tends to do, that complicated everything.

[171] Older i.P. audAx: This was nothing compared to a woman with my name who had seven or eight boyfriends at a time.

[172] Older i.P. audAx: This is an unhealthy reason.

[173] Older i.P. audAx: Ah! How life does change. Life is very different with a jealous boyfriend.

Because wimmin need emotional intimacy to feel sexual, men are the opposite.

For me, being non-monogamous is like being a not-for-profit psychologist prostitute[174], meaning I am a friend to many, a listener to many, and I care about their joys and concerns as a teacher or preacher. But I also have physical fun as well.

My sexual orientation is bisexual, but I have been unlucky in the arena of lesbianism because I have found females not to be very receptive to the idea of non-monogamy. Actually, amongst the lesbian community the worst thing that you can do is to be non-monogamous, so though I am sexually attracted to females I could never actually date one no matter how much I would like to[175].

Some advice: If you are going to be a "slut" stick only with a trusted group of friends. If you are afraid of STDs the group of friends should be mostly virgin. If you are afraid of drama [sic] the group of friends should be mostly polyamory [sic] so that they will not be jealous of one another.

Cons

> "Religions are like people. You can be friends with all of
> them but you cannot date them all."—Me

I like nonmonogamy because there is minimal soap opera, [sic] it is understood from the getgo [sic] that I do not commit to anyone[176], but the problem is that it makes men feel that they psychologically should or could not have deep feelings for me. The problem with nonmonogamy is that the partners think more about sex than relationship, due to the way they are conditioned. Here are my problems with non-monogamy[177]:

- They get jealous. And they can all sing No Doubt's "Ex-Girlfriend" and change the word "girlfriend" to "boyfriend," singing "I kinda always knew I'd end up your ex-boyfriend."

- None can say they love me or all can say they love me but if all do, then the effect is lost.

- They get horny [sic] and I feel that all they want is my body.

---

[174] Older i.P. audAx: or an IPSA certified surrogate partner/counselor. *See* the definition of prostitute in Appendix A: New Terms

[175] Older i.P. audAx: That's not true. I now know two women who are married with mistresses: Lana Jakle and Kaitlyn Ryan.

[176] Older i.P. audAx: I wrote this before I was 22, when I was too young to be committing myself to anyone.

[177] Another one is relationship status. I find that the only reason for a relationship to have an "it's complicated" status is because of the man, which is ironic since men insinuate that women are complicated.

AudAx

- I surely get lonely.

It is imperative to be medically checked and reminded not to be selfish in a lifestyle such as a nonmonogamous lifestyle, or else it becomes an unhealthy lifestyle. It is imperative also to stop doing one-night stands at a certain point due to the unreliance [sic] of doing it with someone whose body and abilities you are not absolutely comfortable with. But it can be practiced without it being a sin[178] or even being negative but it must be practiced CAREFULLY and with ethics.

"Both"

When given a choice
between A and B
I have always chosen both.
And it's endearing
until it happens to you
and the game ends.
And yet I do not see
what is wrong with test drives.
Everyone has different techniques
and if I were to have favorites
then I would not be a good parent,
would I?
So must I change my nature
for different stages in life?
But wouldn't that be inconsistent?
Isn't consistency virtuous?
If it is then you cannot blame me
for committing a sin.

"Don't Let Me Get You"[179]

You say that you want to know me
but you do not know yourself well enough to say that,
you cannot handle my truth,

---

[178] Older i.P. audAx: "There is no sin, but it is you who make sin." –The Gospel of Mary Magdalene, line 26 (This was created before January 1, 1923 and in the public domain.)

[179] Older i.P. audAx: A play on "Don't Let Me Get Me" by P!nk

your desire for truth is a pack of lies.
You say I do not know myself but I do.
I am a sex addict[180] I fear
and you should too
because to really know me
you have to understand
that I fucked your friend
or at least I could
because I would do anything not to sleep alone
and that I am, in your words,
just like every other white girl
and why is it any surprise?
No one is on our side frankly
because we are, as you say,
selfish, only after one thing,
and God help us if we are only children
because that is the only way I'll stay—
only.
You cannot understand my longing for
sex, drugs, and alcohol
and how long I have desired to live without restraint.

I am a Fucking asshole.

Pictures and Pornography[181]

"The stock-boy sits, and studies like a sage
The subject matter of one glossy page,
As lost in curves as Archimedes once.
[…]
Nothing escapes him of her body's grace
Or of her floodlit skin, so sleek and warm
[…]
And how the cunning picture holds her still
At just that smiling instant when her soul,
[…]

---

[180] Older i.P. audAx: Compulsive.

[181] Older i.P. audAx: We interrupt you for a brief moment of Google time. Please Google the Communications Decency Act.

Consents to his inexorable will."
—Richard Wilbur, "Playboy"

After seeing too much porn I have actually learned some valuable lessons. Most everyone's body looks pretty much the same naked so it should be so much more important to look at a person's personality first. Naked bodies are not that beautiful. People look much better with clothes that fit. It is the sensation of sex, not the images, which make the images appealing. It is the connection of the sensation to what is seen while having the sensation. It is very easy to take your clothes off, get in some sexual positions and still not feel sexual.

The sex hobbyist camera of choice is the Polaroid camera so that one does not need to get pictures developed; this could be why pornography is not very artistic most of the time. I have learned from looking at porn that it is easy to lose creativity in that field of artistic expression[…]. The only other thing I dislike about pornography besides its lack of artistic creativity is that it perpetuates the idealization of shaved pubes, which I personally think looks like sandpaper[182]. […]

Platonic [Sexual] Friends

Sabrina Temptress

She and her boyfriend, alias C-S or City Stylez, lived in Arlington and worked in the [nation's capital]. She modeled here, and that is how I met her, then moved back to New Orleans[183] to support her mom and family financially about a year after [Hurricane] Katrina hit. Two of her close friends committed suicide.

Marilyn Totale

I met Marilyn at a Lapdance and Floorshow class held at the Tinselville-DU Fitness Center. The class was taught by a [pregnant] professional stripper[184]. We had a lot of fun afterwards [and] found out that we both lived at the end of the gold metro line. We had a lot in common besides[185] where we were descendants [sic]. Her grandparents were Czech. Her brother became fascinated in Japanese [culture] and lived there for about a year. She enjoyed the animé Merain 3/4. She studied at Maryland Technology College in Fashion Merchandising and worked in Express

---

[182] *See* To Depilate or Not To Depilate in New Olo.

[183] Older i.P. audAx: a.k.a. Nawlins

[184] Older i.P. audAx: Exotic dancer.

[185] Older i.P. audAx: This should say "except for."

as a mini-manager for 4 years before becoming a receptionist at a construction company. She considered getting a master's [degree] in construction.

Premarital Sex[186][187]

"And Isaac brought her into his mother Sarah's tent, and took Rebekah, and she became his wife; and he loved her: and Isaac was comforted after his mother's death."
—Genesis 24:67 KJV

There's actually no such thing as premarital sex. Sex is marital, at least that was its original intention. The harm is done when this is ignored. Scientists have discovered that the first child takes on the height of the first sex partner in mice. Sex partners are judged together, according to the Bible. By having may [sic] sex partners, I am telling God that I want to be judged with mankind.

Because everyone's body pretty much looks relatively the same naked [sic] it is a fool's errand to have sex before consummation and all the more stupid because you only become devirginized once and so it is better to have that first memory with someone you love. Do not have sex before you are married because whoever you have sex with is likely not going to tell you if e has a sexually transmitted disease until e has already had sex with you.

Of course, I have had premarital sex, BUT the first time I had sex was with someone who I loved[188].

Sex Occupations (willing only)[189]

[Exotic Dancing]

"… She wasn't what you'd call
A blushing flower…
[…]

---

[186] *See* Open Relationship/Open Marriage: Shared Infidelity in New Olo for further discussion.

[187] Older i.P. audAx: The only people who seem to accept avoidance of premarital sex are those who have already been disillusioned or burned by it. Not many who play the "no premarital" game are virgins anymore. Another reason to avoid premarital sex: you can't raise a family with dopamine.

[188] Older i.P. audAx: He's still up there, but this was written somewhere between age 18 and 22.

[189] Older i.P. audAx: *See* Sex Workers of the World in New Olo.

She rented by the hour.

[…]

But when I saw her laid out like a Queen,

She was the happiest… corpse…

I'd ever seen.

[…]

And as for me,

[…]

When I go, I'm going like Elsie."

—Fred Ebb, from the musical "Cabaret"

[Prostitution]

Prostitutes are a part of any culture e.g. Geishas, [sic] gypsies, wenches, etc. It is one of the oldest professions in the world[190]. Indeed, it is not shocking that porn constitutes 20% of the Web[191] and is the most profitable.

And do not worry, God does not have anything against them, nor does Jesus who dared speak to them during his time. I guess where it comes to sin they have not violated any parts of the 10 Commandments unless they excite someone who is already married. Prostitutes and the true artists are some of the most misunderstood groups in society that have been around since the beginning of time. I am surprised that a Prostitute[192] has not written a classic. Drunkards have, perverts have, mentally ill people and druggies have, smokers have and blind people have, perhaps Prostitutes are too busy? But I suppose they are more inspirers than creators. Prostitutes, if you read some artist's biographies, have provided an enormous amount of inspiration to the arts pretty much since the institution was official.

As for me, I am a wannabe whore, an idealistic dreamer who has always wanted to be an icon society has forever condemned. It is my terrible fate to desire to make a positive impact in people's lives through a medium that will forever cause a mistranslation. Who in the world beside myself keeps as a role model Jesus and Jessica Rabbit[193] simultaneously? Who else would see the ideal of the [P]rostitute as being a Sumerian high priestess?

---

[190] Older i.P. audAx: Farming, I believe, is actually the oldest profession.

[191] Older i.P. audAx: And is its reason for being.

[192] Older i.P. audAx: Capitalized out of respect, the way the Department of Veterans Affairs capitalizes "Veterans."

[193] Older i.P. audAx: Or Jenna Jameson.

The problem with America's [P]rostitutes is that they do NOT want to be in the profession[194].

If there were more people in the profession who genuinely wanted to be in the profession, then people would not have to waste so much money on such poor quality. I have heard many times that professional whores do not do shit. If [P]rostitution were not illegal, then I would advertise that, unlike many others, I actually enjoy what I do and I would include a table of all the fetishes to which I cater and their prices. It is because prostitutes do not enjoy their line of work that I would have to say that it is far better to be a slut[195] than a whore because a slut enjoys what e[196] does and a whore generally does it to get by, like a cubicle worker. But of course it is even worse to be mistaken for a slut or whore if you are not. All entertainers are whores because they give so much of themselves out to strangers and people who do not care about them and who give them disrespect [sic] but they love to do it. If only I could be a [P]rostitute of a legal brothel, but I have had too much unprotected sex to get a license. I used to have considered prostitution [sic] getting paid for having fun. But I soon realized that I value my independence way too much to do anything so controlled.

What I know about the [sex] profession: Tampa, Florida is the strip bar and lingerie-modeling capital of the South; Las Vegas, Nevada is the adult playground of the West. Many female wrestlers are porn stars. I remember going to a strip club and seeing a police car parked outside with a license plate that was obviously that of one of the strippers[197]. Every [P]rostitute ring is different and there are many variations on prostitution. Some [P]rostitutes make mega bucks and some make at best twenty dollars per person. The [P]rostitution found in nude bars has more dignity (since many are college students who realized that it is a good paying profession) than street [P]rostitution that does not even compare in grace. And being a porn star (not an amateur) is much more rewarding than being a [P]rostitute because you are getting recognition and it takes a lot more endurance than one would imagine. Also, I would imagine that [P]rostitutes would hate both sexes, the wimmin because they look at them differently and the men because they look at them differently.

Prostitution is like any profession. I would best compare it to editing because though one is able to be the very best in the profession, you only give as much as you are paid to give[198]. If you are an excellent editor then you can do all different levels of edit, but if you are given the task of only copyediting or proofreading, rather than comprehensive editing then you will not give your best and will[199] purposefully leave out things that you know should be changed.

---

[194] Older i.P. audAx: The majority, not all.

[195] Older i.P. audAx: I'm a minx.

[196] *See* Appendix A: New Terms.

[197] Older i.P. audAx: Not that I'm lumping strippers with prostitutes.

[198] Older i.P. audAx: unless you're a workaholic.

[199] Older i.P. audAx: May.

AudAx

And with editing, it is a profession that does not get much respect[200] and many people do not know the cost and might think that a good deal is too much, even though it is not.

It took me a long time to learn that people just do not talk about their work life with their family. I lived in a specific society, meaning public and private life is separated, but I wanted to live in a diffuse society where public and private life are intertwined. I suppose this attitude developed once kids stopped telling their family about school or when people felt religion only applied to Sundays. It took me a long time to realize that it is socially acceptable not to talk to my mom about sex but it took me even longer to decide that I felt comfortable being socially acceptable in that way—I would have preferred to talk to my mom the way Frazier's radio friend, Ros, [sic] talked to her mom.

If the world were more accepting, I'd be a porn star rather than a [P]rostitute; I'd want to be known. But if I were a [P]rostitute I'd be a luxury escort.

Any godinterm[201] whore must be a slut first, but any godinterm and HOLY whore is a therapist[202] first. The worst prostitute is a prostitute on drugs because that prostitute has lost any remaining sense of dignity and respect and the sexual Aphrodite/Venus aura is no longer present. All long-term prostitutes have interesting stories to tell that looks deep into human wilderness[203]. I think that my experiences are sometimes on par with some of theirs[204].

Agape and Sex

> "I felt like if any two people had any type of sexual affinity for each other they
> had to sleep with each other immediately, otherwise it was a terrible [...] betrayal
> and waste, you know. I felt [...] well, I spent a lot of time trying to decipher
> what the feelings I had for somebody were [...] and whether I had to sleep with
> them or not[...]. Fortunately, I'm relieved of those obsessions now. It's very
> wonderful. It's very wonderful not feeling you have to sleep with everybody."
> —Leonard Cohen, poet, composer, singer, New York City August 13,1969

---

[200] Older i.P. audAx: I often compare it to dentistry: No one wants to see you, but your job is to make them smile. Most people want an occupation that makes a difference. People want to put a smile on other people's faces. What could be better than putting people in ecstasy? It's way better than just a smile—it's bliss.

[201] *See* Appendix A: New Terms.

[202] Older i.P. audAx: Like an IPSA certified surrogate partner/counselor.

[203] *See* Appendix A: New Terms.

[204] Older i.P. audAx: Especially those of the voluntary, older Christian Prostitutes.

I translate sexual affinity[205] to also be a sort of love. It has been difficult for me trying to decipher the difference between sexual affinity and love. I mean what makes me sexually attracted to someone is the fact that they have something I want… something I am missing… or just the plain fact that I want to understand them on a level that people understand one another when they love that person. I found that those who I am most sexually attracted to are just a reflection of who I want to be. But you see, these feelings do not discriminate […]. I have these feelings for everyone I have encountered. This is my entire reason for being bisexual. This is my entire reason for believing in agape (See Agape Theory in the original book). Everyone wants to love and be loved, but sometimes it is hard to know when you love or when you are loved. This is why people go to so many lengths to find "the One" or to have sex. I wanted to be loved, I wanted to be liked by everyone—I wanted to be loved by everyone and I wanted there to be no barriers about whom I loved.

When you finally realize that God loves you and that you are capable of loving everyone, gosh, that sure is a wonderful feeling and you will not ever be an unstable person ever again[206].

In a way, I think that I have a very Beatle-esque idea of love[207].

Overall

To me, [P]rostitution means giving love without discrimination with the knowledge that you may never ever get any love in return[208].

What I would like to talk about regarding [P]rostitution is the sex industry in general. I have just finished reading *How To Make Love Like A Porn Star* by Jenna Jameson. It is now my favorite book[209]. Basically, it's a story about life. And sex is a great part of life that too often gets stigmatized. I think of it that [sic] there are varying degrees when it comes to prostitution and any job in the sex industry. It all depends upon who, when, where, why, and how[210]. Who, is all about the level of maturity of the person entering the field and their personality traits and talents. When is maturity in terms of age. Where depends on culture. Some cultures have healthier [P]

---

[205] Older i.P. audAx: Also known as rapport. Anyone who is a good salesperson knows that rapport is sexual affinity.

[206] Older i.P. audAx: Realizing and integrating are two different things.

[207] Older i.P. audAx: "All you need is love." —The Beatles

[208] Older i.P. audAx: This is different from codependency, which expects love in return.

[209] Older i.P. audAx: One of my favourite books.

[210] Older i.P. audAx: Or what, when, where, who, why, and how.

rostitution standards than others[211]. Why is a big one. Many people do it for the wrong reasons. They will not survive usually. And how is closely connected with why; it is all about which doors and decisions led to the path of being in the sex industry. Jenna Jameson is a strong person who is not afraid to define herself as the best porn star[212]. She knows that it's who she is [sic] and it is not due to the cause of any life-changing trauma. And she does not have a shred of guilt because her mother was in the business before her and her father gave her the go-ahead. The stories of the people who do not survive in the business are the ones people hear the most, but who really wants to learn about a business from people who failed in it?

As a Goth Christian [sic] I believe that it makes much sense for me to be a sex enthusiast because death and sex are often compared to each other and are interrelated. With sex comes life and death, pregnancy and STD's. But anyways, I am very concerned with my own mortality, though I am not (a person who thinks of disease/death often). When it comes to the Bible, anything Xrated[213] [sic] is inside the pages.

Rather than feel ashamed, I am proud to "know too much." It has been a childhood goal. It gives me a more "human" perspective on things people tend to rationalize and I would never give up my right brain or my childhood perspective. I am a highbrow sex enthusiast, a watcher of porn awards[214], a Playboy reader not a Penthouse reader[215], someone who would go to the Museum of Sex (MoSex)[216] or go to a nudist colony for research, a Geisha[217] not a street whore, the type of person who prefers Brazilian sexuality to American sexuality that is being overruled by consumerism even though every now and then I like American vintage pornography for display[218]. I am the type who could develop a lifelong friendship with a one-night stand. I have never shied away from the term "sexual" like some people do, preferring the term "sensual" even though, to me, it means the same damn thing. I consider the term "sensual" a term for wusses, scaredycats, not for me. I am also a 70/30 femme bisexual with a leaning towards heterosexuality. Though only an official college student for a few years [sic] I will always have the college student mentality, meaning, to me, that I will always be a scholar proud of my sex life.

---

[211] Older i.P. audAx: If I were in the sex industry, I'd go to the Netherlands or France. America's sexual standards (pardon my French) sucks balls.

[212] Older i.P. audAx: I'm also quite impressed with Mia Khalifa, the Lebanese (and only Middle Eastern) porn star.

[213] Older i.P. audAx: Concerning sex or death.

[214] Older i.P. audAx: Uh…not actually.

[215] Older i.P. audAx: Playboy will no longer allow nudity because it no longer makes sense for them to compete at that level in the sex industry.

[216] Older i.P. audAx: in any state, or the Sex Museum in Amsterdam.

[217] Older i.P. audAx: Or Kisaeng.

[218] Older i.P. audAx: Like that of John Lennon and Yoko Ono.

Sex was where my true self came alive and made sense[219]. I was proud that I had more experience at age 19 than Jenna Jameson had at age 19. I had [...] tallied acquaintances to prove my self-worth but it became more apparent when I tallied sexual adventures. I had always desired new things, meeting new people and having new experiences. I was far more interested in avoiding hypocrisy[220] than I was in upholding beliefs that are merely tradition. Sometimes I even had sex for Sex's sake to prove my loyalty to the sex goddess[221]. I rate a nation on their treatment of sex, not just the size of the industry but also the treatment of sex education, sexual expressions in the language, treatment of fetishes, legality of the sex industry, quality of living for prostitutes, criminalization[222] of sexual activities, etcetera.

For some, people do not consider me a slut because I do not better my position through it. Unfortunately, I am often misunderstood by the others[223]. Some friends dare to berate me for doing something "moral"[224] just because they equate sex with sin. They are obviously not very familiar with Sumerian culture[225]. And sometimes I go along because if I just [have] one night [sic] stands with the words "true love" [sic] people would see me in a worse light than if I embraced sin. But as an ex-depressed [226] [sic] I would like to believe that people are capable of loving strangers (*See* Agape Theory in original book[227]).

The Sex Scene

About being part of a sex scene: People interested in all types of ways to have sex after a while will eventually get around to satisfying all of their fantasies because they are determined to seek it.

How to Tell if a Sex Enthusiast is Ethical:

- Person is highly concerned about confidentiality

- Person does not leave when the other person is sleeping

- Person does not lead on a one-night stand

---

[219] Older i.P. audAx: Though I am always becoming my true self.

[220] though I could not entirely

[221] Older i.P. audAx: Not literally.

[222] Older i.P. audAx: And decriminalization.

[223] Older i.P. audAx: Everyone has a cross to bear.

[224] Older i.P. audAx: And vice versa.

[225] Older i.P. audAx: Which came before and was the origin (if I understand correctly) of human civilization.

[226] Older i.P. audAx: Eh...it comes and goes once a month through PMDD.

[227] Older i.P. audAx: The Meaning of a Metaphorical Life.

- Person is honest and upfront about risks

- Person is honest and upfront about monogamy/nonmonogamy/polyamory/polygamy etc.

- Person asks questions about STD safety

- Person uses protection and birth control[228] every time

- Person does not ignore the other person afterwards or treat [the] other person with less respect

- Person does not pressure others or disrespect others' opinions

- Person does not seek out virgins, married persons, and monogamous people who are already taken

- Person does not use sex to advance one's position, normally work-related

- Person does not compete with [an-]other person interested in [the] prospect[229]

It is not godinterm[230] to assume everyone in a field of study thinks alike. My opinions differ greatly from other people's opinions that are in the sex scene. Though I have not been in the sex scene as much as some, I have at times been afraid that what they say is true [sic] and that it really is the way of evil (shudder). If that is so, then I hold this belief: That in the way that partial Christians are twice more sinful than an atheist, partial sex hobbyists are twice more pure than a virgin. If that be not the case [sic] then I hold this belief: In the [same] way that the closer to holiness the harder the fall from grace, the closer to sin the more magnificent the rebirth.

Sex is just another part of life with its own lingo and emotions. It is a part of life as high school is a part of life, or work is a part of life. I find it sad that people need to drink alcohol in order to act the way I do[231]. Alcohol is what people use to be me when I'm sober. Anyone with that many inhibitions has serious problems. The reason that the sex scene seems so evil to those on the outside is because it is being infested with people like this who need substances to do what they normally would not do. If they have inhibitions, then they obviously must feel embarrassed or guilty for doing the things they do. Guilt is sin. Inhibitions should not exist in a perfect world.

The reason that the sex scene is considered evil is because the people most prevalent in it should not be there!

---

[228] Older i.P. audAx: Ah, another reason why I can't be in the industry. Damn contraception from the damned food and drug industry. I prefer natural family planning now, which…yeah…is best when paired with monogamy, like white wine and fish.

[229] Older i.P. audAx: Or client.

[230] *See* Appendix A: New Terms.

[231] Older i.P. audAx: If they are in the industry, and they drink to do their job, they really, really shouldn't be in the industry at all.

[Napoleon Hill:] Sex Transmutation

"Scientific research has disclosed these significant facts:
1. The men of greatest achievement are men with highly developed sex
natures[232]: men who have learned the art of sex transmutation.
2. The men who have accumulated great fortunes and achieved outstanding recognition
in literature, art, industry, architecture, and the professions, were motivated by
the influence of a woman." (Hill N., Think and Grow Rich, 1988, p. 176)

"A: [Emotion of sex] is a virtue when controlled and directed
to the attainment of desirable ends. [...]
Q: Do I understand you to say that knowledge of the true functions of sex and ability
to think accurately are the two things of greatest importance to mankind?
A: That is what I intended you to understand. [...] sex emotion
is the same energy as that with which one thinks."
(Hill N., Outwitting the Devil, 2011)[233]

The reason why religious people are able to practice celibacy is because they have practiced the art of sex transmutation. They place the passion elsewhere where they will be more rewarded. Anyone with great passion has a high sex drive, but does not necessarily have to enjoy the act of it. Sigmund Freud would call what Napoleon Hill refers to as sex transmutation [as] sublimation.

Sexually Transmitted Diseases

Warning: Though I am not a bug chaser, I am not the one to be giving advice and lectures about sexually transmitted diseases because my preferred method of contraception is the Catholic method: coitus interruptus[234]. I am no doctor and I do not quite understand the medical aspects of sex. There is tons of information out there if you only look.

---

[232] Older i.P. audAx: This could account for the high rate of scandals, which, of course, is only confined to the rich and famous. Scandals among hicks are not as scandalous.

[233] Older i.P. audAx: I cannot find the page number.

[234] Older i.P. audAx: Plus the sympto-thermal method. Also, something to note is that some men cannot use condoms due to having a micropenis or issues with staying erect, which is something that is always ignored in sex education.

AudAx

My [Youthful] Opinion on Sexually Transmitted Diseases[235]

I can understand why most sexually transmitted diseases result in infertility and complications with childbirth. The role of a mother and wife is to be monogamous and to not have sex before marriage and to be loyal forever until demise[236]. The role of a single man is just that, to remain single. The two sides should not join because one should always put much care into thinking about giving birth to children, it should never be an accidental thing. If the two sides join, then the result will be disharmony. A single man should[237] never have an accidental birth or a child from someone else who roams around and is not loyal.

The reason that concubines did not have sex with other men, I believe, was because their occupation was to give birth to the male's offspring and to be loyal. If that is your role, then you should play it. The only sexually transmitted disease that really bothers me is the Human Immunodeficiency Virus (HIV), of which there is no cure[238], but as for the others they bother me not, for the worst result is sterility and embarrassment, and after choosing the single life I did not intend nor wish for children and one can overcome embarrassment with some effort. The worst thing that could happen to me as a single person would be to have a child because it is not my place in life; it is not my role. For me, sexually transmitted diseases actually come as a strange blessing, for I wish for sterility most of all[239].

This is thus why I believe sexually transmitted diseases exist and why I think it is godinterm[240] that they do.

My [Youthful] Opinion on HIV and AIDS

As for the Human Immunodeficiency Virus (HIV) and Acquired Immune Defiency Syndrome (AIDS)[241], even they are God-given gifts, to me, and this is why: Since it does not attack right away and may give a person a few years left to live [sic] it was created as a sexually transmitted disease so that people who are in the sex scene, but are not there for a godinterm reason, may take

---

[235] *See* Glitter in New Olo.

[236] Older i.P. audAx: Stylistic preference.

[237] Older i.P. audAx: "Should" being the operative word.

[238] Older i.P. audAx: I now know that many others have no cure either—at least on American soil.

[239] Older i.P. audAx: This is no longer true because I do wish for children and have always wished for children, but before I did not believe I could or would have any. Perhaps the wish for children changes with age. See any source on Law of Attraction.

[240] *See* Appendix A: New Terms.

[241] Older i.P. audAx: Which may or may not have been man-made and which may or may not exist in the way the media portrays.

some time to reflect on their life[242]. It is a godinterm thing for anyone to realize the immediacy of demise and the fragility of life. Woe to the people who are not aware of these things for they will be met with an unpleasant shock.

Social Responsibility

Now as for the darker parts of sexually transmitted diseases: The greatest problem a single person, like me, who does not want children, is met with is the problem of other people. Sex is USUALLY not done alone[243]. The greatest thing to worry about with sexually transmitted diseases is your partner's or partners' safety. And that partner or those partners has/have to worry about his hers or [e's[244]] partner(s) etc. So once someone is infected with a sexually transmitted disease, the chain of embarrassment and loss of trust has begun. And that infects everyone involved with bad feelings toward each other. It is not that I am afraid of sexually transmitted diseases, because I am not, since I am not afraid of demise or sterility and if I die I die, but it is because I realize the responsibility that I have toward my partners who mostly all want to have children and who have other partners to worry about, that after making my research observations on sex so that the rest of the world does not have to, I will (attempt to) abstain[245].

Intellectual Benefits

Another benefit of sexually transmitted diseases is that it gives one yet another frame of reference from which to understand the power of compounding and the power which things we do not even detect may hold on us.

Some Vocabulary (Not a Complete List)

These terms all mean penis[246]:

- Dick

---

[242] Older i.P. audAx: I went to a Sexual Compulsives Anonymous meeting where a man admitted to having sex without telling his partner(s) after diagnosis. Scary! That is definitely when you have to admit you have a problem.

[243] Older i.P. audAx: Depending on the definition of sex, which I define to not be strictly coitus.

[244] *See* Appendix A: New Terms.

[245] Older i.P. audAx: Remember that abstinence allows for masturbation. See Jainism and Opus Dei: Abstinence, Asceticism, and Celibacy.

[246] Older i.P. audAx: Of course, also see the above quote.

AudAx

- Pen15[247]

- Penis

- Phallus

- Quivering member

These terms all mean balls:

- Balls

- Ballocks

- Scrotum

- Testes

- Testicles

- Whirlygigs

These terms all mean vagina:

- Cunt

- Female genitals

- Poontang

- Pudenda

- Pussy

- Quim

- Tom Tom

- Vagina

- Vulva (Edea)

These terms all mean breasts:

- Boobs

- Breasts

- Jugs

- Papilla (nipple)

- Rack

---

[247] Older i.P. audAx: My boyfriend recently told me about "pen island." Ha ha.

- Tits

These terms all mean sexual intercourse:

- Coitus [interruptus][248] (intercourse with orgasm)
- Copulation
- Fornication (outside of marriage)
- Fucking
- Knowing one another[249]
- Making love
- Paraunia
- Penetration
- Sdrucciola (oo…fun!)
- Subagitation
- Sex
- Shooting a wad

These terms all mean oral intercourse[250]:

- Corvus
- Cunnilingus
- Fellatio
- Gamahucheur
- Irrumation

These terms all mean orgasm:

- Acmegenesis
- Climax
- Le petit mort (translates to "the little death")

---

[248] Paracoita is the female sexual partner and paracoitus is the male sexual partner.

[249] Older i.P. audAx: In French, this translates to the verb "connaître l'un et l'autre," thus the title of this book: *Connaître Sacral olo.*

[250] Older i.P. audAx: "oral intercourse" does not make sense.

- Orgasm
- The Big "O"

These terms all mean dildo:

- Dildo
- Godemiche

These terms all mean horny:

- Horny
- In heat
- Rammish
- Ruttish
- Sexually aroused

Posing positions:

- Standing bridesmaid
- The blow job
- The cowgirl
- The dirty doggie
- The doggie
- The piledriver
- The reverse blow job
- The reverse cowgirl
- The scissor
- The scissor mish
- The sidesaddle
- The sixty-nine
- The standing cowgirl
- The standing sixty-nine
- The wheelbarrow

Other terms that are not as commonly known:

- Camel toe a.k.a. wedgie

- Dirty Sanchez- [W]hen cum forms a mustache

- Hitler- [W]hen cum forms a straight line from the nose to the upper lip

- Houdini- [W]hen a man spits on a woman's back while doing her doggy style so that when she turns around he can pop a cumshot.

- Roman helmet- [W]hen a man puts him [sic] balls on a woman's eyes and his dick in her mouth.

- Split beaver- [W]hen a woman holds her genitals open

Techniques

[Gender] Equivalents

[Female   Male]

Clitoral shaft=Penile shaft

Hood=Foreskin

Clitoral glans=Penile glans

Labia=Testicles

G-spot=Prostate gland[251]

General Tips and Techniques[252]

"We human beings are so constituted that when we seek happiness for ourselves, it eludes our grasp[253]. But when we seek to make other people happy, happiness comes and abides with us. If each will seek to give pleasure to his or her wedded partner, the bliss of each will be greatly intensified."

---

[251] Older i.P. audAx: A woman's urethra is not in the clit.

[252] Older i.P. audAx: When asked for a favourite position, people will tend to answer with what works for them biologically (gives them better quality sex). There is no one size fits all answer regarding what's the best position.

[253] Older i.P. audAx: This is a codependent quote.

—Ida Craddock, The Wedding Night[254]

The number one thing before any sexual escapade: Keep water on hand because you will most certainly become exceedingly thirsty[255]. Also keep on hand: emergency pill, birth control, condom variety pack, and pregnancy test[256]. Keep in mind also that men's arms are stronger and wimmin's legs are stronger for sex[257]. I definitely support weightlifting for both wimmin and men in order to be better in bed. I had been quite lazy about exercise and at times it showed painfully when I got tired early from a session of sex. Also it is especially nice to massage the perineum, the area between the main genitalia and the anus. Both men and wimmin have it. But sometimes men are usually ticklish at the base of the spine or the perineum. Also, imagination plays a huge part in sex. I find sex more enjoyable the more people I imagine doing it to no matter how old or ugly (quite perverted, yes?). One last thing: All emotions can be conveyed with muscle tension. During sex we can look farther into a person's emotions and self.

---

[254] Older i.P. audAx: "[A] corrected, edited, and annotated version of this work is included in the new book, Sexual Outlaw, Erotic Mystic: The Essential Ida Craddock by Vere Chappell." (Craddock)

[255] Older i.P. audAx: Avoid juice – too much sugar.

[256] Older i.P. audAx: Well, I think the pregnancy test requires more time.

[257] Older i.P. audAx: I'm kind of the opposite; I can't do cowgirl very long.

Tips and Techniques If Your Partner is Female[258]

"… the bridegroom who hastens through the act without giving the bride the necessary half-hour or hour to come to her own climax, is not only acting selfishly; he is also sowing the seeds of future ill-health and permanent invalidism in his wife."
—Ida Craddock, The Wedding Night

It is generally true that men do not know how to please wimmin. This is why I have included the following advice:

- All wimmin taste differently[259]. Some say that cum is sweet; some say that it is bitter, and some say that it tastes like fish sticks[260].

---

[258] "[A] vigorous fingerbang is a very amateur thing. At this point in the twenty-first century, it's just disrespectful" (Ellis, 2014)

"Don't handle a breast any more roughly than you'd want your balls handled. [...] A very enjoyable position for breast stimulation is from the rear." (Zilbergeld, 1992)

"If you start too fast [...] it can be a turn-off to your partner [...] don't go immediately for the hot spots. [...] If a certain type of stimulation is working, don't immediately rush off elsewhere." (Zilbergeld, 1992)

"Men should know that some women become very still and quiet just before their orgasm, as if they're listening or waiting for it. [...] you should not stop stimulation when she begins to come. [...] When she starts coming, don't stop what you're doing, and don't change it. Just keep on truckin.'" (Zilbergeld, 1992)

"[K]iss, kiss, kiss, then to breasts, back to kissing, then to belly, back to kissing, then to vulva, back to kissing, then to clit, and so on." (Zilbergeld, 1992)

"The most common position for the man doing the woman orally is for him to lie on his belly facing her genitals, but this creates a huge problem: you have to lift your head up, which quickly tires and strains the neck. [...] One solution already noted is for her to be sitting on something with you kneeling between her legs…" (Zilbergeld, 1992)

Older i.P. audAx: I cannot find the page number because the book loan ended.

[259] Older i.P. audAx: Actually, so do men, in terms of tasting differently.

[260] Older i.P. audAx: Mine is both sweet and bitter. It is a bad stereotype that wimmin taste like fish sticks. If they "smell fishy," tell them to go to a gynecologist. That's not a good thing.

- Do not assign a number for how many times you want her to cum[261] (it puts pressure on her).

- Do not use moisturizer as lubrication[262].

- Even though it feels better for you to go all the way in and out, that will dry up a girl faster after a while and will make sex less pleasant for the girl. I know it is hard, but men must learn the meaning of "No." Even I know that when a girl is tired or her vagina is starting to dry up that sex can afterwards become much like agony. I have gone many times beyond my breaking point, the time when I am bleeding and it is not my time of the month.

- Go slow for wimmin and do not do so much side-to-side action with your tongue.

- If you are heterosexual and you want to practice techniques beforehand, then put a cucumber or something long in the vagina in order to practice.

- Ignore the comments about the duration of sex from the movie *Grease*[263].

- It is a downright lie about vaginal orgasms. Masters and Johnson, scientists, "found all orgasms centered in the clitoris" (Dodson, 1996, p. 21). Even though I admit there to being a G-spot, the G-spot is also tied in with the clitoris through muscular connection. The G-spot is more like a male's prostate gland.

Tips and Techniques If Your Partner is Male[264]

- At a guy's climax, suck around the corona[265].

- Be careful with the dick. Wimmin do not understand how sensitive it is.

---

[261] Older i.P. audAx: The only reason this has gone on for as long as it has is because the woman just thinks, "Whatever you want."

Older i.P. audAx: And do not force a woman's head during fellatio (it could make her annoyed). Someone once asked me if it turns me on when I gag on his dick. Um...would you be turned on if you were gagging and couldn't breathe??

[262] Older i.P. audAx: I repeat, "Do NOT use moisturizer as lubrication." Also, do not let the woman douche! Major medical no-no!

[263] Older i.P. audAx: However, if you watch the TV show *Masters of Sex*, it could be true for some people. I actually know of a woman for whom it's even less.

[264] Tips and Techniques If Your Partner is Male (Cont'd):

- Don't grab a guy's crotch unless you're willing to go all the way. I learned that the hard way and had to be saved by someone brawny.

- "It can be a loving gesture [...] if a woman uses her fingers to spread her lips apart..." (Zilbergeld, 1992)

[265] Older i.P. audAx: Sorry, "coronal ridge."

- Be patient!

- Everyone is different. Some men do not get enough stimulation from the vagina whereas the only way for other men to cum is through the vagina. I have had experience with men who could not cum through vaginal penetration and men who could not cum through oral sex. Some men have so much control that they are unable to cum and some men have difficulty having any control at all. Some men are even able to have serial orgasms and ignore the refractory period. It is not impossible for men to have serial orgasms.

- Experiment: circle clockwise and counterclockwise, move side-to-side[266], move in and out, etc.

- If you so desire your partner to have a great sensation rather than the need to cum, then I carefully suggest a technique that could possibly put someone in a coma. In order to truly fire up a man's sensations concentrate primarily on the balls. If you suck on men's balls they will be thrown into the highest form of ecstasy that is possible (though they will not cum from it). Licking, sucking, and stroking do best. Eat the balls as if you were eating an ice cream cone. This will cause a fiery feeling to spread throughout the body, much like what happens when a woman's clitoris is wet and stimulated. Keep in mind that you should not expect to be watched because the male's literal head will be mostly against the bed with eyes closed.

- In order to deep throat put your throat and mouth in a straight line and stimulate the underbelly with your tongue[267].

- One does not have to be horny to be hard or wet; one just needs to be given the right physical stimulation. In order to get a limp dick hard one must suck. This is purely physiological, not psychological.

- Remember to suck the male's fingers. They go crazy for that.

- Since the anus is so tight, usually there are only two camps: those who will never try anal sex and those who cum from anal sex. There is no other group. Be sure to know which camp the man belongs.

- Teeth and nails can be quite painful to a man's dick. Once, I will not tell whom [sic] this happened to, I accidentally used my nail when I grabbed and it made a cut. The guy sneezed and opened up the wound even more so that we could not have sex for a week.

- Use hip muscles only when having sexual intercourse.

- Use spit!

---

[266] Older i.P. audAx: Eh…not so much side-to-side.

[267] Older i.P. audAx: Practice with a banana.

Tips and Techniques for Females[268]

- I dare you to take a picture of your vagina with labias spread. I bet you never knew what you looked like from your partner's angle. I am an upside down triangle with a larger left labia than a right labia.

- Ignore what others say about the clitoris. For a woman who is having vaginal sex and cannot or does not want to massage her clitoris, that woman should pretend that all the tension is going into the clitoris and should make sure that the male's lower belly is brushing against the clitoris[269].

- Keep the vulva spread open and tense, relax, tense, relax, putting all your effort into tensing then letting go before you reach a climax.

- Make sure to arch your back.

- Use both hands under the buttocks in order to press your body, as close to the other's lower body as possible[270].

- Use the Kegel's (Pubococcygeus [PC]) muscle.

Tips and Techniques for Lesbians

There is a thing called "tribadism," that means grinding. [With a dildo] it takes some physical finesse to imitate the cock going into the pussy, but is not impossible[271].

Other Tips and Techniques

If you or your partner is tall make sure that the tall one is wearing socks. Trust me on this[272].

If you feel that you have mastered all there is to master try these techniques:

- Practice squirting (I have done this once and could not figure out how to replicate it)[273].

---

[268] Older i.P. audAx: Sorry men; I don't have a similar section for you, being that I wouldn't really know. If you're interested in tips and techniques, this is not the book for you. You can find what you're looking for on Amazon or even at a library.

[269] Older i.P. audAx: This works great with huskier men.

[270] Older i.P. audAx: A pillow also works.

[271] Older i.P. audAx: Wish I had more to say. No, I wish a lesbian would teach me.

[272] Older i.P. audAx: I don't remember why I said that.

[273] Older i.P. audAx: I can do this more often now, but I still don't know how to control it.

- Practice "serial orgasms" (multiple orgasms do not exist[274]).

- Learn how to orgasm without direct stimulation (I have been able to do this). Learn to orgasm by sexual fantasy alone[275] or from just breathing.

- Meditate at the same time[276].

When Sex is Not Godinterm[277]

Letting Sex Control You Rather Than You Controlling Sex[278]

A lesson for the men out there: Do not let sexual feelings change the way you act toward people[279]. Many children have been abandoned for that[280]. My uncle, Jonathan A. Audax, completely chose to forget his first-born son, Scott[281]. Ralph, a so-called Christian, developed feelings for me although he already had a girlfriend and ever since then had been avoiding me in high school. And it hurts[282]. It is a cruel thing to treat someone you had feelings for, or to treat someone who reminds you of someone you had feelings for, in such a negative fashion. If sex is evil, it is not the act that makes it so, but the way it distorts your thinking. If you let your sexual feelings hinder your ability to show love, then you decided to take the wrong path.

Materialism

Orgasms are like purchases. Items can only be purchased once, and once purchased[,] the value of making the purchase shrinks to nothing and the only way to find immediate gratification is to make another purchase. When sex becomes akin to gluttony, as in becoming an addiction, it loses its holiness. How do you know if it's an addiction? If it's part of the budget, it's not an

---

[274] Older i.P. audAx: I think what I meant to say is that even if you have multiple orgasms simultaneously you'd only be able to feel one at a time.

[275] "On women who can orgasm solely via fantasy, see B. Whipple, et al., 'Physiological Correlates of Imagery-Induced Orgasm in Women,' Archives of Sexual Behavior, 1992, 21, 121-133." (Zilbergeld, 1992)

[276] Older i.P. audAx: This one's the best!

[277] *See* Appendix A: New Terms

[278] *See* New Olo for more information.

[279] Older i.P. audAx: In fact, this, I believe, more than the sexual act itself, is what hurts victims of sexual abuse the most.

[280] Older i.P. audAx: Including several people in my adoptive family.

[281] Older i.P. audAx: Who finally forgave Jonathan after Scott's mom died.

[282] Older i.P. audAx: Even if I understand it. The opposite also hurts.

AudAx

addiction. The greatest sin in sex is when it becomes cousin to gluttony, a cousin of materialism. That is when sex turns evil.

Not Mutual

Physical passion is only godinterm if welcomed by both parties, otherwise it is horrible.

Connections to the World

Animals

Sex is godinterm. But one must keep in mind that it is a wild thing that can never be tamed.

Dating[283]

The stages of sexual intercourse are like the stages of dating: foreplay is the stage of flirting[284], erection is the stage of confessing admiration or love, and the orgasm is the kiss[285].

To me, dating makes no sense because it just makes more sense to get to know someone outside of such a structured unspontaneous societal structure.

I'm not really a fan of online dating, which is the only kind of dating that seems to be formal-ish anymore. With the current rule being that you can now have sex on the first date, I don't like it because you don't know who else or how many [people] someone's dating simultaneously. I also want to say, *"People, online dating sites are not Fetlife. You do realize your employer is more likely to be on an online dating site, right? Please tell me you understand that."*

All the relationship books advise putting off sex, but anyone who has ever tried online dating might find is that the norm is sex within the first three dates. [If so,] [t]his book is for you. Even if you made all the mistakes regarding sex, all hope is not lost, in my opinion.

---

[283] See New Olo for more discussion of dating.

[284] Older i.P. audAx: Texting is a great flirtation method, but sexting is lowbrow.

[285] Older i.P. audAx: If this confuses you, then realize that I was talking about dating *in my time.*

The Fickleness of the Public

I actually admire Christina Aguilera. How is it that she is called a slut but Madonna is called sexy?

Laughter and Tears

Cries of ecstasy are so much like cries of laughter or tears.

Maturation

I do not think sex proves a boy has become a man or a girl has become a woman. Sex is easy. The act of it is easy[286]. The dick goes in the hole and there are lots of nice feelings. Sex has nothing to do with maturity.

Politics

Even in a world of sex one can feel the power of politics [and the economy] all around you, most notably by noting what there is more supply of, what there is less supply of, and what does not exist. From my studies with sex I have discovered that albino porn does not exist. Necrophilia, midget, and handicapped porn are so few that it might as well not exist[287]. The porn that is most plentiful is the least controversial such as plain images of wimmin[288] naked or partially clothed.

---

[286] Older i.P. audAx: It's even easier than stock trading.

[287] Older i.P. audAx: Weirdly, there is far more [fake] incest porn than anything in this sentence, even if there are more handicapped people in America.

[288] *See* Appendix A: New Terms

AudAx

Power

Excision of the clitoris is to reassert man's power over the female[289]. Men usually do not like to know that a woman can be more aroused by genitalia that does not reside inside the vagina.

[Sex] Magic[k]

I imagine magic[k] (not ["]sleight of hand["] magic) to be like getting a penis up; it has to do mostly with the mind.

The Stage

Stage fright makes me horny. I think it is due to the heightened senses.

Stress

Like art, sex relieves stress, except for when it does not. The problem with sex is the stress and anxiety, that I already have too much of from worrying about sexually transmitted diseases and pregnancies.

Unification

Sex is a great unifier of the mind for people with Attention Deficit Disorder (ADD), Attention Deficit Hyperactivity Disorder (ADHD), and Alzheimer's. It is that one thing that all people can understand no matter what their brain deficiency[290].

---

[289] Older i.P. audAx:

> "[M]an's distrust and suspicion were not helped by the fact that women were all along compelled to resort to shrewdness in the effort to alleviate their bondage."—The Urantia Book (The Urantia Book Fellowship 798)

> Regarding power, there are two ways for a woman to maintain power (even post-feminism): via virginity and inheritance or via seduction. Women who marry may hold power only in the household if they are smart enough to be the power behind the throne, but they will eventually lose to the seductresses. It is not the fault of a woman for being manipulative, but it is the fault of a paternalistic society where women were no better than slaves. The same would hold true for men in a maternalistic society if they lacked brawn, which, if Lilith (said to be Adam's first wife) had her way, is where we would be now.

[290] Older i.P. audAx: Or proficiency.

Waiting

Whenever I am ready to stop sucking dick, due to a tired mouth, and when I am getting bored of sucking dick is usually when a guy cums. It is like how [in] every time that I am giving up trying to find something [that] is the time when I find what I am looking for. It is always when I am ready to give up that things work out for me[291].

Wine

Sex is like wine. It can be beneficial and to the point of being holy if used properly[292]. Sex enthusiasts are wine tasters; sex addicts[293] are drunkards.

Fun and Creative Ideas

Here are some fun and creative ideas if you are interested.

Fun Things To Try

- Change speed.
- Create pubic hairstyles with soap.
- Give yourself an enema.
- Grab the other's head with your legs.
- Have sex with your underwear on.
- Hold the dick like a doorknob.
- Masturbate against a pillow or mattress.
- Paint a piano on the body and play it.
- Rub the dick as you would rub a stick in order to make fire.
- Stroke the dick as if you were milking a cow.
- Try a full body massage.

---

[291] Older i.P. audAx: It's interesting to remember how I would feel guilty when my father thought I was a quitter.

[292] Older i.P. audAx: And despite what the young would like to think, sex gets better with age.

[293] Older i.P. audAx: a.k.a. sexual compulsives.

AudAx

- Try all of one type of food for a day or week then see if the cum tastes differently.

- Use a cock ring.

- Use a terry cloth in order to feel friction.

- With an eyedropper get cum and use the eyedropper as a pen.

- Without touching, have literal head an inch away from [the] penis and relax by breathing in and out slowly.

New Olo: Ages 22-34[294]

Ens Seminis: Introduction to New Olo

Disclaimer: The views and opinions expressed here are from someone who didn't understand jealousy until age 32. My ideas of jealousy are based on having a Capricorn moon.

Disclaimer: When discussing couples, I use the hetero "he" and "she"; however, this can be replaced sometimes with "she" and "she" or "he" and "he." When I mean "he/she" I use "e."

Disclaimer: If you are not interested in a chapter in this section, just consider it to be like tabasco sauce in your kitchen, and don't put it in your pie[295].

"For the last 50 years, liberals have been telling me my generation was taught that sex
was dirty—but were we? [...] When anything about sex was taught or discussed we were
told that sex is private, that it is sacred, and that it is between husband and wife."
—Zig Ziglar, *See You At the Top (Ziglar, 1979, p. 357)*

"I like to remind people that everyone's parents fucked. Sex isn't
dirty, isn't abnormal, shouldn't be a source of shame."
—Hand to Mouth (Tirado, 2014, p. 100)

"There are times I almost think
I am not sure of what I absolutely know.
Very often find confusion
In conclusion I concluded long ago
In my head are many facts
That, as a student, I have studied to procure,
In my head are many facts…
Of which I wish I was more certain I was sure!"
—Richard Rogers, "A Puzzlement" as sung by Yul Brynner

"Q. Why did humans spend so much time worrying about what others thought about them?

---

[294] I dated the ego from age 14-33.

[295] A reference to Abraham-Hicks.

A. Why? Does it make us look needy? Because we didn't really care what
anyone else thought. Did that sound cool? God, we hope so."
(Stewart, 2004, p. 119)

"At this time, it is difficult to make descriptive statements about sexual addicts with empirical
certainty. [...] There is no survey technique that can guarantee total candor about sexual
behavior across the levels. [...] Finally, studies of sexual compulsiveness often are done
within the criminal justice system. Obviously, total honesty brings risk in that situation."
(Carnes, 2001, p. 69)

"There are those who make a case that the conflict, competition, and exploitation that erode
our planet will not change until we, as humans, move into more collaborative and cooperative
modes. Such a change in ecology starts with the most fundamental aspect of our relationships:
our sexuality. We cannot evolve further until men and women treat each other differently."
(Carnes, 2001, p. xvi)

Today there are many people who are sexually confused (in more ways than one) and have double
standards they don't even see in themselves (especially wimmin). My solution is to bring these
taboo topics to the surface so that we can have honest conversations about something that makes
us very human.

What does it mean to be human? Well, if we go with the Christian definition, all humans were
born perfect. If that is true, nothing we love is ever shameful or wrong.

"Now, seed are perfect, yea, as perfect as the source from which they come; but they are
not unfolded into life made manifest. The child is as perfect as the mother is. [...]
Perfected man must pass through all the ways of life, and so a carnal nature was full manifest,
a nature that sprang forth from fleshly things. Without a foe a soldier never knows his
strength, and thought must be developed by the exercise of strength. And so this carnal
nature soon became a foe that man must fight, that he might be the strength of Allah made
manifest. Let every living thing stand still and hear! Man is the Lord of all the plane of
manifest, of protoplast, of mineral, of plant, of beast, but he gave up his birthrights, just to
gratify his lower self. But man will regain his lost estate, his heritage; but he must do it in a
conflict that cannot be told in words. Yea, he must suffer trials and temptations manifold;
but let him know that cherubim and seraphim that rule the stations of the sun and spirit
of the mighty Allah who rule the solar stars are his protectors and his guide, and they
will lead to victory. Man will be fully saved, redeemed, perfected by the things he suffers
on the plane of flesh, and on the plane of soul. When man has conquered carnal things
his garb of flesh will then have served its purpose well and it will fall; will be no more.
[...]
Man cannot die; the spirit-man is one with Allah, and while Allah lives man cannot
die. When man has conquered every foe upon the plane of soul the seed will have full

opened out, will have unfolded in the Holy Breath. The garb of soul will then have served its purpose well, and man will need it never more, and it will pass and be no more and man will then attain unto the blessedness of perfectness and be at one with Allah."—*The Holy Koran of the Moorish Science Temple of America*, Chapter 1 (Ali, 4)

This has got to be the hardest time to grow up in history (despite or in addition to the letdown from the economy). Wimmin and men have traded places. Men are the ones seeking security and commitment in their spouses and women are more aggressive and freedom-minded. It puts me at dismay that a reversal of roles brought with it a reversal of fortunes—divorce, as was the cultural Marxist's intention. Whites and Onyxes[296] have also switched places, with Whites feeling increasingly discriminated against. You can either fight or adapt. I hope that I can help you with the latter. It's okay for you to be the way God made you. It's okay to be a man, and it's okay to be a womyn. It's okay to be White, and it's okay to be Onyx, or whatever race or color with which you associate[297].

The only things more controversial than sex are money and anger[298], but since I don't have enough understanding about those subjects, I'll stick with something I do know.

This, Old and New Olo, is the memoir portion of the first half of my autobiography, covering childhood through my early thirties.

New Olo is sex philosophy[299] in a memoir.[300] This is a philosophical research paper used to reconcile sex with Christianity. (Despite the sexual bent of this book, I do not intend to use philosophy as a type of seduction as Gorgias would, but as a way to seek truth.) What this book is not is erotica. This book is not a novel or a book of tips and techniques. This is not about tips and techniques because policies are not built on techniques. Policies are built on philosophy.

---

[296] A more respectful term for blacks. *See* Appendix A: New Terms.

[297] In terms of race, I am black or white inside. I have both black and white [culture] in me, but with breaks for things like work.

[298] "[A]nger is a fact of life, and it can be used to enhance one's sex life." (Zilbergeld, 1992)

[299] Older i.P. audAx: Actually no. I may be intelligent and pragmatic, but I have not been classically trained in logical fallacies and logic axioms. I am like my friends, musicians who can create lovely music but cannot read a page of music.

Even though I may be on the path to becoming classically trained, I, irrationally, believe it would be better to publish this book prior to becoming an expert in philosophy, for there is value in preservation. If not a philosopher, I hope to be the subject of logical statements. That just might be where my power and reason for being lays.

This footnote serves as a disclaimer.

[300] Older i.P. audAx: This book is many things to many people; it is a memoir, empirical research study, collection of stream-of-consciousness essays, a skimmable reference book, and a book of poetry.

AudAx

This book is part of my purpose in this incarnation. I was chosen to relieve people of guilt, a useless emotion for the emoter. I live my life through agape, but I write with saeva indignatio[301].

One of the hardest things about sex is marriage, and one of the hardest things about marriage is sex. Nothing creates more fear, hurt, or embarrassment than sex in a relationship or marriage. I have heard a pastor compare marriage to skateboarding; sometimes you get in a few scrapes. The things that are wrong with society can be traced to what is wrong with marriage, and what is wrong with marriage can be traced to what is wrong with sex. It is this simple fact: no woman can be half sugar and half spice. She's either too much sugar or too much spice. In Myers Briggs' Personality Indicator (MBTI), a "Guardian" type, a Sensor-Judger, cannot be an "Experiencer" type, a Sensor-Perceiver[302]. It is not possible; people can be only one of 16 types, according to the MBTI, and there is no crossover. Wimmin are not happy with being stuck in a role, and neither are the men.

It's a damn shame that propaganda makes wimmin think they need to be married and have kids because they get the short end of the stick. They have to strive to be good in bed, but not too good in bed, smart, but not smarter, and they do way more chores than men, the biggest ones revolving around beautification.

It is this that I believe has devolved into a rape culture, though I do not come at rape culture from the view of a radical feminist, only a sex radical feminist if a feminist at all (they are not the same thing). It is not the fault of the sugary women or the spicy women or the men or a paternal society or feminism or St. Augustine or MTV[303] or the Internet. We didn't start the fire, but we have all played a part in it, and every person is responsible for society's destruction via their own personal sexual attitudes. It is my responsibility, as someone who can see what society needs, to write frankly about sex, not just tips and techniques, just sex and nothing but sex and its many incarnations.

As nations have seen, when drugs are forbidden, they go underground into the black market. The supply increases rather than decreases. The same happens with sex. It is only when all know that sex is not forbidden that we will be able to have a healthy relationship with it[304].

This book is not a story. If people circulate rumors of this book's "fictionality" and my hand is forced, then I will distribute evidence similar to *The Key to Uncle Tom's Cabin*, but there will be a lot of ethical considerations and backlash, so I hope my hand will not be forced. If that were to

---

[301] You know how Tim Allen had "Tool time" in *Home Improvement*? This is Google time.

[302] For a philosopher, it is odd that I would resist the word "think," but I did so because the last person I wanted to be was someone who thought away happiness with internal thinking (Ti). Granted, external feeling (Fe) didn't increase happiness either.

[303] Music Television

[304] Nudists have often argued that nudism would go a long way in healing society's attitude toward sex.

happen I could honestly say it wasn't blackmail because I have no devious political ambitions; it's just the truth bubbling up to the surface. To prove this point, I have dated people on both ends of the political spectrum. People might wonder how I can date people from opposite ends of the political spectrum from as far right as a white supremacist to as far left as a democratic socialist. My answer: political party cannot determine if you'll be a freak in bed. I have my priorities[305]. However, to ease the fears of those I write about, it will not be published while I am still living. This book was written not because it needs to be read, but because it needs to be written[306]. Because this was originally a part of *The Meaning of a Metaphorical Life*, the names I used have stayed the same and identities of people and places have been concealed for privacy purposes.

Samuel aun Weor, Isadora Duncan, Elena Ferrante, and Anaïs Nin: Why Me? Why Now?

"Sex is Not the Enemy"
–title of a song by Garbage, a grunge band

"Let Opinion Be Taken Away, and No Man Will Think Himself Wronged. If no man shall think himself wronged, then is there no more any such thing as wrong."
—Excerpt from *Meditations* by Marcus Aurelius (Aurelius, 1944)

"The great moral theorists in our tradition not only are all men, they are mostly men who had minimal adult dealings with (and so were then minimally influenced by) women."—Annette Baier (Haber & Baier 1993, 362)[307]

"Have I not chosen a delicious way to make more of you? [...]
joy and sacredness do mix (they are, in fact, the same
thing) [...]
You have shamed sex, even as you have shamed life [...]

---

[305] Would this book change our attitudes to things seemingly unrelated to sex, like politics and religion? Undoubtedly. I would fully expect there to be some sort of ripple/butterfly effect. I can only hope that it is a positive effect, but even negative effects are positive in the end. ""Everything will be alright in the end. If it's not, then it's not the end"."—John Lennon or Indian saying

[306] "[D]iary entries are not written to be read. They're written to be written and then to be put in a drawer, eventually to be discovered by one's grandchild after one's death." (Silverman)

[307] Examples of men who had a hand in shaping current day society with minimal dealings with wimmin or views of wimmin being other than are Plato, Immanuel Kant, Sigmund Freud, etc. Ernest Hemingway may have had the most dealings with wimmin, but not as people. What the world needs is an intellectual who has been on the receiving end of a catcall. And, not to brag, but I do fit that description.

AudAx

The feeling of attraction and the intense and often urgent desire to move toward each other,
to become one, is the essential dynamic of all that lives. I have built it into everything. [...]
[...] you don't dare show how much you love it, or you'll be called a
pervert. Yet this is the idea that is perverted.)
[...] this is an experience and an issue of sweeping implications on a
global scale."
—*The Complete Conversations with God*, Book 1, p.125 (Walsch)

Masters and Johnson, the sex researchers who were the inspiration of the *Masters of Sex* TV show, did great things and were pioneers of their day, but they never quite figured out how to make people stop feeling guilty. Everyone has a secret and most secrets relate to sex. But sex is not a secret, and secrets are not mandatory for being human.

If most people desire it, then why must it be taboo? To make it harder to get? To make the experience more valuable?

I am a practicing gnostic Christian whose Life Path and Intensity Number adds up to 7, a holy number. I lay my life on the line in the face of society's beliefs (and it's not the first life in which I've done so). What is there to sacrifice? I spread love around my own way. Sometimes, as with Solomon, I fall prey to my ego, but that often happens with God-given gifts and talents (some would call them genes). I communicate with Him regularly via synchronicity. I also do not budget much for food since God has always provided. I rest my faith in God's grace. Anyone who fails to see my faith is foolish at best and blind at worst. There are many fools, but do not underestimate the seeing blind. They will believe anything they see with their eyes, and anything they are told repetitively. I, on the other hand, have read the Bible twice from cover to cover; I have even gotten my hands on the Masonic Bible. (However, I am more interested in the original texts from the original Christians.) I have read the formerly hidden Dead Sea Scrolls, Sumerian texts, Hebrew texts, gnostic gospels, and Edgar Cayce texts. I have seen the tomb of Jesus. I am familiar with the formerly esoteric Kabbalah, Tibetan Buddhism[308], Tantric Buddhism, and more about the Koran than the average American. I have read the modern *A Course in Miracles*, *Conversations with God*, and *The Disappearance of the Universe*, not to mention *The Urantia Book*. As it says in *A Course in Miracles*, what I want is what God wants. With the right thinking, and esoteric background knowledge, I see none of the conflicts within religious texts that my atheistic brethren have found, though I do see some propaganda scattered about from those in power during the Council of Nicea. Where there is wisdom and truth from the past I will recognize it. I have recognized it in the words of Francis Bacon, Ralph Waldo Emerson, and Sumerian texts. There has been no other time in history when esoteric knowledge has been accessible to all; people just need direction and to trust in themselves. What we know of Christianity today goes

---

[308] The Tibetan views of sex should not be so foreign to Christians for Jesus studied in Tibet under the name of Issa.

92

against all forms of esoteric wisdom, from the gnostic Gospels of Thomas and Mara Mariamne[309] to Kabbalah to Hermeticism to the Rosicrucian Order to the Dead Sea Scrolls to Nag Hammadi. In a strange way, I seek to bring us back to an understanding of sex that is both radical, holy, and radical by claiming it is holy[310].

Since adoption (of Moses and Jesus) also affects Christianity greatly, I think I was born uniquely equipped to provide some new understanding to the people of God.

To all those who have eyes to see, I am from the East and the West, the North and the South. I am from the Far East and the Western hemisphere, I am from North America and the Southern states in my birth country and adoptive country.

I've had about as many sexual (whether with actual sex or not) relationships as I've had lives[311]. I recall or know more than 25 of 97 past lives since Atlantis[312]. In order, some of my lifetimes have included lifetimes as a priestess, geisha (or kisaeng), and, most recently, a mobster's girlfriend. This sexuality has spread over into this lifetime.

If ten thousand hours makes one a master, then I have mastery in spades.

There is no one who understands the term "brotherhood of man" better than I do unless that person is a polyamorous slut ("slut" being a positive term in my book, for lack of a more accurate term). Oh, and I just happen to be a bit of a succubus (like Bo from *Lost Girl*, though I prefer Kenzi's fashion sense). When I see clairvoyant visions, they are for others, not myself. When I heal, it is for others, not myself. My body (and mind) was made for the good of mankind, whether in a sexual way or not.

---

[309] The proper title for Mary Magdalene. Why was Magdalene a popular German Christian name from the mid-16th century to the 20th century in my family tree? They knew something about St. Mary Magdalene that has been blotted out and revised in the 21st century. Multiple early Americans don't name their daughters Mary Magdalene without good reason. That in itself shows that we can't just point our finger to the Council of Nicea. The rewriting of the Bible and the focus on a paternal society void of female influence is far more recent than we can imagine. Just consider how much has changed in your own lifetime.

[310] See Appendix B for spiritual credentials.

[311] Older i.P. audAx: Just because you had a past-life marriage with someone doesn't mean you're meant for each other; it just means that you feel like an old married couple.

[312] I know this statement will discredit me to some and not others, but I don't care

AudAx

My core values are freedom[313] and openmindedness. You can't have either without the faith to know that the choices you make with free will and the opportunities/risks you take will turn out all right in the end (some would call that predestination or optimism). Openmindedness allows the mind to open up to the gray areas, the unknown, which in turn allows us to be more open to love and relationships. Oh, and individualism is another core value of mine. The Law of Attraction implies that I am uniquely qualified to be of help in the lives of people with whom I come into contact, not by doing, not by saying, but by being. I can create a revolution just by being myself, which is easier said than done.

When I do things for a higher cause, I know who I am serving[314]. All I know is that I couldn't not write this book. To hell (or heaven) with the consequences (and damn the rule against double negatives).

Mission

[My mission is to] reveal what is hidden because a lot of people will relate.

How to Read New Olo

If I don't explain a connection in this book or *The Meaning of a Metaphorical Life*, it's because 1) my autobiography serves as a snapshot of my mind, and I don't think by explaining concepts to myself that I already know and 2) we have Google nowadays, which, to use an analogy, means we don't have to treat email as snail mail or a word processor as a typewriter, but can maximize the technology at our disposal.

Like a fiction author, I will imply things, and I intentionally will not explain new concepts or ideas that can be googled. In the age of Google and hyperlinks, I am surprised no one realized how much paper real estate can be saved by foregoing explanations and leaving the homework up to the reader. Not only does it save space, but it shows trust and confidence in the reader.

I'd rather assume that people are smart individually, and all I care about is if I'm getting through at an individual level. I am going to write this book like a German manual, meaning I am going to assume that you are intelligent and willing to do further research if you are interested. If you

---

[313] The collective beliefs of society are limiting, but a desire for freedom may lead inevitably to loneliness. Freedom is not for people who need people. Therefore, I may need to revise this for myself to say that my core values are individualism and openmindedness.

[314] Most people in my generation either start off religious or end up so. My biggest point of pride is that I started off religious and ended up religious. Though I might have neglected my relationship with Jesus or took Him for granted, I never forsook him.

think that, as a womyn writing from a womyn's point of view, that I should consider my audience or if you think my being indirect is manipulative, asking you to read between the lines, passive-aggressive, or a request for you to read my mind, then you probably don't have sex as often because you're missing pretty obvious (and most likely repetitive) clues. If you want to have a sexual experience by reading a sexual book, then you get to participate by either doing the work to understand the references, from a womyn's point of view, or treating the book like your own personal whore. It all depends on the level of sexual experience and philosophical enlightenment you wish to attain.

American History

"Suburbs were where children could be raised in safety and ease. Away from the dangers of city streets, they would have room to play and freedom to roam. Instead, we have play dates and 'helicopter parents,' children robbed of spontaneity and parents hovering constantly above them. Street play is proscribed; in places, even sidewalk games are against the law…. And today's suburban children are denied the pleasures of our generation. They see their friends when parents arrange it; they rarely walk to school…. What now are hallmarks of conformity—enforced exclusion of commerce, rules for setbacks and lot sizes, the meddlesome homeowner association—were created by the dissidents of another era, abolitionists, *sexual pioneers*, seekers of spiritual enlightenment. The residents—abolitionists, feminists, and transcendentalists—lived with no laws or jails and rejected the institution of marriage. The settlement was soon a magnet for cranks and eccentrics, and it become notorious for its unconventional ideas."
—*Dead End: Suburban Sprawl and the Rebirth of American Urbanism* (Ross), emphasis added

"I'm not as free to be as perverted as I want to be."
—Disturbed

Perhaps it's not so much beauty I despise as it is American secular liberal culture. I cannot even take a man's phone number, and thus an opportunity for one-to-one human contact with the opposite sex, without the fear that he only wants sex. I don't think this would have been an issue in a tribal culture.

Debunking the Most Pervasive Sexual Myths

Myth: He can't change.

Truth: He can change if you change. Don't listen to new age feminists; listen to age-old Kabbalah wisdom, which has existed longer than the Bible.

AudAx

Myth: STDs are irreversible.

Truth: As far as I know, I have reversed herpes with a proprietary, homeopathic blend. It was time-consuming but well worth it.

Myth: Every pre-menopausal female needs pads and tampons to get through her menses.

Truth: Tampons cause toxic shock syndrome, and pads cause rashes. Whenever possible, I opt for natural methods to American methods. I use natural family planning, sea sponges, and cotton pads. I even prefer sulfate-free shampoo to going all the way into the no poo movement.

Myth: Breast cancer cannot be prevented.

Truth: Breast cancer is caused by repetitive use of carcinogens. Avoid the carcinogens of synthetic hormone therapy and hormonal birth control, and you'll be fine. According to DNA, I have a higher than average risk of contracting breast cancer. I can't even imagine having a breast removed (but since I have small breasts, it should be easier to imagine than if I didn't). It would almost be like having one testicle. That's called being a monorchid (which I think sounds emasculating, literally).

Myth: Cancer is incurable.

Truth: Cancer is incurable in the United States[315].

Marriage: More Than Legal Prostitution

"But I would have you without carefulness. He that is unmarried careth for
the things that belong to the Lord, how he may please the Lord:
But he that is married careth for the things that are of the world, how he may please his wife.
There is difference also between a wife and a virgin. The unmarried woman careth for
the things of the Lord, that she may be holy both in body and in spirit: but she that
is married careth for the things of the world, how she may please her husband.
And this I speak for your own profit; not that I may cast a snare upon you, but for
that which is comely, and that ye may attend upon the Lord without distraction.
[...]
The wife is bound by the law as long as her husband liveth; but if her husband
be dead, she is at liberty to be married to whom she will; only in the Lord.

---

[315] I think my father almost had prostate cancer. I don't much about it, but I'm sure it affected my parents' sex life (which I always thought was a myth since I wasn't conceived through their union).

But she is happier if she so abide, after my judgment: and
I think also that I have the Spirit of God."
1 Corinthians 7: 32-35; 1 Corinthians 7: 39-40 KJV

A good marriage should encompass everything the word "firm" encompasses through the root "firmus": steady, strong, substantial, solid, secure, safe, stable, mature, valid, loyal, faithful, steadfast, and true.

I remember one time I felt very passionate about something that I was sure my mom would agree with. Well, she didn't. She sided with Dad. Though I was upset about it, it taught me a valuable lesson: put the marriage before the kids. I learned this lesson again when someone gave it to me as advice. The marriage is forever (at least it was designed to be in one's lifetime, whether or not the logic was for survival), but the children are only under your roof for a short while before they have families of their own to which they must cleave. "If we create a child-centered home to the neglect of our marriage and the marriage falls apart, or if we only give the marriage fifty percent of the oxygen it needs and the marriage suffers, the children of the marriage will suffer too." (St. John, 2014, p. 10) I have done enough soul searching (and believe me, it's been a lot) to know that one's self-esteem is rooted in the parents. Anything about the parent, in our minds, reflects on us. If our parents could not maintain a marriage, we doubt our own abilities to do so as well. Don't worry so much about the children. Don't hover, especially in a codependent sort of way (with children or your spouse). Children of even poor or narcissistic families still turn out all right in the end. I know because I've dated them. It's okay to give them some independence; it will be good for them.

Sex in Marriage

Marriage is a pretty big statement. The statement is that 1) marriage is better than being unmarried, 2) that the spouse will be sexually available as long as humanly possible to the other spouse, and 3) that the spouse will love the other past the time when sexual intercourse is possible.

Sex is never a good reason to marry. One does not marry someone because they get a heroin-like or cocaine-like high. No, regular consummation is only a byproduct of a successful marriage. It says, "I appreciate you," not "I want you for your body."

Marriage is a holy union. Any creature designed for marriage was created to be horny. Sex for the rest of your life that your spouse could not refuse (historically)? From a man's perspective, who'd want to pass up that opportunity? Unfortunately, from a woman's perspective (not including me), it seems that many feel that once they have e, e won't get away and she can do whatever she pleases, even if it means no more sex. It seems that men have caught onto this attitude and realize the prison potential it has in tandem with it's nympho potential. According to Redbook, "the women who never have sex [in marriage][316] outnumber the women who have it daily!" (Redbook, 2014). And, this, my dear, is something that needs to change *now*. That's why I wrote this book.

Starting now, there should be no more pronovalence (ability to have sex only in a prone position) unless you're into necrophilia fantasies. I don't want so many people to have erotophobia, fear of sexual love; miserotia, aversion to sex; or hedonophobia, fear of pleasure (unless they have phobophilia, hamartophilia[317], peccatophilia[318], or traumaphilia[319] and get off on hurting others[320]).

This book was partially written for married couples because sex within marriage is a duty, right, and responsibility that should also be fun. Biblically, within a marriage, "not being in the mood" is not a valid excuse to dodge marital responsibilities, but this does not give either one license to coercively rape each other either[321]. Sex is a privilege and a duty within marriage. But marriage was also intended as a safe place to act out fantasies.

Healthy and Lasting Marriage Starting with Courting

"Partners in happy relationships assert themselves, express anger, and sometimes
raise their voices and even yell. Yet they do not fight dirty [...] and there are lots
of positive comments[322] even in the midst of conflict." (Zilbergeld, 1992)

"The vast majority of dating men and women expect sex to be part
of their activity within a few dates." (Zilbergeld, 1992)

"I say therefore to the unmarried and widows, It is good for them if they abide even as I.
But if they cannot contain, let them marry: for it is better to marry than to burn.
And unto the married I command, yet not I, but the Lord,
Let not the wife depart from her husband:
But and if she depart, let her remain unmarried, or be reconciled to
her husband: and let not the husband put away his wife."
—1 Corinthians 7: 8-10

---

[316] They participate in agenobiosis, living with their spouse without sex.

[317] The love of committing "sinful" acts. Heck, I'd rather someone think that vanilla sex was sinful and get off on that, then have them think that extreme nonconsensual violence was "sinful."

[318] See footnote above. These people probably also have stygiophilia; they derive pleasure from thoughts of hell.

[319] I could imagine rape victims having traumaphilia or traumatophilia.

[320] Mutually agreed upon

[321] *See* 1 Corinthians 7:1-10

[322] And affectionate touch

Lots of people don't understand courting. Let me make it clear: courting is an engagement with no sex or optional escape clauses; it's like having an option to own a house that you rent or an option to own 100 stocks. It should never go past one year. And this is why many rich people do not have the same rate of divorce, because they understand that commitment (making the leap of faith) has an appreciating payoff.

Courting is like buying a house (meaning that dating is like renting an apartment). You may want to look inside many houses, but you'll only live in one, or at least will most likely commit to one at a time and have few in your lifetime. Nothing will provide a greater sense of stability. You will have to put down a downpayment with the wedding costs. A marriage is expensive to maintain and repair, so it must be something you can afford over the long haul, but it is worth it in the end. Some will decide to rent-to-own through cohabitation, but there's still a lot to be said for buying outright.

Courting is a lot easier to understand in the context of work. There is a screening interview, phone interview, face-to-face interview, unspoken at-will agreement, verbal nondisclosure agreement, tenure or time before being fully vested, a promotion, and a merger.

To be certain about an engagement around a first date, one has to be able to have wisdom, also known as having a high rate of what can be called prophecy. They must know basic laws of relationships, be very selective (see the Courting vs. Dating table), and trust in actual astrology by an actual proven (certified) astrologer and/or expert in like systems. (Actual astrologers are easier to find in India or Korea, not as much in the united States of America, with a lowercased "u.") It's not as difficult to have all these things in place as it sounds; cultures have been doing this for centuries, far longer than the united States of America has been around. People say that people were fools to use astrology with arranged marriages, but I say that people of today are egotists if they believe that time passed makes right.

One courts to marry; one dates to have fun. The purpose of dating is to learn what works for you and what isn't working so that you can fix it before making a permanent commitment. Be aware that "dating around" is sometimes a key word for nonmonogamy and is a faster way of finding more frogs. In fact, dating is like job hunting; you need to have a boyfriend (or girlfriend) to get a new one. I would call dating, the American way, "sowing oats" or "wasting sperm." My aunt believes that you can date anyone you want if you are not married, that only marriage counts as a committed and dedicated relationship. Dating is a failed American experiment that only courting can solve, even though the intent was to use dating to solve the failures of courting. This may sound unlike me, but I went through the pain so you can go through the gain.

In the beginning of my book, I talk about the book being for the single singles or married marrieds. The reason for this is because addictive behavior shows itself most in the married singles and the single marrieds. It was when I was a married single that I began in "recovery."

AudAx

I write this book to the married marrieds because a sex relationship outside of marriage (or a marriage-like arrangement), whether romantic or platonic, is like cheese with mold. Sure, you can eat around it the way you'd eat around a bruised apple, but in the end you're respecting your health and keeping yourself safe by throwing the whole thing out. That's not to say that you're throwing the baby out with the bathwater. The "baby" is the lessons you have learned, and, like an actual baby, your understanding grows with time. The "bathwater" is the dopamine, which has never saved a life.

This book is made specifically for the married marrieds or those who have made a vow of singleness (of purpose) or have committed to the sex industry. In general, it's made for those who can commit either way[323], for holy singleness requires just as much commitment as marriage, if not more so for beautiful people. There is a time and place for everything (under the sun). I did not write this for people who are "blowing in the wind" and "sitting on the fence," only committed people. Woe to the person who is undecided and without singleness of purpose. If you aren't being as purposeful about a spouse as you would be about a job or a house, with criteria and a "screening interview" or "open house," then you are not in control of your relationship; you are letting the relationship control you.

You can't mix a single life with a married life or a married life with a single life (though not to say it's not possible). If your occupation or experiences dictate, "never trust anyone," then you should not get married. Marriage requires trust. If you believe jealousy is good or are a one-person type of person, then you'd probably be miserable being single or nonmonogamous. Not all romantic relationships were designed with the outcome of marriage, and this is the greatest thing that people need to understand. Communication must be clear from the get-go.

Even consciously thinking about crossing that boundary muddies the bathwater. That is why right-thinking is important in Buddhism and Christianity. However, literally dreaming about it is excusable because dreams do not often have obvious meanings.

When I say "dating," I actually mean going into a relationship without dates, which is what I used to do. Dates in themselves are actually closer to courting because of the element of discernment. The average number of dates before deciding is three. This parallels the number of interviews for a corporate job. The one nice thing about being attractive is that its ability to bring quantity gives one a larger field for the process of elimination and gives greater negotiation power.

Dating, the ritualistic way is superficial with too many rules to memorize for an average person. I have rarely ever dated the ritualistic way. I find it to be a silly custom. It seems to me only appropriate for online dating (gag me with a spoon) in order to root out the overtly wacko (and if I thought the person across from me was wacko, he probably thought the same of me).

---

[323] When choosing your path, the most important thing to remember is the end goal. The end goal of married parenthood requires a different strategy than just having fun.

If someone doesn't accept your dating offer, then it just means they have different "families of origin," different past lives, or a different confirmation bias or paradigm shift. It has nothing to do with your self-worth.

Courting vs. Dating

Courting for Marriage	Dating for Fun
"Good guy"	"Bad guy"
Responsible/good judgment	Fun/impulsive
Beneficial to each other's self-esteem	Challenging karmic lesson
Commitment	Sexual attraction
Compatible families	Compartmentalized
Compatible lifestyle	Mutual interests
Growth	Stagnation
Logical	Illogical
Permanent for one or more incarnations	Temporary
Most Marriageable Personality: ISFJ	Most Dateable Personality: ENTP
Synergistic	Selfish
You are the answer to e's prayer	The answer to your prayer
Unconditional love	Unrequited love

As you can see, courting outweighs dating as a way to find a spouse, for a person who is dateable and a person who is marriageable are wholly and inherently different, though they can change.

If you are still having difficulty understanding courting, due to its assumed banishment from American society, I recommend that you watch *The Quiet Man* or read *Choosing God's Best*, which details the history from courtship to dating with the advent of the motor vehicle. The only reason there are dating rules is because dating came from a combination of courtship plus cars, and courtship was designed for people who didn't know how babies are made. I don't miss rules, but I do miss the innocence of early high school romantic relationships, when it was not possible to have sex (due to having chaperones and living with parents). I imagine that's what no premarital sex is like.

AudAx

Honestly, I also think the reason why we have social expectations for sexual behavior is to protect people who have had a breakup and are going back out into the dating world, to even the playing field.

I cannot say enough good things about waiting for marriage, if marriage is your aim. Courtship was designed for our own protection. Also, most in the sex community know that waiting increases cum production for squirting.

People I know who have practice courtship, including my parents (not all of them are from the expected generations): About 7% of the American population, according to my sample.

Downsides of Marriage

The very definition of "commitment" implies that that marriage is an institution, just like a prison or psychiatric hospital to which one is committed.

People who say their purpose in life is to be married with kids usually don't know their purpose. Maybe at least half of the entire population throughout history were married with kids. That is not, therefore, a unique reason to explain one's specific and singular reason for being born.

The downsides of marriage are the same as the downsides of having children, if you do not know why you are doing it or if you think it will solve all your problems. If anything, your problems could be exacerbated by the very thing you sought out to solve your problems.

Baron Yu[324]: 1 Corinthians 7:7 and Single Marrieds[325]

"And Jesus answering said unto them, The children of
this world marry, and are given in marriage:
But they which shall be accounted worthy to obtain that world, and the
resurrection from the dead, neither marry, nor are given in marriage:
Neither can they die any more: for they are equal unto the angels; and
are the children of God, being the children of the resurrection."
—Luke 20:34-36

"For I would that all men were even as I myself. But every man hath his proper gift
of God, one after this manner, and another after that."—1 Corinthians 7:7

---

[324] Older i.P. audAx: Baron Yu spent only four days with his wife after his wedding before returning to work.

[325] Older i.P audAx: Even the great South Asian Indians who were married left their wife and child.

As Luke 20:34-36 implies, without death there would be no marriage. There would be no birth and no institute would be necessary for raising a child. However, there is no death anyways since we are reincarnated and have lives between lives. In this life (or lives) we have the issue of time and space. In my mind, this means that marriage is unnecessary for those who understand that it is true that we live forever here and now (even though there is no here and now).

Most scriptures in the Bible advocate sex within a monogamous married life and shun anything to the contrary as it would defeat the purpose of a monogamous married life. However, right in the modern New Testament we have Jesus shunning the married life (supposedly). If the way to heaven is not through marriage, then all those things that are shunned because they do not work for the goal of marriage, should be acceptable because they do work for the goal of being single.

So for someone really contemplating an unmarried life, it is obvious that one will be faced with the issues of being seen as a commitment phobe, even with a fearless commitment to Jesus and the issue of being either unmarriageable or the type one wouldn't take home to mother. I think our society needs to revise our understanding of perpetual singles since more are choosing that lifestyle (Read *The New Single Woman*). Originally, when married life was desirable, spinsters were seen as failures. Now that the single life is desirable, the term "old maid" is "old hat" and we must come to understand what makes someone a successful single. I think the first indicator, of course, is happiness. However, I would add that the ultimate successful single, much like a religious monk, transcends the physical world of special relationships and is able to see God in all beings. The comparison with the monk does not mean I advocate celibacy, though it is something to consider. Some people prefer Kantian moral philosophy, as to even allow themselves a moment of relaxing their strict codes of conduct would lead to further relaxation. Others do better with testing the limits and seeing where their boundaries lie.

Some well meaning people tell me there's someone for everyone and that someday my prince will come. Someone told me he was sure I'd get married because I'm pretty. I'm sure marriage requires a lot more than looks. Maybe that's just me. Maybe people can overlook a lifetime of emotional baggage, poor communication controls, poor impulse controls, and could forgive me for being a writer. Actually, I'm sure I could overlook that in someone else, and have.

The thing that's missing from the equation that many people don't get when they "advise" me is magnetism. There are certain types of people I draw to me, and I don't actually want to draw other types toward me because I like playing with fire. I'm just not gonna marry fire. Singleness is a lot safer for women. Ironically, it is men that seek out the single life.

Most people see sex as temptation, especially if they're in a closed marriage. However, I see marriage as temptation because I know my purpose in this world, and marriage is a distraction from it. Marriage would only serve to attach me to this lifetime.

AudAx

Now don't get me wrong. I love the idea of marriage as much as the other girl. Just because I have considered a life of singleness doesn't mean I don't love the idea of marriage. In fact, I relish it. I know exactly how I want my marriage to go; I have the Tapeterest board. However, I know that a ceremony is not the real thing, and I fear[326] that any marriage of mine would probably end "up in flames" since I tend to attract married men and people with psychological disorders. I still jump toward thinking about marriage whenever I get involved in a new relationship, but I know it's just fantasy. As long as it stays in my fantasies, no harm can come of it. It's a lot like edging actually. It's like getting right to the edge, right near climax, and then backing away from the edge of the roof.

Another benefit of being single: It would be a lot harder to do sexual magick[327] if you're married. But strong emotions make it so much easier. And, believe me, single people have a lot of strong emotions.

Longest time without a long-term relationship: Two years

Longest time without sex: Six years (middle school and high school)

Longest time without romance: Two years

Longest time without a monogamous/closed relationship: 10 years (middle school through most of college)

Longest time without anything: One year

Will Fine: Commitment in Marriage

From my experience, I know that love is not enough. Love is only the why, not the how. Commitment is the how. Love is both a motivator and a teacher, but it doesn't tell you what to do day to day.

The way I understand it is that commitment is a tool that helps us escape our destructive "yeahbuts" and comfort zone ("klipa" in Kabbalah). Commitment makes you quit-proof. I do not understand why people would be afraid of a tool, but I do understand that people fear the unknown and that which is outside of e's comfort zone.

---

[326] Older i.P. audAx: I no longer feel that way.

[327] Sexual rites have historically been used for manifestation. The most intense emotional state is at climax. That's when you can launch an intention, decision, or postulate.

An assurance of commitment may not always guarantee quality (in bed). Sex is one of the few skills not practiced in a classroom setting or as on-the-job training, so the only way to ensure quality sex is to be with someone who is experienced.

It's true that all the good guys (or girls) are taken (when I say "good" I don't mean it the way most people do). That's why it's harder to find quality sex when you get older (but when you do it's amazing!).

Will was the only married man who ever turned me down (strangely, single men are more likely to turn down my advances). He was taken by college and married when he was 26. He was amazingly good at turning down my advances without getting weirded out. He knew exactly what I was doing and knew exactly how to respond. I respect him for that.

Faithfulness and Fidelity

"Smoothness of life is simply deadening because it keeps us out of what is real life… [The] indulgent life [is worthless] because it cannot connect men and women with the real springs of strength and of power. No man was ever made against no resistance."—Robert Elliott Speer

"Faithful" is the best word I can think of for being monogamous because faith requires complete trust, and I learned that I cannot be faithful if I do not have complete trust in someone; it is only when I do that I can be.

Faith requires trust. When I was unfaithful to my boyfriend, I did not put my faith in God either. I trusted no one to fill my needs but myself, and the only way I could fill those needs was through other people.

If we are to understand fidelity as faithfulness, then to have faith by necessity means to have one God, and not to be disconnected from Source and not to worship idols.

The word "truth" originates from trëowth/trïewth "faithfulness, fidelity, covenant" from "triwwibö "covenant." A person who is not faithful to e's spouse cannot live a life of truth and has broken a covenant with God.

See www.markmanson.net/disney/ for more information on fidelity.

Loyalty

The ad for the movie Elizabeth states "absolute power demands absolute loyalty." This explains two things to me: first, why sexual fidelity is important to many (especially dangerous) people, due to their ego, and, second, why marriage should be avoided because it is a distraction from God. You cannot serve two masters[328]. That is the basis for Luke 20.

Loyalty does not equal fidelity. If you agreed that it does mean fidelity, then it does—for you, but if there is resistance then other solutions are possible. Loyalty is getting dessert where you had dinner. Infidelity is going elsewhere for dessert.

Regarding Me and Loyalty[329]

I understand loyalty and the value of it. I am loyal to family, friends, employees, companies, service providers, teams, values, causes, and God. I would only hire loyal employees if I were a business owner. I am faithful. Faith is a cornerstone of Christianity and the Law of Attraction. The definition of "faithful" is closely related to reliable. If a spouse is not reliable and cannot be trusted (inside or outside of the bedroom), the foundation of the marriage is built on shifting sand.

I do not know why people conflate sexual fidelity with loyalty. According to an ex, I have never been sexually faithful to him, but I have had the same hairstylist for about 30 years, I continued to make monthly payments to a cause that people people stopped making monthly payments to, I have kept people in my heart and mind that others had long forgotten, and I understood that character was all about committing to something long after the excitement for the moment had passed. My sexual fidelity, in my mind, had absolutely nothing to do with loyalty, because I am a very loyal person.

I am a Virgo. I am loyal. I am a minx, a pet dog. I am loyal the way a dog is loyal. I am loyal to my owner, but I always love to be petted by others. I am thankful that my friends are there when I need them for a pet.

I like to be petted by others but at the end of the day I know who to go home with and I will follow that person to the end of the world. Getting petted by others does _not_ indicate an issue with the relationship. It does _not_ mean I don't love you. I can still love you unconditionally, but I don't want you to punish me for doing and loving what is natural for me to do and love. Punishing a dog for wanting to be petted is cruel and unusual. To ask me not to be petted by others would go against my nature. I am not a jealous person and do not expect my boyfriend or spouse to be either. When I was punished for wanting to be petted, I was in an abusive relationship. When I was free to be me, I was happy.

---

[328] However, two horses increase power by more than double for a carriage. Ponder that.

[329] This was written when I was young and before "recovery." My thoughts on this have changed.

I find money differences to be a good reason for divorce, but not sexual infidelity. Sexual infidelity is never an acceptable reason for divorce in my book (pun not intended), and most royals would agree.

For appearances of following social mores, the only way I would be persuaded to have a semblance of fidelity is through a purely logical, health-oriented stance, but even that would not have the same intention. I do not need to suck a cock in order to suck someone's finger or toe. I do not need to undress to give someone else an erotic massage or to receive one. There are many ways to satisfy. And that which I satisfy is not a hunger, not a beast, but rather the fulfillment of my path.

Divorce[330]

Opposites do attract, but like also attracts like. So opposites, once they get together under the same roof, especially in the first year, just as soon break apart. The most common pairing and break up is between someone who takes life too seriously and someone who does not take life seriously enough. The inevitable result is that children become the opposites of their parents due either to compensation or differentiation. (Other common pairings and breakups are between savers and spenders and people with high sex drives and low sex drives.)

Since Onyx[331] men are mostly raised by responsible single mothers, this contributes to emerging adulthood, the rise of the Omega male, and increased incarceration among black males.

Another factor, and a reason why I'm anti-feminist (or pro-menist), is that a patriarchal society ensures the propagation of the species by ensuring that wimmin need men. When wimmin do not need men, which is quickly becoming the case today, they do not need to propagate the species either. (Nowadays, men need wimmin for practical and spiritual purposes, but wimmin want men in general—with donor insemination and other methods; wimmin no longer need the sperm of their boyfriends or love interests).

Why is the divorce rate so high[332]? Because women have jobs. 'Nuff said. Why is the marriage rate so high despite the divorce rate? Because men don't have to have enough jobs.

It's an ill-fit for all involved because wimmin still define themselves by relationships (or are defined by relationships), and men still define themselves by occupations, but more wimmin are

---

[330] Here's a simple solution to the divorce epidemic: if parents would stop insulting their children, we would have less divorce.

[331] *See* Appendix A: New Terms.

[332] ...besides the fact that Americans believe in love marriages, which produces both a high and withdrawal, or disillusionment.

in occupations and more men are in relationships. So most wimmin and men now have to get over a nagging feeling of being a failure, according to their respective gender stereotype. The feminist movement, along with mandatory schooling, spawned emerging adulthood and Omega males. Along with the civil right movement's and the recession's creation of disillusioned and incarcerated young Onyx males, the society is being systematically destroyed from the inside out. I wouldn't even need to write this if we weren't so confused about gender roles, sex, love, and relationships as a result of these and other factors.

The Role of the Spouse

It is the role of the spouse to keep you aware of society. A spouse that keeps you in the dark dims the light that you can offer to the world. If your spouse is not your best friend, then you do not have a spouse.

Cohabitation

Dating leads to cohabitation, which is a form of concubinage and devaluation of the womyn. (Unless, of course, cohabitation is viewed as a conscious marriage without the paperwork. If that's the case, I think it's safe to say that ideas on premarital sex do not apply.) Cohabitation is an illusion the way college is an illusion; it makes you think and act like you're married when you're not (college makes you think you're financially responsible when you're not). You get the post-traumatic relationship disorder without the commitment (before God) that goes with it. Breakups feel like divorce, and reconciliation feels like remarriage. However, it's all false.

Playing Devil's Advocate: Allorgasmia, Apistia, and Uxoravalent as a Fetish

"But I say unto you, That whosoever looks on a woman to lust after her has committed adultery with her already in his heart." –Matthew 5:28

"Most marriages do not end because of adultery; they end because of neglect." (St. John, 2014, p. 10)

"Just because you're on a diet doesn't mean you can't look at the menu."—Anonymous

Allorgasmia is fantasizing about someone other than your partner. Uxoravalent (as opposed to uxorovalent) is the ability to attain sexual satisfaction only extramaritally.

Have you ever noticed that the greatest romance classics are about affairs—*Casablanca, Dr. Zhivago,* etc[333]. It doesn't take love to make a marriage; it takes love to make an affair. So what? Are we going to accept that the greatest stories in our lives are covered in "sin," that even God wouldn't look favorably upon us finding our twin soul[334]? Ridiculous! Are we going to say that if you loved someone you wouldn't have sex with someone else?

I call BS. The only reason why that myth has lasted as long as it has is because if you love someone you will prioritize them. However, priorities don't reduce the temptation to consider. Most countries already know that the person whose child you have may or may not be good in bed and that people who are good in bed are not necessarily someone you'd want to live with. If you can find someone who is both sugar and spice, then good for you, just don't expect it. Just look at the statistics of how many married couples have sex often.

Well, if you're having an affair with someone you "love" but are still having sex with your spouse, does that mean you don't truly love "the other"? Are we going to say that there has to be a "one" and not a two, three, four, or whatever? I have loved and still love four or more men, not including my father. Are we to say my perspective is not valid? Well, I'm used to people saying that about my life. I don't care anymore.

If I ever get married and have a child and she asks if our love is the greatest love story, I will tell her the truth: All the great classic romance stories are about people who can't be together, so that would not apply to me and my potential spouse. However, what we would have that great fictional lovers don't have is perseverance, dedication, commitment, and the willingness to delay gratification. This also serves to benefit other aspects of our lives.

Not everyone will agree with me because, well, they probably get off on the idea that their partner gets jealous, which could be a fetish in itself. I know someone like that[335]. I think he had zelophilia, arousal from jealousy. It's whatever turns you on. Personally, I'm more interested in candalagnia, watching my partner have sex with someone else, which is different from mixoscopia (watching others have sex). It's on my to-do list.

Ed Steffens and George Mireille encouraged adultery on the woman's part. The former was a sex addict; the latter was a commitment phobe. Could this sentence be reversed? Sure.

I think this is an appropriate place to discuss this. Considering that the last word Jesus had to give people of today was concerning psychology in *A Course in Miracles*, which you may or may

---

[333] See The Word "Love"

[334] Note: A soul mate can be either someone you date or someone you marry. Actually, by now, everyone you know is a soul mate as we have all gone through enough incarnations to be repeating the same relationships. "Twin soul" is a more accurate term.

[335] As well as me in a former life.

not be familiar with, it is my belief that Jesus, and God (whatever you think God is), understand that psychological disorders are the cause of extenuating circumstances[336]. Much of the book discusses the dangers of special relationships, to which any divorcee can attest. I understand the dangers of special relationships too.

Adultery, Divorce, and Lust: Adding an Inferior Element

> "[W]hosoever looketh on a woman to lust after her hath committed adultery
> with her already in his heart. [...] [W]hosoever shall put away his wife,
> saving for the cause of fornication, causeth her to commit adultery: and
> whosoever shall marry her that is divorced committeth adultery."
> —XI. 31. and 35. The Sermon on the Mount, *The Jefferson Bible*

> "If loving you is wrong I don't wanna be right
> If being right means being without you
> I'd rather live a wrong doing life
> Your mama and daddy say it's a shame
> It's a downright disgrace
> Long as I got you by my side
> I don't care what your people say
>
> Your friends tell you there's no future
> In loving a married man
> If I can't see you when I want to
> I'll see you when I can
> If loving you is wrong I don't wanna be right
> If loving you is wrong I don't wanna be right
>
> Am I wrong to fall so deeply in love with you
> Knowing I got a wife and two little children
> Depending on me too
> And am I wrong to hunger
> for the gentleness of your touch
> knowing I got somebody else at home
> who needs me just as much
>
> And are you wrong to fall in love

---

[336] For those not familiar with or interested in *A Course in Miracles*, I would recommend Gnostic literature. Those who disdain Gnostic Christianity know nothing of Jesus' life post-mortem for they know neither Mariamne nor Thomas.

With a married man
And am I wrong trying to hold on
To the best thing I ever had
If loving you is wrong I don't wanna be right
If loving you is wrong I don't wanna be right"
—Luther Ingram, "(If Love You Is Wrong) I Don't Want to Be Right"

I used to be oblivious to the wrongness of adultery. When asked about the topic this is all I had to say:

"Have you ever wondered why God forbids adultery, divorce, and lust? I believe
that He detests adultery and divorce because adultery and divorce is [sic] akin
to idolatry, for it separates the bond between Him and you. The reason I give
for why He detests lust is because lust is earthly, but love is spiritual."

I had a hard time grasping the concept. I thought the societal abhorrence to adultery was restrictive of natural human needs. And that is what put me in the category of "cheaters" in power—those who do not get No's and who don't have consequences. Or the only consequence was a continuous stream of jealousy, which created the very thing it was in reaction to. I was a somewhat financially independent, impulsive self-gratifier dating an epicurean whose self-gratification came in other forms. Now I see that it's not even about sex at all but about trust. Restoring trust is the hardest thing to ever do in a relationship and requires both partners to work on it, even the person whose trust was broken. It casts a layer of dread on every interaction.

Adultery comes from "adulter," which means "toward the other" and has an element of counterfeit (love). It relates to "adulterate," which means to defile or corrupt something "by adding another substance, typically an inferior one," according to the Google definiton. This word comes from "adulterare," which comes from ad+altero, meaning "to alter."

By this definition, someone who adds a superior substance (person), might not be an adulterer, as they might have just had a "starter marriage." If the introduced "substance" is superior, then the secondary provides a service in strengthening one's resolve and courage to do what should have been done without impetus. The secondary then may become the primary.

The people I knew who committed adultery in their heart or body: At least 2% of the American population, according to my sample.

Affairs: Objectification and Illusion

"Affair" comes from "à faire," meaning "to do." I have never "done" anyone, but I have known people (biblically) and misused my rights as someone in an exclusive relationship.

Both "affair" and "engagement" have nonsexual meanings related to events. The process of having an affair or being engaged are both very major events, though for opposite reasons.

Having an affair means trading down. Instead of being with a man who wants the commitment and responsibilities of marriage and children, one ends up with a fun-loving albeit temporary opportunist that will never put you first. They usually don't fit the family dynamic. In this case, love is impractical and does not advance the human species.

The single largest reason against affairs, and this is where I am speaking to my birthmother, is that affairs create lives tainted by shame and destructive, compulsive coping behaviors that take a lifetime to heal.

Cheating: Taking the Easy Way Out

> "You say I'm crazy
> 'Cause you don't think I know what you've done
> But when you call me baby
> I know I'm not the only one"
> —Sam Smith, "I'm Not the Only One"

You know those stories of how people who are truly in love don't feel the desire to cheat? I think it only applies to people with a low sex drive, people with very little sexual experience, or people who have more to lose than a lover. I can say that I have cheated on the men I loved, but when my sex drive slowed down I no longer felt the desire or need.

What is cheating? When people think of cheating in a romantic context, they think of dishonesty and deception, but that is an incomplete view of cheating. If you think of cheating in an academic context, it is asking someone else to do your homework, plagiarizing, using the answer sheet to answer test questions and believing that you've done nothing wrong until you get caught.

So the big issue one should have with cheating is not just the dishonesty, but the fact that someone got something without putting forth the effort. Gee, cheating sounds a lot like socialism. Yes. Anything won without the effort, without the cost, is not expensive and is not valuable. So what happens is that the parties involved with cheating, or extramarital affairs, are devaluing themselves and lowering their self-esteem[337].

Really, looked at it that way, cheaters deserve pity, not because they deserve a second chance, but because they deserve to be looked down upon as someone who is no longer an equal. And

---

[337] Actually, disregard anytime I reference "self-esteem." Love/Belonging comes before Self-Esteem in Maslow's Hierarchy of Needs, so either he's wrong or psychiatrists are wrong. Ignore anyone who tells you that you need to work on your self-esteem. What you need is to feel loved, not self-esteem.

the person who should be angriest should not be the person being cheated on, but the person being cheated with.

I find it so amusing that women are so quick to pin men as cheaters when that is typically my issue, not theirs. In addition, I don't really care if they do; it doesn't affect my income. (Having been to The Landmark Forum, I also find it amusing that people are so hung up on dating and marrying people who are 100% honest because it's such an unrealistic expectation for most people, unless people are put in a completely accepting environment like Landmark Forum, which, for the most part, is composed of strangers.)

Nowadays, marriage means nothing to those who play the field, and most people play the field, married or otherwise. Nowadays, "Are you married?" either means "I want to date/have sex with you but want to see if it's alright" or "You're in a seminar, and I want to make sure that what I'm saying is relevant." I'm somewhat traditional. What happened to the olden days where when people gave out their phone number it meant "Let's go on a date?" Now all it means is "I haven't had sex for a while, and you're the first pretty thing to come along."

It is deceptively easy and at the same time annoying that "No" is no longer understood to be "No." Saying "no" to sex really does hurt a guy's feelings, but even though women don't like to hurt people's feelings, sometimes it must be done if it's not something she wants.

I do not see the parallels between adultery and cheating.

Infidelity[338]: Traitorousness from the Attitude of "What's In It For Me?"

My sexual advances have only been turned down twice. Both times the man believed in the sanctity of a committed relationship. One was married and one was (legally) single.

So about 2-3.6% of men I have blatantly sexually advanced on were not willing to stray; this is a much lower number than one could find with public surveys regarding sexual fidelity, so it's safe to say that most women have been cheated on one time or another.

When at least 50% of the male population, let alone slightly less than 98%, has had an affair once, about equal to the rate of divorce, I think it's no longer necessary for it to be a stigma, just as sex in itself, since most everyone (every adult) has it at some point, shouldn't be a stigma either. A

---

[338] Most (liberal) people can understand and sympathize with closeted gays and transsexuals; they understand that those people felt they had to live double lives to survive. They do not call them duplicitous, but rather misunderstood. How is that different from Tiger Woods? I have heard from many men; especially those who can't get any from their wives that their desire for sex is part of who they are. They too feel that they must lead double lives to survive. Why it is okay then to love gays and transsexuals but not okay to love straight men?

stigma prevents communication from fear of people's perceptions, when in reality there is very little difference between the person who is afraid and the person who is perceiving.

Some Christians believe that sex is only holy within a marriage, which less than half of the country of the united States of America can maintain for a lifetime, with no one coming (or cumming) before. Such a belief in sex goes against God for it makes man a replacement for God and an owner of His equal. And it makes an owner of a man's equal. Some say that Jesus is the bridegroom to the church, and that is not a polygamous arrangement. Everything God created was for our pleasure and happiness. He is not a horrible father.

Sex is arguably a human need much in line with food, clothing, shelter, and love. Can we survive without satisfying these needs? Absolutely, for a temporary amount of time depending on the need. Imagine being afraid of eating from someone who was not your designated food provider because you were told you could get salmonella or the seeds to make more food for yourself? What if someone told you that you would go to hell for eating from someone else? Or how about love? What if you were a dog that was punished every time you wagged your tail and got a petting from someone other than your owner?

I can see how infidelity could be considered a sin however. When infidelity is mentioned in the Bible, it refers specifically to being dishonest in my humble opinion (IMHO).

The issue is that, since the genders are not the same, men have to lie to get the same things women get when they tell the truth. So since not everyone can get things the same way, no one should? I don't know why most men can't do it without honesty and integrity for all parties involved since it's not that big of a deal for wimmin. Refer to the 10 Commandments. If you pay attention, half of the 10 Commandments (1, 2, and 7-10) say this same thing with different words.

However, I don't see why infidelity done in the right consciousness should be a big issue if the other person practices healthy non-attachment or actively participates with e's partner's extramarital experience. (*See* Open Relationship/Open Marriage: Shared Infidelity)

I've come to the conclusion that people say they dislike sexual infidelity because it shows a lack of commitment, but to some people (i.e., me) it does not show a lack of commitment. If it does not interfere with obligations and actually improves performance, then it is useful.

It is popular to dislike sexual "cheaters." They say it is the lying they dislike[339], but subconsciously it is that person's unconscious negative self-talk that seeps off the pores of the desperate to be loved that they do not like. They do not like those who have been told repeatedly at the hands of their loved ones that they'll never be good enough, even if such message is contradicted

---

[339] Lying is a slippery slope into gaslighting.

occasionally, since this is a common thread among those with sexually addictive behaviors. And who would?

Love Addiction

> "Yes, Life is Love and Love is Life
> No Life without Love; no Love without Life
> Our Life for Love; our Love for Life
> My Love, you are my life."
> —Edith Piaf, "La Vie, l'Amour" [English Translation]

> "My chief objection to a quarrel is that it ends a good argument."
> —G. K. Chesterton

No discussion of infidelity is complete without a discussion of love addiction.

I have a hard time accepting that people can be objects of addictive behavior. These are people with whom you may have married in past lives, people whose souls you can talk to, people with whom you have shared your secret fears. How can spirit be an object of addictive behavior? This is hard for me to understand.

However, I know what it's like to be a drug for someone else. Also, "people mistakenly believe they 'feel better' or 'act better' or are 'only happy' when on drugs." I felt the latter with an abusive boyfriend; it was clear I was addicted to him.

Addicted person: Person who seeks other people to make e feel good.

Addictive person: Fun-loving person who does not reality test well.

Love addiction is really fantasy addiction; that's why it goes beyond romance but is usually only recognized in romance situations. Codependence is what really solidifies it. However, the codependence adds a layer of pity. If you have two love addicts clinging for dear life to each other, it is really a relationship not just of mutual abuse but of mutual pity. (I think in one relationship, I got back with him 9 or more times, not including breaks.)

The downside and danger of love addiction and sex is that both provide the illusion of compatibility. People with addictive behavior don't tend to get divorced until they're recovering. Not saying that to deter anyone, but people feel extremely comfortable with illusion.

Those who follow *The Rules* are love addicts pretending not to be love addicts. Those addicted to love do not practice sound courting habits. For instance, they'll start a relationship long distance or date far outside of their age, race, or religion, thereby maintaining a secretive relationship. They may become enmeshed and take everything their partner says as gospel à la the Kennedys. When a relationship ends, they will believe they are still in a relationship and may take up fantasizing or stalking, being either a petty annoyance or a danger.

The person most compatible with you (and at the same vibrational frequency as you) will be the last person you "date."

Love addiction is as potent and as deadly as a hard drug. The only substance that is harder to withdraw from is heroin. If love addiction did not exist, then murder would either cease to exist or the frequency would reduce itself to a manageable number. People say that when they return to their addictive behaviors it is worse than before. Since I have no desire to be murdered by a "loved" one, or extremely physically abused, I take recovery very seriously.

Hera: Jealousy

> "Jealousy…which is the scourge of many a marriage, is nearly always caused
> by self-doubt."—Maxwell Maltz, *Psychocybernetics* (Maltz, 111)

Steve Harvey declares that jealousy indicates that a man is in love, and it even says God is a "jealous God" in the Bible. However, 1 Corinthians 13:4 says that love does not envy (is not jealous), and I do not believe that God is a jealous God. Steve Harvey is wrong; jealousy among men is uncommon.

Myth: Jealousy is innate.

Truth: Jealousy is learned or an extension of a competitive nature or astrological sign.

I can't really use competition as a feeling because it is not something I have any attachment to either. Men have been known to go crazy in the futile attempt to make me theirs, and they have also been known to go crazy when I am already devotedly theirs.

The closest I've ever gotten, for someone with a Capricorn moon sign, to the feeling of jealousy is the feeling of betrayal within a relationship, or envy of a couple people when I was a single teenager. These are the emotions, coupled with the emotion of self-importance, that I used to come close to understanding it.

1-2% of the sample size gets extremely jealous, according to my sample size. Yes, it's that low.

Jealousy and Gender: Code of Honor and Self-Protection

Wimmin disliked "homewreckers" historically because they felt that "if we're in it together, we might as well [follow certain codes]" and "homewrecker" wimmin ignored those codes of honor.

Wimmin were motivated for the same reason most people are motivated to do anything—for survival. Wimmin without men in a paternal society could not survive. They needed men to sign for apartment rentals, checking accounts, and credit cards all the way up until the 1980s. So in this respect, the proper term was really "cheating" because the financial benefits were unearned.

The only people who tell me sex isn't everything is wimmin. However, they could probably tell me that money is, at least a big factor. If you want to understand the world, follow the money.

Money, in my opinion, is on par with sex. Not only do big spenders attract savers, but people with low sex drives attract people with high sex drives. I don't know what it is about opposites attracting.

Since the wimmin's revolution, jealousy becomes more illogical, but it continues to get passed down due to childhood imprinting.

Men, on the other hand (historically), are jealous because they saw women as treasures to be owned, prized for their birthing hips and genes, and "other" men were seen as thieves. And what does the Ten Commandments say about thievery? Thou shalt not steal [or covet]. Since the women's revolution, the two genders are more equal, with women now having more dominance in the economy[340] and in schools. Therefore, male jealousy too is inherited for the only reason for it is tradition.

The Evils of Jealousy

Jealousy cannot be explained away as something that happens because someone is so beautiful or desirable. Pot is desirable, but it is also designed for sharing. No, jealousy is a result of low self-esteem, maybe shame, the result of logic that says that there can be only One, and if you're not it, that you must be unworthy of love, unlovable. It is a similar motivation as sexual compulsion, maybe even with the sense of loss, abandonment, or trauma, but without the fear of intimacy. The only difference is the results. However, one result is similar: poor relationships.

Some say that the number one reason for divorce is infidelity. I would argue against that conclusion. I believe that the number one reason for divorce is jealousy. There is a reason why I put love addiction next to jealousy—because it is dangerous. See the last paragraph of Love Addiction.

I find jealousy to be the forerunner to abuse, and I step over it lightly. Jealousy is the sign of impending abuse or impending divorce (or a break-up). The need to be jealous is a self-imposed, limiting belief, much like the belief that money is not a renewable resource, which, of course, billionaires know is a lie. Jealousy punishes feelings. I think only premeditated crimes should

---

[340] Who does the salesman seek? The wife, who makes spending decisions.

be punished, not emotions. Jealousy indicates distrust, which signals the end of a relationship because no solid foundation has ever been built on distrust. (Ironically, it takes a lot of trust from the non-primary partner to have an affair.) Jealousy is irrational, territorial (objectifies people the way Hitler did during the Holocaust), and causes one to compromise integrity. For example, the one who values privacy, in a fit of jealousy, will stop at no lengths to learn a password, check past phone calls, check past emails, and stalk/lurk on social media. I dare say that the person more responsible for a divorce is the one who claims e did not want it (per the Law of Attraction).

Jealousy is controlling from a place of fear because the root of jealousy will always be distrust; it is never endearing and it is never romantic. However, it is forgivable. If I am going to control my boyfriend's résumé or provide him with my urine to pass a drug test out of my desire to make rent payments, then I am just as guilty of control.

My definition of jealousy is "violating someone's boundaries due to lack of self-esteem when imagining that someone is cheating." The first and last time I was with a truly jealous man, he believe that he controlled my body and took the credit if I was physically healthy[341].

Jealousy goes against my values. It says to the other person, "When you are under my roof, you will be under my control." It is parental control. It creates a prison. Jealousy is a loved one's prison. It says, as the Ten Commandments says, "I am your God, and you shall have no other gods before me," therefore implying that one must choose between the significant other and their God. Taking the Law of Attraction into account, it also states, "I am afraid of what I don't want," thus bringing what is not wanted into reality.

Jealousy is also an excuse for not committing to a jealous person. It brings out nothing but doubt and hard questions for the fiancé(e): Do I really need to get married? Is it worth the hassle? Will I need a prenuptial? Will I stay for the kid(s)? Would I rather be honest and risk hurting his feelings (and mine by proxy)? Would I rather be natural? How much am I willing to go without? Do I even want to try to restrain myself?

Sexual compulsives, the smart ones, try their best to avoid jealous people at all costs. (I've not always been smart.) Jealous people do not fit neatly into a sexual compulsive's lifestyle, and no intelligent person wants someone to tell them they should feel bad or guilty about their nature, the amount of chemicals God gave them, or the amount of difference between them and the other person. To do so would be insane. (In this respect, I've not always been sane.)

In the same way that sexual compulsives can objectify a person, jealousy can too by reducing the other person to a mere possession. The dangerous combination of sexual compulsion and jealousy cannot possibly lead to intimacy. It is only when people are treated as people, not possessions, that there can be intimacy.

---

[341] It's kind of sad that the person most compatible with me, as of now, thought he owned my body.

The Law of Jealousy

The person who is perceived as the reason for abandonment of a loved one will always be the most hated no matter if the hater is not a jealous person, is nonmonogamous, has never seen the person he hates, or is not in a romantic relationship with the loved one.

The Leman

Anyone who is having an affair with a married person out of love (and not one-night stands) falls into the trap of believing the married person to be a genicon, a person who is dissatisfied with e's actual partner. That is not always the case. Actually it's probably rarely the case.

As a spouse, I would have a lot of competition, but I myself am not competitive. Mistresses vie for attention. Are not video games, football, and TV shows mistresses? Unlike most wimmin, I'd rather any spouse of mine have a human mistress. That way he could become more familiar with and understanding of wimmin. That can only benefit a marriage. For no womyn can compete with a womyn who bears her loved one's children.

I have been a reluctant mistress more than once, and I have learned that married women do have cause for concern, for when I was a mistress I got all the attention, but when I wasn't I got lies.

Open Relationship/Open Marriage: Shared Infidelity

"So be mine
And don't waste my time
Cryin', "Oh Honeybear
Are you still my, my, my baby?"
(Don't you dare!)
[...]
No way, can I be what I'm not
But hey, don't you want your girl hot?
Don't fight, don't lose your head
Cause every night, who's in your bed?"
—Jonathan D. Larson, "Take Me or Leave Me" from the musical *Rent*

"When I'm with you I'm with you, and when I'm not with you, you
don't worry about where I am"—Kerry (Silverman, 2010)

"When people say something 'isn't natural,' what they mean
is it's not natural for them." —Mark Manson

AudAx

I believe that it is the idea of "the One," perhaps sprung from the idea that not only can one only be in one marriage, but that one can only be in one religion, is what causes the ills of jealousy within a monogamous relationship. Such idea of "the One" (in marriage or religion) is a relatively new concept in the history of the world, as is the idea of a love-based marriage. Sexual infidelity is only an issue in an American or American-inspired culture that believes in love marriages. Love and sexual attraction have not historically been a requirement for marriage, thus relationships outside of marriage were widely accepted. Americans think nonmonogamy is a new concept when in fact it is a relatively old concept. People used to just call "marriage."

Extramarital relationships have been useful under a variety of circumstances: infertility (which is biblically acceptable), lack of sexual interest due to a marriage of convenience or royalty, erectile dysfunction, sexual anorexia, barrenness, disgust or fear of sex or gender, differing sex drives (and there will always be differing sex drives). Forced celibacy, especially if the person being forced comes from a culture where sex enhances gender, is always cruel and unusual punishment. Abstinence should always be mutual. If one person does not wish to be abstinent, then they should have options. Under all of these circumstances, this should be worked out via communication. Extramarital relationships that did not come from the above circumstances and are not worked out via communication are either the sign of a larger problem within the relationship (which money issues could uncover equally) or maybe just the sign of an enthusiast.

Because of my past lifetimes, I am still very sexual. However, I have also gotten fed up with being exclusive with a man (from a past life) that could have more than one woman. I fought back—with nonmonogamy.

As I learned from my peers, open relationships are the way to go. I get the idea that my understanding of marriage is not a common one (in America) or else I'd already be married. I'm just following the lead of the people I've spent time with but do not know how well their experiments in marriage turned out. So *take my words with a grain of salt.*

I have made it clear that any mistress of my partner is welcome in our house. She deserves respect too, as well as a clean (not inexpensive) bed. I prefer the idea of an open marriage, where the spouse is prioritized as primary (which would be different from say a polygamous or polyandrous situation).

At least with open relationships there's open communication. I much prefer established open relationships to dating. I try to avoid dating as much as possible and only use it as an expression to mean that I'm going steady with someone.

In an open relationship, there is a ton of more respect. It says to the other person, "I trust you to make the right decisions. I know that you will stay safe." Now if the other person does not make the right decisions, and does not practice safe sex, it would make sense to rein that person in temporarily until e is back on e's feet.

With nonmonogamy, "shared infidelity" is an experience that can bring people closer together. Have you ever watched *That 70s Show*? Bob and Midge were married characters on the show that would go on double dates with their spouse. I was amazed at how well the show portrayed real life and real life personalities. The script writers had amazing insight.

Open relationships, though it involves relations outside of the primary relationship, is not even in the same category as cheating. It is a conscious choice to have fun, enjoy life, and accept the risks that the enjoyment of life in such a way could lead to death for one or multiple (i.e., many) people.

The fundamental Christian assumption is that STDs are worse than a monogamous marriage. That's not actually true if you come from an abusive family, whether abused from a narcissist or codependent (though ocnophile[342] narcissist abusers are certainly worse). In the case of marriage, codependents (i.e., anyone from an abusive family) often find themselves jumping from the frying pan into the fire, either being abused again or becoming the abusers, the latter being a lot harder to accept.

If you open yourself to physical risks via nonmonogamy, your emotional risks are low. If you open yourself to emotional risks via monogamy, your physical risks are low. These things must be taken into account.

As I was saying with my friend, who is like me, how do you explain to someone that if you have sex outside of the relationship that the relationship is still going great? No complaints whatsoever. How can you explain that you want to commit your heart and soul to someone in marriage, but that your lower half can't agree? How can you explain that you were not made to be monogamous, but you don't want to give up playing pretend? How do you explain that all nonmonogamists are at heart feelers, at heart dreamers, and that they dream of being normal because they feel it would be a better life? Who would understand? Who would have empathy? Would you?

Or would you disregard someone forever because they do not give you something you believe is believed by most? Would you cut off your dick to please your brain?

There's nothing more disappointing for a nonmonogamist than sharing awesome and excellent news with a loved one then the loved one breaking down into tears, ignoring you for days on end, or labeling you mean things just because God gave you a high sex drive and most wonderful enthusiasm for the most natural act.

The idea of a traditional marriage seems like something I'd do with low self-esteem—to imagine that I would be so desperate for a father for my child that I would allow a source of pride to be a source of shame[343].

People in open marriages make up 5% of the sample size, according to my sample size.

---

[342] Chronically dependent on their lover

[343] I no longer hold this viewpoint.

Marriage of Convenience

I don't actually see anything wrong with a gay man marrying a straight woman. There would obviously be no premarital sex, but sex is not a requirement for marriage, and they could be lifelong best friends. There might be challenges with having kids, but nothing that can't be solved with science. The only major issue is whether or not the man is closeted, for closeting brings shame and is a result of shame. Shame brings addictive behavior. In fact, staying in the closet is addictive behavior in itself. However, for someone who formerly chose sex as a drug of choice, marriage to a gay man is appealing since sex is not the reason I'd get married, nor should it ever be.

How to Do Monogamy

"Familiarity breeds contempt." –Aesop[344]

Before declining sex from your spouse, consider your children. No, not like that! What I mean is if you decline your spouse's advances, where do you think that frustration will be channeled? Into anger? Yes. Rage? That too. Constant rage? Most definitely.

Will that affect the child's self-esteem? Yes. Will that child blame e-self? Yes. Will that affect that child's beliefs? Yes. And how about when that child has a child? Yes, it can go one of two ways, intolerable domestic abuse that ends in disaster, or a dysfunctional family dynamic that gets passed down three or four generations at a minimum. All because your mind was closed to sex.

Do you get why I wrote this book?

I'm sure at one point my father enjoyed my mom, but he no longer respects her, which is a dynamic of which I'm all too familiar, being a sexual compulsive. Studies from Dr. John Gottman, mentioned in his book, *The Seven Principles for Making Marriage Work*, as well as in *Blink* by Malcolm Gladwell, have shown that spousal contempt can even lead to a weaker immune system (Gottman, 1999) (Gladwell, 2005). The words of judgment and criticism are based on making a decision. Condemnation can soon follow and, according to Dr. John Gottman, a marriage cannot survive condemnation. If my mom were to die I would have no doubt that it was somehow caused by a marriage of too much familiarity and contempt.

If you want to learn more, I'd recommend *The Seven Principles for Making Marriage Work*. You can then learn the importance of a term called "bids."

In *Conversations with God* (I think), Judgment Day is actually the day when judgment ceases.

---

[344] I do not agree with this statement anymore, but some people do.

Types of Nonmonogamy

Types of Nonmonogamous Relationships

Type of Relationship	Frequency of face-to-face contact	Communication frequency	Expectations	Employment Analogy
Fuck Buddies	Quarterly	Quarterly texts	Just bootycalls, no friend intros, secondary	Vendor
Friends with Benefits	Monthly	Monthly calls	Sex and real, intimate friendship, introduced as a friend, secondary	Consultant
No Label	Weekly	Biweekly texts	Just sex, just fun, no friend intros, primary	Unpaid internship/ Temporary contractor without benefits
Not committed	Weekly	Biweekly calls	Sex, romance, and light friendship; friend intros; primary	Temp-to-hire with benefits
Secret	Biweekly	Daily calls	Sex, romance, and serious friendship; no friend intros; primary	Part-time paid under the table in cash
Nonmono-gamous	Daily	Daily calls	Sex, romance, real friendship, and intimacy leading to open marriage; friend intros; primary	Full-time

Fuck Buddies

Even though being friends with benefits stretches your mind and the limits of what is acceptable, the idea of fuck buddies is just, no offense, plain stupid, and I don't say that about many things. Perhaps, I think this because of the area in which I live where privacy is of utmost importance in a job. A fuck buddy is not even a buddy. If you cannot trust someone enough to give them your name, address, or any personally identifiable information why are you fucking that person? Now I can say this is stupid because I did this once, without really understanding the arrangement I was signing up for because it was not in the brochure. Even a fuck buddy relationship is a relationship, with all the psychology that goes along with it (especially regarding control in a D/s[345] arrangement). And it involves masterminding. Do you want your income, intelligence, integrity, or spirituality going down the drain because you mind-melded with a poor, stupid, or lying sexual compulsive? No thanks. If you cannot even have a decent "friends with benefits" relationship because all you're focused on is sex, or if having one non-sexual encounter is a stretch for you, then it's time to realize you've got a problem, and I don't use the term "problem" lightly.

Friends with Benefits (Young i.P. audAx's Opinion)

I tried to stay non-monogamous, especially with guys, because of the belief prevalent (opinion) among men (especially older men) that wimmin and men cannot just be friends. American culture has made it a possibility to marry without the goal of reproduction and made it an impossibility for men and wimmin to be friends if they are both straight. Ever since the '60s, we've had the *When Harry Met Sally* mindset. Even *What If?* (spoiler alert) about an opposite sex straight friendship ended in marriage even though the preview seemed to promise that the movie wouldn't end that way. It is not possible to see a movie without some form of romance (though I have seen one that didn't), and rarely mentions asexuals.

I have found that many guys still hold to the belief that friendship with a girl leads to a relationship with a girl, that in turn leads to sex. Men make very good friends, especially gay men. In fact, I find male friends to be the best of friends. However, since I found that these guys would not just start out with a friendship with me, I felt that it was necessary to date, reel them in with the lure of sex, have sex a few times, then break up in order to get to the goal of friendship. I break up with the promise of staying friends afterwards, and it is only then that I could secure a friendship with that guy. Their end is sex. My end was friendship.

Men are motivated to be good friends due to the mutual attraction both sides have, but they know they will not be your prime anymore, so they are also respectful and not jealous anymore. If men can lie about friendship to get in a womyn's pants, is it not fitting for a womyn to lie about sex to get a man's friendship? However the cost of such a friendship is knowing that

---

[345] Domination/submission

such an arranged friendship has a bias. If men abhor the idea of being in the friendship zone, then shouldn't wimmin abhor the idea of being in the sexual zone? Sometimes, even a sexual enthusiast as myself, abhors the sexual zone. I find it all very interesting. Men are generally too eager for sex and wimmin are generally too eager for marriage. Has no one ever put two and two together and realized that marriage can only be between lifelong friends?

It's not so much that men cannot be friends with wimmin, but that people with compulsive sexual behavior will spoil every friendship. In a state of addictive behavior, I related to the masked woman on *Emerald City*, the TV show. She bought her men to own; I bought men who owned me, either romantically or platonically or both. Any female sexual compulsive understands that sex is not the end goal—conversation is.

People feel a lot more comfortable after having sex together, just as parties are a lot more fun after drinking. However, just as alcohol leads to negative consequences, so does a relationship started with sex. The disciplined way is the harder way but also the way that leads to more rewards.

So I had a hard time understanding why people were so against premarital sex and how I could remain sexually faithful but still keep up outside friendships.

The problem with "friends with benefits" is that if you open the door for one person, people will assume that you will open the door for every person. Such a friendship not only kills trust from a significant other, but also from friends. It adds an uneven playing field (as there will always be a top and a bottom) and diminishes each person's godliness and divinity. Each interaction thereafter will be tinged with distraction from a non-sexual topic of conversation.

Confusing church with state is like confusing sex with love, either way you're "fucked." The latter arises from incest and the idea of friends with benefits.

Sex ruined as many friendships as money ruined. I did not consider anyone a friend who had ulterior motives, anyone who wanted my sex, membership, time for activities alone, money, or skills. I wanted to believe that mixing friendship with sex, money, or work one time would stain the friendship forever and that no such person wanted me for me.

When your friends are people you slept with who want to continue sleeping with you, you have to face reality: you don't have any friends, you have no one to console you in your darkest times, no one has your back, and no one will really give a damn if you die except for the dog, but only because when you're dead you can't drop crumbs. I've had the kind of heartbreak a slut has and not a divorcée. More men have told me they loved me than should be allowed, but I do[346] not feel like I have anyone I can talk to. Today (May 1, 2015), I have three men who are desperately in love with me, and three more men who may love me but know the boundaries. There may

---

[346] Did

be more I don't know about. I'm not even that beautiful, and I'm not even famous. I think it's because they can be themselves [sexually] and have fun with sex around me. That's why I wanted to write this book—so that people can realize that they can love themselves without my presence. *I'd rather have one man who loved me and was marriageable than have many men pine for me who are not.*

There are two reasons I didn't stay close friends with my male college pals: either they didn't plan for their future or they were too sex-minded. The typical response from sex partners when I decided to stop communicating with them was that they will pray for me. I didn't fall for it one moment. I no longer associate with people I have had sex with, including people I'm interested in romantically[347]. (I'm not married as of this time.)

But once I eliminated the spoiled friendships, I found I had none left and that perhaps friendships weren't perfect and that I should be thankful to be sought out for having things others coveted as opposed to being dismissed and ignored.

Why be heterosexual[348]? When an entire gender has lost your trust, you cannot afford to lose the trust of the other gender. It is especially important for extroverted women to have female friends and coworkers because introverted men do not understand and/or respect an extrovert's need for platonic company.

I came to realize that it wasn't men who were unsafe, but it was I who perverted friendship, thinking that I had to manipulate to have a friend. It was I who operated out of *quid pro quo*, sex for friendship.

As for myself, I have disappointed myself time and again with my own tortuous proclivity to temptations.

However, I did learn that it's a lot harder getting a guy without coming onto him.

If you can only prove to people that you are worthy by being in healthy relationships, does that mean all your exes are less worthy? I don't believe that some are more worthy than others if we are all a part of God.

When people expect me to forget my exes, I'm confused. I still don't know how it's possible to completely eradicate an ex from one's mind, to feel less for someone you were once intertwined with, and to extricate them from one's self. Apparently, it's possible because Myers-Briggs ISxP types do it all the time; I'm just not able to wrap my head around this brainwashing phenomenon.

---

[347] This is no longer true because I got back together with an ex briefly, thinking that by finally knowing how to be monogamous that he would want me back.

[348] In this stage of my life, I choose men not because I am straight. I choose men because I want my future child(ren) to know and have a positive attitude toward e's grandfather.

If one has already cut off contact voluntarily, there are only four reasons why romantic love for another should get in the way of a current relationship:

1.   The other person gets jealous

2.   You or the other person believes in "the One"

3.   You end up comparing the other person to someone in your past where the current person is not "good enough"

4.   You are more willing to give up on commitment to the other person because you experienced better in the past, even though you yourself knew it wouldn't be sustaining.

Osho says that love is a state of being. If that is so, then love cannot be contained or restricted. So if love were expressed through sex, then it would be natural to be monogamous. However, love is NOT expressed through sex. Love is expressed through caring.

No man can tell me who I can love or not love. Nor can any man take away my love for him, no matter what mean things he does. No man can define for me what love means to me. I can love family I have never met or friends or even exes.

Friends with Benefits (Older i.P. audAx's Opinion)

You know what friends with benefits is most like? A contracting job without benefits. So why is it called "with benefits" if there aren't any? The irony about friends with benefits is that once you have gained a "friend with benefits," the only way to keep your sanity is to treat life as if you are single, meaning that only when I had "unbroken up" could I deal with the emotions of having broken up.

"No Label" Relationships

No label relationships are worse than friends with benefits, which is worse than nonmonogamy. It's like being in a BDSM relationship where your master does not permit you to orgasm (emotionally). And, for me, after having experienced a six-year relationship previous to this one, it was like going from being upper middle class to bankrupt. Out of more than 100 romantic relationships, I have only ever been in a "no label" relationship one time. Probably because they suck, and not in a good way.

Mormons are Christians Too: How to Do Nonmonogamy

Always leave things with the primary better than they were to begin with. This is similar to the rule for being a good guest: always leave a place better than you found it[349].

The difference between a person who has an affair and a person in an open relationship is that a person who only has affairs is unlawful, dishonest, and/or confused. (And a person who has affairs is a person who gets off on having affairs; not a person who gets off on commitment.) A person only in open relationships is lawful, honest, and/or has everyone in their rightful role where their strengths are highlighted. A person who has done both has experienced withdrawal.

Extramarital and Secondary Affairs as Voluntary Service for the Greater Good

If people were thankful to the "Others" (unapproved secondaries), then people would have fewer trust issues because it wouldn't have to be a secret. If we were thankful for our lovers' or spouses' renewed sex drive, and secondaries knew their purpose is one of service to their loved one's loved one, then the world would be a happier place. People forget that secrets hurt the withholder AND the withheld.

Everyone has their place. That means some are made to be primary and some are made to be secondary (and some are made to be both for different people). Some people will never be primary boyfriend/girlfriend material, and a successful nonmonogamous relationship hinges on being able to tell the two apart. Another word for "abuse" is "misuse." So if you use a primary as a secondary and a secondary as a primary, then you have abused both and neither one will feel comfortable wearing the other's shoes. If the primary is traditional, then there is no secondary.

Any person who can neglect one person should not try to take on two people. Only the person who has enough affection for two (i.e., a codependent) should attempt more than one relationship at a time[350]. Another way of saying this is if you don't remember to water one plant, you won't remember to water two.

For the secondary, you must fully understand and be okay with living in the shadows and must not require the primary (your lover's loved one) to live in the shadows. If you are in this arrangement, then the primary is not narcissistic. If the primary is, then it is not a mutual agreement, and this will not end well for any party. The most important rule for a secondary is to be cognizant of the primary's feelings and important dates. Know when there are major events, family events or vacations, and most definitely step out of the limelight on their anniversary and New Year's Eve!

---

[349] Hint: It's harder for the primary or secondary to be jealous after the primary or secondary have had sex with each other.

[350] Since codependents get a bad rap for being unhealthy, by spreading out the attention, it does less damage to either relationship.

Pros of open relationships:

- Allows someone else to fill in gaps and do what the primary doesn't want to do
- Built-in babysitter
- Donors for the infertile
- Keeps people sane
- Satisfies sexual and emotional needs
- Secondary will notify the primary if something were to happen to loved one

Cons of open relationships:

- One downside to nonmonogamy is that one cannot truly level up in nonmonogamy.

Benefits of being primary:

- Ability to plan for the future
- Ability to approve of secondary
- Ability to start or end openness of relationship, keeping in mind its pros and cons
- Allowed some bossiness
- Beneficiary
- Can have unprotected sex
- Clear conscience
- Has a say in major decisions
- Irreplaceable
- Knows loved one has a bodyguard (someone to watch over the loved one) and/or kids have a potential babysitter
- Loved most
- Metaphor: Three-course meal or more
- Mutual decision making
- New Year's Eve kiss
- Permanent, or more permanent
- Public (displays of affection)
- Receives financial support
- Receives legal support

AudAx

- Reminiscent of each other's family of origin (not to be confused with a birth family)
- Sees loved one frequently, if not every day
- Sees the real person
- Sex after marriage (long-term gratification)
- Takes priority with time and money
- Trust
- Usually the official parent
- Will meet the family

Benefits of being secondary (or mistress):

- *Attention*
- Like fish (catch and release)
- Metaphor: Fast food or dessert before the meal (immediate gratification)
- No strings attached
- Privacy
- Sees person at e's best
- Sex without marriage

What I will do for a secondary:

- Shred financial papers prior to e's arrival

What I will not do for a secondary:

- Allow e into my sanctuary (my abode)
- Be called pet names
- Be ordered around like a whore
- Clean the house
- Get a canker sore from sucking
- Get connected to a crime
- Give money, even if e's own momma's broke
- Have sex within two weeks before having sex with the primary
- Put up with stupidity

- Sext

- Send pictures if e knows what I look like

- Spend money on anything over the price of stamps

- Spend too much time with (immature secondaries tend to forget that other people have things like chores and paying bills)

- Wait over half an hour

- Walk a long distance

How to Not to Do Nonmonogamy: A Life-Changing Experience

In an experiment, one day my boyfriend and I switched places. He had a jealousy phenotype, and I had a promiscuity phenotype. However, he became a nonmonogamous noob, and I became a monogamous noob to see how the other lived.

For me, the paradigm shift was easier because I no longer felt the thrill of nonmonogamy and valued genuine friendships over fake ones. But what I noticed for him was that, with his paradigm, there was a lot more deceit involved, even if innocent deceit, in which case it became an affair instead of an open arrangement.

Maybe it's because women don't understand the meaning of secondary or maybe monogamous men don't understand the meaning of keeping to a schedule so that the transition is seamless. They make it harder than it has to be. It's a lot less healthy.

This is the time when Mihaela Furtry found him. She, being the anxious and clingy type, instantly took to Facebook to upstage me after he had led me to belief that he had gotten what he wanted from her and that she was no longer in his life. Not only did she call him when we were with his family on one of the few days I got to see him since we were long-distance, she posted a picture of herself with him on her profile pic, taken at 2AM in the morning in his apartment, and let me, and potentially his family, know when and where they were dating via Threetriangle or something like it. I later found out that she had decided to marry him within the first month or two of knowing him. I took massive and immediate action to make this situation go away[351].

This experience led me to feeling sober, confused, scared, overwhelmed, lost, embarrassed, awkward, ashamed, upset, uncertain, and tentative about the relationship and my future in it. It shattered everything I knew about who I am. For the first time in my life I was truly jealous.

---

[351] Even though I shouldn't have.

AudAx

I used to think jealousy comes about because e doesn't want to be treated the way e would treat someone if they were having an affair. No shit! However, I learned that jealousy was not a fault of spiritual weakness, but something natural indicating strong feelings for the person involved.

From that experience, I have decided that nonmonogamous people do nonmonogamy better. When they do it, it is about transparency. When others try to emulate them, there's this idea that it has to be unspoken, and there's this feeling of guilt. I wouldn't say that affairs or open arrangements are a sin, but I would say that it shows failure to appreciate what you have (Commandment #10). It's much better for people to stick to their own domain before they embarrass themselves. Or maybe it's a gender thing. When I want sex, I'm direct about it, I get what I want, and I'm still able to keep my original schedule.

How to Choose

Choose Marriage: If one's goal is marriage, then a boyfriend/girlfriend is a dead end. Childhood friendships make for the best marriages. The person has already passed the friendship test, you and your family got to know the person well before things got physical, and you are already inseparable, meaning you wouldn't want a life without that person. The transition is seamless. No boyfriend/girlfriend needed.

I have limited time in my life for people, so I only allow myself to open up to one person at a time (generally)[352]. That is the person with whom I spend the most time, not just my primary partner, but my only partner (for most of the time). I guess that makes a boyfriend more like a friend with benefits, because he is my best friend, but I call him a boyfriend anyways because to not do so implies a different set of contrived rules, and he seems to like the label.

Choose Nonmonogamy: If one's goal is to play the field, then someone who is spouse material is a dead end. Both the upside to choosing nonmonogamy and the downside to choosing monogamy is that you can't be obsessed with two people at a time, only one. If you burn at 1000 watts (meaning you're codependent and such codependency will destroy the relationship with the primary), then it's better to be nonmonogamous (depending on the primary partner's feelings). If you're obsessed with the negatives of your primary partner, it should be alright to do whatever you can to get back to being obsessed with his/her positives.

If you're the type of person who's afraid of saying the wrong thing, then you especially need to stick with your own kind so that every romantic interaction is not tinged with manifesting fear.

---

[352] This was not true in college.

132

Marriageable (Primary)	Dateable (Primary if Not Married)	Secondary
Beauty is in the eye of the beholder	Fits societal beauty standards	Fits societal beauty standards
Best friend	Good friend	Acquaintance
Chemical of oxytocin	Chemical of oxytocin and dopamine	Chemical of dopamine
Childhood friendship	Friendship based on similar interests	Mutual friend
Different personality	Similar personality	Similar personality
Emotionally stable/high emotional IQ	Emotionally unstable/low emotional IQ	Emotionally stable/high emotional IQ
Fertile or infertile	Fertile or infertile	Fertile (if primary is infertile)
Flexible (long-term similar interests)	Inflexible (temporary similar interests)	Flexible (temporary similar interests)
Good heart/Good head	Good body	Good heart/good head/ good body
Good roommate	Decent roommate	Bad roommate
Like a home club or team	Like a club or team of which one is a member	Like a club or team that one visits as a guest
Lives in the future	Lives in the past	Lives in the present
Low intensity	Medium intensity	High intensity
Open book but endlessly fascinating	Able to maintain interest	Mysterious
Serious	Fun	Opposite of the primary
Sexual purity before marriage/commitment of fidelity	Multiple partners/open relationship	Open to an open relationship
Similar age	Different age (e.g., extreme age gap relationship)	Young enough to babysit

Marriageable (Primary)	Dateable (Primary if Not Married)	Secondary
Similar amount of sexual experiences	Different amount of sexual experiences	Secondary has fewer sexual experiences (to reduce risk)
Similar culture	Different culture (e.g., ethnic culture or racial culture)	Same race as the primary.
Similar economic class	Different economic class	Similar economic class
Similar goals	Different goals	Similar goals (temporary)
Similar location	Different location	Doesn't matter
Similar religion (e.g., both Christian)	Different religion (e.g., Christian and atheist)	Doesn't matter
Similar work hours	Different work hours	Doesn't matter
Someone you can be comfortable with forever	Someone exciting and/or energetic that you can only take for short moments at a time	Someone you can be comfortable with now
Someone you will gladly take care of when e's body stops working	Someone you cannot burp or fart in front of	
Decades-long marriage	Annulment or quick starter marriage	Someone you will marry if your spouse dies, with your spouses blessing
Sun sign and moon sign connection	Mars or Saturn connection	Venus-Uranus connection
Valid long-term plan	Not a valid long-term plan	Not a valid long-term plan
Wants children	Does not want children	Okay either way

The Artist Formerly Known as Prince: True Christianity

I consider myself a true Christian. *A true Christian is unconventional, subversive, radical, extreme, and rebellious. A true Christian is a vigilante.* E cares not about propriety. I'd go so far as to say deviant.

I practice Christian (okay, Catholic) birth control and have Christian finances[353]. There's no question I'm a Christian. Go Team Christians!

About Atheism

Atheists are ignorant[354], so sue me. (I'm not singling them out necessarily; some "Christians" are ignorant too.) I believe that you exist. I believe I could have sex with you if I wanted. It's kinda hard to have sex with someone if they do not believe a naked person is naked. Duh! I talk with God; He is my best friend. Of course I believe He exists. How could anyone do anything without belief? Any activity would be impossible. The very fact that atheists believe that they exist makes them hypocrites, for God is in all of us. He willed Himself into being through all of us; that makes Him inseparable from us. Only the Kabbalistic ego wants us to believe in a Creator separate from His creation.

Bishop Ambrose's Catholicism[355] vs. Social/Cultural Marxism

"The way of a fool is right in his own eyes[356], but he that listens to counsel is wise."
—Proverbs 12:15 Contemporary English Version

"Take me to church
I'll worship like a dog at the shrine of your lies
I'll tell you my sins so you can sharpen your knife"
—Andrew Hozier-Byrne, "Take Me to Church"

The Catholics[357] and secret societies do not get along even though a requirement to be in a secret society is to believe in a Higher Power. Perhaps some of this has to do with sex. Sex provides secret societies with what nothing else can: intense pleasure and intense masterminding simultaneously. There are a few things I cannot go into in depth, and masterminding is one of them. There are certain things I would rather not disclose, even though this entire book appears to be a mighty big disclosure.

As Peter Kreeft, the Catholic, says, sex has become our religion.

---

[353] As in I listen to Dave Ramsey with discernment.

[354] "Ignorant" here meaning lacking knowledge about Christianity.

[355] Refers to a time when church ruled state.

[356] See the introduction to Dianetics.

[357] "Ecclesia catholica" means "universal church." However, the Catholic Church is not universal.

It is a well-established fact that St. Augustine was a sexual compulsive, or else Sex and Love Addicts Anonymous would not be considered the Augustine Fellowship.

Since Jesus was buried with Mary Magdalene[358], and if we believe she is what the Catholic Church attests that she is—a prostitute, then it should say a lot that the Son of Man[359] was married to her.

I was reading an article about how, according to surveys on college campuses, sex had become a cultural expectation exceeding even the dangerous American experiment of dating. When the society changes faster than the religion, it's no surprise that church membership will drop. The average age in my church is 40; it's certainly nowhere for young people to pick up dates unless they like older men/women.

Social Marxism has become the catchphrase for the moral decline of society. Cultural Marxism does not eradicate God. It does not obliterate Him. God survives any ordeal.

The reason why I can thrive in this time period is because I actually enjoy sex. When sex becomes obligatory for most people, it's no surprise that people will flock to me or someone who enjoys it like a chocoholic enjoys chocolate. That's why I have to say, "No."

Maoists' *What If*: Agape and Sympatheia Unconditional Love

> "Love is "the uniting of 'Nuit.'[360]"
> —Aleister Crowley, *Liber AL vel Legis*

> "Theodore: I've never loved anyone the way I loved you.
> Samantha: Me too. Now we know how."
> —Spike Jonze, the movie *Her*

The movie, *What If*, is the first of its kind to depict a romance that stays in the friend zone (yes, that can be a sort of erogenous zone too). I argue that this is what agape love is like. Now, false Christians would have you believe that no one is capable of agape but God. Such a belief takes away your power and separates you from Source. I believe it is possible and is something to strive for. Both Osho and Thelema have described love as agape love, as a way of being, as an adjective, not even a verb or a noun. (Meretrix, 2003)

---

[358] See the documentary movie *The Tomb of Jesus* from James Cameron.

[359] Not Son of God because all religious heads were called the Son of God back in those days.

[360] Nuit is "the total possibilities of every kind [...] Every event is a uniting of some one monad with one of the experiences possible to it" (Liber AL vel Legis).

Regarding agape love, all people are one. Believe me; I would know, especially for the men. One God or many gods; it's the same thing. One lover or many; same soul.

To pretend that *human* love is entirely without criteria is horse shit. Even if the criteria is intense, deep physical attraction or personality compatibility, there is always some way a person must qualify. If someone thinks another is stupid, ugly, strange, boring, clingy, or creepy, e may not fall madly in love with that person. I say "may" because it takes all types to make the world go 'round. True, the idea of conditional love brings with it more shame, but to see how we want the world to be rather than how it is will only cause disappointment.

Holy love has no qualifications, for all are God's children. God loves the stupid, ugly, strange, boring, clingy, and creepy. That's called grace. He honors us by his presence without us needing to be or do anything to win His love. Do not listen to those who tell you otherwise.

In the same way that love for those outside ourselves makes beautiful music, so too does love of God. It's a shame such love music is forgotten by the mainstream.

True love, in my opinion, comes from the ability to rise above lust, possession, and special relationships[361]. True love is the love a parent has for e's child when e sends e's child off to college or out into the world. True love acknowledges that the presence of this beloved person is not something to hoard, but something to cherish. True love acknowledges that we were all made to share our gifts and talents with many, that we were designed to love many and be loved by many. True love is practically altruistic and philanthropic and is usually an indication of spiritual growth. True love is responsible for making decisions that have far-reaching effects, difficult decisions. True love lets go, lives and lets live.

Now as to how this connects with sex: Sex will make someone feel more accepted and united than talking can ever accomplish. Sexual compulsion is different from non-attachment, meaning attachment to special relationships. Regarding non-attachment, the value of not being attached to people is that your love for a person does not exceed your love for the whole. What this means is that you remain strong under negotiations and when being threatened. No one is your weakness. The church would have you believe that attachment is the way of the Force, but instead it is in actuality the way of the Dark Side.

Holy Indiscrimination

One time I was at a party playing Never Have I Ever with drinking. I hadn't even had a drink early in the game and since most of the people were people with whom I've had sex, at one time or another, I announced that only the people who haven't had sex with me should drink (or the

---

[361] Reference to *A Course in Miracles*.

other way around). I didn't realize it at the time, but apparently, that's not something people do, even in college society. My friend told me that he got kicked out of the party because the hostess thought no decent womyn would say something like that of her own accord.

When I was making out with a 21-year-old girl at a later date, she told me not to have sex with her parents again because they'd have sex with a "300-lb. honky." (I try not to be judgmental.) Once someone told me that I should have higher standards for the people I have sex with, but then that wouldn't make me promiscuous, since promiscuous specifically means indiscriminate sexual relations. Unfortunately, sometimes that leads to anaxiphilia, being in love with someone others would perceive as "a loser."

Though I wouldn't have chosen it personally, I have been deemed as someone who shall teach many men via life-affirming holy relationships, as opposed to ego-based special relationships. It is my purpose in this life to greet the men I taught in my lifetimes as priestess and/or educated geisha/kisaeng and reaffirm the lessons I gave them back then.

The kabbalistic purpose of sex is only to bind two souls together, so what I have been doing by going down my path is binding[362] humanity so that we are all judged together.

False Love

Osho's love is not impossible for it is Jesus' commandment to all. However, love (if based on the word "*lubha*," meaning greed) is what codependents believe love is, which doesn't take into account tough love and other types of love, nor does it account for agape.

Natural Family Planning

Myth: Everyone needs birth control.

Truth: I don't know who told feminists they are winning because it's a lie. Face it ladies, men do control your body. They decide whether you shave or exactly how much you are going to damage your body to prevent a pregnancy—whether you are going to get pelvic blood clots with the ring or massive weight gain with the pill (to the tune of a pound a day). It doesn't even mean one man in particular controls you, but that the very act of considering intercourse with the opposite sex means that you are willing to be controlled by someone, generally a man. Men put the "control" in birth control.

---

[362] Making sex a sort of permanent binding spell.

Birth control causes breast cancer, rapid weight gain, and blood clots. There is nothing less sexy than bloating from the pill. It's no wonder it causes people to lose their sex drive. Believe me, there are many alternatives to ingesting synthetic hormones.

The alternative, championed by Catholics, is natural family planning (not to be confused with family life education), which is a modern rendition of centuries-old wisdom. For more information, go to your local Catholic church.

Teshuvah: Good Deeds

"Above all else, guard your heart, for everything you do flows from it."—Proverbs 4:23 NIV

"Don't you see that whatever enters the mouth goes into the stomach and then out
of the body? But the things that come out of a person's mouth come from the heart,
and these defile them. For out of the heart come evil thoughts—murder, adultery,
sexual immorality, theft, false testimony, slander. These are what defile a person;
but eating with unwashed hands does not defile them." Matthew 15:17-20 NIV

Before choosing to do good deeds, one must know what deeds are good. This must mean grappling with what good deeds are questionable or even controversial. Does cohabitation keep us from a connection with God? Does homosexuality? Does masturbation? Does alcohol? Does pot? Why? These are the questions we each must ask ourselves.

We must also ask, "Who or what is God?" What are His motivations? What are ours? In what actions does ego reside? Do we believe the Bible as literal, figurative, political, mathematical, prophetic? Do we think of it as literature, a manual for life, a direct communication from God or angels? What parts of scriptures have been altered or mistranslated?

Since I do not believe in perpetuating guilt, we must choose to turn to God by making the best choices, with the understanding that even a good choice might not be the best choice, but that a bad choice is better than no choice at all.

"A good plan violently executed now is better than a perfect plan executed next week."
—George S. Patton

It is our actions and choices that indicate who we follow, whether God (Source) or Satan (giving for the sake of receiving).

Ethics and Sex

There are three basic types of ethical decision making: consequentialist, the Golden Rule, and moral Kantianism. This book is an example of consequentialist thinking. The Golden Rule is for safe sex. Jesus uses moral Kantianism. The Josephson Principled Decision Making rolls up all basic types of ethical decision making into one model:

- Caring: Making love, being friends
- Civic virtue/Citizenship: Serving as a model
- Justice/Fairness: Open for both or closed for both (both require and are interconnected with trust)
- Respect: Open discussion
- *Responsibility: Safe sex*
- Trustworthiness: Honesty and keeping promises

Regarding responsibility, the absolute *worst* thing you can do regarding safe sex is to break up or divorce the person who gave you an STI[363]. Most likely they did not give it to you intentionally. It's understandable that it's shocking and difficult to trust again, but consider the logical side. If both of you are released into the wild, consider how much the risk compounds, especially if you date around before settling on someone long-term. If not dating around, you could get depressed because you may feel lonely, which could result in acting out. The best thing to do is to forgive as soon as possible and keep the sex amongst yourselves.

Now I'm not advocating staying in an unhealthy relationship. If this is the straw that broke the camel's back then, by all means, leave, move on. If, however, this is an unfortunate anomaly, realize it for what it is, educate yourself, and carry on.

See the cloud in the silver lining: there is more logical reason for fidelity now that everything's in the open. You won't be able to do as much with someone else as you could do with each other. Make up and have fun.

Greed, Gluttony, and Lust

Being sexually greedy is akin to being beautiful; you never get turned down. Sexual compulsions are often accompanied by compulsive spending/buying or eating disorders. Greed can also

---

[363] That's why you need to be careful of who you have sex with, not just anyone you meet from an online ad, and when you have sex with e, not on the first date.

encompass compulsive gambling[364]. All of these show a lack of control and an Epicurean attitude toward life, or else an insatiable hunger that can never be at peace. Out of the known vices, one could roll these all up into "thou shalt maintain self-control." Other terms for self-control could be "the middle way," "discipline," "self-restraint," and "balance." See Word Choice in Recovery and Habits.

---

[364] I know this is true because I didn't need to gamble in Las Vegas to compulsively gamble with my finances.

Epicene

"You must begin to develop those qualities in you that the opposite sex represents to you."—Jesus, *Jesus: My Autobiography* (Spalding 171)

In a study devoid of societal influence, girls were given cars and boys were given Barbie® dolls. Girls tucked their cars in bed and boys made the dolls action figures. People may not like their gender roles, but life is tough for everyone. Culture, unlike what many would have you believe, is independent of gender. And gender is independent of personality (where men can be feelers and women thinkers) or sexual orientation (which I think carries more of a vibe). If muliebrity, assumption of female characteristics from a male, gets under your skin, politely express that you took offense and move on.

Everyone can agree that sex has something that appeals to both genders. It is both an activity that men like and a moment of intimacy[365] that women like (or vice versa).

Gender (and General) Communication[366]

According to John Gottman's research "only about 30 percent of the differences or problems in a relationship can be fixed" the remaining 70 percent are deeply rooted in the different personalities and histories of the partners and have to be accepted.

Sha'ar Hagilgulim: Wimmin[367]

"The only thing that can fix a stick up your ass is a dick up your ass." —Me[368]

Men and wimmin are certainly not (treated) the same. If there is a case of rape at work in a womyn's restroom, for example, no one thinks to put a lock on both the wimmin's and men's restrooms. Though men do get raped, and I know one in particular that has been raped, it is not usually from a stranger who rapes impromptu.

Men and wimmin have wildly different motivations for sex. If many wimmin don't even like sex because they can't orgasm, and even refuse to give sex to their husbands *before* the men have

---

[365] Talking about intimacy, a company retreat could never bring as much immediate intimacy as a hands-on, experiential sex workshop.

[366] Apologies for forgetting to record page numbers when I was reading this book.

[367] In Chinese, "wo men" means "we."

[368] I reccommend reading *The New Male Sexuality* by Bernie Zilbergeld.

erectile dysfunction, then they only invest into beauty for the financial stability of having a husband. So wimmin don't compete for sex; they compete for money.

Also, I do not know a single female "guru," and that's because only men can get away with saying they love all people, only men can look people in the eye. Wimmin can only look men in the eye if being stern, not if being congenial, lest it be mistaken for flirtation. Men do not allow wimmin to be their trusted friends for even though their feelings for wimmin are between them and God, they blame the wimmin that are most enticing, and the most enticing wimmin are both intelligent and beautiful. What makes a man a guru, makes a womyn an eligible wife.

The reason why we have no female Einstein or Bill Gates is only because her husband probably threatened to leave her if she didn't wear makeup and dress up for him, so she spent all the time that could have been used for productive purposes on keeping her marriage, if not for her, then for her kids.

From my unique perspective, it is not men who are tempted so much as it is wimmin who are tempted (not temptresses). When talking about how a womyn should dump someone who's not treating her the way she wants to be treated, or how a womyn is justified in cheating because of that, I think it's really the wimmin who objectify the men—they make them into objects they can throw away. Very few realize their own hypocrisy.

For example, wimmin, according to surveys prefer men with a good sense of humor, but I think it's ironic that stand-up comedians tend to be depressed. Case in point: Robin Williams. This is an example of wimmin having idealism and getting disappointed.

Why does our society put so much emphasis on dropping their significant other at the drop of a hat if they did not satisfy expectations of entitlement[369], yet tell people to rethink getting a divorce? This is an inconsistent message that can and will only result in the opposite effect.

Dating, being begotten from courting, should, in many cases, be a precursor to marriage, or at least courting itself, so the marriage mentality should precede the marriage itself to set a foundation of loyalty.

However, this is not the case. Dating involves rules, but marriage involves only what works. I never took serious interest in dating books, only relationship books, and never understood why my ex said I played games when he was the only one doing so.

Kabbalists (the heading of this section is in Hebrew) believe that one of wimmin's purposes is to bring men closer to the light. If wimmin can control themselves, whatever man is attached to them can too, by proxy. Wimmin were made to be role models. They do not know where their influence ends.

---

[369] As a womyn, I have done the breaking up many times.

Feminism

> "[T]he deliberate pursuit of pleasure not only improved the quality of a woman's life--these things could also save her life."--Regena Thomashauer, Pussy

> "The solution for the epidemic of powerlessness among women, which neither great success nor higher education is able to solve, is simple: reconnecting a woman to her pussy."--Regena Thomashauer, Pussy

I just saw someone post that backyard farming is feminist. If self-sufficient women is feminist, then why do we need feminism? We only needed it to vote, but what justification do we have to hold grudges about not voting in the past?

Feminism is just another form of imprisonment. It's not so much that wimmin are trapped in a man's world, but that men are trapped in a womyn's world. It is why men fear the institution of marriage—to some it is a symbol of restriction, like the planet of Saturn. When a married man tells me that he's going to cry if he can't get sex and that he doesn't know what to do, it tells me that something is seriously wrong with our society. It tells me there are millions more like him and that people are suffering needlessly at the hands of their loved ones when they don't have to, when they could proactively fix their marriage with openmindedness and acceptance of each other's turn-ons. I imagine many cases of [fill in the blank] could have been prevented if the spouse fulfilled his or her role as spouse and biblically submitted to each other.

Wimmin are trapped there too, in a womyn's world. Poor Emily Dickinson (she was a womyn trapped in a Victorian world—a.k.a. womyn's world). The wimmin's movement might have given wimmin the right to choose, but it did not give them *the right to not have to choose*. In a utopian world, there would be no "tough decisions," and women could have anything they want (which is why we're here in the first place, according to Law of Attraction). In a utopian world, wimmin wouldn't have to choose between work and marriage or love and fame. In a utopian world, single wimmin would not feel "burdened" by a child, and a wife would not feel resentful of her husband. In a utopian world, aspiring sex workers would have freedom to do what they love, freely being able to tell anyone they pleased what they do or did for a living without fear of repercussions or imprisonment. Wimmin wouldn't have to choose between their passion and having a future family. In a utopian world, there would be no restrictions, no force, no status quo, no expectations, and no lack. Where a utopian world is concerned, the wimmin's movement has failed.

Some believed that wimmin's domain was in the kitchen. Since my mom, her mom, my dad, and his mom, didn't cook, I didn't cook. I find that men make better chefs than wimmin and maybe that's the way it should have been from the start. I'm still waiting for someone to teach me how to peel a peach, but luckily I do know how to boil water and could possibly use Sousvide. A domain in the kitchen would cause me to tremble in fear of my inadequacies (as if I wasn't taught to do so already). No, the kitchen is not my domain. My domain is in the bedroom. It is my safe place, as long as it is someone else's bedroom.

I guess that would make me anti-feminist. I am not a feminist. Feminists believe that empowerment trumps commitment. I believe they are mutually exclusive ideas.

No, I prefer to call myself a sex radical feminist or third wave feminist if I were to call myself one at all. I'm a lipstick femme feminist who rarely even puts lipstick on. What a walking contradiction!

However, I don't embrace it, and I don't love it. I'll tell you that I've fully embraced feminism when marriage rates are as high as they were before the wimmin's revolution as true equality is neither a patriarchy or a matriarchy but a partnership. I don't see the trend changing anytime soon.

Cameron Dias: To Depilate (Acomoclitic) or Not to Depilate (Pubephilia), That Is the Question

Pubephilia and Trichopathophilia[370] is arousal to pubes. Most people (usually non-millenials) have complimented me on my bush. I think it looks better as well. If you're sparse down there you can always get a laugh at the idea of using the most outrageous merking (pubic hair wig) you can find.

Much has already been said about this topic. Thank you, Cameron Diaz. I am in Cameron's camp. Men generally prefer long hair and shaved pussies. So which one is it? Hair or no hair? Would men prefer long hair and a bush or a shaved head and a shaved pussy? I can bet that men would go with the former. However, drains clogged by hair gross out only men. Women shed an average of 1,000 hairs per day thanks to the silicone in their shampoo.

My reason for not shaving (fully) is because I am not keen on the idea of a man controlling what I do or don't do, and I refuse to let a man control me. Don't ever let anyone force you to change your hair, either above or below the waist. That is your body. No one else has a right to it. Everyone has a different reason.

If I were in Korea, being shaved would be an insult. In Korea, it is an insult to say someone's bald down there (probably because only prepubescents are naturally bald), but in America (thanks to Hustler's probable connection with the shaving industry), the opposite is true despite how much the triangle is making a comeback among women.

Pubic hair has been a major sticking point in my relationships. It determines if I should pursue, how I feel about a current relationship, and when I need to get out. If I were in the sex industry,

---

[370] Arousal to pubic hair is different from being a furry. Furries go beyond sex. They tend to appear as their animal spirit. They don't even need fur.

it would be a definite part of the contract. My feeling is that if you give a man rights to your hygiene routine, he will take the rights of your reproductive system as well.

An ex went below the belt literally by saying my pussy (which he had never seen, being in prison) reminded him of a rabid rodent. I couldn't even say I was just some girl he wanted to fuck because he ensured, by his actions, that we never would. I was just some girl, period.

But God, I hate having to look like a fucking tween just to get the minutest opportunity of being licked. Everyone knows that hairless mammals are not as cute.

Those who grew up with the desire to shave are either athletes who shave for practical reasons or those who grew up on or currently watch Hustler era porn from the '70s or later. The latter are a product of commercialism, in my opinion.

Shaved pussies glorify pre-pubescence, unnecessary consumerism (of razors), disgust of the natural female body, and paternal societies all in one fell swoop.

We used to preserve food with salt, then the icebox came along then the refrigerator. All of a sudden we think that we need to throw everything in the refrigerator when it used to grow on the vine, on a tree, or in the ground. We used to live like animals with no baths, no showers, no shampoo, and no soap. Then all these expensive conveniences came along. All of a sudden we had soap that lathered, and we couldn't imagine any other kind. So we got used to stripping our hair of natural oils and using conditioner to add a false sense of moisture back in. We got used to using facial products that dry out the skin and using chapstick to pretend we still have some sense of "natural" beauty. Before you know it you're trapped. You feel that you need so much stuff that you're not even mobile because the "stuff" took away everything you already had before there ever was so much "stuff." You can't even escape an attack. You'd be wiped out instantly in a zombie apocalypse. Does "stuff" make you free? No. It binds you. Do beliefs surrounding "stuff" make you free? No. It binds you, then it binds others. Until they believe what you believe, which is what "they" want you to believe.

I understand that past a certain age, people don't change, but if I overheard my son confess in a casual conversation that he preferred shaved, then I wouldn't know if he were gay, a pedophile, Lars (from *Lars and the Real Girl*), or a controlling chauvinist that wants his womyn to die of an embarrassing reason. A womyn's body, in the art world, is only decreed to be lewd if it has pubic hair. Men who prefer a shaven woman have censored preferences or are turned off by maturity. A man wanting a shaved womyn is like a womyn wanting a man without facial hair. It is destructive to force a spouse to kowtow to the wish of making the spouse unnatural. It is akin to being sexually turned on by GMOs, MSG, and high fructose corn syrup.

If you're used to shaving or not shaving, an abrupt change, coupled with tension in the relationship, can indicate an affair or other sexual partner. I've been guilty of this. Even if a guy is okay with nonmonogamy, it hits a little too close to home.

Why I will not shave:

- Creates an environment of shame

- Cultural preference of birth country

- Dangerous to health (Google related articles)

- Inauthentic

- Not life-enhancing

- Not practical when not being given oral

- Personal preference

- Sets the standard for handing over control of my body in a boundaryless relationship

- Time-consuming

- Unhealthy

I've had sex with 78 men, mostly unshaven (26 were romantic interests that got close but did not lead to sex), so I don't think it's as much of a turn-off as some men say it is.

In closing, all I want to say is, "I hate you, Hustler. I'm switching to Playboy."

Men who shave: 2% of the sample size, according to my sample.

North Korea: Cosmetic Surgery

The only reason someone should get a boob job (which, unlike a handjob, does not involve fondling the boob) is if the financial benefit outweighs the financial cost. It would be stupid to get if you did not at least break even because you'll be trapped into doing it all over again in 10 years. Cosmetic facial surgery is different, in my opinion. An ex of mine can spot cosmetic facial surgery a mile away and thinks it's gross. Personally though, I like the way Cher and Nicki Minaj look and wouldn't mind looking similar.

AudAx

Emmenology

A womyn can never forget her assigned sex no matter how well she can pretend to be just another boy because she is reminded every month, in the same way that a boy is reminded of his assigned sex whenever he gets turned on.

I imagine that the only people interested in the study of menstruation (or menses) are gynecologists. I had my first false menstruation (menophania) when I was 9. I think I was the first in my group of friends to get it. Would have liked to have gotten some boobs to go along with it, but ah well.

"Period"[371]

Oh, period,
How you reek of the round moon!
How your screaming offends the sun!
How you end
Subject-verb sentences!

Oh, period,
You are oftentimes forgotten
At the end of paragraphs
Or the end of a bulleted list.
Bullets chase you
In your dreams.

Oh, period,
You are oftentimes forgotten
When men peek up skirts.

How gracious you are!
Despite the Forgotten War
With birth control,
You bestow a blessing
When you are missed.

It is a blessing
Of tortuous puking,
dizziness,

---

[371] I used my own poem to replace Lucille Clifton's "poem in praise of menstruation" and "to my last period."

And cravings,
As if the craving
For lust in itself
Were not enough.

Thank you, period.
I will not forget your birthday.
—Me, from The Raw and Uncensored One

Makeup

The only times you really *need* makeup are when you're in the performing arts (stage acting, drag show performer, exotic dancing, modeling, etc.), a black tie event, or if you're blond. (Damn invisible leg hair. J/k.) All other times makeup is just fun. The irony is that the darker the skin, the more you can get away with and the less you can get away with.

Some men have a makeup fetish, and, for a few with body dysmorphic disorder, the lack of makeup can be a dealbreaker.

Makeup is the perfect example of a consumerist culture, for one does not usually have makeup if it was not store-bought, and homemade makeup is to storebought makeup what veggie burgers are to Big Macs, a cheap imitation.

False eyelashes represents to me how attracting men is an expensive chore, which I used to believe was only for those who did not trust their sexual prowess. The only people who wear false eyelashes are those who care deeply about being liked, or, in my case, those who care about keeping someone who has other traits I like besides superficiality. The reason for this is that it is a nuisance and requires practice to get right. In addition, it tells God that humans think they know better than him how to use lashes, for the act of curling lashes defeats the reason why they're there: to protect one's eyes from sand and dust. God forgive me for idolizing a man.

This brings me to how attracting men kills wimmin faster. For example, it is a well-known statistic that wearing heels puts so much pressure on the feet that it's like carrying around an elephant all day. No wonder my mother gave up walking in old age. Don't get me started on beauty products. Most people know that most beauty products test on animals. I even heard that once a company was taken off the PETA watchlist, they started animal testing again. Then there's the whole issue of mineral oil (crude oil), paraben estrogen that causes breast cancer, and lanolin, which is made from dead animals! This is the stuff found in most beauty products. That's as gross as L-cysteine in food products, which is made from human hair! Perhaps I've been listening to too many Arbonne sales.

In addition, there's a multitude of toxins in every female product. Products for menses either cause weight gain or blood clots, both of which can cause a stroke at an extreme, not to mention toxic shock syndrome. It's called toxic shock syndrome because tampons are toxic (shocker!).

The Pudenda

"There's essentially no limit to how often we can use 'penis,' 'balls,' 'scrotum,' or 'shaft,' but female anatomical language is a big, flapping red flag."—Sarah Silverman (Silverman, 2010)

I don't have much to say in this venture into cunnilalia (talking about female genitals) as much of what I've already said covers it. Most women prefer starting slow and would prefer bradycubia, slow penetration, first.

Faking Orgasm

There was an episode of *Masters of Sex* in with Dr. Masters asks Virginia Johnson why wimmin would fake an orgasm. She said it was so they could go back to doing whatever they'd rather be doing.

Along the same lines, an app, in a scientific experiment, would call people randomly and ask, "What are you doing?" and "What are you thinking?" (kind of a scrum call, to those familiar with Agile methodology). The app would then gather that research study information. The result was that the mind wandered 90% during commuting and work and only 10% during sex. [372]

The G-Spot

"Three researchers caused a stir a few years ago when they gave a label to this sensitive area, calling it the G-spot, and suggested it was a true anatomical structure like the clitoris or nipple. Unfortunately, the evidence for an anatomical structure is shaky unless we want to say that any very responsive place is the G-spot. The vaginally sensitive women I've talked to locate the spot in different places in the vagina. [...] Some women also report that their sensitive spot shifts depending on where they are in their menstrual cycle." (Zilbergeld, 1992)

The more I learned about differences between men and wimmin, the more I realized that despite how much I loved sex, the men were getting their needs met more than me[373]. I didn't realize how other wimmin thought or why. I think the main reason why wimmin don't like sex is that many were designed to reach orgasm by other means than penetration.

---

[372] Wimmin with a weaker sex drive have greater negotiation power.

[373] It's ironic that men are said to think about and love sex so much, yet us wimmin know that in reality they know very little about around half of it; the half that pertains to the opposite sex.

That's when I realized that it's quality, more than quantity that counts, and I'm not just talking about the motion in the ocean. For the first time, I could say, "No" when a man offered me my own cum, which I had never liked to lick from his fingers in the first place. My scent belongs only to me.

Priapus[374]

According to the John Gottman Institute, the average married couple doesn't seek marriage counseling until the sixth year of marriage. I can tell you that is certainly not because the women don't want it, but that it takes six years for men to realize the damage society has done to their gender and how acting like society's version of a man reduces quality of life. When a man struggles with all the pressures society puts on men, it generally does more damage to innocent bystanders than when a womyn struggles with all the pressures society puts on wimmin.

About the Penis

"A man's semen contains all the vitamins and minerals that he needs. One should bring this semen or Bindu up his spine, so that it may become Ojas [life force] and distribute it throughout his body. It takes Eighty bites of food, when fully digested, to give you one drop of blood. Eighty drops of pure blood makes one drop of semen. A man needs 90% of his semen to maintain his body."
–Yogi Bhajan[375]

I will now engage in medolalia; I will now talk about the penis. Even though most heterosexual and gay people love the penis, there are some out there who don't. I've heard wimmin say that they think a penis is gross, and then there's the real condition of spermatophobia, fear of semen (which I guess leads to *really* safe sex). It doesn't say anything about the man.

Abused Men

Even if they used to have maniaphilia, an attraction to insane people, it would not surprise me if an abused man ended up having gynophobia, or the fear of women. As long as it doesn't become misogyny, the hatred of women.

Men ARE Abused Too: 4% of the sample size is abused physically, emotionally, or sexually by a woman (not including other men), according to my sample.

---

[374] I recommend reading *The New Male Sexuality* by Bernie Zilbergeld.

[375] I recommend reading *The New Male Sexuality* by Bernie Zilbergeld.

Acmegenesis

Though many people achieve orgasms (especially men), some people (especially women) have xeronisus, an inability to reach orgasm. For those people, orgasm could never be the end goal. For these people, it is best to practice karezza, gentle lovemaking without the goal of orgasm.

Anger and Angry Sex

Have angry sex if you want, but keep it amongst yourselves. My favorite form of conflict resolution is sex. However, there was a time when the man wasn't ready, and it's only been recently that I've understood why a man wouldn't want angry sex after being an asshole. I mean yelling I can take, but not dick moves. (Puns intended.)

Being Uncircumcized

"Is any man called being circumcised? let him not become uncircumcised.
Is any called in uncircumcision? let him not be circumcised.
Circumcision is nothing, and uncircumcision is nothing, but
the keeping of the commandments of God.
Let every man abide in the same calling wherein he was called.
Art thou called being a servant? care not for it: but if thou mayest be made free, use it rather.
For he that is called in the Lord, being a servant, is the Lord's freeman:
likewise also he that is called, being free, is Christ's servant.
Ye are bought with a price; be not ye the servants of men."
—1 Corinthians 7: 18-23 KJV

1% of the sample size is uncircumcized, according to my sample.

Ejaculatio Praecox[376]

I could never understand the quote from *Grease*, the musical, regarding the time it takes to have sex, until I witnessed premature ejaculation first hand. It was even shorter than what was in *Grease*. I think he came the instant his dick touched my pussy. I guess that's what happens to people who are voluntarily homeless and haven't had any in a long time.

---

[376] I recommend reading *The New Male Sexuality* by Bernie Zilbergeld.

1% of the sample size has this issue, according to my sample. Since the quote has a larger amount, I would assume that meant that people who suffer from this would be less willing to seek out sexual intercourse, which would explain why they did not approach me.

Erectile Dysfuntion[377]

One-third of male college students say they've experienced erectile dysfunction (Hingston, 2012); however, most of the people I've played around with who had this were over the age of 40 (but I have had sexual relations with someone in his 20s who had premature ejaculation. Ever since I "cured" or "healed" one man's erectile dysfunction (he didn't tell me I did until afterwards) and temporarily improved another man's erectile dysfunction without the use of pills or effort, I have prided myself on my power and abilities. I impress myself. If only I could have sex with myself. It's also possible that there was a xenodynamic going on there, meaning that the first guy could only be potent with strangers. Hm…probably not, since we weren't strangers for long. I have never gotten pregnant from premature ejaculation.

Jerry Pur's greatest pride was his duration in bed, and his greatest fears were losing his thickness and stamina, so as the Law of Attraction states, his greatest fears became self-fulfilling prophecies for at least 20 years. I was able to help with the erectile dysfunction issue somewhat, as I mentioned above, but was not able to fix the premature ejaculation challenge.

I met him post-"recovery." Some might think that's ironic. I think it's appropriate. In a way, any man who has ED is a bit like a sexual compulsive; they think about sex all the time. The only difference is that they're not able to act on their impulses. My experience, with the majority of the men I knew with this (not all), were also a bit like sexual compulsives because they cared what people thought of them. I would like to see someone conduct a survey to discover if people who don't care what other people think have ever had ED. I doubt it.

2% of the sample size has this issue. 1% of the sample size has this issue combined with premature ejaculation. 2% of the sample size has the issue of premature ejaculation.

Injections[378]

Injections don't always work, especially if there is a high level of anxiety.

1% of the sample size uses injections, according to my sample.

---

[377] I recommend reading *The New Male Sexuality* by Bernie Zilbergeld.

[378] I recommend reading The New Male Sexuality by Bernie Zilbergeld.

AudAx

Testosterone[379]

Do doctors normally take advantage of the 50+ years of experience that professional bodybuilders have of testing, even synthesizing, testosterone? No.

1% of the sample size resorts to using this solution.

Seamen[380]: Cum Etiquette

A lot of men tend to forget the best way to communicate in a way that is pleasurable before sex is to discuss where ejaculate should go, where it shouldn't go, and how it's cleaned up and disposed of. Should it go inside a mouth? On the face? In the vagina? Since "cum" is Latin for "with," it means that this is a conversation you should have *with* your sex partner.

Small Penis Syndrome[381]

First, let me say that there is nothing more annoying than a partner who complains about the size of his penis.

What baffles me about SPS is that I have had sexual encounters with many men who have micropenises (three inches or less, I believe), rantallion (larger scrotum than penis), or erectile disorder, yet have no fear of the bedroom or of being naked and, in fact, seek out new partners regularly with pride (again, sex does not always imply coitus). Then there are men, of any race, who obsess over the size of their ding dong to excess, never believing that they are good enough. Wimmin know this and, unfortunately, some exploit it. I believe that men with SPS are endowed with squirting powers so their wife can be happily raising a child not worrying about sex.

Men are more interested in size than women. I once met a guy who had an 8-inch cock and thought that was too small. Considering that the average man has a 5.5-inch cock, that's pretty impressive, but not necessarily the most desirable. I'm sure you've heard it before, but I'll say it again: It's all about the motion in the ocean, or phallation.

An Imagined Scenario:

---

[379] I recommend reading *The New Male Sexuality* by Bernie Zilbergeld.

[380] Intentional spelling

[381] I recommend reading *The New Male Sexuality* by Bernie Zilbergeld.

A: I'd like to get down and dirty with you.

B: Do you mind having an audience?

A: No.

B: Are you above or below the average dick size?

A: Well, above, of course!

B: That's too bad. I won't bring home anyone that's larger than my husband.

Penile Exercises for Increasing Size

In my research, I think catatasis, or jelqing, is the best method for increasing a man's size. It carries risk, but not nearly as much as meatotomy or peotomy, surgical amputation of the penis, which is even worse than expensive 10-year breast augmentations. No one wants a bumpy cock that hangs down from Bihari surgery, which involves cutting the ligament above the penis to make it appear longer. A few men prefer increasing the size of their balls instead. This is called scrotal infusion and is like breast augmentation, but for the scrotum.

Pied Piper: Illicit Statutory Rape and Licit Encouragement

Disclaimer: If the person reading this book is under 18, anything described in these pages that e[382] acts on is a prisonable offense (from intercourse to streaking to public urination to sexting), even if the child is old enough to drive, work, compete in the Olympics, die, or do anything expected of an adult. Even though liberal states have the legal age of consent down to 16 (even if they start showing school-mandated pornography to children as young as 7), and might not have Romeo and Juliet laws or laws against nudity, travel can occur freely between states, unless the juvenile is already on probation. If the reader is over 18, any acts involving a partner must require uncoerced consent from a spouse or person over the age of 18.

"The inseam on the same sized shorts in the boys' department was almost 7
times longer. [...] The only shorts in the girls' department that matched them
for length were a girls' size Large (10-12). I had to go for athletic shorts because
they didn't make any denim shorts for girls with an inseam this long.
The problem, besides the fact that we are calling the same amount of fabric Large for girls and
Extra Small for boys, is that those size Large shorts would never fit my 5-year-old daughter
in the waist. [...] I have no idea why an XS shirt (size 4-5) needs to curve like that to show

---

[382] See Appendix A: New Terms

the shape of a young girl's body, a body that hasn't even developed the curves that a woman's shirt in that same cut would be trying to feature. […] While we were at Target we also stopped by the women's and junior's department to measure the inseam on the shorts over there.

Um…

Not quite 2 inches on a women's size 7. Let me remind you that this is less than one inch longer than the shorts intended for toddlers. […] And no, it is not about shorter clothes costing less money to manufacture. The clothes in the boys' section don't cost twice as much, although they have more fabric. […] No matter what, there is no excuse for trying to sell me a one inch inseam. Ever. They literally make underwear with longer inseams than that." (Giese, 2014)[383]

Regarding the Romeo & Juliet laws, have you ever noticed that Disney princesses are often teenagers? Snow White is only 14! Cinderella is the oldest, at age 19. And every animated Disney movie has romance. In South Korea, K-pop artists tend to be oversexualized 13-14 years old, even though they are contractually not allowed to date for up to 20 years, probably because if they were any older they'd be stressed out by exams and regular jobs. Many animé main characters from Japan are in middle school, which is even younger. And yet no one has ever banned Disney or animé because of these things (but they allow Disney to ban tattoos).

With today's cop culture, youth are not allowed to have sex, but they are allowed to die unarmed at the hands of cops or on the battlefield. The only Americans allowed to have sex are those who would have been considered old maids 70 years ago or in another country (like Korea or the Middle East). And those who would be perfectly acceptable in any other country are criminalized in this one. Therefore, when America tells other countries that these are our criminals, those countries imagine far worse crimes than those of which they are capable. In February 2016, our dear President Barack Obama signed into law that our foreign allies and enemies may assume that our streakers, public urinators, and those who had sexual relations with a teen of child-bearing age who have served their one month in jail and the minimum 10 years on the sex offender registry are all pimps looking to put women into slavery. However, in America, pimps can only be convicted if there is a verifiable victim. Foreign countries do not need an "innocent until proven guilty" precedence.

In an election year that focused on the sexual abuse from both Trump and Clinton, why do we still bother condemning and locking up teenagers by the boatload who can't keep up with differing ages of consent in different states? They will suffer far worse in a prison environment than in a political arena. And their suffering before getting to college age will affect the economy far worse than a losing presidential candidate.

---

[383] To read the original article and to see the response from Target, go to this site: http://binkiesandbriefcases. com/target-intervention-behalf-daughters/

In the year 2017, *Time*'s Person of the Year was The Silence Breakers, making an interest in pedophilia and sexual crime *en vogue*.

Pedophilia is as un-American as communism; however, people still participate in it, but deny that they do, particularly in their family. Why is an interest in pedophilia seen as the "worst" crime? If it is the worst crime, why then is pedophilia not mentioned in the Ten Commandments? (Even though the dictionary definition defines it as in interest in prepubescents [yelds[384]], for all intensive and American legal purposes this includes an interest in any teens, including a teen's interest in people their own age, which is just ridiculous[385]. To keep one safe across state borders, this section considers 18 to be the age of consent for adults *AND* teens.) In a society where there are childcare centers in some high schools and midriffs and makeup for children of all ages, I have a problem believing that this is still so taboo. In a society that teaches sexual education through the Common Core even as early as preteen years, or earlier, in a society becoming more sexually active at a younger age, I have a very difficult time with understanding why adults are not even allowed to put sunscreen on a child.

What makes the witchhunt against perpetrators ridiculous is that perpetrators and victims are often two sides to the same coin, for it is shame, victimization, resentment, and often genetics that causes one to act out. Therefore, those most against sex offenders dig their own hole. Just as a

---

[384] Not old enough to procreate

[385] …and in extension the following:

- adolescentilism (playing the role of a teen),

- anaclitism (arousal from items used as an infant)

- autonepiophilia (arousal from being treated like an infant),

- blastolagnia (arousal by young females),

- corephallism (anal sex with a young girl),

- eopareunia (engaging in sex while young),

- ephebophilia (interest in older teens),

- hebephilia (interest in premenacmiums, or pre-teens, and younger teens),

- infantilism (dressing up as a young child for sexual play),

- infantophilia (attraction to babies and toddlers),

- juvenilism (acting out the role of a juvenile in a sexual situation),

- maiesiophilia (arousal from childbirth),

- nepiophilia (attraction to babies and toddlers)

- teleiophilia (interest in people of reproductive age), and

- tithiolagnia (having an orgasm from nursing).

gay Muslim kills gays, the fanatics are the ones that kill America by destroying our constitutional rights.

Keeping in mind that I have wanted to prove my maturity as young as 10, keeping in mind that I lived in an area barren of kids in my childhood and grew up more accustomed to adults, I am a firm believer in considering thirteen-year-olds to be adults. Considering that whenever I talk to people my age or older, their first time with sex, alcohol, or other "adult" things, occurred around the age of 13, that further supports my point. I know I was a lot more perverted as a child going through puberty than as an adult because my imagination had not been beaten down. I do not think pedophilia is pedophilia if the child is the initiator. I know that there were plenty of times when I wanted sex from someone much older. But should I or someone else have been punished for the natural process of growing up? Or should someone else feel shame for someone else's hormonal curiosities?

I have watched the *War on Kids*, read the *Last Child in the Woods*, and am quite familiar with John Holt's teachings regarding unschooling and how kids are a lot smarter than we as a society give them credit for. This is all by design thanks to the relatively recent development of words like "child" or "teenager." (Recent means decades or centuries to me, as opposed to millenia.)

I think what causes people so much shame and repression is the interpretation that, say, seven years of age is too young for a child to respond to sexual advances. My perspective is that seven years of age is the age when children have been beaten down the least from the entire world and still retain a sense of wonderment. The crime, in my opinion, is not so much that a child that age is too young to respond, but that a child loses e's sense of positive wonderment.

The only thing that has ever matured people beyond childhood into adulthood is the fear of survival and the understanding of the seriousness of it, parental neglect, or the value of self-sufficiency. And the only thing that has kept them immature was the term "adolescence," "dating," and anything else that evolved after the creation of the automobile. The invention of the teenager was created thanks to mandatory secondary schooling made available by the invention of the car.

Sloth-like children have surrounded me for ages that take, take, take, complain, complain, complain, and do absolutely nothing to change their status from dependent into independent[386]. Those whom I have found to rise above do so only with the help of a strong integrity.

I have also found plenty of unique children who do adult things. Some children have had both parents die at young ages and have had to provide for themselves and their siblings. Some children are very opinionated and knowledgeable about adult matters, such as politics, finance, and the news. Some children who appear older than they are will sneak into movies, bars, and

---

[386] Older i.P. audAx: Now these people are adults and have not changed much.

anything else with or without a fake ID. Some children, particularly females, and especially with the aid of the Internet, will pose as someone older in order to seduce someone into cyber sex or into having real-life sex. Remember that it takes two—meaning that oftentimes the younger is to blame at least partially and many times they are the instigators, especially online[387]. All these children I have thus mentioned were of the age of thirteen.

Child molesters will serve a lifetime prison term but usually live only shortly after because inmates will beat them up since child molestation is seen as the most horrible crime, which makes people believe it is also rare. However, having been to Landmark Forum, a completely safe and accepting environment where people feel free to disclose, I realize it may actually be the most common and the shame is in the view that it is not.

This makes the false accusers or childhood seducers cold murderers. (And if you wonder how someone could be attracted to someone that young, have you ever fallen in love before seeing someone or knowing their age, or even gender? In the world of technology, it happens all the time.) The pied pipers aren't older; they are younger. They are jailbait. The youth sentence the innocent, who make naïve mistakes, to death, whether literally or metaphorically. There is no life under sex offender registration. None whatsoever.

The pied pipers are usually nymphets, a sexually precocious 13- or 14-year old, or 15-17 year old females born with a "get out of a life sentence free" card who lure people with neanilagnia, a yearning for nymphets. In a "she said, he said" scenario they will always come out on top in the same way that a womyn will usually win a custody battle or a white womyn will be able to convict an Onyx man. They will use excessive force (if action could be translated to litigiousness) against anyone they merely dislike than was ever foisted against them if there ever was. With law, once a charge is there, it's there. There are no second chances. There is no removal of the charge; there is no true expungement. In the eyes of the law, your sins cannot be erased no matter how guilty you feel about your false accusations.

I do not shame victims of crimes, only perpetrators that the law will not recognize as such.

As for boys, the young ones in the gay or Arab communities around or above the age of thirteen are the ones that seek out the older and more experienced men. They are bardajes or catamites. Actually, this is true of both the gays and the lesbians.

A person's sexual maturity has nothing to do with age and legal age has NOTHING to do with sexual maturity. I know virgins who are older than me[388] and might be in for just as huge a shock as thirteen-year-old virgins. When I had my first phone sex with Will, he was only a freshman in high school, meaning that he was around fourteen, and was as well versed in sex as I was, and

---

[387] This is how my ex ended up in a version of *Catfish* that affected the trajectory of his life.

[388] I wrote this when I was 31.

AudAx

I was sixteen. (When I was fourteen, my fourteen-year old female freshman friend was dating a senior in high school, and considering that he has a history of being abused by women, I don't think it happened the way stereotypes would have you believe.) I've even told my boyfriend that I would have liked to have sex with him if I could time travel to where we first met (school). I think he was more flattered than creeped out.

The entire idea of statutory rape of a child is based on the notion that a child is mentally a child and an adult is mentally an adult, but such is not the case. The mother of an ex told me that men in general tend to hover around the age of 14. I have mentioned this to men many times and most men of ANY age will agree that they feel 14 despite what their body says. In Chinese, the symbol for "man" is the same symbol for "child." I dated a man 41 years my senior, and he told me he didn't feel fully mature until he was in his 50s or 60s. Spiritually, an adult could have lived his first lifetime and a child could be on his hundredth lifetime.

Facts About Statutory Rape

Fact: It is well known by parents of young children, especially boys, that children love to be naked and also love to play with themselves. Does having the common picture of the baby in the bathtub that mothers love to whip out to show to their sons' fiancées make that mother a watcher of child pornography? Where do we draw the line?

Fact: In several cultures, and in the past, old men would marry girls half or even one-third their age and it was perfectly acceptable.

Fact: Four Horsemen of the Infocalypse: child pornographers, terrorists, abortionists, and abortion protestors, are used to cite why ordinary people should not have access to online protection from the National Security Agency (NSA). Considering that liberals are known to be pro-choice, and thus abortionists, I'm surprised that more people aren't in arms about this form of political control, this witchhunt, this War on Whatever We Perceive is Real. (Oh wait, it's because the conservatives are the ones known for bearing arms.)

Fact: Several teachers are strippers to pay the bills. If American society valued teachers more, they wouldn't have to seek second jobs.

Fact: Sexuality is very human. It's almost as if we imagine children to be less than human. So would that make the war on make-believe threats to actually be a war on children? Wow, I think we're finally getting somewhere.

Fact: In a world that knows the importance of mimicking in child development, people who mimick Vin Diesel's characters or blow things up à la Michael Bay go directly to prison. The propaganda surrounding statutory rape is similar to the propaganda surrounding violence. Those who are addicted to television and movies watch constant violence and gore on a regular basis, yet even toy guns and theatrical guns can receive punishments as severe as suspension or imprisonment. The pro-molester propaganda comes in the form of shaved pussies and schoolgirl outfits in porn, but the punishment is extreme.

We live in a world where wimmin shave their pussies (initially wimmin who got paid six figures) and encourage men to enjoy the look of prepubescent privates but condemn to death anyone who is influenced by Hustler's propaganda in the '70s or anyone in bed with the NSA-like Gillette company. Oh yeah, it's really smart to make uniforms that are in every man's wet dreams the mandatory uniform for all private schools that house the underage. *Rolling eyes.* Oh yeah, it's really smart to forbid a child from playing outdoors where it has been scientifically proven that that is where he learns best, all because we're afraid of an exaggerated boogie monster, when, in reality, a molester is more likely to come from closer to home. Do you think perhaps that I'm being sarcastic? Do you think that the war against sex offenders is really a war against kids? Do you realize that you treat your children with less respect and expect less out of them when you treat them as if they are helpless, especially if you believe you were helpless as a child? Do you realize that children matured a lot faster when they lived in large rooms with many families where everything was out in the open? Just look up the literature written in that time period and see if anything that we have today holds a candle to it.

Prisoner and Correctional Officer

Under statutory rape I also include mutual sex between a correctional officer and prisoner. (If you can't tell, I consider rape rape, mutual sex is not something I personally consider to be rape.)

Abuse (Sexual)

I don't understand sex abuse. I never understood sex abuse in others, but from reading about it I now realize that the pain comes from the lessons and behaviors it teaches, or the stories we create about it. To me, it was from the parent I trusted; the one who was did not use labels to make people lesser. From that experience, sex was freedom, protection from harm, and love.

I think sexual abuse for pre-pubescents is so traumatizing because they do not have the chemical receptors to make sense of sexual feelings. Though young children may desire affection, they do not understand lust. Another reason it can be damaging is because sex can be easily confused with love, or vice versa.

Now that I am older, I have learned that children do NOT understand sex when they are young. I personally did not understand sex when I was young. In fact, many young kids are too hung up about "kooties" to even consider the other gender in a sexual fashion. Sex, and all the mindset that goes along with being a sex hobbyist is LEARNED, the roots of which originate from the family of origin. But, children, though not sexual, ARE sensual. Sensuality is inherent in children, which I think is what Freud was trying to get at. And after being so involved in being a sex hobbyist, I have learned that sex is not the end, but sensuality is because sensuality speaks of art and love and holiness. Sex is just a physical act, and the ability or inability of participating in it can create shame.

The way that I have learned to understand the concept of sex is by taking experiences I learned sensually from my more intimate childhood years. Everything I am now is just a realization of what I was as a child. I am still the same.

Sensuality is inherent, but lust is in fact not. It is because the media is so full of sexuality that we can no longer see the sensuality, and we can no longer see that the present generation has gone wrong somehow. It has become a psychological need, but it is not a need that comes from the soul. And because it has become a psychological need, so many children [teens] are seeking after it, even those for whom sex is seen as sinful, and they cannot understand or stop this psychological need. It has become a force they cannot control, and so they end up messing up their life because they could not control the desire to get laid, and by messing up their life they mess up their soul because they cannot escape from the guilty feelings[389]. And I am here to bring us back to sensuality, which looks a lot like sexuality on the surface, but is not.

Coitophobia, Erotophobia, and Genophobia

These are the fear of sexual love or sex, a very specific kind of commitment phobia, possibly caused by sexual abuse. I've never run across it, unless I mistook that person for asexual.

Childhood and Subagitation

When I watch "Too Cute" on the Animal Planet, it surprises me how a dog's earliest days on this planet and e's interests match with e's later life. What does this mean for a sex worker's childhood? Hint: If something traumatized someone, they probably wouldn't have a passion for it. Just putting that out there.

Autonepiophilia

Autonepiophilia is arousal from being treated like an infant. As for pretending to be a child, I imagine that would appeal more to adoptees or men more than non-adopted wimmin since non-adopted wimmin may not have had attachment issues or stopped touching at a certain age.

---

[389] Whew! Guess I was pretty passionate when I wrote this.

Comparison of Childhood and Sex

Building blocks => Putting dick in vagina

Barbie dolls and dress up => Dressing up sexy

Make-believe => Roleplay

Candy most desirable => Sex most desirable

Both Childhood and Sex

- Creativity
- Curiosity
- Desire for hugs and kisses
- Ecstatic glee
- Envy
- Fascination with blood, gore, etc.
- Heightened senses
- Imagination
- Jealousy
- Optimism

Non-Sexual Touching[390]

My childhood best friend and I used to kiss and hold hands in a sort of European or Asian sort of way. There was never anything sexual about it. I really don't think there was anything sexual when Judas kissed Jesus. If there were, well, that would change a lot.

What constitutes sexual? For men, giving or receiving any form of touching is sexual. So would they rather their children die as those children did who were never touched for the sake of a science experiment? How is that child going to learn how to have a healthy romantic relationship?

Men consider touch to be sexual and so too do women, but only insomuch as they are in the proximity of men. Being influenced far more by men, due to my distancing from potential mothers (wimmin) with whom I've had mixed feelings, I can relate to the idea of touch provoking

---

[390] I recommend reading *The New Male Sexuality* by Bernie Zilbergeld.

sexual thoughts. It certainly does get in the way of knowing the difference between business-related rapport and sexual interest.

The only people I knew who cried when their dog died, and only when their dog died, were men who have had sex with a lot of women (more than I have had sex with men). The dogs were the only way they could satisfy the need for nonsexual touch. It really shouldn't be that way.

What the fuck is wrong with America? We deprive children raised by men, hormonal teens in schools, and men in general (especially prisoners, of whom there's a lot) of a basic need (touch) and tell them it's sinful, or even criminal, to want it and that they'll burn in hell for desiring a basic need. What?

How I Learned to Drive[391] Without Persephone or Fu Hsi: Endogamy, Exogamy, Sororilagnia, and Syngenesophilia

"No fault can be found with this type of love on the grounds that such affection is unnatural, for other animals mate without any discrimination; there is no shame for a heifer in having her father mount her, a horse takes his own daughter to wife, goats mate with the she-goats they have sired, and birds conceive from one who was himself their father." (Ovid, 233)[392]

The reason why incest is bad is because it confuses the roles we have. A parent cannot teach a child to be independent if keeping him/her dependent as a lover. Regarding incest, I would certainly be hard-pressed to find a sexual partner with whom I did not have a previous familial past life. It isn't the act itself, but the shame regarding that act that led to three generations of family curses.

Since the scent of people biological to a person is *usually* and scientifically proven to be a turn-off, it wouldn't apply to people who marry into the family. Non-genetic incest would include an attraction to a stepmother (novercamania), stepfather (vitricophilia), mother-in-law (pentheraphilia), or parent-in-law (soceraphilia). However, as an adoptee even I would find non-genetic incest to be gross.

It was only after I had sex with my ex that I realized we were in the same family tree and separated by multiple degrees (about 35 degrees) through marriage. He was my first cousin one time removed from the wife of a first cousin of the wife of a first cousin two times removed from a wife of my seventh cousin two times removed. (I like to research genealogy.) If we had a child, I doubt that incest would contribute to an offspring's intelligence; age would probably be a bigger reason. Incest is the only way to perpetuate the family line if only one family is deserted on an

---

[391] A play

[392] Ovid. *Metamorphoses*. 233.

island or is stranded in the desert. All that has been written about it is in the Bible. One time I remember that on a mission trip, the guy whose house we were fixing told me (a stranger) about how he had had incest, with no shame. The other volunteers were obviously turned off, but I listened without judgment, which is what a *true* Christian would do per Jesus' first commandment to love each other.

Royalty has had a tradition of marrying within the family in order to keep the family "pure." And the idea of keeping family "pure" is quite a Hitler-esque idea, and not many people in their subconscious want to be compared with Hitler. Why is it that it is okay for royalty to have incest, but it is not okay for backwoods farmers?

Incest is not forbidden in the 10 Commandments, but scientifically, this is not a godinterm (*See* New Terms) idea because it has been genetically proven that incest causes offspring to be of lesser intellect, which is ironic since royals have believed the opposite. The reason inbreeding is bad is because the combination of both parents' DNA results in more homozygous recessive alleles being expressed, that are defective gene copies that have a loss of function. Also, if the incest is not mutual, it can cause years of psychological damage. And incest does cause confusion and we always try to avoid being confused.

Most people think that it's only hurtful when it's initiated by elders, but it can also be hurtful when it's rejected by elders. There was an instance I read about where a man had sexual problems because his mother rejected his advances and called him a "sicko" or "freak." Sticks and stones might break bones, but a mother's words can hurt too.

However, incest is indeed necessary as a last resort when there are few in a population and the inhabitants mutually want their genes to live on.

The Last Witch Hunts in the Woods[393]: The Sex Offender Registry

If I encountered a sex offender (SO), I wouldn't tell my child to not talk to strangers. I would say, "Hi," and have my child do the same[394]. I would explain that my ex was an SO, and I understand what he's going through and has probably already paid his debt. I would invite him to coffee, with my child, so my child knows how to be a good Samaritan. Why would I do this? I would do this primarily to model to my child how to treat others with respect and, secondarily, for the nation. If we can brighten an SO's life, e will be a better contributor to society. If e's a better contributor

---

[393] This is a reference to *The Last Child in the Woods*, which connects the dots between the sex registry and environmentalism.

[394] In fact, yesterday (March 4, 2018) I just heard a speech that concluded that if others only treated each other as a human being, there wouldn't be any need for gun control because there would be no mass shootings.

to society, word might spread. If word spreads, then other SOs will be inspired, and others won't be as afraid. If other SOs are inspired and others are not as afraid, parents may even let children play outside, as they did prior to the '90s. If parents let their children play outside, then those children will be happier, be better learners, and even have enhanced senses. If they are happier, are better learners, and have enhanced senses, then the prescription drug use will decrease, the diagnosis of anxiety and depression will decrease, and the world will be filled with better minds that can invent things and solve challenges and opportunities. If the world has people who can solve grand-scale challenges, we might even have peace.

Sexual Crimes

It's not difficult for a college student to get a charge for lewd (lenocinant) and lascivious (tentiginous or grivoiserie) behavior. This person would be a lupanarian (at least the day e got caught) or pornerastic (if also typically horny).

Sexual assault means threat, essentially, and sexual battery means unwanted touch (of any kind). Perhaps you too have now picked up on the fact that you too can go to prison for essentially anything if you're not the type who's socially aware. This would apply to people on the autism spectrum or certain personality types.

Sex Addiction is Not a Sexual Crime, Nor Is It Child Molestation

Now I worry about what people think[395], but when it comes to my addiction, I find that more people worry about it and want to keep it a secret than I do. When so many people have it, why is it even an issue? The fact that they want to make it as secret keeps it unhealthy, so while I work on my own recovery, I fear that the act of doing so makes people less healthy of their own accord. By blocking recovery by saying "we want you to recover, but don't tell anyone" is akin to saying "don't tell anyone your parents beat you." This leads right back to shame. And why is one not to tell anyone? Because it gets conflated with sex offenders? Why does it get conflated with the sex offender witch hunt? Because if people truly knew their worth and didn't keep saying, "I'm an addict," but instead said "I have had addictive behaviors," they could eventually become rich because their self-worth could increase. So the lying politicians that be have a vested interest in keeping the addiction machine going. Why else would the Chinese government support the opium trade?[396] So people will let liars rule over the recovery of its citizens just because some lying politicians (or journalists who want to trap politicians) conflate sexual compulsion with very particular types of sex offenders.

---

[395] Older i.P. audAx: This was written by my younger self.

[396] The book entitled *The New Jim Crow* by Michelle Alexander also asserts that the American government paid cartels to bring hard drugs into America to justify the huge spending on Nancy Reagan's War on Drugs, with numbers and statistics to prove it.

Sdrucciola Workers of the World[397]

You wanna get into a debate about the morality of sex workers? Let's talk about the morality of politicians, car salesmen, and Phillip Morris first.

Talking about salespeople, I hear that current sex workers make good schoolteachers—who sell learning—and retired sex workers make good real estate agents—that would make them house salespeople. If one isn't good at sales prior to being a sex worker, I hear they get a whole lot better. So, any debate about sex worker morality should also include whether it's sex that corrupts or sales that corrupts.

The primary reason why society looks down on the sex industry is because most people are envious that they don't have the looks and those who do have the looks are envious because they didn't think to do anything with it.

Most sex workers aren't untouchables because of their social rank. In fact, they can be from all socioeconomic ranks. Sex workers are mostly untouchables because you literally cannot or should not touch them (which puts models into the sex worker category). Most sex workers are NOT prostitutes. However, some are.

The Enthusiastic Ecdysiast

I would want to be in the sex industry because I love sex more than money, which is ironic because most people who get in are the opposite. I am not typical. I do not understand how someone can say they love sex if they hate men. Believe me, the quality of exotic dancing would improve if it were not seen as something poor people do to make ends meet, but as a legitimate career that one can choose like a college major.

Cost-Benefit Analysis

Everything in the world revolves around money and cost-benefit trade-offs. When people realize that, everything makes sense. Why are fashion models skinny? Because they're likely to get hired. Why do skinny people get hired? Because it takes less fabric to clothe them.

Why do some people have body dysmorphic disorder? Because they compare themselves to people who are motivated by money because that is what is "sold" to them via the media. They

---

[397] The only way American sex workers can be safe to follow their calling is to smuggle themselves into other countries. I've considered moving to the Netherlands to find a country that would appreciate the beauty I could offer, but the immigration laws are strict.

do not think, "Oh, everyone should conform to an industry for a select few because those select few make more money" even though that is exactly what they are doing where their body is concerned. If they did that in all aspects of life, they would be comparing their personal finances to those of certified public accountants, their music skills to Beethoven, their athleticism to Olympic gold medallists, and would never accomplish anything because of a fear of failure.

Why do strippers date older men? Because older men have more money and because they're more likely to treat them with more respect. If they're of a certain age they may remember the sexual revolution and may have come to accept their sexual selves more than their younger counterparts. Why do strippers dislike female custies (customers)? Because they don't spend as much money. However, for some reason, they dig me. One girl told me I made her wet and asked me to feel, which I did to confirm, and another girl hugged me before I left the club.

Why do strippers have big boobs (bathycolpian)? Because it increases their earnings. Why do celebrities get plastic surgery? Because it keeps them in the game longer if their aim is to play someone young, attractive, and sexy (usually a main character who will have more lines and get paid more). Why do strippers tan? Because it hides their occupational injuries.

When other girls tan are they hiding injuries? No. They do it because they saw someone else do it[398]. Why do people imitate what they see? Because it is how babies are able to learn. This is not to blame poseurs because that is how we learn, by posing ourselves after the people we observe: first our parents, then our peers. If we really would like there to be peace on earth should we stop imitating others? Try telling that to your children, that they should stop imitating what mommy or daddy is doing. Would we really want to live in a world in which we could not learn?

Joe Redner

America has one of the highest rates of both strip clubs, registered sex offenders, and incarceration (with strip clubs probably feeding the last two). If there's anything that is uniquely American (and I do not say this with pride), it is sexual hypocrisy and sexual confusion. I just think about a male friend's Facebook feed where one post about double standards created an *ad nauseum* conversation. At this point, hypocrisy (or pretending to be someone else) is even more American than the Constitution, which no one in the courts counts anymore (and if they do, they act as pope in the belief that only they can interpret it). I don't understand the fact that people who have babies, and are therefore sexually active, do not want to admit to their child how they created life. It is like denying their children's origin story, which every nation and religion has. Hm...sounds like most people have the attitude of an adoptive parent. With most mothers (throughout history) pretending to be virgins, it is like denying their child's existence, which in itself is a form of abuse.

---

[398] See more discussion on why women shave in To Depilate or Not To Depilate in New Olo.

Stripper Stereotype

> "Of course the kind of cliché downward spiral about poor women is that once things get really bad, they have nothing left to sell but their bodies. That's probably the worst thing most rich people can imagine a poor person having to sink to."
> —Hand to Mouth (Tirado, 2014, p. 98)

> "Guys actually thought I'd be impressed when they told me that they liked me best out of all the women at the club because real honest women wouldn't strip, that it was beneath them to like a stripper. Amazing. Some guys will moralize at you while they're getting a lap dance."
> —Hand to Mouth (Tirado, 2014, p. 100)

I'm not gonna lie. Stereotypes are, unfortunately, not completely unfounded. There are plenty of strippers who are extremely ignorant about their own bodies and sex, which one would think they would have some knowledge about.

However, despite my large vocabulary and Master's degree, I do know what it feels like to be considered dumb (See the section with Mindy Cogsworth and Lew Galosh in the main book, *The Meaning of a Metaphorical Life*). So even if strange things come out of their mouth, there is usually some reason why they are saying it, or maybe they just weren't listening, which I have been known to do on occasion.

If...

If I became a stripper, it would be because I'd reached a point in my life in which I realized that I don't care what people think of me, I'm more important than money[399], that I'm not going to be a wage slave anymore[400], and that I stand up for what I believe in. It could be in my genes. Who knows.

"God's Plan"

God, why would you make me this way?

Why is the world so cruel

that I would be forever banned

from doing what I love to do?

---

[399] Stripping would require a paycut for me.

[400] Meaning doing something that doesn't bring me joy.

AudAx

Was I built to please others so they would never understand

why I'm here and what makes me who I am?

I figure you must have a plan.

Lies Parents Tell Aspiring Sex Workers

> "If you are not doing what you love, you are wasting your time."
> —Billy Joel

"Do what you love," they say. "We want you to do whatever makes you happy. We will support you in anything you want to do."

That's bullcrap. The only way to make it in this world is to subjugate yourself to others: to parents, to society, to the church. They're all big, fat liars, on a road paved with good intentions. It doesn't mean I don't love them any less, but I won't sugarcoat their lies.

What they should say is "You can be anything you want if that's what you want to focus your entire life on to the exclusion of everything else. You can challenge the status quo as long as you won't back down."

Once Upon a Time There Were Punquettos and Molls[401]: Sacred Putanism

"If you do away with harlots, the world will be convulsed with lust." –St. Augustine[402] (Dever)

> "A cold, self-righteous prig who goes regularly to church
> may be far nearer to hell than a prostitute."
> –C.S. Lewis

> "I firstly read the concepts of each feminist category i.e.; Marxist feminism, Radical
> feminism, Liberal feminism, Existential feminism and Social feminism.
> [...]
> Most of these doctrines feel that once society is restructured, prostitution will just go away![403]

---

[401] Prostitutes. A male whore is a spintry.

[402] St. Augustine had a child with a prostitute against his mother's wishes. He only became as we know him because he felt remorse when his mother passed.

[403] Older i.P. audAx: ROFL! If the oldest occupation can be wiped out with a few simple tweaks, then what are the implications? Here, philosophers, have a field day with that one.

[…]
Prostitutes hold within them something that nobody has bargained for, because they
never looked! What they hold is priceless, an ocean of sexual/caring/innovative and
spiritual information. When are we going to pick up the keys and open that door?
Who else gets so close to the most primal and strongest
urge that nature is driven by, than a prostitute?
[…]
If you have a broken leg, you don't visit an [sic] heart surgeon, do you?
Where do you go to get rid of that powerful energy that isn't being dissipated in a relationship?
Where do you go to soothe the troubled sexually confused 'child within?' Which in turn gives
a client self-awareness and therefore a responsibility for balance in ones [sic] sexual appetite?
[…]
Within the 'art' of prostitution lies the very answers we seek in society regarding
our own sexual naivety, immaturity and confusion." (Tansey, 2003)

"In the common practice of meditation the idea is to reject all impressions,
but here is an opposite practice, very much more difficult, in which
all are accepted."[404] —Aleister Crowley, *The Book of Lies*

Historically, prostitutes arose as women who failed virginity tests.

Why is "mistress" (literally "female master") synonymous with unmarried women, "the other
woman," and prostitutes all over the world? They're quite different. But apparently not to a man.
E must feel that any "other woman" is e's master.

Nothing is free. There is no free lunch. Sex comes with expectations of keeping sex fun, having
a relationship, having an honest relationship, or eventually getting married. If you don't know
which one your sex partner expects, then the cost is higher than you bargained for.

What I like about prostitutes is that the expectation is clear. The downside, of course, to putting a
price tag on physical sex is confusing it with self-worth[405], but if the prostitute is wise, e will know
that goods and services have no relation at all to the soul. A good prostitute should think of her
body as a tool. That tool needs upkeep and maintenance and will not stay in pristine condition
forever, but it will be necessary to keep it up for as long as possible. A good prostitute should
also take good care of e's body with or without regulations. This extends beyond the topic of
sexual protection and into the realm of health, sexual or not.

Some think paying for sex devalues people and sex itself. These very well could be the same
people who believe men should pay for dinners. Um…how is that different? The more dinners

---

[404] Older i.P. audAx: Gosh! I seem to recognize that idea. Where did I see it from? Oh yeah, the Bible.

[405] At least they have a price tag higher than $0, which some foster children do not

men pay for, the more sex they expect. How does one value things? By price tag, right? By supply and demand. So rather than devaluing, prostitution actually places a value on sex and the object of affection. Where this is wrong some think is that people are priceless, so doesn't that make all love free? Tell that to a foster child whose parents paid nothing for the service of being that child's parents. Isn't it rather free love that devalues instead of the oldest calling in the history of occupations?

As for me, I am like an escort and have been told that it's surprising that I'm not. People will pay just to be near me and have my company, with or without hanky panky. They think they are hanging out with a friend, but I see a transaction, a trade of equal value. Once I saw prostitution as the best way to deal with insufferable bootycalls, especially since I attracted poor people. I do not consider myself merely a slut, but a priceless middle class escort who is a minx on the side.

However, my dilemma is this: Since the most intimate love can only be given one person at a time, the question that haunts me is, "Will they focus on the love given or the love taken away?" The amount of love I give depends on the amount of love received, whether or not that's the way it should be. The amount of evil I give depends on the amount of evil received. Whether I make this world a better place is up to the givers and receivers.

When I was little, I wanted to be a vet until someone told me I'd have to stick my finger up a dog's anus. This is that kind of moment. If you want to get into sex work, these are the things you will need to be equipped to deal with (as in, you need tools to deal with them): urinary tract infections (UTIs), bacterial vaginosis (BV), herpes simplex virus (HSV), other sexually transmitted infections (STIs) up to human immunodeficiency virus (HIV), pregnancy, sex and love addicts, abusive people (verbal, sexual, physical, and emotional), liars, and self-esteem issues. Every time I have sex is a roll of the dice. Sometimes I get a UTI, BV, or pain from birth control. Prior to sex, I might have weight gain due to hormones or birth control. My sex emergency kit contains the Pill, Queen Anne's Lace, the Today sponge, spermicide, cranberry pills, Valtrex, vitamin C, L-lysine, condoms, lube, tampons, and pads. Anyone who doesn't have a sex kit is in for some surprises.

If sex is still worth it to you, then you have my respect, and I hope others realize how much respect you have earned after you have decided the risks are worth it. You work hard for the money, harder than many. I pray you never have self-esteem issues even when you do not get respected.

Those who love prostitutes most are those who are philopornists with pornolagnia, literally people who love prostitutes; those who have chrematistophilia, arousal from being charged; or even harpaxophilia, getting pleasure by being robbed. The clients, "johns" (that sounds like they're a toilet), have cypripareunia, sex with them. Eassayeurs are men who are hired in bordellos (ficaros) to encourage timid clients to follow their lead.

With the "mancession" (recession where jobs for men were hard to find), I feel that men are unwilling prostitutes. The only men with the right looks (to me at least, in 2008) are the ones who can't afford rent, have constant financial emergencies, or need just a few more dollars to get by. So do I not pay to have sex with them? If I want sex, then I do. Methinks I do. So isn't it hypocritical of them to judge female prostitutes, some of whom have had a higher education than some men could even fathom?

Temple Fricatrice

"What? Know ye not that he which is joined to an harlot is one body? For two, saith he, shall be one flesh." –1 Corinthians 6:16 King James Version

"Historically, intercourse was the act through which male and female experienced God. The ancients believed that the male was spiritually incomplete until he had carnal knowledge of the sacred feminine. Physical union with the female remained the sole means through which man could become spiritually complete and achieve gnosis—knowledge of the divine. Since the days of Isis, sex rites had been considered man's only bridge from earth to heaven. 'By communing with woman,' Langdon said, 'man could achieve a climactic instant when his mind went totally blank and he could see God.'
Sophie looked skeptical. 'Orgasm as prayer?'
Langdon gave a noncommittal shrug, although Sophie was essentially correct. Physiologically speaking, the male climax was accompanied by a split second entirely devoid of thought. A brief mental vacuum. A moment of clarity during which God could be glimpsed. Meditation gurus achieved similar states of thoughtlessness without sex and often described Nirvana as a never-ending spiritual orgasm.
'Sophie' Langdon said quietly, 'it's important to remember that the ancients' view of sex was entirely opposite from ours today. Sex begot new life—the ultimate miracle—and miracles were only performed by God. The ability of the woman to produce life from her womb made her sacred. A god. Intercourse was the revered union of the two halves of the human spirit—male and female—through which the male could find spiritual wholeness and communion with God. What you saw was not about sex, it was about spirituality.
The Hieros Gamos ritual is not a perversion. It's a deeply sacrosanct ceremony....
Admittedly, the concept of sex as a pathway to God was mind-boggling at first. Langdon's Jewish students always looked flabbergasted when he first told them that the early Jewish tradition involved ritualistic sex. In the Temple, no less. Early Jews believed that the Holy of Holies in Solomon's Temple housed not only God but also His powerful female equal, Shekinah. Men seeking spiritual wholeness came to the Temple to visit priestesses—or hierodules—with whom they made love and experienced the divine through physical union....
'For the early Church,' Langdon explained in a soft voice, 'mankind's use of sex to commune directly with God posed a serious threat to the Catholic power base. It left the Church out of the loop, undermining their self-proclaimed status as the

sole conduit to God. For obvious reasons, they worked hard to demonize sex and recast it as a disgusting and sinful act. Other major religions did the same....
'Is it surprising we feel conflicted about sex?' he asked his students. 'Our ancient heritage and our very physiologies tell us sex is natural—a cherished route to spiritual fulfillment—and yet modern religion decries it as shameful, teaching us to fear our sexual desire as the hand of the devil.'" (Brown 308)

I've never understood why people don't respect prostitutes nowadays but they still respected me when I was a slut and gave it away for free. I mean if it's your occupation, aren't you more likely to take it seriously? Some cultures even respected temple prostitutes. How could something so inherently spiritual be relegated to the ghettoes? I could see spiritual leaders being poor if they chose a path of asceticism, but today's American prostitutes (not all) chose a path of lack.

Not every punquetto gets a *Night Shift* (1982) or *Pretty Woman* (1990) ending, and not everyone is as openminded as they were in the '80s, which really wasn't that long ago.

What would have happened if Shakespeare were a female prostitute? Probably nothing. We wouldn't even know about Shakespeare's great works. That could rock the very foundation of Western civilization. But isn't sex itself the foundation of Western civilization? The Urantia Book says, "[S]ex has been the unrecognized and unsuspected civilizer of the savage; for this [...] sex impulse automatically and unerringly compels man to think and eventually leads him to love."

The ability to love all as Jesus commanded is a curse on this earth and a blessing in heaven. I live in the consciousness of many men, and that is where I belong: in their remembrances and hearts for it is in the heart where revolution is first won.

Types of Educated Punquettos[406]

- Escort

- Geisha

- Hetaerae[407]

- Kisaeng[408]

- Oiran

---

[406] I'm pretty positive that I was one of these in a past life.

[407] Simone de Beauvoir writes a lot about hetaerae in *The Second Sex*.

[408] The existence of kisaeng is probably what inspired me to take an Eastern view over a Western view of sex.

Sex Workers in Korea

American society is good at perpetuating lies, one of them being that most Koreans are prudes. Ha ha. Yeah, right. In terms of international relations, it's possible that the whites thought they were the dominant race in Korean adoption because their dominant elite is Rockefeller who believed in rule by mandatory schooling. However, I think it's the Koreans that are infiltrating the world because the passion (love) of one's nature will always be stronger despite how much control is enforced on one's life. It's like how Teddy Roosevelt thought that he was westernizing Japan, but it was Japan that had the more superior attitude and were smart enough to pretend they were swayed to his way of thinking. Yes, a diverse America means gone are the days of Puritanical ways. Between Asia, which comprises about 60% of the world population, and other non-white and more sexual races, it is true that the future will be a non-moralistic society (in terms of white morals alone).

On that note, here's an incomplete list of where one can find various Korean services in the industry[409]:

- Barbershops
- Coffeeshops
- Daeddal rooms (masturbation rooms)
- Delivery (love motels)
- Full salons
- Gangnam BJ joints
- Karaoke bars
- Kiss rooms
- Massage parlors
- Mountain hikes
- Officetel
- Room salons (fancier karaoke bars)
- Whiskey talk bars
- Window shops

Discussion question: In a collective society, what does the plethora of sexual services in Korea mean on a deeper level?

---

[409] They might also offer services in restrooms, or "tea rooms."

Value of a Marriage for a Sex Worker

A stripper once thought that she didn't like the idea of giving free sex to a boyfriend. Let's consider this idea. First, it's optimal to avoid premarital sex anyways so she shouldn't worry about societal pressures (however, he was probably attracted to her because he thought he would get a lot of free sex). Secondly, the average cost of a wedding is $25,200 (in 2014). In terms of money benefits alone, that's worth about 1,260 $20 one-song dances, 168 $150 half-hour dances, or 84 hour-long dances. Considering one $20 dance (with extras) per day, that would be an equivalent to over three years of service. Considering a half-hour dance per day, that would be less than six months. Considering an hour dance per day that would be less than three months. If he pays for it, that saves her three months to three years of work. If they both pay for it, then he has an income and she could even change jobs or be a stay-at-home mom with his support. This does not even include the intangible benefits of marriage.

Virtual Sex Workers

For a customer, virtual reality is the only place where you can get closest to your sexual fantasies. You can have a different body. You can even be an animal with horns and a tail. However, there are still limits because there are real people behind the avatars, possibly with a real need for real money, and one can never be 100% certain that e's speaking with someone in the right age group or gender. There are risks.

I heard that the chance of getting paid in a virtual environment is one in 10, so you better be the best and persevere. Any sex worker needs to have ophelimity, the ability to please sexually.

Fetishization Topics (Sample Size = 107)[410]

Marriage is about long-term stability and survival of a race (human or a subset). Many have married people they did not fetishize. Many dark-haired lovers married blonds, many gay men married straight women. Many a royal was smitten by non-royals, and many a Jew was smitten with a Gentile but did not marry them. Just because I think older men are hot doesn't mean it is practical nor respectful for one of them to father my child(ren). Just because of the high rate of Korean adoptees with whites or Asians does not mean that they have never dated or loved an

---

[410] Disclaimer: Please keep in mind that many fetishes involve other people, are not always in the bedroom, or are there when others least suspect it. In a sense, many people (or at least some people) are turned on almost all the time, turned on by almost all things, or are walking fetishizers (is that a word?). I am putting this out there to encourage more compassion and open-mindedness toward our fellow man or womyn at ALL times.

Onyx (Moorish) or Mexican. And those who married outside their fetish were only unhappy if they thought they were lacking something.

I believe the fetishization of my race, on some level, contributed to making me a sexual compulsive. (Someone who has compulsive sexual behavior does not see fetishization as racist, but rather as an opportunity.) It is a misconception that we know better than God. Following the addictive chemical reaction of love is us thinking we know better than God. Let me tell you, "We ain't that smart."

So, think of this section as something written to the already marrieds since none of these should affect the trajectory of your life.

Softcore Vanilla Paraunia

Normaphilia

If you are only interested in acts considered normal, then I'm surprised you're still reading. However, I can assure you that several of these fetishes, though they have strange names, are normal, or not too extreme, such as the interest in kissing etc.

Aphephilia or Haptephilia

This is deriving pleasure from being touched. I would hope that most people have this. If nothing else, I would believe at least 99% of the readers have this. So, ha! You do have a fetish, and it doesn't make you abnormal. However, a word of caution: fulfillment does not come through the finger.

Aliphineur and Tripsophilia

Aliphineur is using lotion to arouse a partner. An aliphineur is a person who uses lotion to arouse a partner.

Michael Polkfield McGee

I had an ex who was a masseuse. I intrigued him because I was the only one who gave him a massage instead of requesting one. However, after we broke up, my dear ex had inevitably become one of those creepy old men and started frightening one, two, three girls in one night because he offered up his specialty. I couldn't help but wonder if the reason had to do with me, if I had broken him somehow. It upset me that people were so afraid of my exes, and thus afraid of me because I continued to love them, continued to think that they were a part of me.

Basoexia and Deosculation

As Julia Roberts' character knew in *Pretty Woman*, affectionate kissing is more intimate than sex in the same way that true communication is more intimate than either. One should work up to a kiss. Even if, with today's standards and societal expectations, one has sex on the first date, this does not necessarily include a kiss. A kiss should be earned, especially when sex isn't. Instead of it being first base, it should be home run.

Clitorilingus, Cunnilingus, Fellatio, and Gamahucheur

> "Your traveled, generous thighs
> between that my whole face has come and come—
> the innocence and wisdom of the place my tongue has found there—
> the live, insatiate dance of your nipples in my mouth—
> your touch on me, firm, protective, searching
> me out, your strong tongue and slender fingers
> reaching where I had been waiting years for you
> in my rose-wet cave - whatever happens, this is."
> —Adrienne Rich, "The Floating Poem, Unnumbered" from *Twenty-One Love Poems*

To say oral is not sex is ridiculous. To someone with a micropenis or an extremely tight vagina, that is the only way to have sex.

I admit that I first felt uncomfortable with oral sex performed on myself and the idea of performing it on another girl also made me feel uncomfortable, but I have since gotten over that discomfort. I still don't like the taste of my own cum from a man's lips; I prefer the taste of it from my fingers. I guess one could say I'm not a big fan of felching, even the Internet term (which is too much like buffering). It's alright. Kinda like shrimp. I don't really like shrimp, but if someone really wants me to try some I will, but just one.

Some guys, not just mobsters/gangsters, don't like cunnilingus. If someone is known for disliking oral and they do it anyways, that's a warning sign that that person wants to get away with something.

As for fellatio (oral sex performed on a male), it is one of my favourite sexual activities to perform.

More than anything oral preferences tell who is the giver and receiver in a relationship. Takers will only take. Givers will mostly give. And that is how they like it.

I have never met a man who could perform oral on himself. However, I knew one man who was able to cum in his own mouth. Sometimes he missed.

7% of the sample size prioritizes giving and receiving oral sex. 2% enjoy oral on their balls.

Acousticophilia and Ligyrophilia

This is arousal from sounds. I could imagine that anyone who frequents dance clubs gets turned on by loud noises. Once my ex sat me in front of the computer, put earphones on me, and turned on porn. That was a real turn-on.

With noise, I have tried both extremes. I have been as silent as a mouse when I masturbated in my house (that rhymes) or in the presence of a roommate. I have also been practically screaming so much that my voice became hoarse. It is fun to experiment with this to find your preference.

1% of the sample size's Achilles' heel are their ears.

Knismolagnia and Titillagnia[411]

Knismolagnia is an interest in being tickled and titillagnia is an interest in tickling someone. This is another one of those things that is so common, in my opinion, that most people don't even count it as a fetish. A version of this is called pteronphilia (being tickled with feathers), which is a subset of texture play.

5% of the sample size gets turned on by tickling or being tickled.

Gamophobia and Philophobia: Learning The Value of Commitment

"Well, I'm running down the road
Tryin' to loosen my load
I've got seven women on
My mind

Four that wanna own me
Two that wanna stone me
One says she's a friend of mine"
—Jackson Browne and Glenn Frey, "Take It Easy" as sung by The Eagles

---

[411] www.yaqisworld.com

"an intercourse not well designed
for beings of a golden kind,
whose native green must arch above the earth
and subsede corrupting love.
[...]
Oh, courage, could you not as well select
a second place to dwell,
not only in thy golden tree,
but in the frightened heart of me?"
—Tennessee Williams, "The Night of the Iguana"

Gamophobia is fear of commitment. Philophobia is the fear of falling in love or of being loved. I don't know if I have this because on one hand I am polyamorous, but on the other hand I historically had a hard time believing I could feel loved.

It can be a red flag when a partner is seeking someone wildly different from e-self; this could be used as a viable escape plan or excuse for breaking up.

George Mireille was a lovely predator. I thought that I had "love at first sight" with him, in a sense, but later learned that a love at first sight connection just means that there is a Venus-Uranus connection and nothing more. It is not a guarantee of marriage success.

I remember asking him about his exes. At first he was convinced that he loved all of them, but after he started thinking aloud he convinced himself that he didn't love any of them. It's sad what the mind will do if not reigned in.

If you want a compliment, then the very fact that a philandering commitment phobe is attracted to you is enough of a compliment. Married men and commitment phobes are both attracted to successful women, even more than most, and are usually one and the same. What successful means in this context is usually a confident and beautiful business woman. Ask a woman who knows. I know I don't know if the same is true for married women, but it's quite likely.

I used to believe that commitment phobia was truly horrible, but I eventually came to realize that out of the possible disorders people could have, commitment phobia is the safest and most logical. The only thing that's wrong with it is if it reaches other areas of your life outside of romantic relationships, which it does by definition. No goal has ever been achieved with ease, lack of focus, and lack of motivation. (An unmotivated partner won't put in the work in bed or at work. Successful people transmute the sexual impulse into their work. Those who are focused make more moolah.)

After learning that I had been clinging to a commitment phobe I let my hair down and frolicked with everyone from virgins to high-level executives. (This was not the only time I learned that when two people collide, they take a part of the other person with them.) Fear of intimacy is not *all* that bad; it has given me a wide range of experiences that I would not have even considered having if I did not fear intimacy to some extent.

2% of the sample size is afraid of commitment.

Alphamegamia, Anililagnia, Anisonogamism, Chronophilia, Geronosexuality, Gerontophilia, and Tragalism

An age gap relationship constitutes any relationship where the partners are 7 years apart or more. Alphamegamia is attraction to partners of another age group. I wonder if I prefer particular generations of people more than I prefer age specifically. (I loved men that could enjoy any media that originated before 1964.) Not only are older generations more viripotent (sexually mature), but they have more experience and more respect for women (as opposed to millenials or Generation Y). Even if 60 is the new 40, 40 is also the new 20, so that would make 20 the new infant. So either the Baby Boomer generation makes for a better set of mature adults than Generation X or Y, or Generation Y is unmanageable and shouldn't have kids during their fertile years.

Anililagnia is sexual desire for older women, or "mothers I'd like to fuck" (MILFs). Anisonogamist is attraction to either older or younger partners. This one includes marriage. Cougars are anisonogamists. Geronosexuality is 30 years apart of more. Some people are even turned on by wrinkles (rhytiphilia). I have had geronosexuality. Gerontophilia is an interest in "grandparents I'd like to fuck" (GILFs). 'Nuff said.

I have never found someone with obsolagnium, waning desire due to age. I'm very happy about that. Indeed! When people talk about how sex has a shelf life, they're either equating sex with coitus/copulation or have never talked to sexually fulfilled 80- or 90-year-old people. The whole idea of sex having a shelf life is utterly ridiculous to me. I don't even know where to begin.

Also, it has been my experience that male flaccidness starts in the brain and works its way to the body, as with most physical conditions, not necessarily the other way around.

It could also be an argument used when saying you shouldn't pick your permanent mate based on sex. Okay, maybe it's not the most important thing, but to me, I want my man (or woman) to love me for who I am. So if the person's not cool with my sex drive then we won't get along on a permanent, let alone a temporary, arrangement. I knew one guy who was into cross-dressing. It was important to him. If he married someone who was not cool with it, he could be miserable for the rest of his life. Is it worth it? No one deserves to be miserable. We were all made for more than that.

AudAx

When I make a statement, "I have a white hair," the most common response is "Oh no!" I wonder if that's what people said to EmmyLou Harris when she had her first white hair. Fortunately, she ignored the age haters.

The disdain people have for age gap relationships is an assault on tradition and the Bible. When people ask me if I am looking for a father figure when I dig an older man, I do not return the micro-aggression by asking why they think the American way is better than what has been tried and true for centuries all over the world. If anything, my interest in older men is genetic and hereditary, not a reaction to my adoptive family dynamic. However, those who support or are in age gap relationships make a statement against the mainstream.

If one desires large age differences but it is not possible due to political, legal, or social constraints, I suggest that one finds someone who does not look their age. There are many people who look young as adults and old as teenagers. This applies only if you are seriously concerned of the consequences.

Ah! How fun it would have been to be Glenda Jackson working alongside Walter Matthau! I also would have liked to meet Donald Sutherland. I used to like Richard Gere, but I'm not sure about him anymore.

If you are a womyn who can live with or without a man, then you would be a suitable match for an older man or a daredevil.

3% of the sample size has one of the fetishes in the title.

LDRs

If absence makes the heart grow fonder, and familiarity breeds contempt, why are so many people against long-distance relationships (LDRs)? Are they also against military and prison relationships? Are they also against spouses living in different states to make a living?

People who can't handle LDRs are spoiled by technology and are not very creative. Plenty of couples have survived separation even when they were divided by oceans when all they had were ships and snail mail.

As much as I love sex and long-distance relationships, what I can't stand is when physical presence only equals sex. If that's the case, then I can get more needs met when we are physically apart and emotionally close.

If others are my mirror, then I am clearly afraid of intimacy, for every man I have seriously dated has had similar fears that have been expressed in various ways. Most of my longterm relationships were long-distance and many were hesitant to share all of their life with me.

Or maybe I was just anxious-preoccupied, according to attachment theory. My father and his neglect followed me everywhere. When I dated a commitment-phobe, he would share the most intimate details of his life then break up with me the next day. When I dated a guy in prison, he neglected my emotions and also disappeared for days on end. The only time I felt a guy was not neglectful of me was when I was neglectful of him. Then the ex I neglected would start treating me like a sex object, when I was taken by another man, making him the biggest disappointment in my life. *See* Under the Greenwood Tree.

In the words of Carol from *The Last Man on Earth*, a comedy TV show, "Phil, I'm your wife, you can always tell me about your diarrhea," but they would not tell me when they were having diarrhea, which a future spouse has a right to know. Why does our society insist that we put on a mask even in private?

Goth-Related Fetishes

As with most Goths, I dabbled in modeling. Unfortunately, men sometimes think so highly of themselves that they think women dress for them and, therefore, can undress for them. This is especially wrong when women dress for function (like the weather). The mere idea that a woman dresses for men is an insult.

I don't dress for [straight] men; if I dressed for anyone, it would be gay men. I love hair the way an Arab woman loves makeup around other Arab women. Any Saudi Arabian woman can tell you that women dress for women (if they are seeking external approval at all). If a woman dressed for men plural, then they would stop upon getting married to one man, for all he needs to see is her underwear. Women, never dress for a man (who is not gay) and does not appreciate your right to self-expression.

Most people would expect a discussion of being in the closet to be in the GLBT section, but, to me, it applies more to this section. Being closeted is like being a spy; it's like pretending to be a Cowboys fan when you're a Redskins fan or pretending to be a liberal when you're a conservative. How could anyone love you if they don't know who you are? People ask me why I put so much value on having a Goth appearance. It has nothing to do with whether my hair is natural or not and everything to do with authenticity. People say that the desire to be liked is the desire to be loved. I disagree wholeheartedly. It was only when I removed the desire to be liked that I could give people the opportunity to love me as I am.

Faye "Coraline" Viola

My best from 4th grade to junior year of high school, and I had strange similarities. Besides the fact that we sexually fantasized about each other, both of our names were related to an oral sex act. Faye "Coraline" Viola was the first person I knew in high school who had sex and wanted to tell me all about it.

She eventually studied at the Corcoran Gallery of Art. She continued excelling in anything artistic besides sculptures: photography, modeling, singing, playing guitar and keyboard, graphics design, etc. She cranked out a new CD. She looks like the actress from *Casino Royale*, the translucent skin, the skinny nose that reddens with a cold, the skinny fingers and arms, the porous eyelids that cry for eyeshadow. To describe her personality, she is a gentle egotist. On her it is a virtuous trait rather than a vice. She is well suited to be a celebrity. She moved back to Northern Virginia from Connecticut in May when I moved away from Northern Virginia the first time. The second time I moved away from the Washington D.C., she was in the other Washington.

My only concern with Goths is the high value they place on sex and the denial they have that sex, like water, can go too far.

Achluophilia, Lygerastia, Nyctophilia, and Scotophilia

Achluophilia and scotophilia are sexual interest in the dark, but lygerastia is arousal by having sex in total darkness. Nyctophilia is love of the night. What Goth doesn't love the night?

BDSM: "Bettie Page," Cupcakes, and Go-Go

Disclaimer: ALWAYS remember to fill out and sign a domination-submission contract with someone you trust completely prior to partaking of any extreme BDSM activities. If participating in serious BDSM make sure to write up a contract so that both parties understand their boundaries and what to do in case of emergency. Relationship contracts are an amazing way of moving forward with better relationship behaviors. I recommend always having a safe word, even when not involved in BDSM. In certain cases, as with rape roleplay, "no" will not suffice. I highly recommend taking first aid/CPR training in advance, as well as sexual training. If you have never been to formal classes on BDSM, then you're probably not a BDSM enthusiast.

> "I know many, many people who are into kink, and they are the most together people I've met because they know themselves." –Chaz (Riley & Rule, 2015)

BDSM is an acronym for bondage (vincilagnia), domination, servant, and master or bondage, domination, sadomasochism, and masochism.

Love is generally masochistic, as anyone would know whose heart has been broken. Would it not make sense to make that metaphor real?

When Leopold von Sacher-Masoch realized his name would go down in history for the name masochism he was pissed off. That's what happens when you pen an erotic autobiography about being thrashed by a beautiful lady.

Matt Frederick was my worst bully, and he followed me through most grades from late elementary school to the end of high school. He was also good looking. This led to the perverted Stockholm Syndrome idea that I either liked to be tortured and humiliated or that I wanted to give him an STD. The former led to my interest in BDSM, and it's been downhill ever since (in a good way). Yes, good things do come from bad things (and vice versa). Just read the "Story of the Taoist Farmer."

BDSM is all about punishment and humiliation[412]. It is also about domination and submission; it is a game of power. It is very different from rape: BDSM is violence for sex's sake. Rape is violence for violence's sake.

Aggression belongs in the bedroom by either party upon mutual agreement, not elsewhere. Servitude by either party, likewise, belongs in the confines of a mutually loving relationship and with a mutually respectful agreement, not elsewhere. Some men prefer to submit to women (cataphilism) and some women prefer to submit to men.

I do not think that it is the pain that makes it pleasurable as much as it is the fascination of the sensation in itself.

BDSM is THE local flavor for the nation's capital, hands down. The scene for BDSM is as strong here as the scene for swinging is in Minnesota[413]. When people ask me why I'm so into BDSM, I tell them that I was raised in DC. I also like BDSM because the BDSM community is education-minded. I love learning! When one is in BDSM it can feel as if you lead two separate lives. I think this poem explains it well, though it was written for a different audience:

> "It hides our cheeks and shades our eyes,—
> [...]
> And mouth with myriad subtleties.
>
> Why should the world be over-wise,
> In counting all our tears and sighs?

---

[412] Humiliation can include kakorrhaphiophilia, arousal from failure.

[413] "If my girlfriend wants to invite Jim and Sheila over again, I say yeah, because I know that I love my girlfriend and she loves me. If she likes fucking Jim's dick, then congratulations to Jim. I'm cool with that, because I believe that she doesn't love Jim's dick as much as she loves my dick. If either of you doubts that, then you're in the wrong game." (Ellis, 2014) (I cannot find the page number because book loan ended.)

> Nay, let them only see us, while
> We wear the mask."
> —Paul Laurence Dunbar, "We Wear the Mask"

Note: There are too many terms to name under the umbrella of BDSM that I don't even bother.

8% of the sample size is into BDSM. This statistic might be unreliable because my study was conducted in the BDSM capital of the nation.

Japanese Rope

As with anything else in the world, this requires skill. It is difficult to find someone who can teach Japanese rope bondage, and it is even more difficult to find someone who is willing to help someone practice. One must have patience while investing time into tying knots on a regular enough basis to become proficient in it.

Gomphipothic and Odaxelangnia

If there is any fetish that leans toward Goths it's being gomphipothic. It's an arousal by teeth. Besides dentists, people who are interested in vampires would have this, possibly. I went out of my way to have a realistic set of teeth made for me. I'm very proud of them. Fortunately, I got them right before the guy who made them decided to quit due to frustrations.

Of course, if a person has vampire teeth, there will be requests for being bitten, so it helps to also have odaxelangnia, gratification from biting on others, or even hematolagnia, sexual stimulation from blood. Those who are interested in hematolagnia would enjoy blood sports, sex games with blood, but with ebola, HIV, and the zika virus going around that is a life-threatening preoccupation. You might not want oral sex from a vampire. Just sayin'.

Only 1% of the sample size has this fetish.

Sleepy Sex and Necrophilia: Sleeping Beauty

Necrophilia is not disrespectful, it is giving someone love that one was not able to give them in life. Necrophilia to women alone is called necrochlesis. Not that I ever tried it, but I do know it's physically possible for a womyn to do a dead man, with a formaldehyde injection. However, that might cause the dead man's fat to melt, I think.

The only time it really creeps me out is when someone has a sexual attraction to decaying matter, or septophilia. A necrophilia fantasy roleplay could couple with taphephilia, arousal from being buried alive[414], or taphophilia, a love of funerals[415]. Placophilia is similar. It's arousal from tombstones. It might be a little weirder, but it's less offensive to people. It's pretty harmless.

A toned down version of necrophilia is sleepy sex, which is pretty much what happens at fraternity parties in the news, so I do not see why it is such a big deal to fantasize about having sex with dead people. I have a sleepy sex fetish because I find it to be the most romantic, sexual turn-on. It possibly evolved from sleepovers where I slept with girls. A toned down version of sleepy sex is lazy sex. An extreme version of sleepy sex is somnophilia, which is with strangers. I wouldn't recommend it. However, hypnophilia, being turned on by the thought of sleeping, sounds pretty harmless.

Only 1% of the sample size has this fetish.

Group Sex

There's nothing like a foursome to motivate me to wash the bed linens and clean (or hire a cleaning lady).

5% of the sample size enjoys group sex.

Bigynist and Bivirist

A bigynist is a man who has sex with two women. A bivirist is the opposite. I am fortunate to have experienced both sex with two men (twice) and sex with a man and female (one and a half times). The former was more enjoyable due to the circumstances. Women are usually more hesitant about these sorts of things. The trick to threesomes, or other adventures involving more than one, is making it look like it's spontaneous.

2% of the sample size is or wants to be a bigynist. I'm the only one I could count as a bivirist due to the nature of how I accrued the sample size.

---

[414] Now this doesn't have to be under dirt. It could just be under sand at a beach.

[415] Okay, that could lead to some awkward situations if it went beyond fantasy—however, I do know someone who had sex during a wedding. Ballsy.

Marcia Flouncra

We spoke for hours on end online, on the phone, in the car, on the metro without once ever touching. We flirted and said sweet things to each other. I hinted some things. She took the hints without making much fuss. We entered my boyfriend's apartment, drank until we had reached beyond tipsy. We laughed, laughed, laughed, tickled each other, then held hands and kissed—all three of us. Stumbling into the bedroom we fell onto each other in a heap as I tried to remove every garment from every limb. My poor ex. He only got wet kisses and flesh in his bed, but I got the whole deal. I enjoyed her uneven skin and red panties. I loved her long hair with my hands. I licked her. She licked me. But I was the more dominant one. Touching her was like touching myself. Her breasts were smaller than mine, but they still had nipples and moans. I felt frustrated at not having longer fingers and enjoyed her wet insides with my trimmed fingernails. I orgasmed both genders and was satisfied. She was not entirely comfortable with the hovering man with the long hard dick and suggestions. I got used to seeing her back. We slept with my right hand cusping her right breast while she was about to fall off the side of the bed. He touched her waist and me and that was all for the rest of the night. He complained afterwards when she was several miles away and I revelled in my new officialness. She invited me to her home and I knew that I had done well.

Pluralism and Gang Bangs: Snow White

Having an orgy with a football team or in a gangbang scene has been the fantasy of many people.

When I think back to my one gangbang (not an orgy), all I think is, "Man, that was risky!" I think it's safer in fantasies.

I met Robin through a gangbang. It was amusing to me really because, to talk with him, he seemed like the most boring ISTJ suit and tie nerd (or geek?).

To this day[416], I still get notifications on gangbangs. I continued to get gangbang invitations into my early thirties, which I declined. At age 31, I was invited to three gangbangs in a year.

Gang Rape

Gang rape is different from a gangbang. A gang rape is instituted by bullies. Bullies are attracted and drawn to those who want to be liked[417] and those who have low self-esteem.

---

[416] I don't anymore, three years later. I had to make the conscious decision to say, "No."

[417] Such people can be found devouring self-help media

That is all well and good to say, but in the case of bankers, judges, and government, that is not the case. You cannot say an entire nation, nay, an entire world lacks self-esteem or just wants to be liked. (Well, the united States of America does have a history of wanting to be liked[418], but that is neither here nor there.) Yet here we are with bullies in the banks, in the courtrooms, in Congress, in the Senate, and in the White House.

Gynandry and Monoecious Gynandromorphs

I think it's common for people to fantasize about hermaphrodites. I, however, have never met one (or at least didn't know it at the time).

This is a continuation of the Bonobo section from Old Olo. What is natural? Have you ever looked around at the animal kingdom and noticed how much variety we have? Have you ever seen the boxfish? Do you know how a land snail has sex with love darts[419]? Are you familiar with sexual cannibalism of a praying mantis or spider? How about filial cannibalism, which is common in a large range of species? If you really pay attention to the animal kingdom you would realize that God values uniqueness.

One size does not fit all, physically, sexually, or spiritually, as we can see from the Gospel of Judas. Why do you want to be like your peers anyways? What do they have that you don't? What do you have that they don't? Take pride in your uniqueness. If you are in a 1% or 2% of the population, make sure that you are in the top percentile rather than the bottom.

Being born with both the sexual parts of a man and a woman are God-given, natural, and right. However, and I know this is controversial, I do not believe that a woman born as a man can ever be a full woman because she will forever lack menstruation. Perhaps I am a cynic, but as a woman with the potential of the gift[420] of premenstrual dysphoric disorder (PMDD), a precursor to postpartum depression, I cannot accept that Caitlyn Jenner gets it so easy—all the fun without the pain, without PMS, without the ability to give birth, without menopause.

Ipsism, Manustupration, and Onanism

"[W]riting a book is mostly an exercise in masturbation."—Sarah Silverman (Silverman, 2010)

---

[418] No one can love someone who is too busy wanting to be liked. Even if someone is a country.

[419] Watch "True Facts About the Land Snail" on YouTube (https://www.youtube.com/watch?v=VTV23B5gBsQ)

[420] Being sarcastic

AudAx

"Along with the 'feebleminded,' insane, and criminal, those so classified [for eugenics] included women who had sex out of wedlock (considered a mental illness) [...] masturbators [...] and girls whose genitals exceeded certain measurements..." (Hillenbrand, 2010, p. 11)

"[B]eing under the covers, face-down, is one way to make sure that if someone walks in, no one will know what's going on. And sometimes, there's an element of that shame left over [in adulthood]." –Carlyle Jansen

"Leaving that door open means there's a possibility that somebody can walk in — and that might add a little excitement about being discovered." –Carlyle Jansen

"Meetings are an addictive, highly self-indulgent activity that corporations and other organizations habitually engage in only because they cannot actually masturbate." –Dave Barry

Amatripsis is masturbation from rubbing the labia together. Siphnianization is anal masturbation and chezolagnia is masturbation while defecating. Some women like to use dildos for masturbation. That is called bouginonia, unless the woman uses a sausage as a dildo, in which case it's called butulinonia.

There are many different masturbation styles, including exhibitionist masturbation, discreet masturbation, vaginal masturbation, clitoral masturbation, masturbation with toys, multiple orgasm masturbation, masturbation with foreplay, quick masturbation, and no masturbation (Pardes, 2014). I've masturbated daily since I was 14, so I'm pretty familiar with it.

As for exhibitionist masturbation, sacofricosis is masturbation in public via a hole in the pants' pocket. I do have a hole in my pants' pocket and could do this if I wanted, but I'd be afraid that people would notice.

I prefer a combination of vaginal and clitoral and will occasionally do multiple sessions in a row if I'm really horny. In porn, women always have long nails and masturbate by moving their middle finger from side-to-side with the left of their fingers straight. I have never masturbated by moving my finger side-to-side.

The act of sexual intercourse reaffirms separation of gender, but masturbation affirms unity that both male and female, ying and yang, reside in everyone.

I recommend reading *Sex for One* by Betty Dodson.

GLBTCQ[421]: Sexual Orientation

Before we can discuss GLBT, we have to define it. I once knew an Arab who would often (jokingly) sexually harass my ex by making gay jokes, but according to his culture he wasn't gay. In Arab and prison cultures, only catchers are gay (as opposed to pitchers). Young boys aren't gay in Arab societies. Men who consider themselves GLBT are only those who *want* to consider themselves GLBT, especially if they are pitchers or gunzels (a guy who wants to be sucked). These people are willing to refer to their "friend" as a "boyfriend."

Mark 6:11[422], about when Jesus sends the apostles into the world to preach, proves that Sodom and Gomorrah was not destroyed due to sexuality but due to lack of hospitality: "And whosoever shall not receive you, nor hear you, when ye depart thence, shake off the dust under your feet for a testimony against them. Verily, I say unto you, it shall be more tolerable for Sodom and Gomorrah in the day of judgment, than for that city."

The only reason why homosexuality could be a sin is because we were morally obligated to procreate when the population was low and the death rate was high. But the "sin" of not procreating is the same sin for adoptive parents no matter their sexuality. The punishment for not procreating is reincarnating into a sterile or barren body. Only through spiritual merit, according to Kabbalah, can this be overcome. However, since most people reincarnate and do not know what they are here to rectify, then it does not seem to be the most heinous crime.

I do not believe that men need to be with women and vice versa, but I do believe there needs to be a balance of ying and yang energy. Some women have had predominantly male past lives, like me, and vice versa, especially during Ascension.

As for homosexuality, most GLBT people I know have a religious background. Pick up any *Metro Weekly: Washington's LGBT News Magazine*, and you will find ads targeting Jews, Episcopalians, Church of Christ adherents, Baptists, and Unitarian Universalists. Just because people like others of the same sex, doesn't mean they all want to turn their back on their church. They are not godless. They come in all shapes and sizes: gay, Republican, transsexual, you name it.

However, sometimes I think the GLBT audience is superficial. When I dressed like the fashion designer I wanted to be, I had a GLBT posse, and even the flaming gays wanted to date me. I was a fag hag in high school, but I didn't know because I was waiting for them to tell me even though they thought it seemed obvious. When I wore "normal" clothing, I would go to every

---

[421] GLBTCQ- An acronym standing for gay, lesbian, bisexual, transgender or transsexual, curious, and queer.

[422] I wrote this before receiving a package from a gay-friendly church. At this point in time, it should be more like common knowledge, but it isn't.

weekly club meeting and no one would ever talk to me because I looked like a "friend/supporter." It's the same way in the Goth scene.

I've also never seen as many smokers together. What's up with that?

GLBT people tend to have a persecution complex, some of which may have been initially justified, such as the death of Matthew Sheppard, but soon becomes irrational, like someone afraid of dogs. I mean to say that most of their fears are unfounded and have no basis in reality until they make them real. It kind of reminds me of the way a person acts after having been cheated on multiple times. At a certain point, the feeling of being persecuted morphs into an excuse for all kinds of behaviors.

New Girl does a good job explaining how one-track minded people misunderstand people who are not one-track minded. This is the story of my life. Most of the time I am not the one-track minded one, surprisingly, because when I want it, I can just ask. So if I don't ask, it's a result of a man reading in-between the lines (even if they say they don't do that). But my inability to not act when someone else wants to is an expression of my compulsive behavior. These misunderstandings tend to be the most obvious around same sex people, one of whom is gay and one of whom is straight. Sometimes it comes from the gay person, but sometimes it comes from the straight person.

Ambisextrous, Ambisexual, Amphisexual, Amphieroticism, Androgynophilia, and Digenous: Bisexuality

Even though I have a lot of experience with men, I get tongue-tied around women. The last time I kissed a girl, Kaitlyn Ryan, she told me to relax and treated me like a lesbian noob.

An aside: Just recently, my lesbian crush posted a new profile pic. Damn! She's still as hot as ever. (The downside to bisexuality is that not only is it "okay" to objectify one sex, it is now "okay" to objectify all human beings. There is a predominance of female bisexuals in the female "sex addiction" community. I don't know if that is due to testosterone or lack of societal acceptance.)

4% of the U.S. population is bisexual, according to my sample, guys and girls.

Commasculation, Uranism, and Zwishcenstufe: Mid-Atlantic Leather

A jocker is a male homosexual. This is the opposite of an epigamic jock (heterosexual).

8% of the sample size is homosexual, according to my study, which includes a Muslim.

Handkerchief Codes

This is a system used usually by gay males or BDSM practitioners. I'd probably be an orange[423].

Cymbalism and Sapphism: Girlfriends

I love men, and I love women, but the variety of women I like far exceeds the variety of men I like. I like spiky-haired blond butch girls (Kerry Morrissey), long gray-haired older women (Bella "Happy" Beatrice), red-haired vixens (Jessica Rabbit), friendly model blonds (online flirts), butt-length wavy-haired Goth brunettes (Eppie Byrd), and baseball-cap-wearing black women basketball players (Shandon). For men I like black men, older men, or any guy with whom I've developed a friendship. I am proud to say that I was Marcia Flouncra's first girlfriend. That is major because in the life of a homosexual one needs an actual sexual experience with someone before straight people will take them seriously. Of course, cisgendered people do not need to prove anything to anyone.

The reason why I believe that sexual identity is something you are born with is because of "gaydar." Anyone who has a finely tuned gaydar can tell you right off the bat that I am bisexual. Anyone I have met who is straight would never guess that I am. I believe that a gaydar can only work when you have an aura and that aura comes from your innate being. A gothdar is similar.

7% of the sample size is lesbian, according to my study.

Catfighting/Pillow fighting

Catfighting is mostly a lesbian pursuit involving tearing off each other's clothing.

Being Transfeminate and Gynemimetophilia: José

I do not understand why anyone would want to suture the labia majors (episioclisia or infibulation) unless it were to become male. I greatly respect transsexuals. Despite the fact that they do not have menses and may or may not have breasts, it takes a great deal of money and time to get the surgery and to learn how to be a womyn (code for "how to beautify oneself"). I once knew José whose goal it was to not only be a gay man, but to be a singer in a transsexual music band. I also dated a man who had been the delight of a female-to-male and male-to-female couple. Sex with transsexuals may make you ineligible to donate blood for a while.

---

[423] Google time.

6% of the sample size is transsexual, according to my study. This statistic may be biased since I'm a Goth, and there is more openmindedness in that particular group of people. 1% of the sample size has had sex with transsexuals, according to my study[424].

Viva Calipornication at the Banquet of Chestnuts[425]

"When all of your friends are comedians and you spend your life in a club hearing and telling jokes, it becomes ever more challenging to make each other laugh. I imagine it's like working in porn."—Sarah Silverman (Silverman, 2010)

"The reasons for making porn a treat are fairly obvious: Like any image you spend lots of time looking at, it shapes your brain."—Sarah Silverman (Silverman, 2010)

"This is an interesting observation, especially coming from a Kantian perspective. 'Losing respect' for men as a class is more difficult than losing respect for women. The so-called 'double standard' is an affront to dignity. Therefore, it is not sexual desire that is objectionable, but the different attitude society has toward men versus women who engage in essentially the same sexual activities."[426]

[...]

If one accepts human sexuality as a natural and good aspect of life, rather than a degrading and bad aspect, it takes away much of the force of Kant's argument against prostitution. Rather than looking upon sexual desires as flaws which place us on the level with beasts, they can be seen as drives that unite us all. Whatever our station in life, the libido is common property.

[...]

But a consistent Kantian can look upon providing sexual services as morally acceptable, provided no coercion is involved, and provided each participant fulfills his or her end of the bargain." (Ann Garry qtd. in Madigan 1998)

People so desire to be unique snowflakes and/or victims that when they observe something about themselves, they conclude that only they feel, think, say, or do certain things, being oblivious to the fact that most people feel, think, say, or do those things too. A non-sexual example of this is feeling skinnier in the mornings and thinking no one else feels the same way in the mornings. Another non-sexual example is feeling that one gets more attention from others when sick and thinking that no one else has the same experience. In sex, it is easy to continue feeling like a unique snowflake if all they have is porn with which to compare themselves to.

---

[424] This does not include me, even though I had an opportunity.

[425] This is the chapter for grapholagnia, icolagnia, pictophilia, and scoptolagnia

[426] (Garry 1978)

This can go the opposite way too, and people could think that everyone is like them when they aren't. An example of this is believing that all men can squirt if the man making that conclusion can squirt and sees that men in porn squirt.

Pornography creates unrealistic expectation, or for some, goals to aspire to, and a porn-inspired romp seems to me a far cry from making love. The problem with porn is that there is not enough representation, and it is not educational from a homeschooling sexual education perspective. Some people have gotten all their education from something that was never intended to be educational. My current boyfriend[427] got his education from pornography, and it just amazes me what he does not know is normal.

Porn does not have enough representation from the following[428]:

- Curved penises (Peyronie's disease)
- Inverted nipples
- Micropenises (without representation, this leads to small penis syndrome, as well as low self-esteem, which in turn affects relationships)
- Outies
- Pearly penile papules
- Smegma
- Unshaved balls
- Unshaved pussies
- Uterine fibroids

Bet you didn't even know what some of these terms are. See, proof that porn is not helping in your education. Also, pornstars most likely have herpes, but despite that fact, pornography does not teach that herpes is not like HIV and that there's no reason to commit suicide over it[429]. The lack of education, in that case, has literally been a life-or-death situation.

Pornography is a mini-movie. As my dad says when I'm taking a movie too seriously, "It's just a movie." Movies are about storytelling. If I'm watching a movie, I don't imagine that I'm in it.

Personally, I'd be more interested in coprology, the study of porn.

---

[427] Now an ex.

[428] Here's an idea: Post-sex cuddling porn with conversation would make porn feminist-friendly and would find an audience with female sexual compulsives.

[429] Apologies for the double negative.

AudAx

Pornography, it has been said, is a gateway drug to sexual compulsion[430]. That is why it is of utmost importance to be careful with Internet safety, but it is especially important to deal with pre-planning how to address the issue when the cat's out of the bag. By the way, the whole world should thank pornographers. If it weren't for them, the Internet would not have been put on the fast track road of success.

Another problem with porn is what it does to the relation between the sexes. My dad told me that he never saw porn before he got out of the military and went to college, back in the '60s. He didn't know what it was. He said that the reason I am not able to be friends with a man or even mind my own business without someone hitting on me was because of the proliferation of porn. Because of porn, his argument went, the wimmin's movement took two steps forward and one step back.

Sometimes when I feel insomnia, I watch porn, but then I'll watch porn too much and blame it for not getting any sleep. Since computers emit electromagnetic frequencies (EMFs), the only real reason to have a computer in the bedroom is if you are only paying for one hotel room or for porn. However, that person will be more susceptible to harmful EMFs during climax.

I would recommend against constant visual stimulation. As with drugs, it requires more to achieve the initial result. I have met and know of many purviewers of porn, photographers, and people in the sex industries that just cannot get turned on by sight alone anymore. They are desensitized.

I think pornography is best for prisoners. For them, they can even practice furtling (the use of fingers in pictures of genital areas).

I feel sorry for those whose pornography compulsions interfered with doing what they really wanted to do off their bucket list. Sex has never gotten in the way of my motivations or doing the things I want. If I want to do something I just say it, and it becomes a date activity. If I have to strive for it, then I make the time. Maybe that's the difference between a Type A compulsive and a Type B compulsive.

I do not think pornography has an element of spirituality. There can be no emotional connection if the viewer is not also the videographer or photographer. The best porn I've ever seen was pitch black. When they're too into it to hold the camera properly, you know they're in love. Nude artwork, on the other hand, has an element of art, beauty, and grace.

4% of the sample size is enthusiastic about porn. 1% of the sample size is enthusiastic about webcams.

---

[430] This sentence will be taken in different ways according to whether you believe pot should be legalized.

The Plight of Photographers

If there's any group of people I feel sorry for it's photographers. To me, modeling and photography are the kind of things you could love so much that you'd do it even if you don't get paid. So many Goths do modeling, that it's practically an inherent part of our culture and identity. I have known countless photographers who keep it fun, but their wives act as oppressors and reinforce the face that adulthood and monogamy are not fun and that the husbands must be interested in only the spouse by force of guilt. It is a clear sign that if the spouse does not of approve of their husband's art they they do not fully approve of their husband. They do not love them as they are and can only love what the husband can be when pussywhipped.

4% of the sample size is made up of photographers whose spouse does not approve.

"Fetish" by Selena Gomez: Other Fetishes Case Studies for the Spouse (Sample Size = 107 including myself)[431]

"'Fetish' is a term in the Portuguese pidgin language that developed along the Guinea Coast, the coast of West Africa, in the early 1500s...After its origins in the trading language of the Guinea Coast, 'fetish' is picked up in early anthropological accounts in the European Enlightenment, then passes to Marx who used it as a metaphor for the commodity, then to Freud who used it as the prototype for the analysis of deviant behavior." (Ulmer, 2003, p. 160)

"once the imprinting happens it is [...] difficult for it to be reversed[432] [...] men will [...] imprint on [...] things [...] that [...] would have been impossible [...] *The first thing is you need to know that this is a need.*"—Claudius Afterthought, "Making Money on Fetishes" (emphasis added)

"Yet these parapsychological events[433] are fairly common, much more frequent than people realize. It is only the reluctance to tell others about psychic occurrences that makes them seem rare." –Dr. Brian Weiss (Weiss, 1988)

I have a larger sample size than most (107[434] including myself) and, though I do not use a precise scientific method, such a dry method would not have allowed me to have access to the information I want (and the reader wants), which I can only receive within a trusting temporary or long-term relationship.

A fetish is a fixation or abnormally obsessive preoccupation or attachment. I almost included this section as an ode to my state because, from personal experience, I believe that Northern Virginia is the hotbed of fetishes, due to its suppressive nature. This section is especially dedicated to those who think that sex is boring, which is a total lie.

"Fetish" in the non-sexual sense refers to a material object believed to have magical properties that was regarded with superstitious and irrational reverence and obsession. Fetishes originated as a religious idea!

---

[431] Ryan, 2002

[432] I have had people who have tried to reverse my sexual imprints. All I had to do was find someone who accepted them.

[433] Replace "parapsychological events" and "psychic occurrences" with "fetishes" and re-read.

[434] Only about two-thirds of whom I have had sex with, which is not a lot compared with other sexual compulsives.

It has since evolved in the sexual sense to refer to an object of irrational fixation. The reason why I think that the definition for sex must change is because fetishes are the most fun part of sex, yet *many fetishes do not actually require intercourse*[435]. I have been fascinated with fetishes for a long time. Sexual fantasies can be the most telling about a person's real self. I have found that sexual fantasies tell more about a person than most anything else in the world. There is nothing else as revealing. There are many times that sexual fantasies "make sense" or align with one's occupation and choices made in life. There are many times, also, when sexual fantasies totally conflict with one's occupation and choices made in life. The sex world is a private world where people can be who they are not allowed to be in public.

I have known it to be true for heterosexuals to fantasize about being homosexual even though they are not homosexual and vice versa. I have known it to be true for jealous people to fantasize about watching their girlfriend or boyfriend have sex with someone else[436]. I have known it to be true for domineering types to desire submissiveness. Most people find that there is something wrong with having sexual fetishes, although it is perfectly healthy and everyone has a fetish of some sort.

For the fetish lovers: Always make sure that you can trust your partner. Also, if you and your partner do not go about sex as if it were sacred then you have destroyed what possibility it has of it being a spiritual experience. I am certain that there are many fetishes I have not discussed here. I apologize for leaving out the fetishes that I cannot remember or have not come across[437]. Keep in mind that none of these are forbidden in the 10 Commandments, the rules overriding all rules, as long as it is within the confines of marriage, or a similarly dedicated relationship.

I feel sorry for men especially who have less common fetishes and are looking for a wife. For some of them, sexual compatibility will be highly important because it is so much a part of their identity or is an obsession. So by opening the discussion on fetishes, it is my hope and goal that more people (mostly wimmin) will be open to bending their brains a little and increasing statistics of eligible bachelorettes for these bachelors. If the "100th monkey syndrome" can be believed, then I could have already singlehandedly changed the world prior to publication of this book.

Please use the index to find whatever it is that you are looking for specifically. Otherwise, feel free to read in order.

---

[435] Perhaps that is why I like it; so that I do not have to exercise my muscles so strenuously.

[436] I fall into that category.

[437] There was an interesting one mentioned in *Ally McBeal*; Richard Fish's character had a fetish for waddles, the skin that hangs down an elderly woman's neck. However, I don't know the name for that.

Hardcore Sexual Personality by Myers-Briggs Type Indicator[438]

The world was made for extroverts who don't rock the boat, generally ESxJs in Myers-Briggs Type Indicator (MBTI) language. The world is also made for Type A[439], right-handed, visual learners. The government industry is made for ISTJ and INTJ personalities. If the world were only made for certain people, then the world would be made of guilt for all those who do not fit the above descriptions. When reviewing this never-before-seen list of sexual personality types, consider that Mars is inherently different from Venus. Sexual compulsives are usually feelers or ENTPs in terms of personality.

---

[438] This is a well-known personality indicator made popular at work.

[439] The origin of this comes from numerology

Sexual Personality by Myers-Briggs Type (Subject to Change and Based on Personal Experience)	
ISFJ: Missionary position, making love, courting, cyber sex, crossdressing	ISTJ: Missionary position, large people, separate beds, courting, cyber sex, threesomes, teasing, role play, light bondage, spanking, interracial, sapiosexuality
ESFJ: Oral sex, multiple partners, role play, porn, phone sex, stockings, open relationships, virgins, bisexuality Negative: Rape roleplay, gangbang, sexual compulsion, or adultery Note: I have had a long-term relationship with this type.	ESTJ: BDSM, gun play, wrestling Negative: Anger rape or war rape
INTJ: Sapiosexuality, fatties, phone sex, courting, asphyxiation, BDSM, cyber sex, giving and receiving, soft touching, tickling, kissing, flirting, foreplay, technique-related sex Negative: Pro-choice birth mother Note: I may or may not have had sex with this type.	INTP: Sapiosexuality, cosplay, furries, celibacy, cyber sex, voyeurism, erotic kissing, foreplay, experimentation, missionary position, vanilla, softcore porn, cuddling, panromanticism, asexuality Negative: Stalking Note: I may or may not have had sex with this type.
ENTJ: Sapiosexuality, phone sex, courting, BDSM, foreplay, dirty talk, straight relationships Negative: Asphyxiation Note: I may or may not have had sex with this type.	ENTP: Oral sex, flirting, one-night stands, age gap relationships, webcam, squirting, same sex relationships, holding someone while e orgasms, power exchange, watching people of the same sex (e.g., lesbians) make out Negative: Coercive rape, statutory rape, or adultery, sexual compulsion, mixing sex with drugs Note: I have had a long-term relationship with this type.

ISTP: Porn, threesomes, doggy style, texture play, squirting, stockings, polygamy, tattoos on private parts, cumshot, polygamy, fantasies, tattoos on private parts Negative: Extreme sex Note: I have had a long-term relationship with this type.	ISFP: Porn, fatties, cuddling, domination/submission, sexting, rope play, stockings, doggy style, tickling, watersports, interracial relationships, having a lot of sex (quantity) Negative: Power rape or jealousy Note: I have had a long-term relationship with this type.
ESTP: Fisting, double penetration, asphyxiation, watersports, body worship Negative: Gang rape, power rape, extreme sex, double fisting, or sadism Note: I have had a short-term relationship with this type.	ESFP: Porn, doggy style, sex toys, flirting, gay jokes, fascination with menstruation, getting a rise out of people Negative: Date rape or power rape
INFJ (Me): BDSM, switch, multiple fetishes, cyber sex, autogynephilia, extreme sex, swinging, promiscuity, exhibitionism, variety, tantric sex, teasing, stockings, people who fit the gender role, technique-related sex, sapiosexuality, interest in breasts, celibacy, loud music, porn, biting, hairpulling, threesomes, physical attractiveness, fantasy, dirty talk, sexual empathy, aggressiveness, sex in trusting relationships, experimentation, makeup Negative: Sadism, rape role play, beastiality, or pro-life birth mother, sexual compulsion	INFP: Multiple fetishes, doggy style, porn, open relationships, interracial relationships, deep throating, cuckolding, cyber sex, cumshots, bisexual, foreplay, being pinned down, seduction, same sex relationships, sapiosexuality, flirting, oral sex, teasing, transsexuals, rimming Negative: Sexual compulsion, gangbang, or beastiality, mixing sex with drugs Note: I have had a short-term and long-term relationship with this type.
ENFJ: Multiple partners, promiscuity, submission, committed relationships, fidelity, touching, togetherness Negative: Sadism, love addiction, codependency, or pro-life birth mother	ENFP: BDSM (highest pain threshold), missionary position, making love, the most sexual type, multiple partners, promiscuity, infidelity, public sex, threesomes, swinging, sapiosexuality Negative: Valuing sex more when evaluating marriage, religious hang-ups

Acrotomophilia, Amelotasis, Apotemnophilia, and Teratophilia

This is an interest in amputees. Though it's unusual, I'm sure that amputees are thankful that such a philia exists. Amelotasis is attraction to the absence of limbs, amelotation is loss of a limb, and apotemnophilia is having fantasies of losing a limb. Teratophilia is arousal from deformed people. *shrug*

Acrotomophilia would have to be, in my humble opinion, one of the most unusual fetishes. It is an interest in being an amputee. I don't know what to say about that except for the fact that it's similar to teratophilia, or interest in the deformed, as well as dysmorphophilia, which is arousal from the physically impaired. Well, no, I do have something to say about it. I can see where that comes from. I could imagine getting turned on by bravery, and someone who is amputated or deformed, but keeps going despite the odds, is brave.

Also, sometimes, it is only by seeing the less-than-perfect, slightly disproportionate bodies that make one think of sex. The beautiful bodies, unless they are wearing close to nothing and sometimes even if they are, have become too common in TV, movies, magazines, etc. to think twice about. The disproportionate may not have a perfect body but they have at least one area of the body that stands out, anything from hips to thighs to breasts to necks to hands. It is not always sexy to have a perfect body all around, but sometimes it is sexier to have the perfect hips or thighs, and only that or the perfect breasts or parts of the body not usually associated with sex. I do not have a beautiful body, but I pride myself on parts of the body not commonly associated with sex. The men craved for sex or the need to have socially acceptable crushes will not be interested, but the admirer of small details will believe them to be beautiful.

Actirasty

This is an interest in making love under the sky or sunbathing.

1% of the sample size has this fetish.

Acucullophallia and Apellous

This means circumcision. I have only met one person who was uncircumcised and one person who may or may not have been. However, I hear that with someone who isn't circumcised, it's possible to slip a man's foreskin over the glans penis of his partner. This is called "docking." Since most men no longer have a foreskin, a fibula (like a chastity belt for men) is obsolete.

98.5-99% of the sample size has been circumcised.

1-1.5% of the sample size has been uncircumcised.

Advanced Techniques

"Whatever the mind can conceive and [bring itself to][440] believe, it can achieve."
—Napoleon Hill

It is true that one shouldn't judge appearances. However, athletics in the bedroom is well rewarded, especially if you are impressed with brawn (cratolagnia or sthenolagnia)[441]. The man who pushed me to go out of my comfort zone the most was a Virgo, the type that strives for perfection. Jim Gulickson, a man who looks like Rand Paul, taught me how to be fisted. I appreciated it because I always want to improve. Practice makes perfect.

Ask anyone who's older or even dead[442], and they can tell you the mind is of more value than the body. This I do not deny. However, your physical body gives immediate feedback as to how well you've trained your mind. If you cannot train your body then you cannot train your mind.

Anything worth doing is worth doing well. The best of us go the extra mile. Every encounter is an opportunity for self-discovery and growth.

However, don't compare yourself with the best. Those are professionals with years of experience. Also, a warning to the wise: Consider before jumping into the advanced techniques that such an act would make vanilla sex less satisfying. Is the benefit greater than the cost? You must ask and answer for yourself.

Athletic Tricks

If you are interested in say having sex upside down, doing a headstand, you will need to be fit. The best motivator for me to exercise and eat healthy is the potential for sex, or even just maintaining sexiness. I watched my parents succumb to FDA's America, just like most Americans. That was not going to be in my future. No sirree. Then there are people who can only have sex while standing (not sure why). They have stasivalence, which is the opposite of supinovalence (which makes more sense for the bedridden). By the way, I did have a life where I was bedridden. Good riddance! Pun not intended.

Deep-throating Techniques

- Hum. You might find that it's difficult to gag and hum at the same time.

---

[440] I'm not sure if this quote is more accurate with or without the bracketed content.

[441] The opposite is asthenolagnia.

[442] You'd need a medium to ask, unless you are have mediumship abilities.

- Lift both of your legs up: For some people, lifting both of their legs up when they feel the gag sensation coming helps to prevent or reduce it.

- Put a little table salt on your tongue. Moisten the tip of your finger, dip it into some salt, and dab the tip of your tongue with that. Another way to do this is to put a teaspoon of salt in a glass of water, and rinse your mouth with that. Don't forget to spit!

- Take a sip of very cold water: Some dentists say that taking a sip of very cold water before a dental procedure helps prevent gagging. There's no harm done in it, so try this for your next dental visit.

Fisting

I would hope that anyone interested in being fisted also has divertissement or paraphilia, an interest in unusual objects, because practice makes perfect and most of that practice is probably solitary practice.

The vagina is made for simple fisting. A baby is bigger than a fist. However, the anus is not made for fisting, least of all double fisting. If you had a baby-sized shit I'd tell you to go to the ER on the double, no pun intended. If there is anything that I think should be banned it would be double anal fisting. Just say no to double anal fisting. I have. The risks outweigh the benefits. The possible consequences are too severe. The equivalent of fisting for the other gender is using glass catheter tubes in the male urethra. If you won't stick glass catheter tubes up your penis (if you're a man), why would you expect a woman to train to take your fist up her pussy? I'm not giving techniques for double anal fisting or brachioprotic eroticism (fisting with the arm) because I do not encourage it.

This is the least holy, least respectful type of sex I could ever envision, with the exception of scat. If there is any type of sex I would consider a sin, this is it, as well as the use of power tools with sex. When pain exceeds the pleasure, it is time to stop. It just does not make any logical sense.

I despise the coupling of violence with sex as in *AMV Hell Divided by Zero*. This is what creates psychopaths. Violence and sex are completely different. No holy person, and we are all holy, should derive pleasure from another's pain if that pain is not lesser than the pleasure or does not result in transcendence of the physical body, which flogging can do.

I quit learning advanced techniques because I didn't like being barked at by someone who had a restraining order on record.

4% of the sample size is interested in learning and practicing advanced sexual techniques.

AudAx

"Erasure and Closure"

I define myself as a minx.
I value friends over lovers
(and they mostly know each other
even if they don't know
they are part of my territory).
Sex is my friend;
Sex is forever.
Men come and go.
Men try to rule,
try to set standards, expectations,
try to alert us to the beginning of the day.
For some men, desires are commandments.

My desire is to be alone.
Is it?
I am liberated.
Am I?
I am a sex goddess.
Not a sex slave?

I have an emotional bond with strangers.
I cuddle
acquaintances and peers I have seen around
for more than 10 years,
single people who are in love with others
or are on a streak of physical neglect.

I can have a new boyfriend
every day
of the week
or of the year.
What makes you so special?
Your godliness?
Your likeness to me?
Your magnetism?
Only psychoses can be magnetized.

I do not judge you.
In fact, I don't even think about you,

or the way you can make me cum,
except for when you demand
to be part of my schedule
when you are only part of my list.

Sex is my mission in life
of highest importance to the people of today,
but it doesn't feel as holy
when I am with you.
It feels like I have more to learn,
more to try, more to do,
or more opportunities to set boundaries.
Where do you fit in
my line of sex compulsives
and one-night stands?
The only people who matter,
when I reflect on my life,
are those who taught me a lesson.
(And it felt like a life in a life.)

I seek to understand how I can reconcile the pieces
of today,
the world of today,
through the lens of yesterday, like you perhaps,
which I also know I cannot do.

You are not a teddy bear.

No, you are not what I think you are
nor what you think I am
nor even what you think you are.
We are mutual predators of each other,
plotting to detach,
mutually taking advantage of
a need we have
of vital importance--
for you, sex (or is it?);
for me, erasure—
to exhaust all my attachments
and bring them to closure.

Ask me about the meaning tomorrow

and tomorrow.
Tomorrow is another day
and my understanding changes day by day,
and that is a good thing.

Agalmatophilia, Galateism, and Pediophilia[443]: Dames de Voyage

The former is an interest in sex dolls, mannequins, or statues. If you're interested in this, I would recommend watching *Lars and the Real Girl*.

The latter is just an attraction to statues. Got Medusa? This could also relate to androidism or mechanophilia, arousal with human-like robots. See the Japanese animation (animé), *Chobits*.

Pygmalionism

This is falling in love with one's creation. This could either apply to falling in love with a robot or it could refer to the plot of *My Fair Lady*, which is, by the way, my favorite musical[444].

Agrexophilia, Allopellia, Candaulism, Cryptoscopophilia, Ecouterism, Scoptophilia, and Troilism

> "I thought I'd feel jealous and want to be involved, but I'm actually having
> fun watching you enjoy it..." –paraphrase from Marlon Basilica[445]

Agrexophilia is similar to cuckolding; it is arousal from others knowing you are having sex. It is my understanding that this term is mostly used when used as a method of humiliation (asthenolagnia), but that has never been my intent. Ecouterism is listening to others have sex without consent.

A wittol is a husband who tolerates his wife's infidelity. Being a cuckoldress, I would not mind marrying a wittol. One of these days I'd like to be on the other side and have candaulism or participate in troilism, which means watching my spouse have sex with someone else, and allopellia, an orgasm from watching my significant other have sex with someone else.

---

[443] Not to be confused with pedophilia.

[444] It was referenced a couple of times by Marilyn Jenett.

[445] This experience may have motivated him to enjoy an open marriage.

Scoptophilia is voyeurism. If you're undressing in front of an open window, then you want to be seen. And if there's a mutual agreement that you want to be seen and someone wants to see you, then there is no perversion, being that it is mutual.

Cryptoscopophilia is like voyeurism though not sexual. I'm sure we've all seen old movies where the hotel walls were paper thin and the characters could overhear their neighbors having wild sex. The idea of this is what turned me on and led me to have sex with my ex's ex-roommate and friend. My ex was correct in knowing the other guy would not have made the first move. I did. I implied that he could hear us having sex and that it turned him on.

5% of the sample size has this fetish. I am including myself here.

Albutophilia, Hydrophilia, and Undinism[446]

The arousal by water is pretty innocent and possibly more universal than other fetishes. However, I am have been a bit watershy lately ever since I've had hives from hot showers. At least, right now, that's what I believe has been causing issues[447].

Water helps the senses as much as fabric play. Water guns, pools, shower massagers all help.

Allotriorasty

Allotriorasty is arousal from partners of other races or nations. I do not understand white men's obsession with black men's cocks. I have tried both kinds, and neither one is larger on average than the other. That is one of the biggest myths and fallacies of this age. It's ridiculous.

Colorblindness is not the answer to racism. Colorblindness just means seeing everyone as white and ignoring that there will be cultural differences you'll have to deal with farther on down the line. It does not allow for individuality, personalization, or accurate medical attention either. Colorblindness is like treating wimmin as men where you end up with wimmin who will sacrifice anything to be seen as an equal to a man. It is like applying eye makeup on an Asian the way one would apply it on someone with creased lids. It's what makes people change who they are to compete. Wimmin will never be men and men will never be wimmin, even if they're androgynous.

---

[446] Older i.P. audAx: Cytherea (a.k.a. Aphrodite a.k.a. Venus) is said to have come from the sea. Seductive mermaids always come from the sea. What is it with water and sex? Well, scientists speculate that water is the greatest thing we need in order to live and survive. When water was found on the moon, some thought that meant creatures use to live there. So the connection with water and sex is reproduction or basically giving life.

[447] Not really sure when this was since it's no longer an issue.

AudAx

7% of the sample size has this fetish, and probably more since all the men I've dated were outside of my race.

Altocalciphilia, Foutre/Podophilia, and Rétifism: Cinderella

Foutre, or podophilia[448], is a popular American fetish that falls under the category of partialism (an interest in a particular body part). Foot fetishes can mean having a fetish for having the feet massaged or a fetish for high heels. I have both. In order to cum from only the foot being stimulated one must have ticklish feet, lots of concentration, patience, and the ability to stay horny from a long time. I find that it helps to have other sexual images running through my head. It is not impossible to do, but it takes a lot of effort to do it, as it does anytime one wishes to cum without being physically stimulated on the genitalia. Rétifism is using the shoe for masturbation.

I went to a foot party. A man paid me to massage my feet and legs. Some consider that my one and only foray into prostitution.

Amaurophilia

This is a preference for a blind partner. An example of this is in the movie *Black* by Sanjay Bhansali, about a South Asian Indian Helen Keller and her teacher.

Anasteemaphilia: Nanophilia

This is a sexual interest in someone who is taller or shorter. I imagine this is one of those philias that you're born with since if you're on the extreme of the height scale, you wouldn't have much choice anyways. Even though I much prefer to be around men who are taller than me, I prefer women who are shorter than me. Yes, I play into the gender roles. So sue me.

Skeeter Zabuza-Early once posted on his Facebook page about how difficult it was to do online dating when the girls found out his height. What he needed was a female who had nanophilia, an interest in short partners. Someone with the opposite problem would need someone who had macrophilia, an attraction to giants.

1% of the sample size has this fetish, usually due to necessity.

---

[448] Not to be mistaken with "pedophilia."

Andromania, Arrhenothigmophilous, Clitoromania, Coitolimia, and Furor Uterinus, and Satyriasis

> "To Gail, sex was a vehicle for expressing everything—delight,
> anger, hunger, love, frustration, annoyance, even outrage."
> —Peter Benchley, *The Deep*

A hypersexual nymphomaniac has concupiscence, which means excessive sexual desires. Do I strike you as that kind of a person? If this book is any indication I *almost* have pantophilia, arousal from everything. However I have never compulsively cruised for sex partners. If I don't have one, I always have myself.

What sucks about being horny is not being horny; everyone still thinks you are. There's nothing more annoying than sex when you're not in the mood. You know you've had too much sex when the idea of getting excited about sex is akin to getting excited about eating or taking a dump, for sex is a perishable—it can only satisfy for today.

Another thing that's frustrating is being a baby-crazed nympho that never bears children despite all my sexual experience.

Nympholepsy

One time I think I had nympholepsy, sexual frenzy, because I was so turned on that I temporarily lost blood flow in my toes.

Androminetophilia, Autogynephilia, Eonism[449], Transvestic Fetishism, and Transvestophilia

Autogynephilia/transvestophilia, is a type of cross-dressing that includes sexual arousal. Transvestic fetishism is also close (arousal to the touch of female underwear). It's not just an interest in being a transvestite; it is a sexual interest in being a transvestite in the privacy of one's home.

Actually many heterosexual men find this a turn-on. Crossdressing (eonism) is a type of fetish that does not require a partner because the turn-on is the wearing of the clothing. I can relate to this sensation since fashion and appearance are so important to me (as long as it is reasonable).

---

[449] Named after Chevalier D'Eon.

AudAx

Though most people think of men dressing as women, some people have androminetophilia and dig Diane Keaton and Marlene Dietrich, who are famous for dressing as men. See the musical *Victor Victoria* or the movie *Glen or Glenda.*

Pinaforing is a type of forced crossdressing used as punishment against boys where the boys must dress in petticoats as punishment. I believe a prison exists where all the men's underwear is pink. It's the same idea.

4% of the sample size has this fetish. I'm not including Ed Wood, the director famous for making *Plan 9 From Outer Space*; I only include those with whom I have had romantic or sexual relations, plus, in this case, a friend.

Being Agamic[450]: Kita Ripard

I have dated both Jared Self Jr., the horniest guy in the world, AND Matthew Hays, the least horny guy in the world. (Matthew Hays did not like to be touched and thought sex was gross even into his mid-thirties.) I can attest to the fact that not all guys are horny. Same for women. Kita Ripard liked celebrities, but never dated and was not a lesbian, though plenty of bisexuals had crushes on her, me included.

There has been a rise in millenial asexuality, which one can learn about further from the Asexual Visibility Education Network (AVEN). Asexuality means someone who is not attracted to any person, but may still get aroused by things or anything that does not involve attraction to a person.

When I first heard about how common it was for a millenial to be a virgin, I was blown away. I was absolutely shocked. I still don't quite understand it.

Definition of asexuality:

It is possible for asexuals to be isophilic, relating to same gender affection without sex.

Agenobiosis

Agenobiosis is a married couple who consent to live together without sex. So it is possible for an asexual to get married.

---

[450] *See* http://www.asexuality.org.

Autoerotic Asphyxiaphilia and Pnigophilia

In my early days of masturbation I found asphyxiation to heighten the feeling of the orgasm. This can be achieved with scarfing (literally using a scarf to obstruct blood flow). In the same way that asphyxiation involves lack of oxygen, insufflation involves added oxygen. It is the act of blowing air into the vagina, which is dangerous and can lead to a *fatal* air embolism. People who want to choke others for sex might have pnigophilia.

3% of the sample size has this fetish.

Anthropomorphism, Autoplushophilia, Dermaphilia/Doraphilia, Fursuit, Hyphephilia, Plushophilia, Puppy Play, or Yiffy

Furry fetishes are NOT beastiality. Beastiality refers to an actual act of having intercourse with an animal. Furry fetishes only refer to having a fascination with fur on a human being.

Autoplushophilia is similar to being a furry but is more about the desire to be the furry oneself. People who consider themselves to be furries identify themselves with an animal totem or familiar, which may or may not be an animal with fur.

Doraphilia is a love of animal skins. So I guess having sex on a bear skin counts.

I have thick, full pubic hair, and I did not like to shave it and now I give that the reason for not shaving it is, what if I meet someone with a furry fetish? Not every lover likes the same things. There is a fetish out there for everybody. There are so many fetishes for so many different people that it never has to be necessary to conform to any standard of beauty. I was completely satisfied with my body once I had developed the self-esteem.

1% of the sample size has this fetish.

Barosmia, Olfactophilia, Osphresiophilia, and Ozolagnia

These mean arousal from smell. These are some of my favorites. I really love a good smell. That doesn't necessarily have to be from cologne or perfume. A bad body odor turns me off. Strangely enough, I've been told that even my sweat smells good (not just my cum). "Wimmin don't sweat; they perspire," some say. Antholagnia is arousal from smelling flowers.

My ex always loved the smell of cum. I could say that he had bromidrophilia. In a similar vein, osmolagnia is arousal to other body odors, like sweat or menstruation.

2% of the sample size has this fetish.

Belonephilia

Everyone who knew me in college knew that my two favorite topics were sharp objects and sex. I wouldn't go so far as to say violence, just sharp objects. Belonephilia, arousal with sharp objects, is definitely an interest of mine. However, it can be dangerous. I already have somewhat of a history of self-cutting, so this is a fetish I'll have to lay off of for a long while.

1% of the sample size has this fetish.

Clowns[451]

I came close to having sex with a professional clown, but I wanted to have sex with the person, not the clown. He, on the other hand, wanted me to have sex with himself as a clown, and my being turned off by horror clown images turned him off.

1% of the sample size has this fetish.

Draupadi: Bigamy, Hetaerism, Polyandry, Polygyny, and Polysemy

Polygamy is having two or more full-time and/or part-time boyfriends or girlfriends. Monogamy is having a full-course meal. To some, such as for those in prison or military romances, monogamy is having a full-course meal and snacks when you need to stave off the hunger between dinners.

I saw sexual freedom, along the lines of polygamous communes, as the solution to abortion and adoption because it was apparent to me that adoption does not solve abortion but only pushes the problem to the side in order to complicate it later.

I'm a good candidate for a polyandrous marriage. As someone whose main trait is obedience, I have always believed in drawing inside the lines. However, I've also believed that we have the right to choose which page we draw on.

5% of the sample size has this fetish.

---

[451] Older i.P. audAx: I was watching a Funny or Die video called "What Your Political Bubble Looks Like From the Other Side." At the end of the video, both sides of the political spectrum are watching the same porn. The implication here is that it doesn't matter your political leaning; both sides watch porn. Being that I've heard that the funniest humor is based on truth, I would definitely say there is some truth to this implication.

Polysemy

Eris "Odin" Eevlos

This guy was destined to do something large; I just hope that he doesn't get stuck with doing something small due to his becoming a self-hating Jew Internet troll. He was a somewhat famous hacker (though he disliked that name) and invested in gold, thinking that a million dollars was easy to get.

I put him here because he lived with not only his girlfriend, but her boyfriend. Though it was not an easy situation, he tolerated the situation temporarily, and I speculate that he was motivated due to the easier access to drugs. In college everyone knew him as the long-haired short guy who would do any drug imaginable and any drug no one has ever heard of. He finally chose to quit drugs right before he moved to California and swore never to return to Virginia. Quitting drugs, meant quitting everything but weed and LSD, believing that these two gave direct access to God, unlike the other drugs which only gave a glimpse. We talked about robotripping, meaning drinking cough syrup to get high, and he told me to try laughing gas and pure oxygen. He was one of the founders of The First Church of Christ Ruiner.

Bukkake

Bukkake is giving handjobs to one or more people anonymously. There is a wall with a hole for the penis, like a chemise cagoule (a long shirt with a hole for the penis). I went to a bukkake party with a married couple.

3% of the sample size has this fetish.

Capnolagnia, In Defense of

Pot is a healthy alternative to smoking and alcohol. It is medicinal, not poisonous. The only exceptions to this rule is when it is mixed with other products. I could see it being called a gateway drug due to mixtures, but, in reality, prescription drugs are far more of a gateway drug exactly because they're legal.

I have seen cannabis without any desire to use up someone's salary through greed and find that it would be a shame for all that labor to result in jail time. Those who sell earn their money through time spent alone. In California, selling is a fine way of increasing the income and quality of life of someone who never could afford a bachelor's degree, someone who went to a technical school, got an associate's degree, got a GED, or was a high school dropout. However, I would not recommend breaking into the business without a mentor.

AudAx

Pot definitely increases horniness. I'd go so far as to consider it a date rape drug. Cannabis oil is also found to create a mind-blowing sexual stimulant for women. I've heard very good reviews.

My mind on pot: Maybe I'm a god. I mean some religions believe we are God or gods. Maybe I already have created a universe inside my head[452]. Maybe people are worshipping me and praying to me in temples and before they go to bed to have sex.

Carpophilia: Epicureus

Carpophilia is arousal by being fed fruits (think grapes or strawberries). This leads nicely into a conversation about nutrition. I support any fetish that enhances health. I have seen the effects of FDA's America and it's quite a scary sight. Most young people neglect their internal organs because they don't notice anything wrong them, including me. However, when there is something wrong with them, it's too late and you could be dead. I'd rather err on the side of being too healthy than too unhealthy.

Chubby Chasers

The only way for a woman to have clitoral stimulation during intercourse without the aid of hands is through having sex with a large enough man. If both partners are heavyset it helps for the heavier person to be on the bottom.

Claustrophilia

I can understand being aroused from being in a small space; that's practically what it's like having sex in a car.

Amomaxia

This is having sex in a parked car.

Cloridectomy, Colobosis, Ederacinism, Exmuliebrate, and Spadonism

The only person I knew who personally castrated himself was the man behind the Oxford English Dictionary in *The Professor and the Madman: A Tale of Murder, Insanity, and the Making of the Oxford English Dictionary* by Simon Winchester. I honestly don't know much about eunuchs or why

---

[452] That's for another book.

one would want to be (even if someone explains it to me). Too much eviration (emasculation) for me to stomach. Cloridectomy is too much defeminization for me to stomach.

Coitobalnism

I have had sex in both a bathtub and a shower. A bathtub is a little harder (in both senses of the word). I imagine the romantics like this one, as long as they remember to blow out the candles surrounding the tub and use underwater lubrication.

Contortion

I once came across a guy who could drink his own cum. He showed me. I was quite impressed. I would be even more impressed if he could show off autopederasty, the insertion of his penis into his own anus.

1% of the sample size has this fetish.

Coprolalia, Coprophemia, and Lalochezia

Some people get really turned on by being told how "bad" they are. In this sense, the worse you are, the better you are, or at least the more turned on. I would call dirty talk "cuss words," not "expletives." The origin of the word, "expletive" is "explere," which means "to fill up," like filler words. However, in this case it's intentional, not a habit of upbringing, so "cuss words" makes more sense. Fescennine means "vulgar," which also does the trick. A vulgar person would have no problem with calling someone a bastard (nothosonomia). Coprography is like talking dirty, but in written form.

3% of the sample size has this fetish.

James Joyce's Love Letters: Coprophilia and Urolagnia

Talking about shit, Westerners do everything wrong, from breathing to orgasms. We don't even know which flags are for wartime and which ones are not, how to capitalize our country's name, or how to write an address on an envelope correctly. We even poop incorrectly. According to scientists, it's healthier to squat than to sit on a commode.

Who the hell came up with the name scatology? Is that person trying to make fun of Onyx people? Are they trying to call Onyx people shit? Fuck that.

I can see the fascination some may have with scatology (a.k.a. brown showers and defecolagnia)[453] Even though scatology does not turn me on, I see no moral grounds on why this fetish should not be allowed. Anyone with a fascination with grossness, à la Ren and Stimpy, would be fascinated with either.

The appeal in watersports is that it simulates squirting. Any man who wishes to be cummed on may find watersports fun because most wimmin cannot, or do not, squirt cum. Though not a golden shower per se, I had an ex who was proud of the fact that he could sit while urinating, so sometimes we would share a toilet seat together when we timed it so we both needed to do #1 at the same time.

I believe it is necessary at times to invest time studying the most "vile and repulsive" in order to better understand the human mind and body. If one were to create a completely realistic human body and mind with his own hands (what technology seems to aspire to according to movies), then it is completely necessary to understand the "vile and repulsive" entirely. There is nothing bad with being interested in "gross" things (just take a look at several guys) because it is our body and it should be natural to be interested in your own body. Hey, when before you are a baby you have not been in a body before, so it is pretty fascinating to know what it can do.

Something I find to be right up there with scat is the arousal from vomit (emetophilia), flatulence (eproctophilia or flatuphilia), or enemas (klismaphilia). A close second is automysophilia, molysmophilia, mysophilia, or salirophilia. This takes "dirty sex" to a whole new level.

4% of the sample size has a fetish with this, not including an ex's ex-wife, but mostly with watersports.

Bundling and Spooning

Bundling is sleeping together clothed without sex and spooning is sleeping with one partner's back facing the other partner's front.

---

[453] ...as well as the following:

- coprophagy (consumption of feces),
- coproscopism (watching someone defecate),
- defecolagnia (arousal from defecation),
- mysophilia (gratification by filth),
- osphresiolagnia (arousal from bad odors),
- renifleur (arousal from the smell of urine or used underwear), or
- watersports (a.k.a. urophilia or urolagnia).

Cuddling is a field dominated by feminine (not necessarily effeminate) men and women. Men who relate more to the gender of wimmin tend toward a cuddling preference, as opposed to other forms of sex.

3% of the sample size has this fetish.

Chanukah, Elohim, and Shiva: Sexual Illuminism, Urban Tantra Buddhism, or Quadoshka[454]

When two people make love, there is a transfer of sexual energy and a mastermind is created. A team is only as good as its weakest link, and so it is with sexual energy. Only the common denominator is transferred (from my understanding), meaning the person with the higher vibration (the more positive and happy person) will receive the lower vibration (from the person who is less positive and happy) and that lower vibration will remain in that person's body until it is cleared. This sexual energy can be transformed into *chi* (or *qi*) energy. This has been studied at length in Tantric Buddhism and explained in *Ra: The Book of One*.

Kundalini is similar to Azoth in alchemy. Tantra Buddhism is associated with kundalini yoga, which is associated with Carl Jung (or vice versa), whose works were the basis of the Myers-Briggs Type Indicator (MBTI).

One time I was able to literally feel my chakras being aligned from an orgasm. That was one of my most amazing sexual experiences. The crazy thing about it was that I didn't even stimulate myself with anything, just the intense thought of orgasm (psycholagny) was enough to have it.

Cyber Sex

Cybering is a very godinterm[455] way to start before having actual sex; it is like the gateway drug marijuana (which I actually think is more like a date rape drug, for myself). It is the ultimate anonymous safe sex. It is also the least serious of all types of sex, but you must have an imagination; it is as make-believe as a role-playing game. It is mostly made for the imaginative and the ones for whom sex is still beyond amazing. It is also godinterm for those who get bored and have nothing else to do but be horny. Cyber sex is the easiest way for a woman to fake orgasm. For other people, cyber sex does nothing.

In the beginning, cyber sex was very wonderful to me. After a while though, it was fun (because anything sexual is fun to me), but I was not all that into it. Cyber sex is one of those things where

---

[454] American Indian tantric sex

[455] *See* New Terms.

a man can get very horny if they think that you are doing what they tell you to do or what you tell them that you are doing. I just let the man on the other end believe that I am doing whatever I say that I am, while I type up essays and do my homework. It's kind of the ADD/ADHD way. The easiest trick to get someone to think that you are interested is to hold down the "O" key.

2% of the sample size has this fetish.

Demisexuality, Epistemophilia, Phronemophilia, Sapiosexuality, and Sophophilia

"It is that which one takes for granted that has the most value. This is how the powerful hide their secrets." –Me

Sapiosexuality means being turned on by intellect alone (the opposite is savantophilia, which is being turned on by people with mental disabilities). Of necessity, this requires conversation, either verbal or written. Sometimes it is heightened by a little banter, whether intellectual play with words and references or slightly facetious wit. In order to be involved with sapiosexuality, it is necessary to be into epistemophilia, phronemophilia, or sophophilia—attend a school of higher learning and read/think A LOT.

2% of the sample size has this.

Dave Gomez

Respect for someone's intellect does not always have to be a requirement for a happy life together. Jesus has never been in awe of someone's intellect. Most of the time his comments can be misconstrued as condescending or, more likely, instructive in a fatherly way. He sees us as naive, foolish, or forgetful (the way we would see a relative with Alzheimer's).

Dermaphilia

This is arousal to skin color, texture, scent, or appearance. I have already established that I am turned on by a good smell and have dated black men in the past. I have also dated two people who had eczema. Because of this I have actually gotten used to people with rougher skin, so that when I would touch normal (especially female) skin, it felt like silk.

Domination/Submission

A Dom is someone who is bossy and enjoys giving commands. E knows what e wants. Sometimes there is a fine line between Dom/sub. I have known Doms who ask permission, and I have known demanding subs.

2% of the sample size has a fetish for domination.

Learning How to Love Depressing Movies and Music: Subs Gary Staton and Kim Yoo

A sub is someone who is obedient and enjoys being obedient. Though usually a sub (because being a Dom makes me laugh), I can be a tad pushy myself. It is a misconception that only the Dom has control. It is completely possible to be a liberated sub female with 100% control.

5% of the sample size has a fetish for submission.

Edging

Edging was introduced in *Orange is the New Black* (which doesn't even use orange jumpsuits by the way). Edging is like watching 10 years of TV episodes that end with "to be continued" and still wanting more. Edging is getting to the point of orgasm without actually doing it. Stripping is a bit like edging. Stripping without extras, with a boundary, is like making the fantasy as real as possible without actually manifesting it in the real world. It may even be more satisfying than edging. Who knows?

Edging is also the best technique for those who have the issue of premature ejaculation.

1% of the sample size does this.

Ergophilia, Kopophilia, and Ponophilia

Ergophilia is the love of work, ponophilia is attraction to overwork (workaholics), and kopophilia is arousal from exhaustion. I would categorize kinesophilia, arousal from exercise, under this title.

Since I have considered myself a workaholic, that would mean that 100% of people from my sample have this, but I do not think that is true, so I will not estimate what percentage of the sample size has this.

AudAx

Erotomania and Stalking

"Stalked in the forest too close to hide
[…]
High blood Drumming on your skin it's so tight
You feel my heart I'm just a moment behind
[…]
In touch with the ground
I'm on the hunt I'm after you
[…]
I howl and I whine I'm after you
Mouth is alive all running inside
And I'm hungry like the wolf."
—Duran Duran, "Hungry Like the Wolf"

"My fantasy has turned to madness
And all my goodness
Has turned to badness
My need to possess you
Has consumed my soul
My life is trembling
I have no control
[…]
I will collect you and capture you"
—Holly Knight and Michael Des Barres, "Obsession" as performed by Animotion

De Clerambault's syndrome, or erotomania, is developing an unreasonable love for someone not interested in them. In other words, it's unrequited love.

I love ice cream. Ice cream doesn't love most people back. I love Denver. It doesn't always love me back. I love Goths; they don't always love me back. I love men; men sometimes have a hard time expressing that they are able to love me back. There's something to be said about unrequited love.

Daniel Lincoln's stalking behaviors came from social ineptness misconstrued as stalking behaviors.

Tom Hellen's stalking behaviors came from his love addiction.

Jake Clusspud's stalking behaviors came from an attraction to the idea of taking care of someone else.

Stalking behaviors are typically more acceptable to people who grew up in boundaryless families, which I knew was at least true for one of the above three.

4% of the sample size has this.

Korean Adoption: Bong-Ki Eun

Among those who had unrequited love toward me, Bong-Ki Eun, a Hawaiian I met at a Korean adoptee event, sent me a birthday gift AND a Christmas gift over a year after he first met me, even though I do not recall giving him my address. He was not the first Korean adoptee to assume I liked him more than I did. Some people who think they are "different" do not seek others who are different in the same way, though some do. For example, I never sought to date other Korean adoptees even though I sought to date other Goths. In the former case, I (and people who don't seek out people with similar differences) never considered the possibility that I'm really that different or prefer to think of myself as relatively "normal."

Ecdemolagnia and Hodophilia

These two words are about sexual arousal when away from home. I've heard, from Dallas Clayton's paraphrase quote, that you have to "get out your house to get out of your head." I try to travel when I can, but can't say I get aroused by it.

Agoraphilia: Bushie Mall

This is having sex in an open or public place.

2% of the sample size is into this fetish, according to my statistics.

Vardhamana: Gymnophilia and Omolagnia

The best way to instill body self-confidence is to be a role model and show comfort with nudity either by walking around naked, being a nudist, or doing nude modeling for art or photography. I've found that the person I knew who was a nudist had a perpetual inner boy. Boys love to be nude, I've heard. However, it's usually men that are more afraid of undressing in front of people (misapodysis).

Some people think that if I love sex I must love being nude. No, I just find that it requires less supplies, and I don't like hassle. I prefer fashion if it makes a bold statement. No, I love fashion.

AudAx

2% of the sample size is into this fetish, according to my statistics.

Sky Clad Mahavira: Adamitism

Adamitism is going naked for God. See *How An Appropriate Use of Nakedness Can Promote the Goals of Religion, Spirituality, and Personal Development* (Miller, 2014).

Alloerasty and Peodeiktophilia

Alloerasty is using someone else's nudity to arouse someone, but peodeiktophilia is general sexual arousal from exhibitionism.

Apodysophilia

This is a feverish desire to undress. I only had this when I was at a college party. (Gynonudomania is a feverish desire to rip off a woman's clothes.)

Atronudia

This is arousal by exposing themselves to a doctor. I get this. I do get turned on when I go see the gynecologist.

Autagonistophilia

This is arousal from exposing one's naked body on stage or while being photographed. As a nude model, I would say that I fit that category to a tee.

Pope John XII: Exophilia and Neophilia

I would hope that everyone who is married has a bit of neophilia, an interest in new things because it's good to keep things interesting. However some people, exophilists, are more willing to try new things than others, and that can get them in trouble if one of those new things is new people or something very unusual or bizarre. I think the enthusiastic Enneagram 7 type is more likely to have neophilia than others.

1% of the sample size has this, according to my statistics.

Nomavalent

I imagine that those who are big on experiences, ambiance, traveling off the beaten path, or urban exploration would have arousal from doing it in strange places. Claustrophilia is the love of small spaces. It would be the opposite of claustrophobia. Chasmophilia is more specifically an attraction to nooks, crannies, crevices, and chasms.

2% of the sample size has this, according to my statistics.

Fabric Play

I do not know if there is a name for it so I will call it fabric play. Though not as popularized, it is especially a godinterm way for the sensuous to reinvigorate their thankfulness for the sense of touch. Sometimes people like to have sex with circles (See New Terms) in order to get that sensation of extra skin around the genitals.

2% of the sample size has this, according to my statistics.

Amychesis and Dermagraphism

I think that the sensation of being scratched is similar to fabric play in that the focal point is on the epidermis. Hlipsosis, arousal by pinching, is similar.

Another sensation, which has no clinical name, is rubbing vaseline on the body. This was explored in the movie, *Striptease*, starring Demi Moore.

Fetishturgy

Fetishturgy is fetish as logic. Is that what this book is?

Formicophilia, Arachnophilia, Entomophilia, Melissaphilia, and Phthiriophilia

Formicophilia is a sexual interest in having ants crawl over you and entomophilia is a sexual interest in using insects for sexual play. Ew! I definitely don't have that. Arachnophilia is a sexual interest in spiders and scorpions. I hate spiders. Then there's phthiriophilia, an attraction to lice. This is also related to melissaphilia, which is an interest in bees. (Some people use bees to sting genitals.) I feel sorry for anyone whose name is Melissa right now since not all Melissas will like bees (even if the word can mean multiple things). Who comes up with these names?

Frotteurism and Gregomulcia

The word "frotteur" used to refer to a person whose job was to clean floors by spinning around with brushes strapped to his feet. How it became what it is today is anyone's guess.

Frotteurism is an interest in rubbing against an unsuspecting person for sexual pleasure. Gregomulcia is the opposite, the desire to be fondled (or fammed) in crowded areas. They go really well together. They also go well with ochlophilia, which is arousal from being in crowds. The problem is when a frotteurist meets a non-gregomulcia person. Then you've got some trouble because then it's not consensual.

I remember being on my high school bus and sitting next to a quiet Asian teenage boy. We were sitting close enough that it was easy to think about the fact that we were touching, but, of course, no one said a word. The only way you know if someone likes it is if they don't move away (considering they have plenty of space and opportunity to do so).

Gender Reversal

Why do I love control? I have learned control from my controlling parents (who willingly admit they like control). I love role reversal a lot in sex because I wish to turn the tables over and be the one controlling the controllers, and see how they like it!

Harmatophilia

This is arousal from others' clumsiness. It makes me think of the movies *Good Luck Chuck*, *Hitch*, or *Hello Again*.

Hentai/Yaoi

Hentai is to animé as a square is to a rectangle. It is a type of animé, but animé is not a type of hentai. They are nowhere near synonymous terms. *Bible Black* (blasphemous title, I know) would never be found in the children's section. I find it interesting that older people still associate animation with children since that is so not the case. I'm sure a lot of people are into this, since I have spent so much time at animé conventions, but I have not put a number to it.

Ishtar: Hierophilia and Staurophilia

Hierophilia is arousal from sacred objects. Staurophilia is a form of hierophilia, arousal from the cross or crucifix. A few people I've dated wouldn't know a [marriage] sacrament if it bit them on the leg.

Hoarding

Lithophilia

This is the love of stones. Does rock collecting count? I used to be a major rock collector. I also collected nail polish even though I bit my nails and couldn't (or didn't) even use them. Perhaps that would also fall under the category of hoarding.

Thesauromania

This is arousal by collecting women's clothing. This would also fall under transvestitism.

Homilophilia, Teleophilia, and Uranophilia

Teleophilia is an affinity for religious ceremonies and homilophilia is an arousal to sermons, and those have to be played very carefully since it's more public. Uranophilia is arousal by heavenly thoughts. Hey, Jesus is husband to the church, they say. So if you're going to be a monk or nun you better have uranophilia or else life's not gonna be too pretty.

Hygrophilia

Hygrophilia is arousal from bodily fluids and secretions. I've always been curious about drinking a cocktail, or cum from a glass. I think it would be easier with a group of men, but those days are over for me. (However, the idea of an enema cocktail turns my stomach.)

Kabazzah

This is a technique I can do. It involves contracting the vagina to "milk" the penis during intercourse. I love it. It really helps to do Kegel exercises prior.

Kainotophilia

Getting pleasure from change is something that we should all have in an optimal universe, at least according to the Kabbalists. However, an addiction to change makes things we don't want in our life to persist, according to The Landmark Forum.

Katoptronophilia and Spectrophilia

These are both an interest in having sex in front of mirrors. I actually think this is so common that people don't even think of it as a fetish. It just goes to show that even if people don't think they have any fetishes, they probably do.

2% of the sample size has this fetish, according to my statistics.

Kleptolagnia

A good example of a klepto fetish would be the scene from *Breakfast at Tiffany's* where Audrey Hepburn's character steals items with her lover.

Kokigami

Kokigami is origami for the penis. It's definitely one way of making a man feel special.

Lactaphilia and Maeieusiophilia

Both of these relate to pregnancy. If you know what lactation means, you can probably guess what's what. In my opinion, I would hope that every woman's spouse has these fetishes, or at least the latter. No woman wants to feel unattractive when they have hormones coursing through their body. Some say, "If mama ain't happy, ain't nobody happy," from Tracy Byrd's song, "When Mama Ain't Happy."

Laliophilia

I love speaking in public and have various trophies from various speech contests and various advanced designations, but I would never say that it turns me on. I don't even imagine people naked. I guess if you imagined people naked, then it could turn you on perhaps.

Lovertine: The Casanova and The Minx

"You expect me to just let you hit it
But will you still respect me if you get it."
—Nellie Furtado, "Promiscuous"

Boys just come and go like seasons
[...]
And I know I'm coming off just a little bit conceited
And I keep on repeating
How the boys wanna *eat* it."
—Fergie Duhamel, "Fergalicious"

"Daddy Issues"

Parents make a difference in sex. "Daddy issues" precede promiscuity. I can assure you that people who have daddy issues will have challenges with those whose parents are divorced since those might result in conflicting self-told stories. Studies have shown that girls with daddy issues begin menstruation earlier to prepare for the search for another male figure. I believe this is why sexuality is so prevalent on MTV and the like, especially for the Onyx culture because that is where children are more statistically raised by single mothers.

Wimmin with daddy issues live ironic lives. They have sex to feel loved, but they're hard to love because they love to have sex to feel loved. More and more people come from broken homes than before (about half of the population is divorced) and for others, abuse doesn't disappear overnight. There *will* be more people like me. There *will* be people who cannot handle the innate contradictions inherent in existing as they are. There *will* be suicides. But I hope that with my words there will be *fewer* suicides and more of an understanding that everything happens for a reason, and all of this emotional chaos is actually holy and sacred.

Menophilist

Even for someone as nympho as I am, I still become a bit more shy during my time of month (even if I am hornier). However, despite that fact, it has never deterred anyone from having sex with me. Not that I can recall at any rate. This goes against the practice of niddah, the prohibition against sex during menstruation. It literally means "one who is excluded."

More than 2% of the sample size has this, according to my statistics.

Metrophilia

This is getting turned on by presbytorean[456], an erotic poem. Heck, if you like the poetry in this book, you should totally check out *The Meaning of a Metaphorical Life*. See ya there.

Narcissism

A narcissist, in the terms of Narcissus, not Narcissistic Personality Disorder,

Narratophilia

Narratophilia is having an erotic conversation. I guess that could also fall under phone sex. Reading erotica and romance novels would fall under this category. My granny was a big fan of middlebrow romance novels. At the age of 21 she began a five-year marriage. During that time she had three children (two that are still living) and a divorce. She told me how she would pray that she would never even be interested in going on a date ever again. She died at the age of 91. She had at least 80 years of life that were without intercourse, maybe more.

1% of the sample size has this, according to my statistics.

Nasolingus

You know cunnilingus, right? Please say yes. I would hope that you know. Anyways, this is nasolingus, which is sucking on a nose. I don't think of this as anything weird. I think of it as something one just does when they're trying to touch every part of you.

Nemophilia, Potamophilia, Pteriodomania, Thalassophilia, and Ylophilia

Nemophilia and Ylophilia is a love of forests, thalassophilia is a love of the sea, and potamophilia is a love of streams/rivers. Then there's pteridomania, which is an intense desire for ferns. I imagine that anyone who has a 7 Life Path in numerology is more inclined toward this, as well as any environmentalist. I've had sex in a forest. Well, it was more like a park.

---

[456] God, I just love these names. I wonder how a Presbyterian would feel about it.

Nosophilia[457]

I believe that *The Road to Wellville* by T. Coraghessan Boyle and a Christopher Pike book dealt with a romance between those who were in a hospice or were terminally ill.

Objectophilia

This is falling in love with things. I think it's a step beyond beastiality but could be similar to agalmatophilia, interest in a statue, doll, or mannequin. According to an ex who became a sex counselor, a person is not a sex addict if they do not have objectophilia. When he said that, I felt better, but nowadays I would beg to differ.

Oculolictus

I love the name of this one because it's pretty obvious what it is, licking eyes. I admit that I did enjoy licking my ex's eyelids. It would only make sense for this to be coupled with oculophilia, which is arousal by eyes. I've been told that my eyes are my best feature.

2% of the sample size has this, according to my statistics.

One-Night Stands

One thing I've learned about myself is that I'm capable of having sex when I don't feel turned on at all and even then can still turn on the other person. I think this goes back to people not being able to tell what emotion I'm feeling, which relates to the days when I had smiling depression in high school.

Ophidiophilia

This is an arousal from snakes. I can honestly say I've never met someone like that. My mother is afraid of snakes (but she is willing to watch parts of *Indiana Jones*). I have know four people who owned snakes, someone in elementary school; Wolf Baile, a model from my high school class; my ex, Ed Steffens; and a coworker. When I think of getting turned on by snakes I think of the movie *Striptease* where getting the wrong snake can go very badly.

---

[457] Not to be confused with nasolingus.

Particular People: Rapunzel

Sometimes a man's fetishes are actually a type of person, like a hermaphrodite (Hermes+Aphrodite), transsexual, midget, handicapped man, pregnant woman (cysolagnia or tocophilia), someone with a particular body type (like "fatties"[458] or circles[459]), or someone with a particular hair colour[460] or length. People who are the subject of the fetish sometimes know all too well and attempt to use this knowledge to their advantage. (I was once told of a transsexual who refused to talk to females because e35 was only interested in males.) Other people find it annoying. It is always very dangerous to have a fetish for a particular man. I myself have a fetish for hermaphrodites, but probably resulting from dreams in which they signified something else.

Partialism

Crurofact and crurophilia is sexual arousal from legs. Such a person would be interested in penis-between-legs (coitus intrafemoris) or penis-to-thigh sex (femoral coitus). There is also coitus a mammilla, penis-between-breasts. I think I should find someone who has alvinolagnia, a fetish for stomachs and match e with someone who has body issues. Axillism is the use of the armpit for sex. It would probably pair nicely with hirsutophilia, arousal by armpit hair.

I knew a guy who got turned on if I just licked his ears. It was nice to know that at least one guy had an "on" switch, but it's easy to take advantage of. Gynotikolobomassophilia, is sexual pleasure by nibbling on a woman's earlobe. Try to say that ten times fast.

2% of the sample size has this, according to my statistics.

Starfish: Anisonogamist, Anocratism, Anomeatia, Arsometry, Buggery, or Sotadism

> "active, eager, receptive to phallus
> coke bottle, candle, carrot
> banana & fingers—
> Now AIDS makes it shy, but still
> eager to serve—
> [...]
> still rubbery muscular,
> unashamed wide open for joy"
> —Allen Ginsberg, "Sphincter"

---

[458] The heavier person has to be on the bottom.

[459] See New Terms.

[460] My personal preference in spelling

232

"Abracadabra: The anus.

[…]

Use your fingertips, mirrors. See what you're hiding

from yourself. Use spoons to reflect:

[…]

Embrace your exits, where bloom

virginities of every orifice. Where bloom oracles: We are all full of shit.

We could choose to make this space in us so small no digit, no wind, no

x could ever pass through. Or we could open a world any finder or tongue

(yours?) could enter into and speak."

--Jessamyn Birrer, "A Scatalogy" from *Ninth Letter (Alexie, 2015)*

"The poor anus was the last part of our bodies to ever get any love and attention. Too many people ended up going through life without discovering this exquisite erogenous zone."[461]

Prior to performing anal, consider anal hygiene. Rinse the anus and butt crack after every bowel movement. Consider using an enema. Anal is the only way to cum inside a womyn (or man) without fear of pregnancy. It is also a powerful, though initially painful, feeling. If you let your partner cum inside your anus, then the cum will break up whatever you have left inside the anus. It is an interesting feeling. Don't be alarmed if the anus hurts afterwards. It can take up to nine days to heal. I think there's even a colloquial expression about it.

Analinctus, Anilingus, or Anophilemia

This is a pleasurable alternative for homosexual men, or anyone. If rimming goes to far for you, you can always start with anophilemia, kissing the anus.

Retrocopulation (Androsodomy, Anomeatia and Coitus Analis)

This is doggy style. Androsodomy is man on man. Anomeatia is man or woman on woman. Knissophilia is the specific sexual pleasure from enemas.

5% of the sample size has this, according to my statistics.

---

[461] *Ibid.* 82.

Pygophilia: Anaconda, Jack and the Beanstalk, and Little Red Riding Hood[462]

"I like big butts and I cannot lie."
—Anthony Ray, "Baby Got Back" as performed by Sir Mix A Lot

Pygophilia, or an interest in large butts, is the opposite of mammagymnophilia or mazophilia, which is…you guessed it…an interest in large breasts (related to macromastic). Someone with a big butt is a callipygian. For the other sex/gender, this would be the equivalent to phallophilia, an interest in large dicks. A mentulate would probably possess a lobcock, which is a large, relaxed dick.

America especially wants everything to be bigger. Most anyone is familiar with this because men are constantly complaining about their dick size and some wimmin feel so inadequate in breast size that they get their breasts enlarged. It makes sense for a stripper or someone in the sex industry, not so much for someone who works in a white collar job.

Parthenolatry and Pucelage

Parthenolatry is virgin worship. Ed Steffens loved virgins (maybe he had anophelorastia, arousal from defiling someone), but he was not a stupprator (man only aroused by virgins, which I imagine applies to some Arabs). One time someone called him the devil for devirginizing young wimmin.

Virgins do not miss anything because they do not know what they are missing. They understand sexual jokes and can look at naked people. They may or may not be jealous, become easily annoyed by cutesy couples, and they are confused about why some people act so differently in relationships. They find anyone who speaks about sex freely as a pervert in a negative sense and are uncomfortable with and unused to the change of mood and tone to that of a sexual mood and tone. They find sex unimportant to marriage.

2% of the sample size has an interest in deflowering virgins, according to my statistics.

Depuscelating Daniel Lincoln

"It ain't nothing like the first time
I'm tryna tell you I can blow your mind
Baby if I touch you here and kiss you there
Gonna fall in love shorty, best beware

---

[462] Older i.P. audAx: Pun not intended.

234

[…]
Wont [sic] you let me introduce ya to thug karmasutra
This aint [sic] no lovey dovey (nah) but watch how I seduce ya
[...]
Once you climax, you feel the aftershock
(i know I got you hooked on this lovin [...])"
—Robinson, Jasiel/Thorton, and Carlos/Benny Tillman,
"1st Time" as performed by Yung Joc[463]

Daniel Lincoln was Napoleon Dynamite crossed with Harry Osborne. He hates artists and philosophers. His favorite heroes are all practically almost invulnerable: Superman, Wolverine, and Achilles. He has somewhat of a split personality: one personality feels everything passionately while another is more composed. In his life he has never had a serious injury or illness. His belief is that everyone wants to survive. His motivation is loneliness. His goal is to settle down in a house with a wife and kids. A major factor too is that he constantly moves. He will do things if asked, but not commanded, unless by a higher-up. He holds to the belief that "no one understands me." He compares himself to Napoleon or Caesar. He is a moderate Republican (my dad says because there is too much stigma attached to being a conservative Republican like himself). His only other friend, a Republican named Valerie, was attracted to him and talked about me a lot, making him surmise that she was bisexual, but he was not attracted to her despite the size of her breasts. He is often quiet because he is often deep in thought (he was nicknamed "Danny Darko" in college but he hated the name). Despite his quietness, he finds my silence disquieting, which I find amusing.

When he became a second lieutenant and came to visit while he was on leave, I became hit with the horn-dog bug. I gave him his first kiss and a few more, with even a few horny moans thrown in. It's nice to be the first.

Before I had all this stuff in my head about what to say: "Theoretically, would you rather kiss someone who you could never have and to whom you must vow secrecy even if it's not under optimal conditions?" If he said yes I would then say, "It is my belief that I make major decisions based on more than one factor. Promise me that you won't think about what I do until the next day. Please forgive me." If he said no I would then say, "I ask because I want to kiss you. I can think of several reasons why you wouldn't want to, but I can also think of several reasons why you would. First, I can give you a lesson in how to kiss a girl. Secondly, life is too short. Third, it's better now before I get married or you get killed, in a worst case scenario. Fourth, if a guy can bite me when I'm sitting on Chocolate Candy's lap then a little kiss won't bother him, as long as

---

[463] These lyrics were found on http://www.completealbumlyrics.com.

there's no touching below the belt[464]. Fifth, I'd rather you talk about me than a girl who wasn't worth your time." Then afterwards I would say, "Did I ever tell you I was young and selfish? Please don't let this get in the way of our friendship[465]. It is best to stay friends because I have already made up my mind about who to be with, but friendship with a little sexual tension is fun. Maybe I could be inspiration for your creative works or help you feel more comfortable kissing women." I eventually just asked, "Would you kiss someone you could never have?"

He told me that he expected it, and he was surprised that I didn't do it sooner. He said that he knew what was going on the moment, a year ago, that I asked him on a date (that was when I was non-monogamous, and he turned me down for that reason). He could also tell when I asked him once if he wanted to watch porn; he knew what was going on but feigned awkwardness.

The last day I saw him after he was on leave, once he became a second lieutenant, I put together wine, cheese, and Oreos for us to eat, but never brought it. I reserved a hotel room but never went. I knew what I wanted to say: "I know why you cannot get a girl. I think the saying is that the rich get richer and the poor get poorer. Girls like guys with experience. What I like about you is that you are pure. Beyond the obvious meaning, I also mean that you are pure of heart. More than anyone else, I know your greatest desire is to be loved."

But I never said it. Maybe in another life. He told me that he felt uncomfortable with what I had done. We then moved onto the discussion of the Israel conflict, but he would not admit to being scared, nervous, or worried. There was no more touching that day until the very last moment. He surprised me with a goodbye kiss before he returned to Fort Banging for leadership training.

Next time he returned from Fort Cocks[466]. I tried to hang out with him with other people so we wouldn't be alone. But alas, we were alone anyways. We walked around my neighborhood in the dark and cold. When we got to the local pool he told me that he thought a lot about me. We started kissing and touching (but not on any private parts). This time there was no Frenching. He talked a lot about getting a room. I was partially surprised and partially not surprised.

It only took me a night of thinking to realize that I had to say "No." When I realized it, I text messaged Jared, and also Jake. After the failed threesome with Marcia and Chocolate Candy, I realized that a woman could say "No" to a man and still be in a threesome with him as long as

---

[464] Older i.P. audAx: That was a lie; it bothered him greatly, and he told me I couldn't have any male friends. Even though I willingly chose not to have male friends in 2017, I was not ready for it ten years prior.

[465] Older i.P. audAx: He did anyways. He broke off our friendship because he thought my coming on to him made me sound like I was drunk, though I doubt I was at the time. Ironically, he put me down as a long-time friend on his security clearance application, so I had to pretend I was his friend for the sake of the security investigation, though that in itself was still a lie.

[466] Older i.P. audAx: Yes, those are obviously made up names to conceal original names.

all it involved was kissing and nudity. So I gave Jake the offer, but realized after my encounter with Daniel that it wouldn't be so easy and that the regret was not worth it.

The regret would be lifelong because I knew that in my heart of hearts that if I did not have Chocolate Candy, I would sterilize myself and go into the sex industry. I was not ready to be that lonely. And I would not be able to give Daniel what he wanted, which was marriage and a family because I loved him but not in that way. After I said "No" to two offers, I called up my boyfriend and told him in the least embarrassing terms what had happened with Daniel. I had finally got Daniel where I wanted him, where any sex lover would have wanted him, I had finally got him to the point where he wanted me to devirginize him, but I could not act on it. I had to end the friendship with Daniel and with Ed, from whom I had raised on a pedestal for his ability to devirginize wimmin, and with anyone else who knew me in the past and could see me only as someone for whom nonmonogamy was a religious belief. And I used to think it was a religious belief so I guess you can say that this was the time of my conversion—the last day of 2006[467].

> "After just three days (just three days)
> One great kiss (One great kiss)
> It's way too soon
> To be obsessin' like this
>
> I should be sleeping, 'stead of keeping
> These late hours I've been keeping
> I've been pacing and retracing
> Every step of every move"
> —Shaye Smith and Lisa Drew, "I Should Be Sleeping" as performed by Emerson Drive

But the story doesn't end there. It's not like I dreamt about him, unless you could call daydreaming dreaming. I daydreamt that he would marry a Korean, like me. I told another male friend of mine, and he concluded that I still wanted him to want me, but that was not all of the story. Daniel touched me in a way I never knew I would be touched, not physically, but spiritually. He connected me to my past. He physically reminded me of Scotty Ledger and Scotty's black curly hair. I was only really friends with Scotty in elementary school, but it bothered me that we never remained friends, even until now. And he connected me to a deeper past that I would not have thought about a few years ago. He connected me to my Korean past. I believe he was sent to me so that I would understand the relationship my birthmother and birthfather had with each other. I am not really at peace with that past, and I do not know if I will be until I meet at least one of them, but understanding is a step toward peace.

---

[467] Older i.P. audAx: I had many more "conversions" per se, before I was clean.

Matthew Hays[468]

My friend Matthew can get depressed by movies like *Clerks II* or *The 40-Year-Old Virgin* because it makes him feel that he has wasted the majority of his life.

Daniel (DL)	Both	Matthew (MH)
Almost 25	Knew for 3 years by 2006	Almost 23
Never kissed before age 24	Virgin	1 short-lived girlfriend (if that)
Deals with loneliness by surviving	Lonely and wants a wife/kids more than anything	Deals with loneliness by animal companionship
Top physical condition	Body tends toward skinniness	Collapsed lung prevents much aerobic activity
Enjoys *Utena*	Enjoys animé	Enjoys anime conventions
Told me "no" when I asked if he wanted to watch porn	Has experienced my kisses and sexual advances	Actually thought we were dating when we weren't. If we did someone should have told me.
Had his first wine at age 24; fears his family's alcoholism	Afraid of alcohol	Beer makes him sober because he fears its effects

---

[468] Older i.P. audAx: When I wrote this, he was 23, but now he is 34. He has, in a sense, wasted his life of his own volition, and it makes other people not want to be around him because he hasn't grown up (he still lives with his dad) and is a bit of a bore, but at least that's good for finances. He's worse at making friends and keeping them than even I am post-recovery, since I no longer make friends through sex. He thinks that a hair transplant would help, but he's still the same person even with more hair.

Some think he is autistic, but, if he is, he's in denial. Autism would not be what keeps him a virgin. Daniel had autism, and he's no longer a virgin from what I've heard, quite the opposite. My boyfriend's younger brother is autistic and dates plenty.

It's not like I never came onto him or tried to touch his cock, come on, but when I did, he actually forgot about it! This was because of cognitive dissonance; it didn't fit his story of life. Despite what I had done, he was the only male friend I did not purge from my life in 2017. I really appreciated having a male friend for whom the idea of having sex with me would never even cross his mind, nor would the idea that I had already attempted to have sex with him once.

Deflected my sexual advances and desires a wife who is pure	Has a halo	Thought *Pirates of the Caribbean* promoted bad moral values
Wore a trenchcoat often before entering the army	Slightly goth-like	Got totally gothed with the makeup and clothes but quit because black is hot in the summer
	Often wears shorts and sandals	Wears sandals even in the snow
Can say "I really enjoyed it" in a monotone voice	Distinct voice	Often cracks jokes
Admires invulnerability	A favorite hero is Superman	Enjoys comic books and wore a Spiderman mask to *Spiderman 3*
Deals with depression by being angry at others	I have seen gone through his most depressing time	Deals with depression by feeling bad for himself
*Sometimes I feel that my love for both of them is love for one person who was put on different roads.		

Telegony

Though often discounted in the scientific world, the idea of telegony has made a recent comeback in October 2014. Telegony is the theory that a woman's child will be influenced by the mother's first sexual partner, has some basis in reality, and may be used as an argument for staying sexually pure. The idea dated back to historical Greek times. When studying fruit flies, scientists at UNSW Sydney found that the size of the female's child was determined by her first sexual partner and not the one that inseminated her.

Penis Play

Certainly there's a word for using the penis without insertion. And, I found it: genuphallation, insertion of the penis between the knees of a partner.

Phone Sex

4% of the sample size enjoys this immensely, according to my statistics.

Pity

Homelessness: Larry and Tim Lassly

I gave Larry about $20 every day because he staked out a place between where I worked and where my client worked. Larry would come onto me occasionally. I stopped giving him money after another homeless person told me that he wasn't homeless. I totally believe that because he would claim that he couldn't eat fried foods because he had had double or triple bypass surgery. I have no idea how he'd be able to afford that.

Tim Lassly ran away from home when he was a teenager, maybe 15? When I met him, he had just returned to his father's house. The only music he liked was heavy metal and thought that everything else sounded "gay". Tim came the second his penis touched my vagina (when we were in his father's house).

I've known other homeless people personally by name, but these were the only two who showed sexual interest in me, and I'm keeping to the theme of this book.

Polyiterophilia

This is repetition of the same act with different partners. Conventions are a great way to find a large resource and selection of sex partners. I can easily have two one-night stands during a weekend convention and no one's the wiser. That's called polyiterophilia, getting off on having sex with a series of partners. It is not unusual for both to sit down together with me without any knowledge of this fact.

I would say that I'm the only person I've met who has been an actual "con slut," so I'll chalk this up to 1% of the sample size.

"The Bind That Ties"

Being a slut
is a prize,
a talent, and a source of pride.
Don't let anyone tell you otherwise.
God's hatred
is a pack of lies
that I despise.
This is something you'll realize
when you can see you with the vision of God's eyes.
Do not listen to those that minimize.

You were born alive,
but seek everyday
for transformation and demise.
The Law of Attraction always applies.
If something makes you happy then time flies.
Whatever is you, under everything underlies.
You may wonder why,
but don't be shy.
This is you, surprise!
Your friends and family will deny, chastise, generalize, surmise, and imply.
Do not listen to what they advise.
Do not believe your own disguise.
Do not comply and compromise.
Instead mesmerize.
Do not be sucked into society's replies,
the bind that ties.

Your power and destiny is yours, arise.
One day they will decriminalize.

Props

Do not underestimate the value of props where fetishes are concerned. Sometimes (though people often do not take this into account), sexual acts that may be related to fetishes are limited by resources and sometimes money, e.g., if someone wishes to be tied up and there is no rope around, then one must buy the proper type of rope. If someone wishes to be handcuffed, or have hot wax put on them, or be involved with role-playing, or cross-dressing, then the necessary props must be readily available or else one cannot continue to execute their fantasies. Objects that can be physically used for sex include candles, Barbies, guns, tampons, scissors, writing utensils, water guns, hairbrushes, drawer knobs, Vicks inhalers, magazines, ice, scotch tape, a kooshball, flavoured condoms, carrots, etc.

Wigs

Wigs are like modesty headscarves, but for people in the sex industry. An example of a wig wearer in the sex industry is Jamie Lee Curtis's character in *Trading Places*. The only person who knows what a wig wearer really looks like is the spouse or significant other.

Psellismophilia

This is an interest in stutterers. I could actually see this. Stuttering kind of makes someone seem like a virgin, all nervous and innocent.

Rape Fantasies[469]

> "If [Scotty] raped me it wouldn't be called rape."—Faye

I had rape fantasies before actually being raped. Fantasy and reality are *extremely, extremely different.* This is closer to agonophilia, arousal by a partner pretending to struggle.

2% of the sample size has this, according to my statistics.

Rhabdophilia

This is finding pleasure in being criticized. Sometimes I feel like I should find someone like this. For a meticulous editor raised by a perfectionist and someone who finds no one to be his (or my) intellectual equal, stuff comes out from me from time to time. And I'd like it to give someone pleasure, but I have never found someone who enjoys it except in BDSM.

Role Play

Role play is much like improvisational acting with better costumes. Possible role-play options: Doctor, dentist, teacher, incest, police, French maid, cowboy, gender reversal, famous couples, Catholic schoolgirl (I know of no man who does not like this one), scout, alien, angel, etc.

Sexting

A coworker once told me that when she found a picture of her son naked she threatened to use it as a desktop wallpaper right before relatives arrived from out of state. It was a firm lesson to him not to sext.

1% of the sample size, that I would be involved with (remember that I prefer older generations), does this, according to my statistics. I'm sure it's probably more in reality.

---

[469] A discussion of rape will come later.

Sisters

I have dated a man who has had sex with more than one set of sisters and has dated sisters at the same time. However, he never had a threesome with them.

1% of the sample size has had sex with more than one set of twins or sisters, according to my statistics.

Sitophilia

Heck, who doesn't derive pleasure from eating? I'm a foodie. Mmmhm…good.

Stockings

Gets turned on by stockings: 3% of the sample size, according to my sample.

Strap-ons

Strap-ons are hard to control[470]. If you are going to get one, then plastic is better to control than rubber.

Switch

2% of the sample size is a switch, according to my sample, including me.

Squirting

Can squirt or like it when a womyn squirts: 3% of the sample size, according to my sample, including me[471].

---

[470] Older i.P. audAx: I just had this conversation about how wimmin don't realize how much work the men put into sex, but, with a strap-on, a womyn can get an idea.

[471] Not on demand, of course. It happens rarely and only with certain stimulation and positioning.

Fakir Musafar[472]: Tattoos and Piercings

Tattoos and piercings are forms of body modification, which is illegal in Korea[473] and used as punishment in China (facial tattoos). Another form of body modification is cicatrization, or scarification. I do not recommend skin stapling.

Don't modify your body because of fear (I'm looking at you, anorexics who get cosmetic surgery). Do it because it's fun. If it is done with the right consciousness, as with anything else done in the right consciousness, I cannot argue with it.

2% of the sample size has this fetish, according to my sample, including me.

Prison: Ted "Rad" Radian

I dated someone with a tattooed dick. He considered getting piercings in them too. I cannot fathom what that would feel like. Since we're on the topic of prison, I did have arousal from writing love letters (erotographomania).

Thassophilia

This is an attraction to sitting. I think my mom is attracted to sitting, but not in a sexual way.

Threpterophilia

I had an ex who always thought that nurses were hot. Unfortunately, I never got around to dressing up as a nurse for him.

1% of the sample size has this, according to my statistics.

Timophilia

I don't see this much because I'm not famous (yet), but with the prevalence of rap music combining money and sex, I'm fairly certain that being turned on by wealth is a very common fetish. When taken to an extreme, it becomes arousal from gold, chrysophilia. This goes well with amaxophilia, being turned on by cool cars. It doesn't really apply to me. I'm the opposite.

---

[472] Fakir Musafar is a Master Piercer with 60 years of research and 40 years of experience.

[473] Older i.P. audAx: Thank goodness I live in America!

I blame it on codependency, whose root is aphilophrenia, feeling unlovable[474]. I could imagine that narcissists have timophilia.

Toxiphilia

I would say that most Americans are attracted to poisons. However, only a few are aware of it. Sugar is close to the top of the list.

Toxophilia[475]

This is a love of archery. Though it was my favorite unit in physical education, I would not say that *Catching Fire* or the other *Hunger Game* movies turned me on.

Toys and Vibrators

> "Silently she opens the drawer
> Mother's little helper
> Is coming out for more
> Strategically positioned
> Before the midday show
> The back is arched
> Those lips are parched
> Repeated blow by blow"
> —James Reyne, "Boys Light Up" as performed by Australian Crawl

My first introduction to vibrators was the shower massager. Vibrating toothbrushes are also nice substitutes. Ovipositors are something out of this world (McCasker, 2015). And I have recently been introduced to the wonders of the Realdoe (Feeldoe?). You know what else is a sex toy? Barbie. If it weren't for sex toys, there would be no Barbie™. Just look at the earlier models.

Wind and Temperature

No one ever mentions this, but I find it a real turn-on whenever someone blows in my ear, in my vagina, on my feet, or anywhere.

---

[474] Older i.P. audAx: This was written by my younger self.

[475] Not to be confused with toxiphilia.

Cheimaphilia and Psychrophilia

This is an interest in being cold. I'm not a big fan of the cold, so I do not get turned on by it. I would say that wanting to have sex in the snow would fall under this category. It's within the realm of possibility, but at this moment I would have to say, "no thank you."

Pyrophilia and Pyrolagnia: Ray Bradbury's **Fahrenheit 451**

Pyromaniacs have this. Pyrolagnia is specific to watching fires. Even though I'm afraid of dying by fire, I understand the appeal of fire. On a metaphorical level, I have perfected the art of playing with fire. I'll play with fire until it turns blue. (I'll fall in love with narcissists and sociopaths even.) The blue flame is what tells me I have to put away my matches. To me, the risks are worth it because I want to feel alive through the process of feeling strong emotions.

Thalpotentiginy: Hot Candle Wax

The extremes of temperatures heighten the senses as much as fabric play. Extremes of temperatures is also a reason why some people prefer to have foreplay in a Jacuzzi.

Wrestling

Wrestling is a place where drama meets violence. I do not know of many men who do not admit to liking the idea of watching two girls wrestle or mud wrestle. Due to the desire for weightloss and self-protection, more wimmin have been learning how to kick and punch properly. I don't know if that is good, bad, or neutral because even though they can defend themselves, they can also instigate violence in their own home because once a woman punches a man, it's often downhill from there.

1% of the sample size likes being punched, according to my statistics.

Xenophilia

This is an attraction to foreigners. I could see that. I'm attracted to the South Asian Indian customs and traditions and have yet to date a South Asian Indian.

Xylophilia

This is arousal to wood or wooden objects. My favorite smell is sawdust. I guess that could fall under that category. I guess this would make the phrase, "a long, hard woody" quite literal.

Yoni Worship

I found it interesting that Tom Hellen was into pussy worship because, out of all of the men I had sexual encounters with, I believe he had the potential to be the most dangerous, even though he was relatively safe.

1% of the sample size has this fetish, according to my statistics.

Zoophilia and Zooerastia: The Frog Prince

Breeders who breed cats know that cats should not stay in heat for too long (besides the fact that the noise can drive anyone crazy). In order to stop a cat from being in heat, breeders actually have to get cats off with a Q-tip.

Canophilia is being turned on by dogs and cynophilia is sex with dogs. Aelurophilia is gratification from cats. I'm allergic, so I'm not going there. Blissom is having sex with an ewe. Coitus à cheval is having sex on the back of an animal.

For those who do not wish for the actual thing, a toned down version is always role-play. It is quite fun to make animal noises in bed. This fetish is not to be confused with any fetish related to furries, though it may be complementary.

2% of the sample size has this fetish, according to my statistics.

The Fetishes I Take a Stand Against: Non-BDSM, Non-Consensual Violence

Now these philias I would have to take a stand against, and there aren't many philias that I take a stand against.

Fetishes That Still Require Compassion

Domestic Abuse

> "Raindrops keep fallin' on my head
> Just like the guy whose feet are too big for his bed
> Nothing seems to fit
> [...]
> Cause I just done me some talking to the sun
> And I said I didn't like the way he got things done

247

Sleeping on the job
Oh, raindrops keep fallin' on my head
Keep a-fallin'"
—BJ Thomas, "Raindrops Keep Fallin' On My Head"

There is more "sin" in domestic abuse than there could ever be with lust. I never encountered the Devil[476] face-to-face before I was in a domestic abuse situation. However, I had encountered lust many times without adverse effects.

Sex is evil when it is a distraction from manifesting your dreams—this means that the end result is manifesting fear instead. That is not the case for me, generally, for sex is part of my purpose on this earth and is the easiest dream that I can manifest.

People who wonder why others stay in abusive relationships sometimes underestimate the power of sex. I had one mutually abusive relationship (yes, I do take responsibility because it takes two to tango), but throughout it all, our sex life was never an issue.

Horrible people can be amazingly charming and very into sex. Even Hitler and The Bird (from the book, *Unbroken*) had wives. Abusive people are often amazing, amazing people, charming, fun, magnetic, electrical people on the surface. But it's when you're already wet from tears that their electricity can really shock you. Is it electricity's fault? It's when abusive people shed their skin that you realize what breed of animal they really are.

For the minor abusers, the 10-20% part that's downright scary (almost nightmarish) does all the work of wanting to stay away from the 80-90% that's good and worth remembering for a lifetime. When you have one abuser in your life, you have them all, both literally and figuratively. You don't "gotta catch 'em all," but you probably will anyways because, see, you're magnetic now too. It's the first one, usually in the family, that opens the floodgates to a world of consistency (or inconsistency rather, depending on type). And this results more from confirmation bias and the assignment of meaning than it ever did from that one family member.

Someone told me that my ability to confront my abuser indicates I will no longer be abused. I was not so sure at the time. I thought that perhaps I would be doing the abusing instead. I did not believe I could be with a "healthy" person.

See, name calling, for instance, is a dealbreaker for healthy people, which is a shame because abused people can't modify their impulses, behaviors, and neuropathways overnight. Haven't they been through enough just to be shunned by emotional health nuts? Abused people let negative comments slide off their back as if it were a perishable that they'll just eat the next day. They exonerate because they understand what it was like when the abuser was in their shoes. Abusive

---

[476] In the study of demonology, this the Devil is different from Satan and Lucifer.

people can be forgiven because people cannot be evil; only "satan" (ego) is evil. Only powers and principalities are evil[477].

Only fucked up people can love other fucked up people, or at least get as close to a semblance of it as possible. I'm not saying you cannot or should not surround yourself with positive people who are going places; I'm saying you won't grow to be where they are unless they have been where you've been. This is partly why marriageable people are those with similar backgrounds and upbringings.

Because of Jesus's prime commandment, I doubt that healthy people will make it into the kingdom ("healthy" as in those who do not know pain). They cannot forgive if they do not understand. Isn't the expression, "seek first to understand, then be understood"? As much as I would like to be loved, when it comes down to it, I'd rather be understood. Love, if I've ever felt what healthy people have felt, is not as satisfying as being understood. It's not something I seek after as fervently. Sometimes being understood requires people who cannot love properly. But that's okay. Let me do the loving. Give the task of loving to someone who has a knack for it[478].

Raptophilia and Stupration

Contrary to belief, I have found that there is no gender difference in injustice. Men are raped. To think otherwise is to come to rape with the false assumptions that it is strictly a physical act. Some men have experienced emotional abuse at the hands of their friends or romantic interests. Men can be relational bullies as easily as relational bullies bully men. Some men have a version of body dysmorphic disorder as a result. A version of this is small penis syndrome (SPS). The only difference, from what I can tell, between men and women is that men usually don't tell.

To feel that my sex drive came from somewhere, I attributed my birthfather to being a rapist or my birthmother to being a prostitute. Neither happened to be true (or at least it's rationally unlikely).

Coercive Rape[479]

> "My first time I [coercively raped someone] it was the
> first date and my partner did not want sex.

---

[477] However, protection against evil makes no sense because the desire for protection of the body, the ego's shield, is what creates much evil.

[478] Older i.P. audAx: Now that I'm a different person in a new unit of time (quite literally because none of our cells are the same cells that we had over seven years ago), I would no longer have said what I said in this paragraph.

[479] I recommend reading *The New Male Sexuality* by Bernie Zilbergeld.

So I began by sucking, and I argue that genitalia can be stimulated by touch over will, and so I suppose it is possible for a woman to rape a man. Honestly, I have no fear of being raped. Anyways, when I die, I would prefer it to be from something sexual (rape, asphyxiation, a sexually transmitted disease, heart attack after sex, etc.). But I am afraid of being the [coercive] rapist because it can be hard to tell when not to have sex. I get awfully irritated when guys will not make a move and I am obsessed with having sex with a girl. The closest thing I have had to rape is being played with when I was not in the mood, when my vagina was dry, or when my muscles ached from having too much sex already and being forced is just damned annoying, but I secretly like it[480]. The only times that I do not feel in the mood is when I am very stressed or very self-conscious, usually due to my period. The whole fear of, and negative psychological consequences of[,] rape I believe comes from Victorian ideals of chastity. My worst flaw is that for the life of me I cannot comprehend why rape has such a damaging effect[481]. I cannot comprehend sex as a bad thing. It feels so amazing. Since I cannot understand I am afraid of being the predator and how horrible to know I unconsciously caused such psychological damage to someone I cared for!"
—Old Olo (cut and pasted for organization's sake)

As for coercive rape, rape is mostly about nonconsensual acts[482], and inasmuch as lack of sexual consent is painful, so is the lack of consent with the government ("Sexual Assault Prevention and Awareness Center" 2017). Being multiplied by each person the government affects, how much more painful is its laws.

Rape means that something happened without consent (usually). However, children are told to obey the educational system without their consent, tried and true culture that's lasted for millennia is taken from a nation without the citizen's consent, people are imprisoned as part of the drug war without the individual's consent. But worst of all, an entire nation or nations of people are made slaves through an economic system based on lies and deception without the people's consent. So why is it only the young, the women, and the elderly get attention if they are sexually molested without consent? Does the rape of a nation matter not?

Voluntaryists by idealogy are anti-rape/rape culture. Rape is bad because sex binds two souls together and forces an unwilling soul to reincarnate with the rapist's soul so that the trauma is repeated over and over again, either to the rapist or the person who was originally raped.

---

[480] Older i.P. audAx: This was prior to age 22. Things have changed.

[481] Older i.P. audAx: I understand it now.

[482] Statutory rape can be consensual, but it is still considered rape.

Biastophilia

Biastophilia is arousal from violently raping victims. Blastophilia is very different from coercive rape as it involves terrifying a stranger. An anoraptus is someone who only rapes older women.

Fetishes That Require Serious Intervention, Professional Mental Help, and Imprisonment

Amokoscisia

This is a sexual frenzy with the desire to slash or mutilate women.

Autassassinophilia

This is arousal from orchestrating one's own death by the hands of another.

Anthropophagy and Vorarephilia: Hansel and Gretel

Cannibals say humans taste more like pork. Is this a coincidence? Anthropophagolagnia is rape with cannibalism. Nothing good comes from this, except maybe survival during the zombie apocalypse.

Though not regarding cannibalism specifically, modern day carnivores live a very different life than they did in the past. There is something seriously wrong with our world if we fear eating raw meat due to salmonella or e. coli. (There's also something wrong with our world if Obama's Secret Service needs to fortify the White House when Abe Lincoln allowed British tourists to walk right up to his cottage and visit him when he was in his night clothes, though that's another topic unrelated to sex.)

Bestialsadism

This is cruelty or mutilation of animals.

Avisodomy

This is breaking the neck of a bird while penetrating it. Those who love birds, or have ornithophilia, would be absolutely shocked. An instance of this was mentioned in *Unbroken* by Laura Hillenbrand.

AudAx

Dacnolagnomania or Erotophonophilia

This is a lust murder.

Dacryphilia

This is arousal from seeing tears in the eyes of a partner.

Dippoldism

This is sexual arousal from abusing children.

Dystychiphilia and Symphorophilia

I'm not really clear on dystychiphilia. It means deriving pleasure from accidents, but I don't know what "accidents" means specifically. Symphorophilia is clearer—sexual pleasure from accidents or catastrophes.

Ecorchement: Self-Flagellation

An example of self-flagellation is ball dancing, a practice of hanging fruit from hooks in the skin.

Erotophonphilia

This is sexual satisfaction from murdering complete strangers.

Executions

Some people have known to become aroused by watching executions. I'm sure this was much more common during the Middle Ages or in prisons.

Hybristophilia

A woman who is attracted to men who commit extremely heinous crimes is a hybristophiliac.

Picquerism

Picquerism is sexual gratification from stabbing someone repeatedly. Yuck!

Snuff Films

Snuff films are showing actual murders in movies without the aid of special effects.

Suttee

Though cultural, I do not condone widow burning and don't even see why that would be considered sexual. Ugh!

Summary Table for Fetishes and Sexual Conditions[483]

Fetish or Phobia	Percentage
Acousticophilia and Ligyrophilia (Sounds)	1%
Actirasty (Making Love Under the Sky or Sunbathing)	1%
Acucullophallia and apellous (Circumcised Males)*	82%
Advanced techniques (Athletics, Deepthroating, and Fisting)	4%
Agoraphilia (Sex in Public Places)	2%
Agrexophilia, allopellia, candaulism, ecouterism, scoptophilia, and troilism (Witnessing Others have sex)	5%
Alphamegamia, Anililagnia, Anisonogamism, Chronophilia, Geronosexuality, Gerontophilia, and Tragalism (Age Gap)	3%
Allotriorasty (interracial)	7%
Androminetophilia, Autogynephilia, Eonism, Transvestic Fetishism, and Transvestophilia (Crossdressing)	4%
Ambisextrous, Ambisexual, Amphisexual, Amphieroticism, Androgynophilia, and Digenous (Bisexuality)	4%
Autoerotic asphyxiaphilia and pnigophilia (Cutting off circulation)	3%
Anthropomorphism, autoplushophilia, dermaphilia/doraphilia, fursuit, hyphephilia, plushophilia, pupply play, or yiffy (Furries)	1%

---

[483] Sample Size=107 including myself

Fetish or Phobia	Percentage
Barosmia, olfactophilia, osphresiophilia, and ozolagnia (Smell)	2%
BDSM	8%
Belonephilia (Sharp objects)	1%
Bigamy, hetaerism, polyandry, polygyny, and polysemy (Multiple People)	5%
Bigynism (Sex with more than one female)	2%
Bivirism (Sex with more than one male)	1%
Brothers or sisters	1%
Bukkake (Anonymous handjobs)	3%
Clowns	1%
Contortion	1%
Commasculation, uranism, and Zwishcenstufe (Homosexuality)	8%
Copralalia, corprophemia, and Lalochezia (Dirty talk)	3%
Cymbalism and sapphism (Lesbianism)	7%
Cyber sex	2%
Defecolagnia and urolagnia (Scat and watersports)	4%
Domination	2%
Edging	1%
Epistemophilia, Phronemophilia, Sapiosexuality, and Sophophilia (Intellectualism)	2%
Erotomania (Unrequited Love)	4%
Erectile Dysfunction	2%

Fetish or Phobia	Percentage
Erectile Dysfunction with Premature Ejaculation	1%
Exophilia and Neophilia (Newness)	1%
Fabric Play	2%
Gamophobia and Philophobia (Fear of Commitment)	2%
Gomphiipothic and odaxelangnia (Teeth)	1%
Grapholagnia, icolagnia, pictophilia, and scoptolagnia (Porn)	4%
Group Sex	5%
Gymnophilia and Omolagnia (Nudism)	2%
Gynemimetophilia (Fetish for Transsexuals)	1%
Jealousy	1-2%
Katoptronophilia and Spectrophilia (Using Mirrors)	2%
Knismolagnia and Titillagnia (Tickling)	5%
Menophilist (During Menstruation)	>2%
Narratophilia (Phone Sex, Erotica, and Romance Novels)	1%
Nomavalent (Traveling)	2%
Nude photographers whose spouses do not approve	4%
Oculolictus (Licking Eyelids and Arousal by Eyes)	2%
Partialism (Interest in Body Parts)	2%
Parthenolatry and Pucelage (Virgin Worship)	2%

Fetish or Phobia	Percentage
Phone Sex	4%
Polyiterophilia (Same Act; Different Partners)	1%
Premature Ejaculation	2%
Psycholagny (Orgasm by Thought Alone)	1%
Rape Fantasies	2%
Retrocopulation (Doggy Style)	5%
Schoolgirl Fantasies*	84%
Sexting	>1%
Sexual Anorexia (Fear of Sex)	1%
Sitophilia (Pleasure from Eating)	100%
Sleepy Sex and Necrophilia	1%
Squirting (Can Squirt or Has it as a Fantasy)	3%
Stockings Fantasy	3%
Submission	5%
Switch (Can be Dom or Sub)	2%
Tattoos and Piercings	2%
Threpterophilia (Nurse Fetish)	1%
Transfeminate (Transsexual)	6%
Uncircumcised	1%
Webcams	1%
Wrestling	1%
Yoni Worship (Pussy Worship)	1%
Zoophilia and Zooerastia (Beastiality)	2%

AudAx

Fetish or Phobia	Percentage
Total (with an allowance for fetish overlap)	179%

*Seventeen percent of the sample size is female.

Sex and the World (Listed Alphabetically)

Abortion and Adoption

Abortion is death now. Adoption is death later, whether literally or figuratively. Abortion is choose a new life now. Adoption is choose a new life later.

If "bastardize" means to corrupt by adding new elements, then it would make sense for an illegitimate child to be seen as an heir to those who are not blue bloods.

I relate with sexual compulsives more than I do adoptees, even though adoptees they are a close second.

Artificial Insemination

Kerry Morrissey

When I was researching about Single Mothers by Choice, I found out that my lesbian crush was not longer married to her wife. Though she wasn't a single mother by choice, she was a single mother who had been donor inseminated. I never actually saw her mothering skills, but I had the impression that she was a terrific mother, which made her all the more hot. Despite the fact that she was a single mother, I had very serious doubts that she would have a challenge getting back on the marketplace. She always knew women lusted after her, even as a butch.

Donor Insemination

I hate to say, because I know I will just be seen as part of the War on Men, but most men's laissez-faire behaviors and narcissistic tendencies have not shown to me that they are necessary in child-rearing. Nice to have, sure, but not as useful as one or two women (unless the woman herself is not interested in raising her own child). I am a good candidate for insemination since I can teach my child how to live with unknowingness. If I have a child by insemination, will e still hate me? Undoubtedly, and I will be proud of raising e in a safe environment where e can express e's feelings.

Astrology and the Hermetic Religion

I had a counselor for two years. I specified that I wanted a Korean Christian counselor so I would feel better and be able to connect. We got into a disagreement about astrology. I am a firm believer in astrology and see it as a background check or akin to meteorology. Compatibility is important in the bedroom, even if it is between two fuck buddies (which is a type of relationship I don't actually recommend having).

Considering what I said above, a background check is regarding the past, not what is to come. I would never get involved with a toxic star combination, which is more important to me than uncovering a criminal record[484]. Most of the time I find that astrology only makes sense in 20-20 hindsight. Astrology is best for intellectualizing the past so that you can understand where you want to go, why you want to go there, how you want to get there, etc.

Future predictions can only be understood in the past and are for the past alone. The reason why (why is always the most important) fortune tellers were banned in the Bible is because of this confusion. However, dreams were not banned, could not be banned, for dreams tell you how to prepare and preparation is made for the future.

God made the stars. It would be ridiculous for him to forbid us from reading them. But keep in mind the dangers of using astrology, or even prophets, for future predictions. Even the predictions of a prophet can only be understood in hindsight.

And, when you get down to it, true compatibility goes way beyond astrology. The question is not, "Do we have compatible personalities," but "Do we have compatible psychological disorders?" because everyone has one even if they're in denial.

Beauty[485]

Looks also have nothing to do with sexual maturity. Plenty of pornographic-looking wimmin are as prude as an old maid and some old maids are as wild as a porn star. (I hope to be the latter.)

When I was young, my dad said when I got older he'd have to beat boys back with a stick. It was a twofold curse: everyone and his best friend had wet dreams about me, but I had never even been engaged, though I tended to have long-term relationships between a year to four years[486]. I'm sure a lot of it had to do with the fact that no one could overcome my dad's hatred of them.

In my opinion, you know you've got that special something when you're reclusive and all you want is to be left alone (is that so much to ask?). Sometimes I feel as annoyed as Megan Fox. I

---

[484] As with any womyn who digs "bad boys," I have an extensive history with dating convicts and felons, though I do not condone what brought them to that point.

[485] Beauty has nothing on entrepreneurship.

[486] Older i.P. audAx: Lately I've been having shorter-term relationships with a minimum of a month.

can't even tell you how often guys do NOT take "No" for an answer[487]. I recommend filing that [conversation] away for sex-ed class when they talk about rape.

Sex appeal is like a Pokémon Go incense or lure that cannot be turned off. Though it can provide the gift of power, it is a manipulative power that should be used sparingly lest it boost one's ego and provide a false sense of self.

Unfortunately, it is this sex appeal that has made me hesitant to exercise lest it increase magnetism, much to my detriment.

Being beautiful is tiresome[488]. Being attractive should be an undesirable, unless you're a person who likes a challenge, because being attractive limits quality courting prospects in the same way that being Goth can limit employment prospects[489]. It is far more difficult for an attractive person to sort the wheat from the chaff. And the majority, if the end goal is marriage, are chaff. If I weren't attractive, then I wouldn't even have had addictive behaviors with sex. Or perhaps, I'm

---

[487] The way God made me is not an invitation for compulsive behavior.

[488] Beauty makes people do weird stuff. It makes people want to kiss someone or ask someone out in front of their significant other or spouse. It makes people want to pick up people from a bus stop, as if they were a streetwalker. It makes people change walking direction just to ask for someone's name. It makes people ask someone point blank if that person is looking for a relationship. It makes people think that an invitation to buy a product is an invitation to their residence. I have experienced all that and more.

My eyes are dangerous because when I don't pay attention to where I'm looking, men in my line of glazed-over sight will look back with the wrong sight.

I know I'm not a supermodel, but there's just something about me that brings all the creeps out of the woodworks to leer at me and drop very un-subtle hints no matter how modestly dressed I am. The opposite of a woman in a hijab is a leering Mexican man in a dark alley (because they find it to be culturally acceptable to flirt openly).

No attractive womyn should need food stamps from the government; all they need is to go on dates with straight male traditionalists, especially the kind that will absolutely refuse to left a woman pay, much to their own detriment. That is called legal whoring, which is mutually acceptable.

The part about Denver I loathe is its Menver aspect. The one thing I missed about the DC area in hindsight was that people wouldn't even comment if you changed your hair because they were worried about sexual harassment lawsuits.

I get more stares due to my unwanted beauty than because I'm Goth, so I'm not so courageous as I seem; I just choose to be the me I've hidden for so many years and get stares for who I am vs. who people want me to be. I've found that when I am fully myself, I get asked out far less often. Thank God in a way. Sometimes people are not interested in Goths or not interested in how I style my hair. At least we are upfront with each other in advance (visually).

[489] Older i.P. audAx: I'm not saying that being a Goth is an undesirable. Being a Goth is a calling and, therefore, unavoidable.

attractive to overcompensate for daddy issues revolving around disapproval of my race, culture, and orientation.

That's partly why I don't wear makeup—to decrease the annoyance level I have toward the opposite sex. I would hate to be Playboy beautiful. It would make men 10 times more annoying and block-worthy. The idea that a womyn should look pretty for a man is beyond ridiculous to me. It's not true that wimmin wear makeup for men; most wimmin like makeup, but most men don't.

I have never had to wear makeup for a man[490]. If men lost their attraction to me because I didn't wear makeup or gained some weight, then I wouldn't be a sexual compulsive. I have rarely needed makeup or weight loss to have a lot of sex. The times I wear makeup are when I had a bad day the day before and needed a "pick-me-up," when I'm modeling or on stage (and, therefore, making money), and when I'm bored and trying to finish off a beauty product that I spent money on.

I have a distinctive face. If people cannot recognize me with a new hairstyle, then I know they never bothered to pay attention to my face. Unfortunately, this is common among men.

My mom thinks I should marry someone ugly. She thinks I'm too superficial. However, I just can't imagine having sex with an ugly person three times a day or more.[491]

The Curse of the Beautiful People:

- Being mistaken for someone's significant other while single.

- Being tired of being asked on dates by people not seen as potential spouses.

- Being put on a pedestal and falling from grace unawares.

---

[490] Older i.P. audAx: That is no longer true.

[491] Beautiful people can only find their perfect match if they are not superficial both in their interactions and in their love interests. Seek only that which never fades.

I'm sure we've all heard it said that beauty fades. But that does not tell the entire story, for intelligence fades too. Yes, just look at any facility dedicated to brain disease, brain tumors, brain damage, stroke, and memory loss. If a sapiosexual decides that seeking brains over brawn is a superior strategy than that of those who are honestly superficial, then they will be sorely disappointed and disillusioned when that which they sought is not permanent.

For me, I prefer character traits. Some might think I am superficial to seek wealthy men, not knowing that I was often the provider in past relationships. I do this because truly wealthy men, when their financial wealth is taken away, have such wealth of character that they will regain their former glory and then some, for what they value is more gold than gold. However, for those who have a spirit of a slave, they will always be slaves no matter if they win the lottery. (Older i.P. audAx: Even this has changed over time. I have learned to be thankful for what I have and to see the character traits in those I already love than to seek out a fantasy.)

- Taking for granted things not easily acquired outside of a sphere of beauty, such as sex or the receiving of favors.

Computers

In the same way that the availability of Internet technology exceeds our ability to keep up with cybersecurity and Section 508 compliance (for accessibility), our biological drive exceeds our wisdom and risk management abilities.

Emerging Adulthood

Before the concept of a child and primary school, people married before they hit puberty. When the concept of the child and primary school began, people had children once they hit puberty. When the concept of the "teen" and secondary school began, people had children when they were teens. When the concept of college began, people had children when they hit adulthood. When the concept of the emerging adult and graduate school began, people had children later, and then the laws *forbade* teens from having sex. If wimmin had kids after the age of 40, there is a higher risk of brain damage or mental illness in the child, so shouldn't it make more sense for a society to forbid older people from having sex? If older wimmin were to breed extensively (or have incest), our society would look much like the society in *Idiocracy*. We can't let schools dumb us down anymore. And we don't need to speed it up genetically.

Food

I thought of sex as a completely different activity from loving; I saw it more like eating, as a daily activity where masturbation was survival food and group sex was a multiple-course meal at a fine restaurant. Or masturbation was to group sex what *matcha* tea was to *sencha* tea. I saw public displays of affection as eating with your mouth open. Just because I have a favorite restaurant (primary) didn't mean I couldn't eat fast food (secondary). I didn't realize that I shouldn't mix foods.

When a man wished to restrict my sexual diet, I thought of it as "How dare you tell me what to eat or who to eat with?" It took time to realize that sex was more like sugar than protein, and not so essential to daily life.

Heaven

Heaven has neither time nor space. Without time, there is no age. Without space there is no sex, neither intercourse nor gender. The only thing that's certain about death is the life review. The life review is a review of the lives you touched. What matters is neither age nor gender. What matters is how good or bad you made someone feel, sexually or otherwise.

How to Manuals

I love reading sexual how-to manuals for a good laugh. It's kinda like enjoying a really good zombie mermaid wrestler boy band movie with deadpan commentary. Good time for popcorn.

Money

Money circulates. It circulates like blood, oxygen, *chi* (or *qi*). It is the life force of a nation. The issue should not be how much blood one can get from his donor (employer or customer or client), but how thankful one should be at knowing that strangers want to make sure you are vital. A rich man is someone with an increased quality of life, like someone high on oxygen or feeling good on double red blood cells.

Now to relating it with sex. There are systems in place to make sure blood is safe. Money captures energy from its owners. A greedy (not necessarily) rich man who gives and acquires money without blessing to the recipient, or thankfulness to the giver, is like a patient without nursing staff (or an employee without a payroll system). The negative energy collects, gets tainted, and, yes, could kill. Just like HIV (human immunodeficiency virus). HIV destroys one's immunity against disease. In the same way, a "lover of money" is now wide open to "evil," predatorial forces.

If we were to look at sex as unsecured credit card debt, being non-monogamous with a monogamous person or vice versa would be "bad debt" because the value would depreciate over time. However, a non-monogamous person with the same[492] or a monogamous person with the same would be "good credit" because the return on investment would be higher than what you put in.

When a monogamous and nonmonogamous person meet and decide to date, that is called abuse. Both sides are responsible if they knew about this going into the relationship but did it anyways. I define abuse as whatever produces shame because shame produces addictive behavior and further abuse in turn.

I use this as an example, but it can also be replaced with goals. A couple with different goals has a depreciating value, both to each other and to the world. A couple with similar goals has an appreciating value to themselves and the world because they appreciate each other and others.

---

[492] Don't I sound Indian-American now?

How I Feel About Special Relationships

I do not choose a married life, not just because God and I agreed to it in 2001[493], but because I cannot morally agree to it. To center your life around one person is to put that person before God and before others[494]. You can tell how much one person values another by the amount of time given to that person. The amount of time between your significant other and your neighbor vary significantly, but they are all God's child. I say "God's child" because "God's children" would imply separation between us and Jesus or us and each other, when it is a biblical principle that that is not so. *See* Matthew 25:40.

> "And the King will reply to them, Truly I tell you, in so far as you did it for one of the least [in the estimation of men] of these My brethren, you did it for Me."—Matthew 25:40 (from the Amplified Bible)

It is through special relationships that the rich get richer and the poor get poorer.

Now, I am not advocating a redistribution of the wealth. Money must not be distributed equally for that would go against God: God gives money only as much as is appropriate and suitable. Anything more or anything less than what you can handle now would cause more of a curse than a blessing. Be happy for what you have.

I am making a differentiation between money and love. Though there are some parallels, money must be earned via meritocracy[495]. Money is only given as much as you have worked for it via hours or via steps up the ladder[496]. Love is given by grace. Everyone has it as babies and children. *See* Matthew 18:3-6.

> "And said, Truly I say to you, unless you repent (change, turn about) and become like little children [trusting, lowly, loving, forgiving], you can never enter the kingdom of heaven [at all].
>
> Whoever will humble himself therefore and become like this little child is greatest in the kingdom of heaven.
>
> And whoever receives *and* accepts *and* welcomes one little child like this for My sake and in My name receives and accepts and welcomes Me.

---

[493] However, there was a stipulation that can be overcome.

[494] Older i.P. audAx: Even a child.

[495] Among other ways.

[496] Depending on what you were taught.

AudAx

> But whoever causes one of these little ones who believe in me *and* acknowledge *and* cleave to Me to stumble and sin [that is, who entices him or hinders him in right conduct or thought], it would be better (more expedient and profitable or advantageous) for him to have a great millstone fastened around his neck and to be sunk in the depth of the sea."

> —Matthew 18:3-6 (from the Amplified Bible)

They have more love than adults, or at least they recognize it better at times. Children are not born with money.

Our Temples

Our bodies do not always do what we want it to do, much like a car or other tool. For many, that means losing weight. For the older people, it could mean most anything. For me, it means having severe allergies when I want to go camping or having bone issues when I want to skateboard.

Parenting

> "I've heard a lot of young women give that reason for having their babies, actually: love." –Hand to Mouth (Tirado, 2014, p. 117)

> "The idea of privacy among nuclear family members is actually pretty new. Parents used to share a bed with their kids—and still expand their families somehow." —Hand to Mouth (Tirado, 2014, p.110)

> "[A] not-insignificant percentage of advantaged people have a hard time understanding that shame is a luxury item, because there is a point at which things are so bad that you lose all sense of shame." –Hand to Mouth (Tirado, 2014, p. 163)

Small children, boys or girls, touch themselves often, as well as other people, and it's important to talk about sexual mores in a way they can understand. I remember my cousin used to play with his mother's boobs often, and she would allow it. It was a bit distracting when you're trying to have a conversation (Grover 2017).

The Rules

Results of the Rules:

- Potential lovers would call multiple times to thank me for a date or write cheesy poetry.

- Male friends would ask for more hugs than usual, give me free sex toys[497], or talk about doing "it" with him AND his father.

- Coworkers would pass by my room just to say, "Hi."

- Waiters would lean across me to pick up other people's plates or would walk nearby to listen in to my conversation and pretend that they thought I was talking to them.

("Playing Hard To Get | Dating 'The Rules' Vs 'The Game' | Soulmates | The Soulmates Blog" 2014)

How to fend off the opposite sex (or same sex) when you have too many people on your plate: Still working on that with three married men and two stalkers[498] (one is both).

Sexual Appeal

Sexual appeal is what I wanted for so long as a youngster, before I knew what sex was. I do not want to discard that which I tried so long to manifest. See the Beauty section for irony.

Spirituality

> "I state unequivocally that it [sex] is a connection to the Divine
> Mind."—Jesus, *Jesus: My Autobiography* (Spalding 197)

In marriage, people may get to the point where one does not want sex because they do not think it is in keeping with spirituality. This is a book to reconcile sex with spirituality so that there is no more guilt or shame, both useless emotions that hinder our relationship with God[499].

If you think sex and religion are incompatible and cannot understand my thinking, then your assumptions are incorrect (and you probably think science and religion are incompatible too).

Sex cannot be tied neatly in a bow, as the church would have it. One of the issues here is that the church views sex as physical and not spiritual, but it is far more spiritual and psychological than physical at all. If sex were merely physical, then there would be no enjoyment and there would not be as many fetishes. As you see in this book, the proliferation of fetishes is proof that sex goes beyond the physical. Sex has nothing to do with the body and everything to do with what

---

[497] There are two things I don't buy: sex toys and pot; people just like to offer me stuff.

[498] Not all stalkers are single. I had one who was married and another who was coupled. I no longer deal with three married men and two stalkers. What worked for me was a spiritual clearing. It was apparently tied in with karma.

[499] Some people may disagree, particularly non-anarchist libertarians.

is between your two ears. I have had sex with someone without a working member and enjoyed it. If it were about the body, you could have sex with a doll. If sex were merely physical, as a sex addiction counselor and ex told me, you could have sex with a tree (dendrophilia). Take away the brain, take away the connection between the sensors and the brain, or damage it in the related regions, like the hypothalamus, then tell me how much you enjoy sex. It has never been about the body. Because I know the connection between sex and spirit, I will never become jaded[500].

Sex is a study in psychology. There is nothing intimate with the physical body. Only the mind can be intimate with another mind. Case in point: I can have sex with an inmate without ever touching him or being in the same room.

My ex, the same sex addict counselor, said sex is not related to spirituality. Why then is the 8th house (in astrology) the house of sex and spirituality? To me, sex is like prayer and prayer activates a wish in Law of Attraction.

Posture, Breathing, and Walking

Why is posture, breathing, and walking a part of a book on sex? Sex is inherently connected with health. Without good posture, you could injure your neck or back and make it difficult, if not nearly impossible, to continue the sexual acts you performed previously.

The correct way to do anything is to do the opposite of what is taught. This is true for building fires, swimming, weightlifting, etc. Read the *4-Hour Body* and *4-Hour Chef* by Tim Ferris.

Most things we learn in school are false. Take the food pyramid for example. Vegetarians reject meat. Paleos reject dairy. Atkins and Paleo followers reject carbs. Some are allergic to dairy. Some are allergic to nuts. And so on.

Breathing should never be forgotten. The Christian West has emphasized guilt in sexual pleasures, therefore resulting in the phenomenon of an entire society of people holding their breath during climax. This is absolutely the wrong thing to do for the health of one's spiritual body. Breathing is most important during the climactic moment of orgasm. Repression of breath is repression of sex itself.

Walking should be relaxed. With tense walking it should be no surprise that a result would be tense sex.

---

[500] Older i.P. audAx: What was I saying? When one's only connection to the outside world (outside of work) is via booty calls, one wonders if everyone is as crass, or a scrub (*See* "No Scrubs" by TLC). It really helps to get out and meet new people just to believe in humanity again.

King David, Wilt Chamberlain, Zeus, Fleabag, and the
Prodigal Daughter: Notes from Idolatry Recovery[501]

"When an individual's external sexual protective boundary is nonexistent, he cannot say no to any sexual approach and is sexual with anyone who wants to be sexual with him. [...] When an individual does not have an external sexual containment boundary, he makes sexual advances without permission or in the face of the other person's refusal."—Pia Mellody, *The Intimacy Factor* (Mellody, 2004)[502]

Recovery Notes 2012

These are notes from when I thought I had a sexual addiction. I'm still not sure if I really do[503]. If sex is a vice, then I love my vices and would not even consider myself addicted if that were not so. Strangely, the person who taught me to love my vices was none other than an alcoholic smoker.

I am not nearly as much of a sex addict as those who first taught me about sex. Both men who taught me about sex had had sex so often before, during, and after me that their cock had become numb to sensation. I would have to squeeze their cock with my mouth or suck it on and on and on to the point of boredom.

If I compare myself to those who are worse than me, I am definitely on the low end of the scale, if anything. If I compare myself to celibate churchgoers, then, at least to them, I am out of control. It's all a matter of perspective.

I consider my sexual addiction to be secondary, meaning that my sexual addiction stems from dating and having relationships with sex addicts. I have not yet reached the 100 mark[504], yet I dated someone who had by at least age 24. I have not gotten to the point where I focus on sex 24/7 to the exclusion of other things. Perhaps part of that is that I intellectualize sex and mentally relate it to other things in my life. I had sex with someone who did focus on sex to the exclusion

---

[501] When people say a product or food is addictive, they mean that it's good and makes people feel good and happy. Yet the end result of addictive behavior is feeling bad and shameful, which results in labeling the drug of choice as bad even though "nothing is either good nor bad but thinking makes it so" (Shakespeare). If Jesus gave His disciples wine, we can deduce that alcohol is a sacred blessing. It is a crime (sin) for it to be less than sacred, just like sex.

[502] I first learned about boundaries in 2008 and began applying it in 2016.

[503] Older i.P. audAx: I'm pretty sure I had sexual compulsive behaviors back when I wrote this, and I'm pretty sure I was in denial.

[504] Older i.P. audAx: I had finally reached that point in my thirties, maybe 2016, right around the time when I was slowing down.

of life. For me to get turned on, as a female, I need at least the illusion of a relationship, some character development. Video pornography[505] does nothing for me unless it is only used as a supplement to enhance the moment. I have never paid for sex. I do not want to hurt myself or someone else to the point where a hospital visit would be inevitable. I have never gotten involved with the criminal system or had anything on my record besides minor car incidents. There are a lot of things extreme things I do not do.

To a celibate churchgoer, of course, everything I mention here is extreme, but I assure you that in the sexual community it's not. The only reason I would consider that I have a sexual addiction is that I practice unsafe sex at times, but I always confide about my health (even if soon after the fact). I have nothing uncommon or deadly. Also, there have been times when I have put myself in physical and emotional danger because my lust for sex was such a powerful [sic] to be reckoned with, to the point where doing something stupid was better than doing something dangerous.

Since the Christian religion was largely affected by sexual compulsives, such as King David, King Solomon[506], and St. Augustine, and since lust may have questionably been the first and most financially profitable and enduring sin[507], this section should be of particular note.

All sexual compulsives start life with a sense of already lost something or someone, such as a mother, or virginity[508].

At least from a womyn's perspective, sexual compulsion arises from a deep need to connect with God (love), meaning that they can become great followers of Christ once they understand HOW to love. In fact, whereas the prohibition against premarital sex seems a restriction to most others, it is such a blessing to those whose lives have already been damaged through the unfortunate consequences of sex (such as abortions, STDs, affairs, etc.) It is only sexual compulsives who can truly understand and embrace God's teachings regarding the sanctity of sex.

It's easy to imagine that among every couple is one sexual compulsive, that is one person who has a genetically higher sex drive, one person who has a slightly greater resentment, one person whose loved one refuses to please and problem solve.

The bad news about sexual compulsives is that you may distrust them, feel jealousy, and they can put your life on the line. But the good news is that, if reeled in with limits, the "dry" sexual compulsive can please your every sexual need for life.

---

[505] Non-70s video pornography

[506] According to Rabbi Akiva, the Song of Songs is the holiest book of the Bible.

[507] Older i.P. audAx: And holy sin, if we believe that Sumeria is the first civilization.

[508] Older i.P. audAx: My hymen broke prior to first having sex, due to an injury on the playground.

Word Choice in Recovery and Habits

I have never resonated with the words "abuse" and "addiction." Another word for "abuse" and "addiction" is "bad habit." Bad habits, like cancer cells, can be overcome with good habits, and healthy cells.

There is a huge connection between sex addiction (compulsion) and other addictions or compulsions, such as workaholism, narcotics, debting, gambling, etc. I've been addicted to many things over the years: nails, rage, people, emotional dependency, sugar[509]. I've also witnessed many addictions: romance novels, video games, television. But it was only sexual compulsion that got me to the 12-Step Program[510].

I feel like all habits are compulsions because they get into motor memory and, as creatures of habit, if we don't do them, then we feel weird and compelled to do them. (Compulsion relates to "compulsum," which comes from the root of "compel," like "The Power of God compels you.") Thus, I learned that it was not enough to call myself a sexual compulsive, but to admit I had an "addiction."

Most people do not like the word "sin" but if sin were understood in the context of, or even replaced with, "abuse" or "addiction," then we can understand finally that "we are all sinners" means we are all capable of abuse (misuse) or we are all addicted to a person, thing, or behavior. It is with this realization that a 12-step program is a true church and has fulfilled all the promises the modern church has failed to fulfill.

It is with the context of abuse and addiction that we can understand why we shall have no idols and why we should not lie to others (and if Jesus were here, he'd say why we should not lie to ourselves.) Sex, or any behavior, is a sin when it is an idol, a priority, a bad habit.

When one considers that anything, anyone, any behavior, and even any thought can be addictive, one realizes that the only way out is through… meditation, through the removal of even our thoughts. Meditation is the only truly good habit.

I have also never resonated with "sacrifice," "surrender," "pain for gain," "delayed gratification," "letting go," "compromise," or "giving up [something]." These words do not resonate with me. But I am okay with "discipline," which relates to "disciple." Others words for discipline are "self-control," "self-mastery," "self-awareness," "commitment," "discernment," "prioritizing,"

---

[509] One interesting thing I've found that people with addictive behaviors have in common is indiscriminate eating.

[510] A sexual compulsive I talked to once speculated that 10% of the population has a sexual compulsion, but, sadly (especially for the wimmin), only 1% of them go to Anonymous recovery groups.

"setting boundaries," "cultivating good habits," "being the tortoise," "showing love," "allowing for freedom," and "developing character."

I do not like how the 12-Step Program downplays discipline because, for someone who has had affairs, that was exactly what was needed: the discipline to say no. In fact, it was such discipline that helped me in all aspects of my life.

Discipline flies in the face of the idea that humans are here to be happy because discipline is hard work and often requires that we do things we don't want to do, but it is oh so necessary.

In addition, I understand the concept of choosing suffering for the sake of compassion and patience, which both comes from "pati-," meaning suffering.

About Excessive Enthusiasm During the Rise of Self-Help and Recovery[511]

I was first introduced to sexual compulsion the same time I was introduced to sex. It's easy to be a compulsive when the other is too, but the person you are with does not always stay. A life with a compulsive is to the monogamous majority what college is to the real world.

My ex-boyfriend wondered how I could get sex at the snap of a finger, but it wasn't difficult. One time, just from meeting someone and recommending a good restaurant, he wanted me to suck his cock. Men take very little prodding and don't even need the intention of flirting to get turned on. All they need is a nudge, or a breath, not even a wink.

Sexual compulsion may lead to philandering, but that is not necessarily seen as bad. The thing about sexual compulsion is that you can never tell which is the lesser evil: the compulsion or the lover himself[512]. A true compulsive will find the compulsion to be the lesser evil.

The only truth about compulsion is lies, and those lies start with the rationalizations you make to yourself. Lying to others might just be the result of lying to yourself, the result of desires motivating rationalizations.

The groundwork for a proclivity to your drug of choice is laid out nearly at birth. A family life steeped in denial is the perfect soil. In talking to similar people, I would say that a common thread for us is verbal abuse, sexual abuse, distrust of women, and/or genetics, all things that begin with the origin family.

---

[511] The problem with having too much sex is the inevitable result is that it takes forever to cum, so it's best to stick with existing lovers who are patient than to bore new ones. Also, for wimmin, a vagina once expanded may not contract to its original size.

[512] I think it's the compulsion.

Sex, more than any other addictive behavior, is intricately connected with verbal abuse and with abandonment, almost to the extent that you cannot have a conversation about one without the other. Since sex is tied to a life of receiving verbal abuse, it is intricately connected with shame because of name-calling statements that begin with "you are."[513]

However, the combination of the three are a lot harder to recover from than physical abuse and alcoholism, I think because internal boundaries regarding communication are harder to understand and set than external boundaries or mere abstinence.

A life lived in escapism is an indicator and a symptom. Self-gratification and selfishness outweigh the desire for intimacy, as a motivator though intimacy is what we truly seek if we are all part of God and God is love.

I rationalized my desire for self-gratification as being the same as a desire for intimacy. I had sex as a shortcut to making friends. As an introvert who was often taken advantage of, I didn't know how to make, keep, or be a friend, so I took advantage of others' sex drives because it was what I knew. But in the end I realized that they didn't really love me[514], and I wasn't really that pretty.

Even that was not necessarily good. The problem with distrusting the ulterior motives of men is that it significantly reduces the woman's teachability, or ability to gain wisdom through discussion.

Compulsion means that what you consciously seek gets in the way of what you unconsciously seek. Or, in other words, the ego binds you in a web of illusions that are too good to be true. Anything that can result in withdrawal is probably an illusion.

As much as I dug myself a hole, I was the answer to my own prayers. Only pain at the right time was enough to get me out of the game.

Pregnancy Scare: Who Do You Listen To?

Anger Stage of Grief

Why am I repeating bad behaviors? Why can't I complete recovery? Why can't I have a nice relationship with nothing to worry about? Why can't I get my act together? Why am I repeating the same mistakes? Why am I caught in Groundhog Day over several lifetimes? Why is my life getting out of control? GODDAMMIT! I want to be healthy! I want to be in a healthy relationship!

---

[513] The Landmark Forum calls this a "superstition," or "is-ing people."

[514] Older i.P. audAx: Okay, I admit that some did, but I could only find that out by taking a break from them.

AudAx

Codependency

What Is Codependency?:

My 2012 Definition:

A compulsion with people and things in a way that takes normal behaviors to an extreme, such as the following:

- Compulsive giving
- Compulsive loving
- Compulsive resentment

Why Revisit Codependency?:

- Fear of having an STD
- Overwhelment with email inbox
- Struggle with finances
- Struggle with fidelity
- Struggle with having attractive, healthy people
- To be as healthy as possible if willing to pursue a relationship with another codependent[515]
- To be more discerning about marriage prospects
- To learn to trust feelings and judgment
- To stop attracting busyness

Lingering Sings of Codependency:

- Alternating between being super responsible and super irresponsible[516]
- Difficulty in completing projects (to-do lists)[517]
- Difficulty in having fun[518]

---

[515] Older i.P. audAx: This sentence does not make sense to me at this stage because it wouldn't even be something I'd consider.

[516] Older i.P. audAx: This one is still an issue, but I think everyone struggles with adulting.

[517] Older i.P. audAx: Hm, I didn't realize I had an issue with this previously.

[518] I find it to be more unnatural to be happy all the time. It "feels better" not to force myself to be happy. Feeling good when I don't feel good doesn't feel good.

- Feelings of being different

- Having a best friend who is a codependent

- Lack of self-confidence in making financial and romantic decisions

- Occasional nailbiting (what precipitated self-cutting)

- Reacting

How to "Heal" Codependency:

The only way to "heal" codependency is by putting up boundaries (not walls), not through self-love. The term "self-love" is deceiving for it expresses itself via boundaries (actions), not via feelings[519].

Codependency Is Not Bad:

- *Gift of the Magi*

- Magnificent obsession

- Superpower:

  o It's "bad" when you can't control it and that causes shame

  o To whom much is given, much is expected

- You can't be a poet without angst

Are All Pop Singers Codependent?

Yes, I believe so. We already know that one would be hard-pressed to find a musician who didn't use drugs (addiction=>codependent). We've all heard stories of musicians who cross boundaries. And the love songs they sing or write are representative of their hearts (love addiction=>codependent).

Summary of Emotional Health Assessment Results:

Recovering codependent with higher than average anger who can improve.

---

[519] However, it can be argued that love is a verb, but not everyone will agree even if it sounds good.

275

AudAx

Codependent and Sexually Compulsive Events: My History and Timeline (First Step)[520]

"Before Birth: Past lives as a priestess and geisha (or kisaeng); others lives were mostly on the fringes of society and/or I was single during many of them

9/17/83: Received trauma via the primal wound theory

1983-Present: Raised by conservative persecutor dry drunk and rescuer[521]

- Suppressed anger for 21-23 years[522]

Age 0-5?: Inappropriate kissing from mother

Elementary School

1988-1997: Acquired ten bullies; see 1997-2001

Age 5-15: Felt ugly due to interracial adoption and verbal abuse; had 10 bullies to whom I felt attracted; never had a sexual conversation with Dad

Age 6: I was new to my first grade class

High School

1997-2001: Mainly befriended outcasts and friendless people

- Friendless autistic girl who I have blocked from Facebook
- Romantically unlucky girl
- Foster child

---

[520] I think having an obsessive personality is more related to sexual compulsion than having an addictive personality. Have an obsessive personality can extend to new hobbies or even worry. Even as a child, I had an obsessive personality; I would obsess about a new hobby for at least a month then move onto the next hobby.

[521] A family that has verbal abuse is a family that has sexually addictive behavior, even if it skips a generation. I didn't even learn about the sexually addictive part of my family until I was in my 30s because all the skeletons had been kept in the closet and denied. A person cannot be a sexual compulsive if they haven't been abandoned in some way. It was this rampant childhood abandonment that I didn't discover until I hired a genealogist. (However, I was well aware of the rampant serial marriages, but I found there were even more in indirect branches.) A sexual compulsive is likely suicidal at some point when reminded about family curses.

[522] Older i.P. audAx: This is a longer time than I had to get double shots for seasonal allergies.

- Homeless teen

- Homosexuals

- Goths (incl. a bipolar girl)

1997-2001: Only "enemy" told me she hated me because I was "perfect"

Age 14: Learned how to masturbate and learned how to get past porn blockers; masturbated daily

Age 16: Had phone sex with a freshman.

Age 17: Made a promise with God that he would find me a husband my freshman year of college.

Excerpts from my diary:

- "Today I received a letter of acceptance from MWU, but for some reason I was depressed. I don't know what came over me, but I felt like crying. It was so strong an emotion I could feel my eyes watering up. I tried not to let anyone notice, by keeping quiet and turning my eyes away to my food or drink or something. *One day I will find a heaven here on earth in one person.* Oh God! Oh God! I tired consoling myself by telling myself I am not alone I am not alone I am not alone. I refused dessert and headed upstairs [...]. What if I cried at school? My thoughts were flooded with horror. Never ever ever every [sic] ever cry at school [sic] you will never hear the end of it and who knows what else? Oh God! GOD!"

- "Sex compared with portions of life [sic]

    - Anticipation: Internal butterflies in stomach (may continue even during process)

    - Excitement (Climax): Hot burning sensation

    - Releasing (Resolution): Soothing thick liquid

    - Exhaustion: tiredness of muscles, need of sleep to rejuvenize"

- "Since we already have this inborn proclivity towards sin [sic] sex could be a device used to satisy [sic] our sinful urgings yet healthily [sic] keep us from harm. Even daydreams, if not acted on, healthily [sic] keep our desires sinful enough to not be sin unless abused."

- "If you can understand the concept presented in Brave New World [sic] about conditioning[,] you can understand how people's minds function. Once [sic] might think his ideas are ludicrous, but it is only because of the strange words and habits. But this is really how it is. We are conditioned to either be stupid or lonely. Freud, Huxman [sic], and polyamory have a certain idea that is not far off. Instead of loving one and despising any show of love to anyone else because it is socially wrong, [i]t would be better, I think to love all but only have the act of sex with one who you will live with for the rest of your life and who will be the father of your child."

AudAx

- "I know I will find the perfect husband who I will love (even if I'm married to him one day before one of us dies) because I tell God my wishes (prayers) each day and I know that if you ask without ceasing, that eventually you will get your wish, even if you ask all your life and then you die, you will get your wish even if you are dead."

College (2001-2007)

2001 (Age 17): Lost virginity to a sex addict (or rather, I initiated against his will and essentially coercively raped him) and was about to marry him.

2001-2005 (Age 17-21): Dated two sex addicts simultaneously plus two others at any given time. One was sexually abused by his sisters and had about 100 siblings due to his father's sex addiction. The other was 7 years older and more experienced and used a condom. The second sex addict had far over a hundred sexual relations, but with a condom. Both may have had 100+ partners when I started dated them. In addition, I always had four boyfriends at a time; I had two open slots for other partners who rotated. Promise with God would have made my husband one of the two sex addicts, but it didn't work out with either. Without them I never would have known about my codependency. I worked from a fear of being infertile.

2001-2007: Mainly befriended and had sex with outcasts and friendless people

- Socially inept friendless virgin
- Deaf girl (only close female friend; the most sane)
- Angry Goth penpal

2001-2007: Only "enemy" told me she hated me because I wanted to be loved

2001-2013 (Age 17-29): Average 4-5 sexual partners per year

2003 (Age 19): Started dating a monogamous man[523].

2004 (Age 20): Ended two 4-year sex addict relationships[524].

2004-2008: Dated [a] (mostly) monogamous unemployed narcissist[525]/sex offender/ex-convict

- *Became a self-cutter*

---

[523] Older i.P. audAx: I italicized the parts that involved my longest total relationship.

[524] Older i.P. audAx: I was pretty sure that I told my monogamous ex that I was already in two relationships, but by 2017 all of that had been forgotten.

[525] Questionable

- *Brief bulimia and inappropriate kissing (2005-2007)*

- *Had anger management issues, starting in 2005 or 2007*

- *Still keeps as a friend*[526]

- *Was promiscuous three times (once with friendless virgin)*

<u>Young Adulthood</u>

2005-2008 (Age 21-25):

- *[H]ad an emotionally abusive relationship with a jealous man who wanted me to get rid of my friends with benefits*

- *I had sex with his friend and former roommate because I had gotten addicted to sleeping with him*[527]

- *I learned to associate monogamy with dysfunctional love and addicted relationships*

2007 (Age 24): Started working in a male-dominated field (only female with male engineers)[528][.]

2008 (Age 25): Ended a relationship with a jealous man who emotionally abused me. I would not tolerate him telling me to get rid of my friends, who also happen to be my sexual supply and ex-lovers. I would consider sex with 22 of them. I have had 48 lovers in my life. I'm friends with 26 of them on Facebook. I ended up associating monogamy with abuse and love addiction. I found nonmonogamy to be safer. Sex addicts were the only people I didn't feel codependent on. During the relationship I had sexual encounters with two men and a romantic encounter with another. This brings the count to six people I had sex with while being in a monogamous relationship.

2008: Started publishing poetry about past relationships[.]

2008: [F]lirted with going to Anonymous groups in 2008 and 2012 but didn't get serious until 2016.

2008-2011 (Age 25-27): Dated a commitment phobe/ex-convict and had counseling. I dated someone I wanted to be monogamous with because he accepted that I was not, but he tried to get me to date others against my will[529][.] [In addition, the following occurred:]

- [I] [s]truggled with overvolunteering

---

[526] Older i.P. audAx: Not anymore.

[527] Older i.P. audAx: I didn't know that he went to court when he was not around because I didn't know he was a sex offender.

[528] Ended up even more comfortable with men

[529] Older i.P. audAx: Later, in 2016 or 2017, Chocolate Candy said that I just didn't give men what they wanted.

- [I] was overworked/harassed by two female bosses (did not feel comfortable with women)

2008-2012: Struggled with impulsive spending[.]

2009 (Age 26): I allow my last ex into my apartment and he rapes me. I stopped believing in cohabitation.

2010 (Age 27): [E]nded a relationship with a commitment-phobe (some sex addicts are this way)[530].

- Could see myself as monogamous with him but he didn't want me to be and pushed me to date others, so I raped myself, using others as props. I practically raped myself by meeting people on a dating site and having sex with them; it made me feel nauseated (when I didn't want to [have sex])

- I stalked him

- [I] [s]till keep [him] as a friend

Late 2010: Gave $1K to a [different] codependent dealing with an ex-narcissist

2010: Gained an angry adoptee penpal

Spring 2011: Communicates with ex-heroin addict/convict

10/2011: Dated an illegal immigrant alcoholic briefly

- Still keeps as a friend

Early 2012 (Age 29): Returned to first sex addict (partially to avoid the dating game and partially to satisfy parents). I dated him again at age 29 but did not feel sexually aroused. He had two girlfriends, and I had two boyfriends (including him). My other boyfriend had a girlfriend.

4/2012: Started a relationship coaching business for Goths

5/2012: Gave ~$5K to [a] fraudster and invested $500 without due diligence

[6/]2012: I break up with the original sex addict boyfriend after June.

6/2012: Dated [a] codependent with narcissist mother

[11/]2012 (Age 29): [H]ad a pregnancy scare.

---

[530] Older i.P. audAx: He actually broke up with me after showing me all the places that was important to him.

12/2012: Compulsive buying and gambling addiction; sex addiction

[12/]2012 (Age 29): [B]reak[s] up with the other boyfriend because he was too codependent, like me. I took a sex addicts anonymous test and did not test as positive because I don't feel guilt. After finding out that my ex was a severe codependent, and while putting us on a break, I had three one-night stands in a row to get rid of the pain […] prior to the dating site[.] I posted a profile […] after [the] breakup stating I was specifically seeking an open marriage (which I consider normal among my swinger friends). My parents encourage dating around and not putting all my eggs in one basket. They buy me a subscription to Match.com, and I feel that I should use it since they paid money for it.

[12/18/]2012 (Age 29): The first guy who responds has sex with me on the second date. He admits to being a [sapiosexual] commitment phobe who catches/releases. I say it's okay, but then say something sexual afterwards. He pins me down with insatiable urge, and I ask him to put on a condom three times. He ignores me. I end up with a sore perineum and get tested for herpes.

[12/27]2012 (Age 29): [M]eet[s] the man of my dreams[531], but disclose about the herpes scare, which happens to be his dealbreaker. He breaks up with me in the New Year.

[3/]2016 (Age 32): [G]ave my boyfriend (a previous ex) a chance to try non-monogamy, but he cheated instead. The bottom line regarding non-monogamy is boundaries and trust. Without those two, even the desire for non-monogamy will result in disaster. This is the impetus for starting my journey with the recovery movement.

[6/]2016 (Age 32): In order to realize I had a problem, I had to remember all the people I forgot I had sex with while being in a seemingly committed relationship.

[11/]2017-[1/]2018 (Age 34): Closed the chapter on trying to get back together with the same man. He breaks up with me in the New Year via ghosting.

Summary: My longest relationships were dysfunctional, but they were all <u>wonderful</u> people, and I'm thankful they were in my life."

Patterns and Characteristics of My Codependent Relationship in 2012[532]

My Denial Patterns

- I have difficulty identifying what I am feeling.
- I can take care of myself without any help from others.

---

[531] Older i.P. audAx: Really? I think not.

[532] Source: Co-Dependents Anonymous

AudAx

- I do not recognize the unavailability of those people to whom I am attracted.

His Denial Patterns

- I minimize, alter, or deny how I truly feel.
- I perceive myself as completely unselfish and dedicated to the well-being of others.
- I mask my pain in various ways such as anger, humor, or isolation.
- I express negativity or aggression in indirect and passive ways.

My Low Self-Esteem Patterns

- I have difficulty making decisions.
- I constantly seek recognition that I think I deserve.
- I perceive myself as superior to others.
- I look to others to provide my sense of safety.
- I have difficulty getting started and completing projects.
- I have trouble setting healthy priorities.

His Low Self-Esteem Patterns

- I look to others to provide my sense of safety.
- I have difficulty getting started, meeting deadlines, and completing projects.

My Compliance Patterns

- I remain in harmful situations too long.
- I put aside my own interests in order to do what others want.
- I am hypervigilant regarding the feelings of others and take on those feelings.
- I am afraid to express my beliefs, opinions, and feelings when they differ from those of others, but can express them under other names.
- I accept sexual attention when I want love.
- I make decisions without regard to the consequences.
- I give up my truth to gain the approval of others.

His Compliance Patterns

- I am extremely loyal, remaining in harmful situations too long.

- I am hypervigilant regarding the feelings of others and take on those feelings.

- I make decisions without regard to the consequences.

My Control Patterns

- I freely offer advice and direction to others without being asked.

- I become resentful when others decline my help or reject my advice.

- I lavish gifts and favors on those I want to influence.

- I use sexual attention to gain approval and acceptance.

- I use charm and charisma to convince others of my capacity to be caring and compassionate.

- I pretend to agree with others to get what I want.

His Control Patterns

- I attempt to convince others what to think, do, or feel.

- I adopt an attitude of indifference, helplessness, authority, or rage to manipulate outcomes.

- I use terms of recovery in an attempt to control the behavior of others.

My Avoidance Patterns

- I use indirect and evasive communication to avoid conflict or confrontation.

His Avoidance Patterns

- I allow my addictions to people, places, and things to distract me from achieving intimacy in relationships.

Fear

What Is Fear?

- It alerts one to red warning flags or true danger

- It can be fun in entertainment form

- It can be illogical

AudAx

- It can be overcome with neurolinguistic programming
- It can override another fear
- It causes you to manifest what you don't want
- It doesn't really exist
- It is rooted in the past
- It motivates

I'm Afraid of the Following

- American economy and what that will mean for a first-time mother
- Attracting drama to my life, which indicates that codependency is still an issue
- Being a responsible parent to a dependent child
- Being controlled and manipulated even if by well-meaning intentions
- Being judged, rejected, and abandoned by family and friends
- Being perceived as crazy[533], especially if perception is reality
- Being vulnerable emotionally and financially
- Current physical stress (neck pain and TMJ) from all the fear of uncertainty
- Dreamstealers
- Enmeshment and entanglement
- Fears my father will implant in me
- Feeling the weight of things left undone
- Financial pressure
- Getting on this rollercoaster
- Having a breakdown due to stress
- Living off faith alone
- Manifesting negative events even while trying to focus on my motivations
- Miscarriage or birth complications
- My parents' poor health, [resulting in the feeling[that I may be left alone without family or friends (since current friends are acquaintances)

---

[533] Older i.P. audAx: It is as common for a man to call a woman "crazy" as it is for a womyn to call a man a "narcissist."

- Never starting a business or getting a business of the ground or never profiting in a business

- Not having a completely healthy anger management system in place

- Physical results of pregnancy on my body

- Potential consequences of a codependent relationship, such as job loss, homicide, or suicide

- Relying on family and friends because I see it as being enabled and not being able to learn from the consequences of my actions

- Repeating the past I had when I cohabited

- Small print and interest rates

- That in disclosing my fears I will create fears and worry in others

- That someone will find out that I don't work very hard in the office

- Uncertainty, even though the mix of certainty and uncertainty plus the motivation of love and fear is what it takes to succeed

What Is Courage

Courage is having faith despite fear of uncertainties.

Friendship

I don't understand why people hate the "let's be friends" conversation because a friend is someone you can call in the middle of the night or is someone who will take care of you when you're in a car accident or will tell you when you have something in your teeth. Also, with some people, friends are friends with benefits. So, how is that a downgrade? Considering the rate of divorce and how difficult it is to live with someone the first year, I'd consider that an upgrade[534]. It's certainly a lot less stressful but no less intimate. Now, if people had the "let's be acquaintances" conversation or "let's be in each other's network" conversation or "let's keep our relationship to Facebook" conversation, I would understand why someone would be upset, but no one ever says that.

Goals

Main Goal

Control my behavioral addictions this year. In a nutshell, be healthy in every way.

---

[534] Older i.P. audAx: I don't agree with this anymore. It really depends if there really are benefits or if it's a title with a bunch of fluff.

AudAx

Questions[535]

What would I like to have happen next month? Introspection into how codependency has affected us.

What would I like to accomplish next month? Read at least one book about codependent couples.

What good would I like to attract? Sanity and sane, stable people.

What areas of growth would I like? Financial growth and the ability to communicate.

What blocks would I like removed? Inability to sell.

What would I like to attain? A healthy marriage.

Where would I like to go this year? Nowhere this calendar year.

What would I like to have happen in friendship and love? Find someone I can call a true friend.

What would I like to have happen in my family life? Closeness with my dad and possibly do some fun activities.

What problems would I like to see solved? How to reconcile our codependency traits over the long term.

What decisions would I like to make? I would like to decide if I should keep my boyfriend.

What would I like to happen in my career? More interesting things at the same pace.

What would I like to see happen inside and around me? Better honesty with myself

Goals for Continued Recovery:

- Appropriate disclosure
- Appropriate nutrition
- Communicating clearly, directly, and honesty
- Dry hair
- Gratitude
- Having fun during leisure activities

---

[535] Older i.P. audAx: I am surprised that in 2018, the answers to these questions are mostly the same.

- Logical/pragmatic thinking
- Make bed
- Reasonable expectations of self and others
- Responsible financial decisions
- Wear makeup/jewelry

Healthy Assumptions

- Accept help/delegate when overwhelmed
- Arguing for the sake of arguing is not active listening
- Be self-sufficient when underwhelmed
- Everyone does the best they can with the information they have available
- Everyone is a part of God
- Everyone wants to love and be loved
- Focus on what you want, but do not be afraid of fear
- Give to those who give and take from those who take
- Have an objective (act, do not react)
- Search for the intention, meaning, visual, or feeling
- Understand differing word definitions by their synonyms
- We are equal, and we both have valid beliefs
- When something isn't working, do the opposite of what you normally would (Kabbalah)

List of My Addictive or Obsessive Behaviors

- Biting my nails
- Debting
- Gambling
- Love
- People
- People who are Projects
- Projects
- Self-cutting (in the past)

AudAx

- Sex (meaning I don't enforce discipline)
- Shopping
- Sugar
- Work

Note: According to my DNA, I am genetically inclined toward heroin and must avoid it at all costs.

Messages to Tom Hellen After 12/15/2012

- Chill!
- If you want me, you need to help me fulfill my life's purpose.
- I will date you if one or more of these conditions have been met (I will marry you if all three have been met):
  1. Break up with Cherie out of your own desire to be emotionally well (but you are free to date anyone else).
  2. Disclose that your reaction to my physical status (possible pregnancy) does not result in increased love addiction
  3. Score well on the emotional health assessment.
- Otherwise, we will joint parent without cohabitation.
- Just because you feel good about something or someone doesn't mean that's the end result you are seeking; it might just be a stepping stone to get what you want.
- Right now I need a confidante and neither a friend nor a lover.
- True love doesn't feel like heroin.
- We are *created* to *create*. If we are not creating, we are not productive and happy.
- What are you willing to *sacrifice* and give up? Without this you will never be successful, but I know where you're coming from. Seek always to be in a win-win situation.
- You don't want a woman who loves you; you want to feel loved. BIG DIFFERENCE.

Statistics

Fifty to eighty percent of counselors have not addressed their own codependency issues. (I have no idea where I got this statistic.)

Strengths and Weaknesses

Strengths	Weaknesses
Ability to manifest food and sex	Ability to manifest money
Ability to reveal what's hidden	Accounting
Appearing to listen	Asserting/expressing/conveying
Beautiful	Anger
Beginnings/focus on origins	Befriending women
Caring	Black and white extremes
Compassion	Bringing the inside out
Creativity	Cooking
Cuteness	Complaining
Darkness	Compulsions/impulsiveness with money and food
Devotion	Diet and nutrition
Efficiency	Discernment
Etymology	Enabling
Existentialism	Exercise and physical fitness
Focus on freedom	Expressiveness
Grammar (editing/writing)	Gullibility/naïveté
Honesty AND Secrecy	Knowledge of legal or political system
Idealism	Leading myself
Imagination	Listening
Individuality	Listening to the right people
Initiative	Making people laugh
Intellect	Marketing/advertising
Introspection/"reflection" (seeing myself)	Nagging

AudAx

Strengths	Weaknesses
Knowing social expectations	Not smiling
Language	Physics
Love of art	Putting up boundaries
Love of learning	Reading body language and other cues
Love of reading	Science
Metaphors	Setting priorities/priority management
Networking	Teaching the wrong people
Nudity	Wanting to be right
Openmindedness	
Playing with dogs	
Poetry	
Sex	
Social skills	
Spirituality	
Study habits	
Varied interests	
Visionary	
Visual learning	
Work ethic	
Working with men	

Spending Habits

- Attraction to filling out forms and pressing buttons
- Complete weakness in face of smooth-talking salesmen
- Compulsive with "free" food and other things
- Concerned about affording Christmas gifts

- Enabled by mother

- Not able to afford rent at one time

- Not able to prioritize to-do lists

- Past tendency to hoard things I never used (nailpolish, rocks, jewelry, and makeup)

- Thousands of dollars have been spent on "get rich quick" schemes in order to spend more money on others

- Took advantage of getting free rides

- Unlike sex, spending is not connected to my life's purpose

Compulsive Spending Test

Valence Compulsive Buying Scale: Since my score was 37, I am likely to be a compulsive buyer.

Richmond Compulsive Buying Scale: Since my score was 25, I need help.

What I Am Willing to Do[536]

- I will consider a long engagement but will not consider a quick elopement

- I will consider an open marriage but will not consider a closed marriage

- I will consider moving to California, but will not consider cohabitation without marriage

Why I [A]m Thankful for the Break

- It allowed me to examine my life and see how well I was doing with "recovery"[537]

- It allowed me to see how important sex was to my life and helped me prioritize core beliefs

- It gave me a chance to consider why I would want to be in a relationship and also understand potential strengths and weaknesses in such a relationship

- It gave me a chance to really identify what I'm feeling emotionally and physically.

- It gave me a chance to take a step back from my businesses and realize that "it's all small stuff" when compared to war.

---

[536] Older i.P. audAx: This has all changed.

[537] Older i.P. audAx: I put "recovery" in quotes because it begs the question, "What are you recovering?" Most people in recovery do not want to revert back to an older time, but would rather look toward a positive future.

AudAx

- It gave me an opportunity to realize the need to acknowledge the past and transform the relationship with my family to one of greater trust, honesty, and disclosure.

- It gave me the opportunity and time to realize that I wanted a child after all (even though it's sort of unrelated)

- It shed light on my spending habits and allowed me to acknowledge my compulsive spending

- On the surface, it might seem as if I stopped all productivity, but in reality this has been the most productive time in my life because I'm focusing on what really matters.

Random Notes After Pregnancy Scare (2012)

- "If you're not growing, you're dying," [quote by Lou Holtz].

- It's okay if people don't agree with me; it doesn't mean they don't like me. It's okay to give opposing viewpoints; it shows people where you stand and who you are.

- Give people a chance to learn and show openmindedness

- Korean adoptees are in a soul group. When I heal, I help all adoptees heal.

- Lying about myself to be liked is manipulative and shows that I'm unreliable and untrustworthy.

Pregnancy Scare: Finding the How

About Terry[538]

- He gives a quote out of context and claims that it is credible because it comes from a wise man. The Bible came from wise men, but even the Bible can be used for manipulation.

- He said he finished a book in two weeks that's not a book one can finish in two weeks; it's a book that takes a lifetime to finish.

- He says that he gets mad when affection is taken away from him.

- He sees "codependent" as a bad word and will not associate himself with such a term, meaning he is still in denial.

- He surrounds himself with people who are obsessed with money and may be codependents themselves.

---

[538] Older i.P. audAx: Ironically, Patton thought this man was the best man I'd dated, years later in 2016. Read through the rest of this section and draw your own conclusions.

- I felt that he was controlling my thoughts and feelings when my thoughts and feelings differed from his.

- If his intention was to warn me about worry, that is good. But if he tries to warn me about analysis, that would go against my star nature. We do not see eye to eye.

- I will not marry a liar.

About His Girlfriend, Chou[539]

- He cannot relate to her parents' passing and the mourning she must go through. He may even be prolonging her mourning by telling her not to mourn.

- He says he keeps her because he would feel guilty for making her fears come true, and he hopes she'll change. This is classic codependency.

- She doesn't trust him, as she shouldn't. He has been lying to her ever since we had sex.

- She is not as interested in sex but wants to see him every month, talks to him every day, and they are connected on Facebook. This does not look like I am the primary relationship.

- She said he's the reason for all her issues. That could be true to some extent if he enabled her, which he has.

- She told him he talks too much. Yes, he does. He's not that teachable.

- There is a possibility that she gave him an STD.

Addictive Behavior with Money (Mostly Mine)

"Money is probably our single most powerful *nurturance* symbol."—Unknown (emphasis added)

- $6K no longer seems expensive to me; I just can't afford it

- Even with a large increase in salary, I am still concerned about making ends meet

- His addiction is rooted in his mother's hoarding and kleptomaniacy

- I go to all the self-development seminars, which always have plugs to buy expensive stuff, which I do

- I have no savings

- I will never have a joint account: this will protect me from overspending for someone else and will protect me from overspending someone else's money

---

[539] Terry, as long as you stay in a relationship that has lived past its usefulness because you think she can be changed/fixed, then you also must think that I can be changed/fixed. This means you do not and cannot love me the way I am.

AudAx

- Money has two basic elements: discipline and nurturance, but I do not have the discipline and focus with money and sex (maybe with relationships if I can break up)

- We are both "job whores."

Adult Child of a Narcissist[540]

"If you don't want to slip, don't go where it's slippery."—Unknown

- Acted as the parent to his mother

- Considered homicide

- Desire to be right

- Does not like the words "sacrifice," "forgiveness," "creation," "philosophy," and "newness"

- Does not understand the purpose of negative emotions

- Felt he must be artistic to survive with his mother

- Felt love was in short supply

- Felt powerfully "depressed" when viewing an addict

- Like me, felt that he had to be nothing in comparison with his parents

- Like my father, his mother is sensitive to criticism

- Rejected by his mother for not being like her

- Prefers intellectual sparring

- Said he was surrounded by drama (psychologically crazy people)

- Said his parents' job is to be critical

- Says exes consider him a talkative love addict

- Says he is very compliant

- Says it serves him to do the opposite of what his mother says

- Thumbs his nose at societal restraints

- Wants "money" (status?)

- Wants me to conform to his thinking like with his mother (devoid from reality/intrusive)

---

[540] Other related thoughts:

- I do not want his mother as my mother-in-law, and I do NOT want the mafia stalking me.

- I will try with him again if he can break up with his girlfriend. Otherwise, I'd be in over my head.

- Wants no boundaries
- Wants to be set free
- Was a loner in high school

Automatic Writing (Spirit Unknown)

How is he feeling? Dismayed, disillusioned, disdained

Is he going to work on his codependency issue? Only time will tell.

What will help us get through this time? Patience, patience, and more patience. Patience without action.

Does he know that I care for him? That is a good way of putting it. He knows on one surface and not on the other.

Can you send a message to him? Sure, what can I send?

A feeling of comfort and knowing that everything will be okay. Can do. Do you want fries with that? Are you willing to give up one chief aim for another?

I think yes. It may depend largely on what gives results. "He that will lose his life will gain it. He who seeks to keep his life will lose it."

Wait. Before you go…where would I go if I'm everywhere you are? How may I help you? Am I up to the task? Certain things will have to go certain ways.

Chill!

- Don't be the thought police
- Honesty over politeness

His Signs of Codependency

- Being a nurturing caretaking
- Being told he's a love addict
- Being told he talks too much
- Getting calls to help others and solve their problems
- Giving money

AudAx

- Having a narcissistic mother
- Having anger issues
- Holding onto a relationship that's not working with the belief that it can still be fixed
- Identifying himself as someone who fixes things
- Nagging
- Overworking
- Tendency to counsel/coach and give unsolicited advice
- Thinking that he knows best
- Wanting to be right
- Willing to stay in a relationship when it become unhealthy

Letter to Terry

Terry,

Are you man enough to be my man? Can you handle being with an alpha female? Are you willing to do the opposite of what you have done while feeling out how to communicate and relate in a healthy relationship? Failure can mean death to society since I am giving society a new language, culture, fashion, food, religious text, etc. My last boyfriend was willing to be the king of my new country but did not have the spiritual enlightenment to anchor him. Do you have what it takes to be married to a philosopher queen? Do you have what it takes to bring darkness to light? Control over my thoughts and feelings means that you are trying to change that which is for the good of society, that you are trying to change that which you do not understand. Are you willing to say that you do not know what you do not know? I am willing to do that for you and for me. Engulfment, smothering, control is the death of 98 lives that have culminated into this one life. Lack of control over your own actions and decisions can murder the lives leading all the way back to Atlantis. When you attempt to make my past lives and star constellation into yours you have altered the future and the fate of the world. Every person I had sex with touched my life, and I touched theirs, and we remain connected through quantum entanglement. Do you want to be my poison or do you want to be my prince?

Logic for Being with Him

I am/was codependent. Most relationships I attract (romantic or platonic) involve someone with a serious issue. If a relationship does not have a serious issue, I would find that person to be stale and boring. I have tried to choose stale and boring (low attraction) but have found I would rather have high attraction instead.

His issue is severe/extreme and could be a challenge. However, he haas all the traits I wanted: a teacher, someone who can handle my wattage, flexible, a spiritual guru, an intellectual, a good dancer, a good cook. The challenge is not the least of the evils, but it is one I understand fully and live with every day. However, it will force me to force myself and my own hypocrisies at times, and it will cause him to face himself and his mother.

Worst Case Scenario: Complete overhaul of entire belief system, death, insanity, loss of job, proximity to a narcissist, sacrifice, unlimited cost, unlimited time

Best Case Scenario: Perfect, permanent, honest marriage

The risk is high, but the benefits are great. Knowing my attraction to danger, I will probably choose the risk, whether or not is is wise to do so because now I find commitment phobia to be worse and not the sign of a successful person.

Love Obsessed Triad/Wizard of Oz Analogy

"Parasol means 'for heat.' Put away the parasol if you don't want a heated argument."
—Me

"Give to those who give and take from those who take."
—Me

"Just because someone does something loving does not mean they are and vice versa."
—Me

Codependent (Tinman)	Narcissist (Scarecrow)	Commitment Phobe (Cowardly Lion)
Wants a heart	Wants a brain	Wants courage
Lover	Attention-getter	Self-protective
Anger	Sadness	Fear
Only you can love yourself	Only you can admire yourself	Only you can assure yourself
Gullible and overwhelmed	Entitled	Unfaithful
Organized	Videogamer	Likes old stuff
Busy	Lazy	Unreliable
Chameleon	Physically Sick Human	Horse

Codependent (Tinman)	Narcissist (Scarecrow)	Commitment Phobe (Cowardly Lion)
Beaver	Monkey	Bird
Rich	Rich or Poor	Poor
Neglected as a child	Too much attention as a child	Felt betrayed as a child
Giver	Taker	Taker and giver
Fear of being controlled	Fear of abandonment	Fear of entrapment
Clingy	Clingy	Withdrawn
Partners are unsuccessful	Partners may or may not seem successful	Partners seem successful
Demands proof of love	Demands entertainment	Demands space
Overly responsible	Neglectful	Not willing to take responsibility
Rescuer/martyr	Victim	Persecutor
Liable to be clean cut or abuse drugs	Liable to abuse drugs	Liable to abuse drugs
Coach/counselor	Star	Varied resume
Wants to mother	Wants a mother	Wants a father
Abused/used	Abusive/user	Ambivalent
Fixer	Broken	Broken
Enabler	Enabled	Enabled
Can be a narcissist/ commitment phobe	Can be codependent/ commitment phobe	Can be a narcissist/ codependent
Difficult to communicate with	Emotional abuse	Mixed messages
Passive	Aggressive	Avoidance
Tidy living space	Messy living space	Empty living space
Worries about others	Worries about appearance	Worries about freedom

Codependent (Tinman)	Narcissist (Scarecrow)	Commitment Phobe (Cowardly Lion)
Critical	Manipulator	Perfectionist
Desire to be right	Desire to be cared for	Desire to be safe
People pleaser	Likes having an audience	Likes being anonymous
Sacrifices for others	Demands sacrifices	Will not sacrifice
Self-sufficient	Self-entertained	Selfish
Avoids praise	Wants praise	Gives praise
Avoids delegating	Loves to delegate	Is delegated to
Audience	Performer	Behind the stage
Alternates between independent and dependent	Dependent	Independent
Selfless	Egotistical/Selfish	Shameful/Guilty
Hard on from giving (oral)	Hard on from receiving	Hard on from thinking about sex
Prefers missionary/catcher position	Prefers pitcher position	Prefers receiving oral
Shopaholic, sex addict, sugar daddy, cutter, etc.	Kleptomaniac, prescription pill addict	Claustrophobic
Dates more attractive	Dates less attractive	Dates more successful
Nagger	Blamer	Whiner

All are controlling/manipulative, addicted to love, afraid of intimacy, and tries to change a person with charm to suit them.

Our Family Trees and Past Relationships

His Family and Past Relationships:

- Past relationship with a drug-addicted circus girl
- Son of a divorced narcissist who is the daughter of a narcissist and alcoholic codependent

My Past Relationships:

AudAx

- Alcoholic ex and grandfather
- Commitment phobe
- Narcissist[541]
- Sex abuse survivor and codependent sex addict
- Sex addict

Note: I never tried to change sex addicts, making relationships with them the only relationships that "worked" and were strangely less intense than relationships in which I tried to change someone.

Our Similarities

- Black and white thinking
- Compliance due to perceived conditional love
- Desire for authenticity sprung from repression
- Desire to be right
- Desire to give
- Difficulty believing we can be loved
- Distrust of wimmin
- "Dry drunk" parents who are sensitive to criticism
- Fixing things occupationally
- Gullibility
- Loss of what we could have had
- Parents whose personalities are very strong (very opinionated)
- Workaholism

Positive and Negative Signs

Positive Signs:

- He can embrace fear in a healthy way
- He can take self-help answers to codependency and apply them
- He may be perfect for someone else, but is he good for me?

---

[541] Questionable

300

- He seeks wisdom from people who have results

- He shows a willingness to listen (but is he teachable?)

- Surely, if he believes he's healthy, he'd have no issue with taking a test to see if he is or is not a codependent.

- Would he settle for a generic womyn?

Negative Signs:

- Breakup is scheduled for March 15th if he thinks he can make me be someone I'm not

- He feels anger when he does not get my love

- He is convinced that I'll always be in his life before I commit to it (DANGER=STALKER)[542]

- He is in denial (this is the most dangerous and insidious)

- He is probably still dating his girlfriend

- He is still assigning good and bad judgments with the words that come out of my mouth

- He sees "codependent" as a bad word and does not want to associate himself with it

- He talks past me

- He talks without listening

Potential Pitfalls

- He could be passive aggressive

- We will "feel good" about stupid decisions

- He will get frustrated at my inability to identify feelings

- He will hide an inability to feel loved behind obsession

- He will pretend to be okay with my promiscuity, sex drive, desire for alternative lifestyles and group sex, my BDSM hobby, and friendship with exes without expressing if he is truly jealous

- He will try to control my emotions and thoughts like his mother

- He will try to help me get rid of ego

- His communication could overpower mine

- The road to hell could be paved with good intentions

---

[542] He did in fact become a stalker after I broke up with him, after I wrote this.

AudAx

- We will get ideas from the good idea jar but will be on the journey to our destination longer than necessary

- We will not accept help

- We will stay past the time when we should break up and call it quits

Terry vs No Terry

Stay	Leave
Even if I break up with him, he could have a tendency to be persistent	Breaking up would show intelligence
I find "normal" people boring and have no sex drive for them	Can keep as a friend (perhaps)
I have to repeat my lessons over and over again until I learn them	He would end up with an addict, which is not good for a codependent
I know what I'm getting into	I am keeping my boundaries regarding sex if I do not put myself in a position where I will be pressured to be monogamous
I may always have an addiction to something. Maybe it would be good to mutate my shopping addiction to an addiction to someone who gives instead of takes.	I am protecting him from myself (since I could end up spending his money)
I need someone who can handle my "wattage"	I don't want to repeat past experiences.
Now we know how to relate to one another on an intimate level	If we married, I would have a narcissist for a mother-in-law
Taking the risk would show courage	I will have more time to give to society rather than to squelch all that time with one person
We don't know any other way to be and can keep being ourselves, as we see fit	Large potential to be a toxic relationship
When you heal your parents, you heal yourself	Staying would not make him feel secure; it would make him stressed

Stay	Leave
	We will enable each other
	We will overstep boundaries without knowing it

Summary: It still depends on his willingness to break up with his girlfriend, work on himself, etc.

Was It Unplanned?

Terry,

We have unprotected sex. Then you tell me you have a track record/history of getting girls pregnant by accident. This implies that your sperm is active, the women were not on birth control, you did not fully withdraw, you prematurely ejaculated, and/or you are good at manifesting pregnancies because you secretly want a child. You mentioned your dream of her acting as babysitter/guardian for my child. I'm not fond of someone who sounds/appears to be emotionally unstable watching over my child. However, it may be necessary due to our strange circumstances and logistics.

Codependents may be unintentionally or passively deceitful and manipulative. Did you want me to get pregnant? You are, after all, older and more desirous of settling down. You also mentioned finally being mature enough to be a father. And you rushed into talking about marriage.

Are Our Love Addictions Compatible?

Him	Me
If I just find The One, all my problems will disappear and life will be magical. She is the One. I will make her see that we are made for each other. (I will make her pregnant so she will feel like she cannot leave me.)	Monogamous relationships are dangerous. Having multiple partners is safer; the worst case scenario is not abuse, it's just infertility. However, infertility is good because it breaks the cycle of pain. Jealousy is the first sign of abuse, but cuckolding is fine. This is what I learned from the relationship I had with a narcissist.

AudAx

Summary: He will project his disgust of his mother onto me because eventually he will see our similarities (in terms of our attitude toward sex). He must forgive and accept his mother. In order to do so, he must know what forgiveness and acceptance is and is not.

Compromise

If you do not accept me the way I am, you will become one of my conquests and friends.

If you accept me the way I am, then I will introduce you to each of my male friends so that you can approve them and/or set up a test for them to pass. I will put them on speakerphone when it is appropriate (i.e., inside the house). We can also discuss what you feel comfortable with me doing with them. I am willing to reduce my sexual partners in order to reduce my chances of becoming infertile now that I realize my desire to have a child. If you want me to be more motivated, then I will require an explanation as to why monogamy is safe and secure in words that I can understand.

What I Want

- Ability to be comfortable with gray thinking

- Be at peace

- Calmness

- Care with words

- Equality

- Love independent of chemicals

- Loving the self

- Low maintenance

- Respect of boundaries

- Satisfaction

- Security

- Tough love when necessary

Why December 15ᵗʰ Return Date

- It gives me time to decide if I want to continue a relationship

  o It gives me time to change my mind again and again before needing to commit to a decision

- It gives me time to raise my vibration and believe in us again

- It gives me time to reflect and get over trauma

- It gives me time to schedule a gynecologist appointment before having sex again

- It gives me time to see how much I miss you

- It gives me time to take a break from everything, not just the relationship

- It gives me time to work on myself

- It gives us time to cool off

- It gives us time to experience solitude

- It gives us time to relax before getting into deep intense recovery

- It gives you time to make the right decisions

- It reminds me when to send out Christmas gifts

- It takes 40 days to change a habit

- It took that long for *me* to believe it could work and plan future trips. If he wants to be secure, does that mean he is insecure?

- It's not too long and not too short (it may be too short for recovery if anything)

- Not knowing what was in store, it also gave me the exact amount of time to focus on making money

Why Return?

- Need to learn my karmic lesson

- Believe you also want to learn how to have a healthy relationship too

- If I can have a healthy relationship with his mother, I can have a healthy relationship with anyone

- It's a test

- I have a codependent radar and am unable to date anyone who is not from a dysfunctional family of origin

- I am not sexually attracted to people from healthy families of origin

Random Notes About Relationship (2012)

- Black and white thinking can create enemies.

- Confusion leads to brainwashing, which leads to self-doubt, which leads to emotional abuse. Telling me to be happy when I'm upset is a form of emotional abuse.

- Consider the fact that I do not feel loved if I feel that someone is trying to change and/or control my thoughts and feelings.

- He started overgiving early on by fixing up his grandmother's place.

- His strengths: Frankness and ability to acknowledge feelings.

- If he can't stand up against her [his mother], he won't be able to stand up against me. If he can lie to her about me, what can he lie about to me?

- If he'll take anything, I can give him anything to take.

- Society tells men to be white knights, heroes, and Mr. Fix-Its.

- With him, I feel like I'm fighting for my life. Every time he takes away the meaning of my life, I have to restore it. I spend too much time redoing what he undoes. Why would I date an enemy?

- Question: How does judging my sex drive honor his dead ex's legacy?

- Question: If he tries to control my "negative" emotions like anger, what does he do to her [his girlfriend]? Is that keeping her in grief longer?

- Result: Overstepping his invisible boundaries and having less respect for him.

In Defense of Who I Am: Why Sex is Important and Why I Need to Be Careful

Executive Summary

If you ask me to be monogamous with you, as you would do if you were healthy, then I would resent you forever. But if you tell me that you accept me the way I am, I would know that you are in denial and are unhealthy. I can only be monogamous with you if you can be monogamous, and I can only trust your words when you do not try to change me. I will never marry someone who lies to me or to himself because the truth will come out eventually.

Advice to Self

- Be patient and believe in delayed gratification

- Establish boundaries

- Focus on the big picture

- Take small steps

Benefits and Uses of Sex

Sex has given me many benefits, from the sacral chakra to the number 5 to the fifth letter, hei (or E).

- Balances intellectual drive

- Connected to love

- Connected to many past lives (not often married)

- Guiltless – why should I apologize for my God-given nature?

- Hobby like being a foodie

- I'm a "minx"

- Monetizable

- Needed like breathing/eating

- Newness - to me, anything can be a fetish and anyone can gain a new fetish

- Nonmonogamy keeps me sane. Monogamy drives me crazy. I can only be monogamous with someone who can accept my nonmonogamous nature.

- Power in manifestation

- Power of healing

- Power over other sex

- Sex is how I make true friends, the kind that will stand over me after a car crash and tell me everything has been taken care of.

- To me, anything can be a fetish and anyone can gain a new fetish.

- Transmutable into money

- We are sensual beings (six senses) in the physical universe

- *You* cannot change that which you liked so much about me. I have lived as a priestess and geisha (or kisaeng) and have found that sex is *what I want*. I will not have someone take that which I want against my will. I will only choose/decide to change if I have an STD scare or pregnancy. If you have a problem with sex, you have a problem with me. I am sex personified. I have seen sex from every angle, and it is good. It is people's attitudes that are wrong/bad.

Boundaries

Boundaries are closely connected to how well do you know yourself.

- "Acceptance" means loving non-attachment (care but not that much). "Tolerance" means putting up with or enabling in this situation. True compromise can only be done through acceptance.

- "I" statements express boundaries. "You" statements express the desire to change somebody or [is an] antagonism.

- Codependents tend to be people pleasers and will be less inclined to say what their boundaries are.

- I do not feel guilty for the way God made me. I was born this way even if society doesn't think I should have been made that way.

- If one can respect boundaries, they are showing that they love and respect who that person is.

- The more someone says "don't," the more someone will "do" (e.g., Tom Heller and his mother) – resulting in getting what you don't want.

- The more you say "I would appreciate it if…" the more you are stating "if you do this it will show me that you love me and care for me." Therefore, a person will be more willing if they loved and cared for that person.

My boundaries[543]:

- At the age of 31, I have finally decided that NO ONE is ever allowed in my apartment. I'm tired of human stray cats overstaying their welcome, "friends" (a weak word nowadays) exploiting my weaknesses and taking advantage of me sexually, and people inviting themselves in that think they're my friends. Even females aren't allowed because the only females who want to be in my apartment are pregnant psychobitches who tell me about running into cars when they were on drugs or organic hobos who lost their job and spouse (because they bought a car without telling the spouse). It is my apartment. It has my bed. My bed is my bed alone and no one shall sleep in it but me[544].

- Don't bring in third parties (put too much weight on friends' opinions).

- Do not judge others/be openminded, but not too openminded

- Do not make promises you don't intend to keep

---

[543] With addictive behavior, I had no standards for romantic relationships, but I feel that, much to my father's approval, that now my standards are too stringent, as if no one really deserves what I could offer as a wife and mother.

[544] Older i.P. audAx: Some people think the womyn should allow the man to come to her and that by making this rule, I send the wrong message. People think I am disrespecting myself by coming to the man, when in reality I am respecting myself by not allowing the man to come to me until he is worthy.

- I cannot be married to someone who wants a closed marriage while being hypocritical and judges me for having a high sex drive (which is based on chemicals produced by DNA). But [I] can be in a closed marriage if one can accept that my body produces more testosterone than most.

- I control the frequency of sex and who I have sex with and that is exactly the issue here. I have almost always initiated and always called[545].

- I don't want to be in a relationship where I am violating someone's boundaries and not knowing it because I don't want to wait for resentment to come out.

- I will not be in a relationship where our boundaries conflict.

- I will not do anything I feel is not for the best interests of those I love and care for even if they ask me to do it.

Crossed boundaries:

- At a drinking game, I told people to drink if they've had sex with me because I know they had.

- I embarrassed someone for implying she was manly in a public game.

- I forced myself into bed with a friend against his will.

- I lost a friend because he didn't want me coming onto him.

- I shared a couple's sexual secret with one of their friends.

- I tried to devirginize a friend against his will.

- My friends are a source of sexual supply.

Circle

Inner Circle Behaviors[546]

Middle Circle Behaviors

- Asking how long it's been
- BDSM with chastity devices
- Massages from casual acquaintances
- Staying out late

---

[545] Older i.P. audAx: That could and should change.

[546] Older i.P. audAx: The fact that I did not record behaviors I would avoid proved my denial.

AudAx

- Sleeping with someone (new)
- Inappropriate jokes
- Ignoring others' boundaries due to marriage or their values
- Phone sex

Outer Circle Behaviors

- Platonic friendships
- Confiding in someone close
- Complete openness/honesty with family
- Deep discussions about finances, politics, or religion with family
- Celebrating holidays with family

Codependency and Sex Addiction

- Having friends with benefits is safer for my emotional health but not good for my physical health. Solution?
- If monogamy is not safe and nonmonogamy is not safe and commitment phobia is not safe and love addiction is not safe, then what is?????????
- I now know one narcissist[547] in person and three narcissists through association.
- I now know that I am loved, but I abuse my support network.
- My desire to be liked is what causes me to keep exes[.]
- What the hell is interdependence???????

Everything Has a Reason (and a Purpose): My Philosophy

If this book were to be based on any philosophy, it would be the existentialism of Kierkegaard, Sartre, or his wife, de Beauvoir. If people say that philosophers' theories are useless because they are merely theories and in the same breath say that the brain, which thinks, is the most important part of the body, then I think it is clear to me that too many philosophers get hung up, not on using logic as the means, but in using logic as an end in itself.

Being a guilt-free Christian leads to freedom, which means you are loved and can do no harm. Unfortunately, responsibility is the "burden" of freedom, according to Sartre. You are responsible for openmindedness, learning, and forgiveness.

---

[547] Older i.P. audAx: This is questionable.

Why Philosophy (Love of Wisdom)?:

- Beauty

- Foundation for congruency

- Plato's philosopher king

- The motivation

How I Am Unlike Others With Sexual Compulsion

- I "love" everyone I have sex with *unlike others*

- I am a sex goddess

- I am glad that I can talk about it openly; I have waited so long to unite the two halves that are me. Christianity's attitudes toward sex were based [on] I Have a Right to Negative Emotions.

- I can use it to my advantage

- I create through my feelings

- I enjoy it

- I love the darkness as a Goth, poet, and person whose Saturn is in Scorpio. Men come and go; but sex is always available.

- I take 100% responsibility over my life and will not allow emotional control from anyone

- It helps me to focus

- It helps me write poetry and songs

- Repressing is unhealthy

- Sex is the easiest thing to manifest

In Defense of Creativity

Here is my response to the forced positive emotions that come from the Self-Help Industry:

- How would you rather be remembered? Would you rather be remembered as rich or as someone who changed the future for good?

- Just because duplication [of positive emotions] makes money faster, I'm not going to discount my life.

- We are created to create. If we are not creating we are not happy.

AudAx

In Defense of My Decision-Making Abilities

My father rewards distrust. I will not allow myself to be cajoled into such behavior.

However, I do not blindly trust anyone. What they say must resonate with me at a deep level and be confirmed through one or more sources that are not connected or have no knowledge of the first source.

In Defense of Sex[548]

I will not feel bad about something that makes me feel good. The best way to control people and keep them at a lower DNA vibration is to do exactly that. America started with the 3 Ps: Puritans, Pilgrims, and Protestants. The church is responsible for putting negative thoughts into the field.

Learning

I said that I loved learning, if I learned from a book, but I actually hated learning life lessons. I tended to learn things the hardest way.

It's been said that physical abuse is easier to overcome than verbal abuse, but I chose parents who thought they chose me who allowed verbal abuse to occur. And when I say verbal abuse, keep in mind that the same word can either be empowering or degrading depending on how it's used.

It's been said that alcohol addiction is easier to overcome than sexual addiction, but I had sexual addiction.

It's been said that it's easier to overcome addiction when you've hit rock bottom, but I chose to overcome it when I was ready to grow up and get on with my life.

Lessons from Mark Constron:

- Be disciplined as if in the military
- Financial solvency is my birthright
- Have higher standards/don't settle
- Take pride in appearance

---

[548] See *Defending Pornography Defending Pornography: Free Speech, Sex, and the Fight for Women's Rights* by Nadine Strossen

Life Purpose According to Astrology: Why I Won't Listen to Conventional Views on Sex

Saturn (Mastery of Sex)

My "ultimate purpose is to transform and heal the culture by exploring and naming the darkness, uncovering what is hidden, and helping others to identify what truly matters." Temptation is a desire the ruling class does not want people to have, so that is what I choose to bring to the surface.

- Bring to light what is hidden/repressed (Why I have a proclivity toward secrets, the unseen, "the subconscious," that which cannot be explained, and invisible forces of power as well as why I am a codependent, since I need to feel safe to reveal my inner truth.)
- Come to terms with death and rebirth (change)
- Study tantric arts and become acquainted with healing and transformational potential of sex

Gemini (Mission)

According to a Tarot.com reading, "[My] mission is to teach others about the power of the invisible, and to serve as a messenger between the conscious and subconscious realms" and be a part of history. If anyone wants me, they need to help me do this.

- End attachment to being right
- Newness
- Openmindedness

Sagittarius (Mostly Single Past Lives)

- Hone communication skills to reintegrate into society
- Listen/socialize
- Practice saying "I don't know"
- Realize my "truth" is only one perspective
- Speak from my extensive experiences living beyond the bounds of society rather than from generalities
- The power of past lives motivates me

AudAx

Listening/Talking

The goal is communication, which requires a sender and receiver (listening only concerns the receiver). When an idea is communicated, the receiver should receive an epiphany, revelation, or new understanding, and the sender should (optimally) feel understood. If the sender does not feel understood, and the receiver didn't gain new learning/understanding, then no communication occurred. This is basic Communication 101.

- Being right is not important
- I'm not interested in how much you know, and you're not interested in how much I know
- Interrupting indicates fake listening[549]
- Listening more than speaking protects your privacy

Mandala Results

Question

What can I expect from my money and love sectors in the near future?

Warning: Take responsibility for feelings.

Advice: Keep balanced; play it safe.

Body and Mind

Warning: Lack of intuition/sense of aimlessness.

Advice: Watch your diet.

Beliefs

Warning: Past dominates and causes you to question relationships. Attitude toward sex leads to higher understanding.

Advice: Live in the moment and clear out memories. "The past has passed."

---

[549] Older i.P. audAx: I continue to do this unconsciously.

Sacrifice

Warning: News from the gynecologist will change my sexual behaviors. There will be philosophical, psychological, and occupational changes.

Advice: A guardian angel may appear.

Summary

Romance: Open communication lines. Talk about sex (and get over my anger).

Finance: Play it safe with spending, but there is potential for making internet marketing my new occupation.

My Thoughts

- Codependency is gray; only I can decide what behaviors are acceptable, no one else.
- Everything about me is codependent; I cannot be separated from it if I tried.[550]
- Everything that is important to me is not valued by my parents.
- Everything that is normal to me, everything that makes up my behavior, they think is not normal.
- I am afraid my parents will pathologize non-problematic behavior. Deviant behavior is not always problematic.
- I am not what I do, but what I do is dictated by who I am.
- I seek lovers out (or tend to be with lovers who match) based on my values, which include nonmonogamy and herb.
- In my world, I am the only womyn men want to have sex with.
- It will be tricky to make a stand for what is right and not get it confused with what I deny.
- My mom punished me for my honesty; the only way to recover is with honesty.
- My parents do not like the person God made me.
- My parents don't know what they don't know.

Random Notes About Me (2012)

- Feelings of ugliness is a root cause of sexual compulsion.

---

[550] Older i.P. audAx: This leads into an as of yet unpublished book.

AudAx

- Gray areas: It's dangerous to think the rules don't apply, but at the same time, the people we worship, idolize, and admire in history were outside the norm.

- I am a BDSM hobbyist and nude model.

- I am a minx, not a slut; I like to be petted by others but will return to my "master."

- I am hardwired to have a high sex drive.

- I beat someone who thought he couldn't meet someone who has done as many sexual things as he has.

- I feel that my spiritual calling and life's purpose is related to talk[ing] about fetishes publicly in a book, which will be scriptures.

- I have dated every sign except Aquarius.

- I *have* the beliefs of someone who *is* who I am.

- I have tried every fetish except scatology and fisting[551].

- I kept the first sex addict partially to keep my lifestyle. Sex is the best thing to make me feel good and powerful.

- I practice agape with polyamory.

- *I require sex to balance out my intellectual nature.*

- I will take opportunities offered to me (food, sex, or herb).

- Poor logic: Sex for sex's sake is flawed rationale.

- The only time I was not the initiator was with the man I lived with.

- Those who *have* not are those who *are* not.

Signs of Recovery

- Ability to say "no"

- Better discernment

- Better personal appearance

- Discipline

Triggers

- Animé conventions and events

---

[551] This changed around 2014 (?).

- Alcohol and pot[552]

- Attractive people (Warning: new office mate is attractive - worst case scenario is being fired from my job)

- Dating sites

- Feeling restricted AND feeling unrestricted

- Massage (Is massage not both spiritual and sexual?)

- Needing to talk

- "Zealousy"

Where I Got My Sexual Supply (Total: 15)[553]

(List does not include frequency)

---

[552] In Defense of Pot

- It's organic.

- It's a painkiller.

- If everyone took it, we would have peace.

- I would go to jail for it willingly.

- I should have said "I won't quit" rather than "I can't." Codependents want to believe there is something to fix when it ain't broken.

- I use it infrequently, but I support the cause.

- It is an issue of state rights and stat laws and is legal in DC.

- What I do in my personal life is my own business.

- I would put it before a job.

- I have never paid for pot.

- I never have more than one ounce at a time.

- It is not possible to be chemically addicted to pot.

- Prescription drugs are more a "gateway" drug than pot.

- However, it makes me horny.

[553] A sexual compulsive is someone who keeps a steady supply of people, especially for times of resentment.

AudAx

The Men Who I May Ask for Sex (7)[554]

Earl Carroll: One-night stand stranger

Gary Stanton: Submissive alcoholic

Jerome Hanseler: Lives nearby, had sex with more than ten years ago

John Listen: Comes with a wife and a small penis and invites me to bukkake parties

Indie: Infrequently interested and thinks I try too hard to put on a show

Patton Jack: confidante who had lots of experience but now has erectile dysfunction

Sir Jackie: Comes with a girlfriend and mistress

Skeeter Zabusa-Early: Infrequently interested and a narcissist, from what I've heard

The Men Who May Ask Me for Sex (3)[555]

Raafi Muhammad Yousaf: Calls me for booty calls when he's tired of dealing with his wife, twins, and job and seems to have erectile dysfunction

Omar Soph: Open to a long-term relationship, with his wife's stamp of approval

Exes I Mail/Talk To On The Phone (4)

George Mireille: Commitment-phobe who may have phone sex or webcam sex and is supportive but with no strings

Ed Steffens: Recovered sex addict that prefers virgins and whom I talk to infrequently

These two will flirt with married women.

Slim Roche: Narcissist who may have phone sex

Rad Snail: Prisoner who will flirt with me until I get married[556]

---

[554] Older i.P. audAx: The number here was written in 2012, but I had 22 throughout my lifetime up until now.

[555] Older i.P. audAx: The number here was written in 2012, but I had 19 throughout my lifetime up until now.

[556] Older i.P. audAx: I do not stay in touch with the two latter.

Male Friends (2)

Both male friends are virgins. Matthew Hays dated one girl in his lifetime. Usman Hassan is a virgin due to religious beliefs.[557]

Summary

Longterm exes keep their distance but know the best, the only time sex has tainted friendship is with Patton, but it was inevitable. Three friends have small penises or erectile dysfunction so I find them to be harmless.

Recovery Notes 2014

Autoerotica and Kalopsia: Vanilla Sky and Tsukiyomi

The reason why fantasies will never die is because entire multibillion dollar industries run on fantasies alone, and it is only through our fantasies that we can be brainwashed. If fantasies weren't so swell, people wouldn't sell them. But they do: wedding planners, strip clubs, pornography, romance novels, romantic movies, erotica, regular movies, commercials, etc. Fantasies are what create tortured artists, which I am, I'm afraid[558]. But I refuse to quit. I will never give up on my dreams.

I am a fan of *Naruto Shippuden*, a Japanese animation TV show that starts off light and ends up very serious. All the "evil" guys want to put the world in a dream state because reality is just too harsh and cruel. However, even the "good" guys were delusional, always believing that a former friend would change his ways and just be their friend again, as if nothing had happened. We all have fantasies, some more than others.

Today (September 20, 2014) is the first day I truly understood sexual compulsion. I can understand why people would believe in sin because addiction really feels like you sold your soul to the Devil. As a sellout, I believe I've had to sell something to be the way I am now. (However, may I note that sin means being cut off from Source, and it is impossible for a soul to be cut off from its holy source, since the Creator "consider[s] thoughts so that no one be banished from him" (II Shmuel 14:14).)

---

[557] Older i.P. audAx: However he asked me later for oral when I was taking a 90-day break from sex in 2016.

[558] Was

AudAx

I have an addiction to comfort. The people who say you don't want it badly enough have not faced the pull of comfort. I have[559] enough money to save to make my dreams come true. I know exactly what I want and how to get it, but I still don't have it. And does anyone?

Sleep is an example of comfort. There are a lot of things I would've done differently if I didn't love my sleep[560]. You cannot have an addiction to comfort without idealism as well. A perfect example of what life is like in my head is this:

In my head I am an exotic dancer who eats ice cream, chocolate cake, and donuts; worships at the feet of carbs; and doesn't exercise, but loses weight in my stomach and gains it in my 34A boobs (I'm pretty planistethic, or flat-chested). I am happily married with children that I homeschool. I have just shared my deepest, darkest secrets with the entire world, and I make millions of dollars from it (at least $5 million per year). I have as many responsibilities as a child, even though I have children of my own. I have sex multiple times a day without getting tired or sore. I have excitement *and* comfort. I never worry about money. I have it all. I <u>am</u> *The Secret Life of Walter Mitty*. Then reality strikes…

My friend actually saw a guy urinate on honeysuckles. :-o! How could anyone do such a thing? It's a crime against humanity. Oh, how the world is so cruel! Why would people be so cruel? And why can't guys and girls be friends? Why can't I have any solid female friends?

This, my friends, is idealism. And this could be why I'm still single[561]. I have always strived for an ideal. All of a sudden it struck me that the people we emulate are not as happy as we thought and that if they were, time moves on for them as it does anyone else. Just look at Demi Moore or Nicole Scherzinger of The Pussycat Dolls. Even with a perfect body, they're still not satisfied. I bet that a few millionaires would rather be happy in a trailer or may even have peniaphilia (erotic fascination with poverty).

Sometimes, as with the Goths, a group of people is stricken down silently in different parts of the world, slowly exterminated without a word and without media attention. Anyone striving to be an endangered species, like me, must strive also for survival, which leads us back again to comfort addiction. All the things that are wrong with this world is the instinct of survival. (See *Dianetics*, not in this book.)

The only difference between humans and animals is consciousness of our desires and that consciousness (along with assignment of meaning) has brought suffering to the world. According to Kabbalists, the world was created because we (humanity) didn't want everything handed to

---

[559] Had

[560] Still do, not from a desire to avoid the day, but as a desire to cuddle up in a warm blanket.

[561] Legally

us on a silver platter, and we wanted to earn it. I was telling my friend this and he said, "I veto their decision." Why does dissatisfaction have to make the world go 'round?

Recovery Notes 2016

"One of the strongest bonds of the addiction is its secrecy[562]. Perhaps, with
the secret broken, addicts can know the peace and self-acceptance that comes
with knowing *it can be talked about*." –Patrick Carnes, *Out of the Shadows*
"Neither filthiness, nor foolish talking, nor jesting, which are not
convenient: but rather giving of thanks." —Ephesians 5:4 KJV[563]

I was always the one who thought that if I could stop attracting alcoholics, commitment phobes, codependents, narcissists, sociopaths, etc., then I could get married. They were always the one with the intimacy disorder. What I discovered in the end was that it wasn't them; it was me. I was the sexual (and love) compulsive.

When I discovered that I really was a bonafide sexual compulsive and love addict, it was both ironic and sad that I realized I wouldn't have been with the boyfriend I cheated on if I were not that way. It's the ironic thing that when an addict, of any kind, recovers, they realize that the person who wanted them not to be was part of the problem and that they were only together because of the addictive thinking. This is because a dysfunctional relationship requires a balance of flaws (*See* "Issues" by Julia Michaels). If someone fixes their major flaw but the other doesn't, then the disproportion makes it impossible to hide behind a veneer of equality. Because what has been found out is that co-addicts are together so people cannot see their real addictions.

---

[562] I learned to lie about everything that makes me who I am by omission because I was a bad liar and lying by omission doesn't require telling tall tales. By keeping secrets, one controls information, and by controlling information I could control perception, so that people could only perceive me as good. Now, secrecy itself is not entirely bad, for even Jesus talked about doing good deeds in secret. But here were are discussing unhealthy secrecy. When I learned in my early 30s that I could share my unpopular opinions, like how I don't believe in vaccines, and still be loved, I made some mistakes. But I'd rather make mistakes with rigorous honesty than through lying by omission. (Older i.P. audAx: I have later learned that keeping secrets limits others' freedom of choice.)

[563] I include this scripture verse that prohibits jesting and silly talking (check out the etymology) along with fornication for it is verbal abuse that leads to the desire to be loved, which leads to addictive sexual behavior.

AudAx

Also, co-addiction is addiction in and of itself. The addiction was the glue that bound me to my only real monogamous boyfriend. Without it, there was no balance, nothing to hide behind, nothing left[564].

Can an addict be charming? Absolutely, one person always loved to hear about my "drama" as if I were a TV soap opera and put that expectation into the ether to be fulfilled.[565]

I have a hard time understanding "healthy behaviors" because to me, unhealthy behaviors seem like "common sense" because it's common and instinctive[566].

What invariably happens is that you read all the literature about attachment theory only to find out two years later that you embody the traits of your partner who before seemed so opposite of you. For example, the co-addict is invariably an addict and vice versa. Or the anxious attachment type is actually the avoidant attachment type and vice versa. The roles reverse. In the end, one realizes that all "sin" (addiction) comes form the same source—a broken heart (See Proverbs 4:23 NIV).

Shame (about who you are as a person) leads to anxiety (usually social). Anxiety leads to coping. Coping leads to addiction[567].

Shame of any form has always existed (whether or not it is denied). That is why Jesus exhorted us to love one another. For anything less than love is abuse, for what is abuse but making one feel bad for how God made them?

When people say something is or isn't normal, I have to question it. Isn't "normal" based on "majority rules"? Aren't I the one who's had sex with more men than the average advice-giver? Wouldn't I know better what is "normal" for a guy? If the majority of Americans have become "Nazi-esque," as some say with the rise of the Trump, then what the mass thinks should not determine my actions as an individual. I would much prefer people use the term "healthy" as

---

[564] I disagree with this statement in hindsight. Some believe in romantic soulmates (or rather, twin souls) and others believe that damaged people attract damaged people. I believe both are true. I believe we agree to reconnect with our loved ones, but with obstacles in the way. I believe we specifically design our families pre-incarnation (or someone else does on our behalf or in cooperation with us) so that our loved one is like our parents (in the ways that we view them) in both good and bad ways, to ensure that we will find each other again.

[565] The problem with soap opera TV shows and serial novels is that the financial need for viewers/readers and the susceptibility of the viewers/readers cyclically promotes the idea that one needs drama in their life to go on.

[566] Older i.P. audAx: No, unhealthy behaviors can be instinctive because they are based on behaviors modeled to us as children.

[567] "Fear leads to anger. Anger leads to hate. Hate leads to suffering."—George Lucas, as said by Master Yoda in *Star Wars*

opposed to "normal." If 75% of the entire world has a mental illness or psychological problem, then being in a "healthy" relationship means being in a "less unhealthy" relationship.

Being a Female Sexual Compulsive

I spent more than 19 years of my life, from 1997 to 2016 with an active addiction to sex. It's harder for wimmin to self-identify as addicted to sex because, unlike wimmin, men prefer being used because they dislike strings. Also, men are reluctant to admit that they were coerced into sex after the fact. A female sexual compulsive has to be ever vigilant due to the nature and socialization of the male gender.

Facebook: The Desire to Be Liked

Another term for addiction could be "the evil of obedience." It's very hard to withdraw from approval when one is so used to waiting for someone else to tell them what to do because someone is so used to the fact that everyone has an opinion on who you are, who you should be, what you feel, what you are supposed to feel, what you think, and what you're supposed to think. In my experience, those who want to be liked have their parents' disapproval, either directly or indirectly, consciously or subconsciously, or via perception.

The desire to be liked is a survival instinct. It ensures that your tribe will stick with you. It also enhances order. The natural way of humans is to be wild, for they too are animals. The militaristic instinct for order ensures that there is no breakdown in society, or that there is one less person to worry about so that things run as smoothly as possible.

Since an addiction to sex or love is really an addiction to being liked, it can also be connected to talkativeness[568].

First Step (2016)

I was adopted before I was born (it takes 6 months to adopt and I was adopted when I was 4 months old). The inability to be held by my mother caused developmental trauma to my brain. I'm a product of an affair, or so I've been told[569]. I suspect my mother had me as a product of rape since she refused to meet with me even after I found her through my adoption agency, but that's speculation. She might have been a sex addict herself, since addictions can be genetic. I

---

[568] Older i.P. audAx: Even after I dealt with the issue of being liked, people continued to complain that I didn't listen to them, and such traits were still visible in my cursive handwriting.

[569] Older i.P. audAx: This does not hold up under classical logic.

was adopted into a verbally abusive household. That was when I learned to lie by omission, not just about an addiction, but about my feelings, opinions, interests, and everything that makes me who I am. (However, I cannot lie if asked a direct question.) To this day, I have never told my father my opinions if they conflicted with his or if they were socially unacceptable for someone in his economic class, since we still have to walk on eggshells around him[570]. For a long time, I felt like I couldn't tell my parents about my sexual orientation. My mental health affected my behavior more than my acting out could have ever affected my mental health. One time when we vacationed in Tennessee, my parents said they would support me in anything I did. I felt like my family could not love me because even though they said I could be anything; I knew they didn't mean a porn star.

My father's alcoholic father lost his mother because she kept her brother and abandoned him. My father's alcoholic father also named my father after his long-lost brother. My father's mother's mother lost her mother through death in childbirth, when giving birth to her younger brother. And, of course, I was abandoned by my birthmother (and/or birthfather).

I come from a family where multiple people in my tree have had three to five spouses. My father's mother, on the other hand, was a romance addict and sexual anorexic.

When I was young, my mother walked around nude and would kiss me until I couldn't breathe. When I was about 5, I started having crushes on boys, lifted my skirt on the request of older boys, and idolized Madonna. From 1st to 4th grade and from 4th to 6th grade I had two long-term crushes. From age 6 onward, I had up to 10 bullies who harassed me practically daily, so that's why I always befriended the friendless and appeared to not have standards. Bullying was such a normal part of my daily routine that I welcomed the (mostly male) attention and never thought to tell anyone. When I was about 8, my parents gave me a book that they didn't know had a page of naked children. When I was about 9, I started to have a larger quantity of friends and thus ended up befriending the wrong people because I emphasized quantity over quality. I also started my period earlier than all the other girls. From about 4th grade on, in murder mystery parties I was always typecast as the more sexual person, perhaps due to my race. When I was about 10, my cousin, seven years my junior, showed me his penis and told me to squeeze it. I didn't and told him, "no." I told me best friend, and we had good awkward giggles over it. Due to various childhood experiences, sex and relationships represented comfort, safety, confidence, rest, sanity, and relaxation.

When I was 14, my grandmother died. She was the only one who brought relief from my father's verbal abuse, and actually enjoyed playing with dolls and board games with me, and ever since she died I, as a love addict, sought a connection that would bring relief from anguish.

---

[570] Older i.P. audAx: This was in 2016, I think, and we have a better relationship now.

The same year I had my first boyfriend. I also discovered masturbation. I started with a pillow and moved on to the shower head. Soon after I discovered that, I could find a way around parental control software to find porn. Because a girl at school bragged about having a boyfriend, I thought I was behind everyone when it came to dating and that everyone was dating except for me. I was extremely envious of those who bragged about having boyfriends. [Censored]

When I was about 15, I went from shy to confident because I got positive attention from guys. I read a bestselling fiction novel that had an account of child molestation. When I was 16, I was friends with an extreme female love addict who even I found to be too much. I also had phone sex with a freshman. Despite the risk of prison, I had probably broken the Romeo & Juliet laws, which I didn't know existed. When I was a senior in high school, I had depression (hate turned inward), and I realized that love was an escape from depression.

When I turned 17, I met the first man I would have sex with. He was my verbally abusive "friend's" boyfriend's roommate. I couldn't really say it was a defloration since I was the one who coerced him. He happened to be a victim of sex abuse at a young age and had more than 100 siblings. He was even an uncle to someone one grade below him.

Since the first boyfriend I had sex with was nonmonogamous, I ran with it. I became an acting out partner to not just one, but two sex addicts simultaneously for four years. The second just met the qualifications for a 7-year age gap and last time I checked had had sex with 300 women.

Between the two sex addicts, our typical response to "how was your day?" was a description of our sexual conquests.

The 2nd sex addict eventually married when we were dating, but divorced because the wife found a tape of us having sex. Then he became a sex addiction counselor, but told me I wasn't addicted because I wouldn't have sex with a tree, so I believed him. Since he was nonmonogamous too, I had at least two other relationships via cyber and at most five others throughout my time in college. The cyber relationships were focused on the more extreme fetishes like crossdressing, scatology, or necrophilia, things one would be less likely to really act out.

In college, I found a group of sex addicts that covered up the name of their organization with something unrelated to be college-sanctioned. I found them because it included acquaintances from my group of friends in high school. The parties were more wild than the other college parties, and this was at a party school. Whenever we had live-action roleplay games[571] (LARPs), I always asked to have the role of the more sexual person. I've always prided myself on not needing to be drunk at a party to take off my clothing. I often justified most of my behaviors as "it was what I knew." Or "it was normal for the people I hung out with." This was ironic because the people I spent most time with were actually the only virgins in the group. College was the last

---

[571] Similar to playing those murder mystery games in elementary school.

time I had female friends[572]. This group would host annual camping trips of debauchery, where our anthem consisted of one guy taking off his pants. Since some of them brought their children, spouses, and lovers to the event at the same time, I thought that nonmonogamy and polyamory was a lifestyle that could legitimately work. When my addiction was getting worse, I was at a party and we were playing "Never Have I Ever," and I told people to drink if they'd had sex with me, which probably ruined any good reputation I had.

I was also part of a GLBT organization and for two years had a crush on a womyn in the organization[573].

College was when I met my only long-term monogamous boyfriend. He was not part of the organization I was in. I thought I told him that I had at least one (or two) other boyfriend(s), but maybe I forgot or it was forgotten since we ended up sleeping together from the first date onward, which happened to be right after a threesome with a guy who was hitting on me before he arrived at his own house. This was a day after I hooked up with a female who called the cops because she thought I'd gone missing.

With him, we risked arrest by having sex in public areas, such as a park, library, and eventually on a plane. Providing oral when he was driving was another level of danger.

That's when I started clothed and nude modeling and met most of my male friends through that. Many of them gave me free sex toys, because they had contracts with the manufacturers. Also, one non-photographer male friend gave me his porn collection. My parents took pictures of me often as a child, so I was a natural model, and photographers often preferred to work with me because of my enthusiasm and creativity.

It was through modeling that I also met "guys with cameras," which are guys who are not good at photography but like to see naked women. One of them violated my boundaries by sending nude pics over Facebook. One day this "man with a camera," called me out of the blue for sex, or for pictures as a cover for sex. Moments later, I received a frantic call from a crying wife and deduced that he had been in a car accident. She had assumed that I was a friend, since I was the last phone number he had dialed before the accident. I was, even though it was a bootycall, and his wife called me thinking I was his friend so I had to console her when she thought he would die. Later, he *tried* to contact me to let me know that his wife had divorced him and that he was free. Why do men think that saying such things would be enticing? No womyn would be caught dead with someone else's refuse. This was my most embarrassing experience.

Eventually, I had to break up with my two sexually addicted boyfriends. You know you have an intimacy disorder when a sex addict accuses you of being too selfish and not being able to open

---

[572] Older i.P. audAx: And then after recovery.

[573] Older i.P. audAx: She's still hot to this day.

up during a breakup. However, the same man, my first, was to become my best friend and acting out partner for 15 years[574]. The other one, who promised to always be my friend, disappeared from my life.

I got so addicted to sleeping in a dorm room with my monogamous boyfriend (which violated his roommate's boundaries), that I had an affair with another one of his ex-roommates when he was going to court for a sex offense that I didn't know about at the time. This ex-roommate just happened to like pleasuring women, which my boyfriend did not (and still doesn't).

It was with my monogamous boyfriend when I lost about 45 lbs. and went from a size 18 to a size 8. At the time, I also had a food (or comfort) addiction and recovered from the food addiction to make up for my infidelity with his roommate.

I thought my boyfriend had forgiven me when we had moved in together in 2008, but his goal was to monitor me. He believed in revenge so strongly (and still does) that the entire time we were living together was his revenge on me. It was ironic because I was so tired of being with someone overly romantic that I ended up with someone not romantic at all. I gave him a sleep number bed (which we had temporarily since we ended up having seven different residences[575] in one year) and all the gifts my father gave me. He was not able to express empathy toward me during that year so I mistook him for a narcissist, but found out he just "didn't feel like it" since he didn't trust me. The feeling I had of being used for money (whether or not it was true) and feeling my parents could not love me due to their reactions to me dating black men (my first and last[576] sexual partners are both black), including my first sex partner and him, led me to expressing anger for the first and for the longest time, and I eventually rained all the rage I had toward my father on my boyfriend. That led to every kind of abuse. I even abused myself (and him by proxy) via self-cutting and kept asking him why he didn't love me. It's interesting to me that something as innocent as nailbiting out of nervous habit led to self-cutting and thus emotional abuse. I was sexually abusive with him when I specifically told him that I was going to have sex with someone else because I was unhappy in the relationship, and he was sexually abusive with me because one time he wouldn't stop having sex with me out of a desire to control the uncontrollable (after we had broken up). The only reason why I stayed so long was because the sex was still good. Well, actually, I also probably stayed because he could stand up to my father, unlike the man before him.

We mutually abused each other, were codependent on each other, and were addicted to each other. In terms of love addiction, I recycled anger to express resentment, and he had an obsession with revenge. I had difficulty with taking care of myself, and he had difficulty with reality. Both

---

[574] Older i.P. audAx: When I removed my block on him post-recovery, I found that he had gone through something similar and missed having someone he could talk to about it.

[575] Or more in a shorter amount of time.

[576] Last as in last one by the time I went into recovery.

of us have focused on each other and tried to avoid intimacy via another addiction, whether sex or underearning. Both of us fought with each other because we experienced repeated disappointments for each other's (perceived) failure to love and were compulsively driven to get the other to tell us we were loved in spite of our own immature, irrational, and offensive behavior, such as his plans of retaliation. I ranted about my boyfriend so much throughout our entire dating life that people avoided having conversations with me and accused me of being enmeshed with him. He especially has a hard time with letting go, because he is afraid of dating, so the only way I could sever ties with him was to disappear in 2008.

When I left him it took me until December 2009 to pay off at least eight credit cards with about a $10,000 high balance total. I stopped owning a car when he put a combination of chemicals in the gas tank, and even without that, he put so much mileage on my car (instead of using his) that it would not have been worth it to transport it.

When my first sex partner swooped in and rescued me when I left the abuse I was living with in 2008, I thought about attending Sex and Love Addicts Anonymous (SLAA) but didn't act on it. It was then that a photographer friend convinced me that I was nonmonogamous and didn't have to change. It was my counselor who suggested I was a codependent and should spend time getting used to being alone. This was around the time that I told my parents about my sexual orientation and who I am. They soon forgot.

When I left him in 2008, I continued dating a man who helped me feel that it was safe to leave. This was a former coworker with whom I'd had sex with at work once (and also a *very* distant cousin that I didn't know at the time). I still love him, and that has been a major issue when I got back together with my only monogamous boyfriend. When this other man broke up with me the day after showing me all the major landmarks in his personal history, I went into the online dating world with the intention of having meaningless sex and using men for free meals. I think 2008 was also the year I had no more female friends.

When I was doing online dating in 2010, I literally felt like throwing up because I did not find the men I dated attractive and did not really want to have sex with them. It was like raping myself. There was no end to messages in the online dating world, and it got old. My mother even crossed my boundaries and set up a dating site for me. I thought I was gonna be sick. I eventually contracted herpes from a man who graduated summa cum laude in his class, but my gynecologist (who my mom trusted) told me not to tell anyone since it's so common. This is the same gyno who prescribed Prozac to me when I thought I might have PMDD, which all the women around me told me was too dangerous and that I should fire him.

I found out in 2016 that in 2011 I took off my clothes at a party after one drink of alcohol, where it was not okay for me to take off my clothing. The hosts of that party told me people would no longer attend their parties if they knew I was coming. I don't remember who witnessed this, but they mentioned a virgin who bootycalled me in 2016 who I thought could be trusted not to do so. It was a sad state of friendship that no one would tell me about this incident.

It was in 2012 that my first sex partner and I got back together. He told me about his experience as an accidental pimp and pornographer, which all sounded interesting to me. We got back together after he went on a bout of sexual anorexia and talked of becoming a Catholic priest through a program so he could get a scholarship to go back to college. Marriage would have been easy. He treated me well and never abused me, but, after being used to the relationship in 2008, he was too nice, and I walked all over him. The first time we were dating it was all about the sex, but then I realized I wasn't actually attracted to him without sex, so I continued to tell him I wasn't interested in having sex. At the same time, he would fly to Texas to have sex with a porn star who had had sex with Ron Jeremy. (Remember, we were nonmonogamous.) He would later get a proposal from someone when we were dating, and I really wish he had taken it[577].

In the same year in 2012, when I was with the son of a narcissist at the same time, who would later stalk me, I had a pregnancy scare. The STD and pregnancy scare got me into the door of Sexual Compulsives Anonymous (SCA). This might have been around when I discussed what the Bible says about premarital sex with my officemate, who I discovered went to sex-related anonymous meetings. I only attended one meeting. Despite hearing a man talk about having sex after contracting AIDS, and knowing the risk of death, I continued having unprotected sex, sometimes without birth control.

The year 2013 was the time when I discovered that my father's father's first wife had kids, despite my father's secrecy about that side of the family. Her grandkids referred to her as a witch, one of her grandkids thought my father was an odd child and wondered why her mother arranged a marriage for her in America, and her great-granddaughter changed her name so as not to be associated with the family.

It was in early 2014 that I was held captive in a hospital for a week due to suicidal ideation because I got in my head that I had inherited my father's verbal abuse. My first sex partner comforted me by telling me about his suicide attempt a few years earlier and his similar stay in a mental institution. It was that year that I confronted my father about his verbal abuse, which improved temporarily soon after then finally became consistent.

Early 2014 was when I felt like I lost my ability to be happy by myself, so I subconsciously sought the only man I thought could make me happy regularly. That's right, the only long-term monogamous boyfriend I ever had. Before and when I got back together with my boyfriend I lived with, in late 2014, six years later, I was contemplating a career in stripping, online and/or real-life, or maybe even surrogate therapy, since those were the only things I could imagine that

---

[577] Especially in hindsight because when he proposed to someone after we had dated, she rejected the offer.

would really give me joy, after working through career questionnaires. Before I got back together with the boyfriend I lived with in 2008, my first sex partner took me to strip clubs when I was scoping them out and deciding where I would want to work. I ended up spending money on setting up an LLC to do taxes as a stripper, as well as gathering supplies for stripper bags so I'd be ready for an audition. One of my photographer friends bought me a pole. When I was asking strippers questions about stripping, one of them told me that my best friend and first sex partner was a misogynist. At this time, I also became penpals with a former escort who encouraged me to get paid through sex, but I told her I wasn't comfortable with that.

The intense fear of poverty and desire to provide for two or potentially three people, were there a child, fueled me to waste tens of thousands of dollars on every get rich quick schemes and pyramid scheme possible, in the name of love. I also had a buying compulsion due to my desire to trust people I shouldn't and lack of discipline, discernment, and patience. Lack of discipline, discernment, and patience led to difficulty with managing finances. I did not have the right character for being fiscally responsible due to the destruction that dopamine from the sex addiction had on my frontal lobe, which was responsible for judgment and short-term memory.

In the second go-round, my boyfriend and I were both hoping to enlighten the other. Since I wrote him a letter about how nonmonogamy was in my blood and was who I was, he opened up to the idea of nonmonogamy, but his rule was no kissing, which I didn't feel was nonmonogamy. So I would keep testing his boundaries to see if I could marry him, meaning to see if I would feel restricted in a marriage to him. Along the way, I casually introduced him to acting out partners as "friends" as if it were no big deal and intentionally tried to get pregnant with my boyfriend without discussing it.

More recently, my photographer friend with erectile dysfunction, the same friend who told me in 2008 that I was just a nonmonogamous person and could not be changed, gave me a dildo to use on a woman. In the desire to use it on a woman, the man I lost my virginity to, who had been hosting sex parties, said he could provide a womyn, a particular type of womyn from my wishlist, as well as his friend who wanted to have sex with me and was well endowed. (As a side note, my first sex partner kept coming back to me because his girlfriend at the time would cum too quickly, and he couldn't get any satisfaction from sex with her. He would keep telling me how committed he was to his girlfriend but in the same breath said I was worth it.) I announced to my boyfriend that I had made a unilateral decision to have a foursome, would let him watch, and that he could say "No." Since I had already made the decision, he never said no but protested by not calling for a week. When the day came, my first sex partner told me that the womyn wasn't able to come, but by then I felt like I was locked in. Soon after my photographer friend, who I had known for about 9 years, talked about his desire to become more intimate and that was when I found out that he had been married the whole time I knew him.

My addiction started rearing its ugly head on Christmas when I went to bed angry and announced in a yell to my boyfriend that I would never be monogamous.

I ended up having UTIs and painful sex. I began to loathe my own beauty and at the same time didn't feel like I was beautiful. When I had severe psychosomatic symptoms after the last time I cheated on my boyfriend and started to view most men with disgust, condescension, and irritation instead of lust, I realized that something had to change.

I realized I had a problem because his girlfriend, who he said he wasn't seeing anymore, called while we were with his sister, and he lied about it twice to my face. I found out that she posted a pic of them in his apartment as her profile pic, taken at 2AM a day after I sent him $400, as well as online check-ins with him. I also found out that they talked about marriage, naming kids, and his sex offense after she'd only been with him for a month, even though I'm the one who paid thousands of dollars for him to see his family overseas. It was the first time I was in his shoes, and I didn't like it. Since he wouldn't end it, I ended their relationship for him[578].

In the end, I found that I could no longer trust my friends because of my habit of using sex to make friends. Not only could I not trust that I wouldn't be taken advantage of sexually or time-wise, but since all my friends were males who I have had sex with, I couldn't trust that they honestly loved me for me. My boyfriend in turn couldn't trust that I honestly loved him for him. I'd already cheated on him about ten times even though I was able to be faithful to men who didn't get jealous.

The first time I lived with him, I lived with constant anger and resentment. The second time I lived with constant worry, anxiety, and fear of returning to the past, so I made him sign a no abuse contract, just as I had done with my father exactly two years earlier.

Activities that had been part of my rituals were daily masturbation (where I would sometimes fantasize about past sex), unprotected sex, one-night stands, friends with benefits, having sex with one person a day at anime conventions without the other sexual partner knowing, and saving sexual websites. I have had to delete my account on a porn site, a sexual hookup site, a nudist site, and Yahoo. I have also had to scrub Amazon, a bookmarking site, Facebook, Finder, iTunes, Safari, Twitter, and iPhone apps and contacts. I have had struggles during the 90-day celibacy fast. For example, when I deleted the porn account and links, I got sucked in.

I am mostly a sex addict and codependent, but in terms of love addiction, I have a history of dating men with criminal records. My long-term relationships of two years or more included two hardcore sex addicts, a sex offender, a commitment-phobe 41-years my senior who did cocaine, and a prisoner in maximum security who was there due to heroin. I was also with an alcoholic and the son of a narcissist for a short time. I have been close to marriage five times. Looking

---

[578] Which I know now wasn't healthy.

back, it's possible that all the above were sex and love addicts. All in all, I have had sex with about 55[579] people but had sexual interest in about 98. I was with 10 of those people when I was with my boyfriend, whether in terms of one-night stands or full-blown relationships. An obvious result of this is that I'm not as tight as I used to be.

I have been with my last boyfriend from 2014-2016 but he told me not to tell my parents until we were living together, since he broke a very serious boundary with my father at the beginning of our relationship and since the last time I was with him they thought they would never see me or that one of us would die due to suicide or homicide. Telling my parents I intended to marry him could cause irreparable damage, a possible heart attack, transient global amnesia due to high blood pressure, danger to my mother because my father is her caretaker, the possibility of being disowned or having an altercation, and harm to the relationship with my aunt and uncle, far more damage than telling them about my sex addiction. It was during the time I was with this boyfriend a second time that my father complimented me by saying I was no longer acting like an N-word. However, my boyfriend got upset that I told them about the sex addiction first. I was in a dangerous situation because we planned an overseas vacation that I couldn't tell my parents about, so I told my coworkers to make sure I come back safely since he had deprived me of sleep out of revenge prior to the trip. I budgeted $300/mo on "crisis" prevention for him and pay for a plane trip with or without hotel every other month to visit him, and resent him when he asks for more trips just so that, one one hand, he can monitor my progress, and, on another hand, because he cannot honor my 90-day commitment to my recovery. In total, I have or expect to spend $11K on him this year, not incl. gifts or the two timeshares I used to "save money" on travel. I am also the only one who calls or initiates sex. It is a relationship that wouldn't exist without sex or my addiction because I had to keep the door open for him to return.

I stayed with him because he laughed a lot, which I associated with my childhood best friend before I started hanging out with the wrong crowds and because I wasn't allowed to express exuberance and joy at my parents' house. When I eventually broke up with him, I blocked him for three weeks, but he thought we were still dating so I eventually had to tell him flat out that we were done.

As far as progression goes, I ended up violating my own values when I started having sex with married men. Only one married man ever turned me down, and I respect that. I have used sex as currency. I have given out sex in exchange for a cheaper hotel room or tent when I wanted to be at a social event or to return the favor of rescuing me from someone worse. I accepted money when I allowed foot fetishists to massage my feet and considered selling used underwear around when I had to get food stamps. I have stalked and been stalked by multiple men. I put myself in a dangerous position when I allowed myself to be fisted by a man with a restraining order on his record who I had no interest in being in a relationship with. I violated a couple's boundaries

---

[579] Could be 74 by now, and we know that my final number of sexual interests came out to 104.

when I told someone I was dating, who also knew them, that we had participated in a particular form of anonymous sex with others at a party. They were government contractors and parents. And eventually, I was only interested in porn that involved incest, which a sex therapist told me was part of my sexual template and couldn't be changed. I can't afford to act on such fantasies because my boyfriend is already on the registry for life in Virginia, even though other states would have already forgiven him by now for something he did when he was in college, and the consequences of acting out on such fantasies could lead to losing any future children I would have, thus recreating the cycle all over again.

I put myself at risk of STDs, unplanned pregnancies (even though I secretly wanted a child), assault, death, arrest, prison, and breakup.

I violated people's boundaries: I coerced men to have sex with me, I kissed the 18-year-old daughter of a couple I had sex with at their party, had sex in someone else's house when their kids were sleeping, flirted with a friend's fiancé, made out with a woman in front of her boss (even though I didn't know it at the time), had sex with an ex-roommate and best friend of people I had dated, but most of all violated everyone's boundaries when I acquired an STD. People have also violated my boundaries. For example, one guy talked to me because I was the only person who didn't judge him for liking cross-dressing, but non-professional therapy sessions quickly turned into sex talk. He didn't understand why I blocked him after that.

I'm thankful that I have support, and I'm thankful that I found Sex Addicts Anonymous (SAA) before I could be risking divorce.

I have an extremely hard time forgiving my father, boyfriend, or birthmother for their trespasses against me, but I have been told I cannot fully recover if I cannot forgive the unforgivable[580]. I still abuse my boyfriend because of my inability to see the ways he is connecting and don't know how to stop misunderstanding.

It didn't dawn on me before recovery that all the behaviors I had came from shame; I thought that was just something birthmothers had. But I exhibited all signs of shame: feeling unloved and unworthy, and it made sense in terms of my origins as the child of an affair (or rape) and of a verbally abusive household.

Intimacy Disorder

Sexual compulsives are said to have an "intimacy disorder"[581].

---

[580] Older i.P. audAx: Now I'm at a point in my life where I don't feel that there's anything left to forgive, since I have already gotten past them.

[581] Which is ironic because sexual anorexics are said to have an intimacy disorder too.

AudAx

Sometimes sex is not very intimate, even if it's great for health. Strangely enough, physical intimacy sometimes keeps us from true intimacy, the kind that can be had without premarital sex[582]. Sometimes, especially for wimmin, sex is foreplay for cuddling.

That which we neglect (communication) is the most important, not just talking but telepathy, the ability to listen without hearing a word, or at least the ability to be silent together[583].

The recovery literature for sex and love addiction implies that I have an intimacy disorder and goes on to describe everything intimacy isn't without ever really describing what it is, as if it is an elusive concept. So I looked up the definition. Besides one of the definitions being sexual intercourse, the primary definition is closeness and familiarity, which is definitely not an issue for a love addict in a 6-year relationship because the love addict is too close and too familiar. From a philosophical perspective, I think the term "intimacy" is as clear as the term "soul" or "self." I took an entire philosophy class on what the soul is and could never quite figure it out and did not get an A.

As a love addict, I take offense to sex addiction being labeled an "intimacy disorder" when I have always been the one pushing for intimacy. When avoidants (of all people) say I was not intimate with them, I think that maybe they strive for an unattainable goal of unconditional love (or positive regard). I was the one who wanted to talk. I was the one who shared things I'd never shared with anyone. Yet I am the one labeled with an intimacy deficiency. I call bullshit.

Another word that relates to intimacy and is required for intimacy to occur is authenticity. My experience with the Landmark Forum shows to me that most people are, or start off as, inauthentic, whether or not they intentionally lie. One must strive to be authentic and intimate on a daily basis, and very few people do, at the time of this writing.

---

[582] Since sexual compulsion is considered an intimacy disorder, having affairs is no worse than playing video games or watching football to avoid intimacy. That is not to say that affairs are not serious, but that other forms of escapist behaviors are just as bad when used addictively, meaning as a way to avoid something else. (Older i.P. audAx: My ex would not like me saying that, nor would he like me bringing up scientific studies of the effect of video games on the brain.)

[583] I can cite both "Enjoy the Silence" by Depeche Mode and *The Good Earth* by Pearl Buck. I think men appreciate silence more than wimmin, at least my Dad is a man of few words.

Reasons for Self-Management and Recovery Training (SMART) Recovery: Anti-Twelve Steps[584]

In the Twelve Step meetings, it is not acceptable to have a good sense of humor, but it is acceptable for people to pretend to have addictive behavior. Even abstinent, asexual, or low libido[585] people can give their first step. Their asexual behavior never put their life at risk, never cost them any money, never destroyed their friendships, never gave them anything to apologize for except for being rigorously honest about their libido. I knew someone who thought she was a "sex addict" because she finally accepted that she was bisexual. There are so many things wrong with that. Instead of thinking about what that implies about bisexuals, I thought about what it said about her and how she was willing to throw all like-minded people under the bus.

I prefer the philosophy of the SMART Recovery to the Twelve Step Program, which focuses on mastering thought. Christopher Perrin, in *The Art of the Argument*, states, "[A]fter you have mastered the logical fallacies, you won't be so easily tricked [by yourself]." (Larsen, Hodge, & Perrin 2010).

Other concerns about the Twelve Steps:

- For the long-term attenders, having addictive behaviors leads to joining a social club (like a church).

- I don't understand. I was so ecstatic when I had sex, but in recovery I am depressed and cannot smile. I feel lost because I cannot have fun around my parents or at meetings, and the only person I can have fun with is someone I'm not allowed to see.

- I think there is a lot of confusion regarding whether or not to trust oneself. Many Christians feel that only God can be trusted and that atheists and Satanists are wrong to follow a life of self-sufficiency and freedom of speech. However, an irony I found during recovery is that to recover one needs to trust themselves (as opposed to others, even if it's a sponsor). I think what would clarify this is differentiating the Lower Self from the Higher Self. The Lower Self, or the ego, is separate from Source. But the Higher Self is so close to Source that relying on it is close to relying on God.

- The problem with recovery is that they use sexual words to help one abstain from destructive sexual behavior, words like "baffling," "cunning," and "intimacy."

- There comes a time when ROI from recovery peaks, after which it is no longer good for mental health to go to recovery groups as the recovery itself becomes a mere stand-in for the previous addictive behavior. Such new addictive behavior may result in an abundance of

---

[584] It is no mistake that the words "baffling" and "cunning" relate in some way to a woman's nether regions.

[585] Low libido is a medical symptom that would have been unheard of during the time of the Puritans and many other original Americans. Indeed, it would be a blessing.

misused time, money, thoughts, materialistic spirituality, and inappropriate relationships or relationships below a desirable standard.

Rigorous Honesty

I find it interesting that there were so many sexual compulsives in one meeting that there were not enough chairs and that people kept trailing in after the start time. It was about two classroom sizes in capacity.

However, therapists and parents tell us, sexual compulsives, who are encouraged to be rigorously honest in the meetings, that we must hide who we are forever. Men even censor their sharing on behalf of wimmin, wimmin who are not lost on the fact that female genitalia is censored more often than male genitalia. Even if people "recover," they are told to deny their recovery in the larger family unit called society or country, headed by power-hungry politicians, for life. It's no surprise that power-hungry dictators promote fear, denial, censorship, punishment, and revenge. It's probably how they themselves were raised. How can one fully recover if the cage one escapes from is locked inside another cage? Isn't it ironic that the Catholic Church built its ideas of sex on the basis of a recovered sexual compulsive, St. Augustine, yet even recovered sexual compulsives are shunned? Or that Jesus married a former "supposed" prostitute?[586]

With 12-Step Programs, I wouldn't be surprised if the majority of Christians and believers in the future are recovering compulsives. Since faith is radical, I sometimes doubt if people are honestly following the 12 Steps and being radically honest.

Signs of Addictive Thinking[587]

- Easily offended
- Likes being liked[588]
- Takes everything personally
- Sees self as a unique snowflake[589]

---

[586] See the documentary movie, *The Tomb of Jesus*, directed by James Cameron.

[587] I realize now that my love/hate philosophy arose from an addiction mentality. Something related to addictive thinking, but different, is recovery mentality. Recovery mentality is rife with slippery slope fallacies, which is necessary in the first 1-7 years, but becomes unhealthy after that time and can generate that which one wants to avoid.

[588] My neighborhood friend as a child, Laura Griffith, was more like my addictive self as an adult: she liked being liked and developed faster in puberty.

[589] This is also a sign of general immaturity.

- Shame

My definition of an addicted person: An addicted person is someone who feels morally superior either through resentment or revengeful forgiveness.

My definition of addictive behavior: A coping mechanism for reacting to other people not doing what we expect or hope they would do. Or it covers up a deeper addiction to caring what other people think and/or denial of reality[590].

My definition of sexual repression: Sexual repression is not a repression of sexual or aggressive impulses, but a repression of affection and openness.

Spirituality

It is important to recover from compulsive sexual behavior to move up through the chakras. Had I not moved past the root, I would not have gotten to the third chakra. The highest (of the basic) chakras are related to the head, brain, and mind. This is why I consider learning logical fallacies to be so key for the recovering compulsive (though it's not everything). Some called me manipulative, which I thought was abusive to do so, but I realized that I was because I was not trained in logical fallacies.

After my recovery, I got multiple invitations to church services instead of parties from my Generation X peers.

Why Did God Create Dopamine?: Dopamine's Effect on the Brain

The most dangerous thing about sex is that it hijacks your brain. That is why sex should be reserved for a trusted spouse, known as a best friend, prior to sexual intimacy because, one hopes, there is less likelihood of being blackmailed or manipulated.

When someone told me that lusting was sinful, I thought to myself, then how are spouses physiologically able to make babies if the man couldn't keep it up? What I realize now is that it isn't being attracted to each other that is sinful, but rather dopamine that caused one to sin. Lust/infatuation is essentially "drinking to get drunk."

The reason why arranged marriages were so successful all these years was because it bypassed love addiction's addictive dopamine, which caused people to view those who were "in love" as

---

[590] Sex is not the problem for a sexual compulsive; it is how one medicates the problem. If your partner or family member is addicted to sex, it's possible that the problem is you. Take responsibility for how you create your life and who you draw in.

diseased. (America has a lot of diseased people by that definition.) My therapist described "puppy love"[591] to me as projection of idealism, so that is why the first year of marriage is so difficult for people—the letdown, juxtaposed with the daydreams, is too great. Arranged marriage, without premarital sex, bypasses not only dopamine but also the crash and burn commonly associated with addictive highs. Ask any unhappily married couple if they had sex before marriage, and I bet they'll say yes.

Sex is like a drug because the first time, after virginity or extended celibacy, it doesn't do much. You need a second hit to get a buzz.

People high on dopamine have a defective frontal cortex. The frontal cortex relates to spontaneity, judgment, and memory. One weird thing I've noticed about sexual compulsives right off the bat was that they all seemed to mention having a lack of short-term memory, including myself. Teens don't have a fully developed frontal cortex either. So a sexual compulsive's brain (or the brain of any addictive person) gets stuck in the teen stage (not just because of dopamine), even if they are in an adult's body (if they weren't it could be a criminal offense).

I can understand why Puritans avoided anything pleasurable. First, pleasurable things cause dopamine, which in large doses, especially in teens with underdeveloped front cortexes, can lead to insanity. Second, it was a compliment to have good character, and a part of character back then was discipline, which can mean doing what you don't want to do for the sake of delayed gratification.

The reason why saving "love yourself" doesn't work for a love addict is because the love addict must first purge e-self of dopamine before the brain's judgment center can be restored.

People living in an addicted state act like animals, with a reptilian brain (amygdala) and *nefesh* soul, which is self-centered and sees the world as something "to be exploited for the self's own needs" (*God According to God* p.102). People who have "recovered" graduate to the front lobe/cortex and the *neshama* soul, which focuses more on making choices from an understanding of unity with others.

Regarding normalcy and addiction, let's look at the statistics of addiction:

"[S]ubstance abuse leads to more illnesses than any other preventable health condition. [...] drugs are linked to more ER visits and hospital admissions than any other single cause— [...] Drugs are also the number one cause of crime. [...] Drugs are involved in from one-half to three-quarters of all incidences of violence, including child abuse, spousal abuse, homicides, rape, and close to 100 percent of date rapes. Drugs are at the center of myriad other social problems. It's estimated that at least 60 percent of homeless people suffer addiction, [...] The

---

[591] Actual puppy love is safe as long as it's only love for an actual puppy.

total overall cost of drug abuse in the United States exceeds $400 billion a year, mostly in health-care and crime-related costs and lost productivity."—David Sheff, *Clean (Sheff 2014)*

The mixed messages about sex are on par with the mixed messages about drugs. However, I'd rather write a book where I dedicated myself to something that had, at least, a slower chance of killing me.

I think that the Native Americans gave youth peyote because overcoming addictive behavior is a rite of passage.

Men and wimmin can be friends, but only if neither has had regular doses of dopamine within a 90-day period, and they are not alone with each other.

There are also good benefits to showering without dopamine (without using the shower head as a tool for self-stimulation): helps with muscle pain, insomnia, itchiness, hair, and longevity.

If the brain is designed to seek pleasure, the question remains: "Why would God give us addictive brains?"

Withdrawal

Addictions will always be based on using good memories to mask bad ones. So the pain of withdrawal is not in giving up bad memories, but in giving up good memories.

Between my mother who kissed me too long, my grandmother who taught me that relationships were escape, and the sexual attention I got as a teen, sex to me represented comfort, safety, and confidence. To take sex away was uncomfortable and made me feel unconfident. In order to change, I had to give up what I loved. I had to give up modeling, even though I was the most enthusiastic of all models. Withdrawal also made it difficult to sleep because I used masturbation as a sleep aid. Taking away sexual partners took away my ability to express my emotions safely or to diffuse the intensity of codependence. I have no coping mechanism for handling stress. One thing of which I am certain is that one must have a pretty rough life for a coping mechanism to be a Higher Power and closest friend. And that is why I had a nervous breakdown. In summary, I felt uncomfortable, unsafe, unconfident, tired, insane, and stressed with withdrawal.

But I am willing to go through extreme discomfort in the hope that it is a temporary discomfort and that I would be able to learn my way to having boundaries.

To a person who is addicted, sex quickly goes from having the Midas touch to having Medusa sight.

AudAx

I never felt more human than when I was recovering from addictive behavior. You know you are human when you can be addicted to "necessities" like food or sex. Sex is a necessity for an animal, but a hobby for a human. To animals, they cannot be addictions because food and sex are the most important parts of their day-to-day life, but in humans, survival "essentials" can interfere with our priorities and well-being. The goal of an animal could very well be to procreate, so sex would not distract from that goal. However, in a human, for example, one's goal could be to move up the corporate ladder ethically or to have a long-sustaining marriage, in which case certain sexual choices can interfere. The very act of writing this book illustrates René Descarte's quote, "I think therefore I am [human]."

Between the generally unsavory characters and people my addictive behavior touched, I had to block 104 people on my phone and Facebook. The only group of people I knew larger than that was work associates.

Sacrifice and Celibacy

It wasn't until recovery that I understood how my ex got in prison *after* he got clean and why another ex's girlfriend would cum too quickly even though she had a sordid/storied past with sex (celibacy will do that).

Giving up self-stimulation to reduce chemical dependency and tolerance was the hardest part about recovery since I'd been doing it daily since I was 14. I was no longer able to put myself to sleep or relieve myself of urinary infections. I had to rely on other means.

Taking a hiatus from masturbation was difficult. It was a slippery slope when I tried to go to sleep, laid on my back or stomach, had to urinate, itched, had BV, got stressed, had PMS, or received a compliment on appearance from a male. It was a surprise that breathing oxygen was not a trigger. I certainly couldn't track my fertility during that time, and I had to wear underwear to bed.

I am actually glad that I slipped up enough times (regarding masturbation) in my first month of recovery that I had a memorable recovery date: the day after Independence Day, which is quite appropriate.

Celibacy was a great tool to enhance nuances. I regained my ability to orgasm without self-stimulation or fantasy. It passed through me like a solitary hiccup and lasted just as long.

I believe that celibacy was made for the side of the couple with the higher sex drive so they could get the pleasure of not always being the one to initiate.

Mutual celibacy, not political celibacy, is best saved when you have doubt in your relationship. It sorts the wheat from the chaff. Celibacy was the greatest gift from God because it gave me the ability to judge people on the content of their character rather than the quality of their sexual performance or prowess.

If the idea of celibacy scares at least 50% of all Americans, then wouldn't that make them all sexual compulsives?

Under the Greenwood Tree: The Return of the Sexual Compulsive Ex-Boyfriends and Other Exes

Sexual compulsives attract sexual compulsives. For example, the exhibitionist attracts the voyeur. It is the combination of "see and be seen." When I dated sexual compulsives, I always knew the extent of their addiction, but I didn't think it was a problem since I had addictive behavior too. I couldn't begin to imagine what it's like for all of that to be concealed and for someone to find out about it later[592]. It makes my head spin. I never really related to the whole "double life" that sexual compulsives talked about because sex was my life and everything else was gravy[593]. Life was where my passion was. To give up my passion for something even more fulfilling…well, that just tells you how amazing I believe my future could be.

Most men I dated had shame[594] that came through with their music choices, such as Pink, Linkin Park, Nine Inch Nails, Tool, or the blues. I've heard that the people we date have the same psychological vibration as ourselves, and it's very possible that I dated sexual compulsives that were not as obvious as those I dated who were.

Sexual compulsive exes have been the biggest disappointments. Let me repeat. Sexual compulsives absolutely will disappoint at one time or another. For exes, they were the people I thought I could always be friends with long after the romantic relationship ended, but in the end, they both proved me wrong.

Looking back, it's possible that the only people I ever dated, at least long term, were sex and love addicts in different forms. Personally, I think it was unintelligent of me to find a sex addict attractive because sexual compulsion is intimately tied with a history of receiving verbal abuse, and that cannot be good if the person is not self-aware. One thing I learned is that I only dated those who didn't respect others' sexual boundaries. *If* there is a slightly higher percentage of sexual compulsion in the GLBT community, then that would explain all the stories I have heard from friends of their controlling or verbally abusive same-sex lovers.

---

[592] Which is exactly what happened to me later with Roche Slim.

[593] But I did eventually get used to that being a man's modus operandi.

[594] Most people deny they have shame because they do not know what it is.

AudAx

When I get depressed at how miserably abnormal I am, I remember that most of the 55[595] people I've had sex with were my equals. That's why it's hard for me to understand what normal (or healthy) is, because I happen to know such a large number of (American) people who aren't.

Considering all forms of addiction (there are 44 separate anonymous or other recovery groups in existence), and if we assume single addictions and add up all the statistics, I'm sure we could get to 100%. What is normal if not 100%? And then what if we added statistics for those not considered normal, perhaps using statistics on disabilities? No, the trick is not to be normal but to be healthy.

A Kaurava: Jared Self Jr.

The first person I had sex with was a self-confessed slut. He was born from a man who had fathered about 100 children within a long-enough timespan for Jared to be an uncle to someone who was close to him in age. This man, my first serious boyfriend and first potential fiancé, had an obsession with porn and having sex with strangers, or even enemies. Multiple women wanted to marry him even when we were dating.

He dressed more like a metrosexual and when I saw him the first time in years he wore a wrinkled suit jacket and dress shoes even though it was a casual occasion. He never finished college and vowed to leave the country, cutting off all ties to anyone who lived in America, but never did.

I have always wanted to recreate the type of relationship I had with my first sex partner and potential fiancé—I have always wanted to share the sexual experiences we have had with others. We used to talk about our sex outside our relationship, and I am fortunate to have been able to find someone else with whom I can have that much of an honest relationship. It was the basis for relationships that would come after (or at least the ideal to which I compared relationships that were not working), even though others were less than impressed.

Snapshots in Time

10 May 2007[596]: Jared took me to Fort Boggs, where he smoked marijuana with his friend Marky who used to call me "AB" for "Audax Bitch," and we had sex. He told me that he planned on going back to school and moving to Inchon, Korea. He added that he did not plan on ever having kids[597]. Jared neither saw me drunk nor high before then. He never saw me fall asleep either because he always fell asleep first and got up last. I fell asleep for the first and last time for him while we watched *Guntoting Mamas.*

---

[595] The latest number is 74.

[596] This is when I was dating Slim Roche.

[597] He probably said this for the same reason why I would say I would always be single—lack of belief.

A conversation with Jared after we had broken up the first time and were friends:

i.P.:"How are you doing?"

Jared: "Good and you?"

i.P.: "Good."

Jared: "That's where my lawyer is." [pointing]

i.P.: "Why do you need a lawyer. [sic]"

Jared: "Well there was that accident where I sued people at my workplace for injuring me in a car accident. He's also good to talk to for legal advice."

i.P.: "What legal advice did you ask him about?"

Jared: "There was this one situation where I was dating a girl at work who was stealing money from the company but I didn't know until later. I found out because I was being interrogated about it. They never did anything to me because they realized I couldn't help them but they didn't entirely trust me because I dated her. She disappeared to New York and later moved out of the States."

i.P.: "So what do you think about the next presidential election?"

Jared: "I want Hillary to win."

i.P.: "I prefer Barack Obama."

Jared: "He's too young. He'll have another chance. Mark Warner's too young too."

i.P.: "Who do you think will run for Republican candidate?"

Jared: "People are talking about... [text is lost] But he's Republican in name only."

i.P.: "My parents said they would vote for Rice or Guiliani."

Jared: "Guiliani is a Republican in New York. He's Republican in name only. Are you still thinking about the Air Force?"

i.P.: "I don't think now would be a good time. Too dangerous."

Jared: "Have you noticed how this is all our parents' generation's fault? This wouldn't be happening if our generation was their age. They ruined it for all of us."

i.P.: "I agree. If we were their age *Adult Swim* would be on the major networks instead of the news. Or if we still had news it would be like *The Colbert Report.*"

i.P.: "So tell me about pimping[598]."

Jared: "Oh that. Well I was with my friend Thomas, looking to pay a prostitute when this prostitute says she needs a pimp. I [sic] light goes off in our head and we instantly agreed to be fake pimps." (He faked being a pimp for some prostitute who tried to commit suicide on a daily basis and eventually disappeared to California.)

Jared: "It went pretty well. She split the profits with us, but since we couldn't put it in the bank we had to spend it on frivolous things like computer games. We only had a problem with this one guy who tried to not pay..."

i.P.: "Tried to avoid paying."

Jared: "Yeah. So she had us on her speed dial for just this occasion and would only have sex in places that we were familiar with."

i.P.: "What about the part about acting like a pimp? How did you know what to do?"

Jared: "We watched a lot of movies. The most informative movie was a movie with Snoop Doggy Dog. I knew how to talk like a pimp, just use the word 'bitch' a lot. But we both knew that someone had to slap her so we drew straws."

i.P.: "I can't imagine you as a pimp. You're too nice."

Jared: "Well, I have my dark side," he said twiddling a napkin.

Later, I talked with him about the rough times I was going through with my parents when the time had come for me to move in with my boyfriend. He told me that every time he went to my house he was scared for his life. That said a lot right there, in addition to the fact that my best friend would park far from my house if she were coming to pick me up. Jared also confessed something else. He confessed that when it was clear that I was cheating on him (with either Ed Steffens or Slim Roche[599]), he cheated on me with two Indian girls. He is now dating an Egyptian who wants sex even more than him[600].

---

[598] Older i.P. audAx: "Pimps is an ugly word. We can call ourselves 'love brokers'."—Lowell Ganz and Babaloo Mandel, *Night Shift* (1982)

[599] Since we had an open relationship, "cheating" meant changing who was the primary partner.

[600] I don't remember when I wrote this.

Jared Self Jr. and Ed Steffens were the only men I knew whose sex drive exceeded my own[601]. It surprised me when I was with Jared that I could get tired of having sex. Surprise, surprise! Anything's possible.

Despite his high sex drive, he would go through periods of sexual anorexia. Then he told me how he considered becoming an Anglican priest or Catholic monk so he could get money to finish college. He was an extreme sexual compulsive who aspired to be a monk and didn't see the conflict in those two ideas. Even though I will be eternally grateful that he saved my life on one occasion, he has a tendency toward misogynism that even he doesn't realize.

You know sexual compulsion is bad when another sexual compulsive, suffering from the same intimacy disorder, complains that you could never open up.

Ed Steffens

My second serious boyfriend had had sex with about 100+ people by the age of 28 and 450-500+ people by the age of 36. He would have had a much larger sample size for serious study and research, but I'm the one who decided to write this book. He had become a sex addiction counselor. He also leads a youth group[602]. Even though we dated for four years, we had never gotten in an argument during that time or been to each others' place (only to hotels). For a serious, long-term relationship, it was still somewhat superficial, just like college life, which was when I started dating him (while still in the relationship with Jared about the entire time). He said we would always be friends, but after we broke up we never were[603].

He had a sudden marriage during the time when we were talking daily in a romantic relationship and divorced soon after because his wife found videos of me. Why they were still lying around I'll never know. He had divorced his new wife. He expanded his business to include Texas and North Carolina. He also went through months of lung problems from the average cold to bronchitis to having his tonsils taken out. The last thing I heard, he got in trouble with the law for selling products with steroids.

---

[601] Between the three of us, I should have had every STD on the planet. It just goes to show that probability does not work the way it's taught in the classroom; it can be manipulated with Law of Attraction.

[602] As with Jared, he didn't see the conflict in those two ideas.

[603] Though I tried.

AudAx

A Few Select Exes

Roche Slim

My relationship with Roche Slim was my longest relationship ever, and also an anomaly in that it was the only (failed) monogamous relationship I had seriously attempted. He was not a sexual compulsive but might have been a love addict (since he was with me). I include him at the top only because the relationship I had with him deserves to be highlighted more than the others. I met him when I was dating the two men above and had just slept with a woman the day before.

Regarding one man in particular, I was mismatched with him both on astrological and personality levels (Myers-Briggs Type Indicator), and I am eternally grateful for having that karmic experience with him. Unlike with Ed, we had extreme conflict. In total, we had three major break-ups and ten minor break-ups. Had I not had the experience of being with him, I would not have leveled up spiritually. This ultimate goal of leveling up spiritually is what some people do not understand who resort to name calling and negativity. That is why they have not accomplished what they are here to do.

"Snail"

We had written to each other for three and a half years, with one and a half years in a romantic/intimate capacity.

If he made any mistake the first year out of prison, he would get 30 years of probation, due to Virginia's insanely strict laws when compared to the rest of the country. He acted like a fool when I implied that he might get 30 years of probation. He never heard that I had planned my life around being with him for 30 years, that I knew the laws in my state well enough to know that no one could know all of them well, or that if you don't plan for worst case scenarios that you might as well just wing it. No. All he heard was that I doubted his abilities and decisions. I guess he thought he was Superman, able to get past a year of probation in a single bound. Anyways, that's when he threw me a sexual insult even though we'd never had sex. No one I could remember had ever stooped so low in such a direct way. It was then that I considered that his earlier feelings for me had been a foil. I might not be able to please one, but if I have pleased about 87 others, then I think I'm still in the game[604].

---

[604] Older i.P. audAx: I don't want to be too negative here. I probably wrote this when it was fresh, and I was hurting. It really was such a lovely relationship, that I thought I could recreate it with a different penpal but never could.

Jack Manning

My friend says things like, "My friend's feeling depressed so I'm gonna rob a bank," which is not too much weirder than when Jared Self says, "I want to be a monk and own a porn video company." Anything I do is tame in comparison.

Jake Clusspud

He was a certified taxi driver but was a New Jersey driver. I relied on him for all things car-related, but he wasn't the best with directions. I was told that he looked like Brad Pitt before he got slightly tubby and that he used to be terribly mean and still is when he's drunk but I only saw him as the sweetest, nicest person to ever meet who got along with everybody… that is until we talked politics.

Differing Views of Sex

Disclaimer: I use the term pervert as a good thing.

Me: I am an imaginative and creative pervert who goes into sex with a child-like joy. I use sex as a joyful distraction. I am driven by *joie de vivre* and curiosity. I have sex with objectives to find the wisdom of the world. I am accepting of other perverts even if I do not understand them. I still retain a strong sense of morality, even though I find being responsibility-minded a pain because it reminds me that it is not all fun and can have serious consequences.

Jared: He puts much importance on marrying a person with similar sexual tastes, as I do, but reality may be somewhat different from his ideals.

Ed: He is a masculine pervert who uses sex as his main form of distraction and can function well without it. He is driven by power and control. He highly objectifies women, in a kind sort of way, and has sex with as many people as possible whenever possible wherever possible. He has no comprehension of the thinking of virgins. He desires to devirginize others. I see how someone could interpret his lifestyle as encouraging the loss of sexual morals. He sees sex as helpmeet to fill out his manly role.

Roche Slim: He is both a silly and a serious pervert who uses sex as a tool of communication—he uses it as a way to say "I love you" and as a form of self-expression. He is driven by the feeling of the moment. He is a contradiction between old school beliefs held by his parents' generation and a product of his own generation with its own ideas of gender roles. In the same way that having sex is a way to forget about the concerns of the world, sex brings with it additional, if not primary, concerns that may at times seem insurmountable.

AudAx

Snail: He is an imaginative pervert who uses sex as something to think about out of fun or out of fear. He is driven by the primal need for freedom, but restricts himself with the primal need for acceptance. In no way does jealousy ever cloud his thinking because he sees jealousy as a problem with the person who has the jealousy.

Others

Michael McGee: He is a romantic pervert who prefers to give. He is very sensuous and enjoys the use of his senses. He is nowhere near as sexually driven as I am.

Knight Labistre: He is a hobby pervert. Sex is literally his hobby.

Relationship Patterns (Age 22 to 29)

Before this section I had six out of thirteen one-night stands, whereas Roche, my boyfriend at the time (2004-2008), had three out of seven one-night stands (almost half). My six were Bing "Cosplay" Sully, Gambit Ogeguri, Eris "Odin" Eevlos, Evan "Vikas" Runner, a skirt-wearing goth guy, and Knight Labistre.

The people I had sex with in general between age 21 and age 29 were Jared, Ed, Dwayne, Jerome, Jason "Dom" Privater, Michael M., Roche, Skeeter, George M, and Gary. The people I had romantic relationships with but did not have sex with were Matt M., Matthew M., and Daniel.

Patterns with boyfriends: movie fans (Matt M., George, and Gary), visual (Jared, Roche, and George), anime (Freddie, Matthew H., Jared, Roche, and Gary), and obsessive/addictive personalities (Jared, Ed, Roche, George, and Gary).

Men who said they loved me in January 2012: Gary, Larry, and Snail. The people who love me in 2012 represent alcoholism, homelessness, and drug addiction respectively.

Sportfucking[605]

> "Those who try to make room for sex as mere casual enjoyment pay
> the penalty: they become shallow."—G.E.M. Anscombe

I used to think of sex as a hobby. I am an enthusiast. Here was my thinking: Many married people are lucky if their spouse shares their interest, but if not that's okay. Sane spouses do not get upset if you have poker night with your friends, if you play golf with your friends, or if you

---

[605] Older i.P. audAx: I know that my ex will take offense to this, but here were my thoughts on the subject anyways.

go shopping with your friends. Sex is no different. You're either interested or you're not. It's not the end of the world if you and your spouse share different interests. If someone came home and said, "I got a hole in one!" the natural response should be "Congratulations!" However, when I say, "Honey, I have wonderful news! I'm going to be part of a foursome/gangbang" I get a cold shoulder instead. It doesn't make sense. I wouldn't tell someone, "You can never watch football for as long as you're married to me. If you so much as think about football, we're through." That's not a marriage; that's a prison. Sex is not an addiction, distracting one from marriage. Marriage could be the real addiction, distracting one from sex.

Now that I am older and more experienced (and also not as horny), I don't see sex as the hobby I used to see it as. If my husband died or if I got divorced, believing biblically that there should only be one spouse[606] per lifetime[607], I would view sex as a profession and be free to penetrate the sex industry even if it's with something as approvable as surrogate therapy.

Sportfucking was fun, but when I did it I was not completely happy. Free love comes at a cost, whether it be pregnancy, STIs, or both.

BV

Something about as common as herpes and something just as annoying is BV. Some women are lucky enough to have it constantly (I'm being sarcastic), or at least every time they have sex, or maybe just every time they have sex with a particular person. It is not an STD, but it can still cause issues with a pregnancy. However, what makes it most annoying, besides the stench, is that in order to treat it one must have a medical prescription because treatments cannot be found over the counter.

Cypridophobia: Glitter

Dicks are like a box of chocolates; you never know what you're going to get until it's too late and you've hurt someone's feelings by the look on your face. Coitus reservatus (withdrawal) does not prevent against venereal diseases or pregnancy.

Sexual compulsions are born of bad habits that formed when you realized how easy it was to be hedonistic. These bad habits solidify when you care nothing for consequences, believing yourself to be invincible and all-powerful through urge alone.

---

[606] Not one boyfriend (or girlfriend)

[607] According to the Bible, when I go to "heaven," I will be judged along with the human race because I have "known" the human race.

AudAx

I have had HPV, BV, and herpes and consider myself lucky.

The Catholic, Peter Kreeft, argued that religion is sex or sex is religion when discussing the issue of homosexuality. If that be the case, then can a religion of sexuality really be called an addiction? Or is it a healthy obsession? Am I really an addict if I have an STD or am I merely a statistic and result of a roll of the dice. I'm not a bad person; I just clicked on a bad website that infected my computer.

To me, herpes was an indicator to write this book and to settle down in a monogamous marriage via non-coital courting.

Many people do not realize that they do not test for herpes during usual check-ups. I researched why that was. The medical society felt that the cost outweighed the benefit. The benefit is that the more people know they have herpes, the more they can prevent the spread of herpes. The cost was that it had reached such stigma levels of high proportion that several people would commit suicide upon the discovery of the virus.

The actual results? About 20% have tested positive for HSV-2, the genital version, and 80% have tested positive for HSV-1, the cold sore. Since most people do not even know if they are carriers, then it's quite possible that herpes could be affecting over half the population, making it…normal. I would compare it to pot: it's common, it's soft, about a quarter to a half of the population have tried it (whether or not they were aware), and it strikes fear in those who [think they] haven't.

Surprise Gift: Being Enceinte

As for surprise gift pregnancies, I do not believe it is the government's or any religion's choice to decide, even if the person is a repeat offender (multigravida).

If it is only a surprise to one party, then it is considered abusive to have unprotected sex with the intention of getting pregnant. However, I would not blame someone who did so. Men do not understand the pull of the biological clock. It's *very* powerful.

Other Risks

I remember a man regaling me and others with a true story about a girl's braces getting stuck in her girlfriend's vaginal piercing and how he had to explain why they were in the emergency room to both families. Quite hilarious after the fact!

Other real hazards are fainting and getting scratched by teeth or nails (whether or not during intercourse). I've fainted about twice in my life. It never hurts to have a glass of cold water nearby. Oh, and it might be nice to dim the lights.

On another note, priapism, a painful erection, is pretty serious.

Post-"Recovery"

External Expression

When I stopped caring if people liked me, I attracted three men who cared so much about appearance that it hurt the relationship. The first one broke up with me because I held his hand at work on a day when no one else was in the office. The second man broke up with me because I was "earthy" and didn't wear makeup. The third man broke up with me because I changed the color of my hair to a naturally non-occurring color.

Prior to "recovery," I didn't believe anyone anyone could love me no matter what e did. After recovery, I didn't care if anyone loved me because I loved e enough for the two of us.

Sartre was wrong. Freedom is not a burden due to choices, since I actively believe there's no such thing as a wrong decision (because it is an unlimiting belief that removes excusitis). Freedom is a burden because when you're free (like Anita Moorjani) most people can't relate.

Sexual Anorexia

"A person who can't is on a path of rediscovery, a person who won't (or will too much) is on a path of reform, and a person who will in moderation is on a path of restoration."—Me

I did not have this, for that would not have been recovery, but I ended up in an open relationship with someone who had ED due to anorexia and someone who had sexual anorexia[608]. The former was far easier to date because we could cuddle and even shower together. The fact that I felt I could not do that with the other man motivated me even more to publish this book.

Regarding sexual anorexism, Buddha was wrong. Nothing comes from the middle[609]. It's "rags to riches," not "middle class to riches." Those you hate can just as quickly and easily be those you love and vice versa. Fallen angels are synonymous with demons. When things fall, they fall all the way. Those, like St. Augustine, who are celibate now were lustful creatures in the past and can just as easily go back there again. So if the church does not want to see pedophilia run rampant, then they should be like the Protestants and choose someone who's already married to lead[610].

---

[608] I wondered if being with anorexics (of any type) was a way of restricting myself. I hadn't had intercourse that lasted beyond a minute for 11 months now.

[609] Older i.P. audAx: I disagree with my younger self.

[610] Older i.P. audAx: We've already had married popes, so what's the big deal?

Post-puberty, sexual anorexia (or sexual deprivation not used as BDSM) can be achieved only after a long time in which sexual desperation and insatiability has not been satisfied. This is a similar pattern that people go through with hunger. By the time the threshold of tolerance is reached, all desire comes to a halt due to a belief that what one desires is not likely and cannot come to fruition. In this way, it relates to the Law of Attraction in that it illustrates the idea that fear of loss creates a move toward loss.

Sexual Anorexia and Shame

Sexual compulsives in recovery tend to think that sex is more like alcohol than food, believing celibacy to be the only answer. They then apply the same standards to non-compulsives, since they don't realize that not everyone was abandoned by their mother and experiences pervasive shame (a commonly misunderstood word) the same way they did.

Unfortunately, this has an effect opposite from the desired one. It is in fact recovering sexual compulsives, such as St. Augustine, that create another generation of sexual compulsives. It is these sexual compulsives who successfully destroyed the church, eventually forcing millenials into agnosticism or worse. And even though it was the politics of greed (not allowing anyone to inherit anything upon death) that made priests and nuns celibate, it was the celibacy itself that created sexual abuse in the Catholic church.

Guilt easily turns into shame from which all acts of guilt arise. Unhealthy behavior is shame-based, or based on the idea of being unworthy or unlovable.

The celibacy itself creates shame, which creates sexual compulsion, and the recovering sexual compulsive thinks the answer is celibacy[611]. That's some circular logic. Isn't it clear then that celibacy is not the answer? And that even occasional (as in not habitual) masturbation is preferable to crossing someone's boundaries, hurting someone's feelings, contracting STDs, or having unplanned pregnancies?

How can you please your spouse if you become celibate? What did they do to deserve punishment?

I would not recommend this method of celibacy for those with obsessions with weird fetishes. What those people need is acceptance from others. Sexual compulsion comes from shame, but if shame comes from sex, I do not see it as a sexual compulsion, but a call for charity and acceptance, much like what we see for homosexuals.

Even though both groups have shame, abstinence, which is good for sexual compulsives ready for recovery would make a self-hating fetishist go crazy. We all know what happens to self-hating

---

[611] Addiction is a vicious cycle. Stress create addiction. Addiction creates stress. The only way out is to not be stressed? If anyone can find a solution to stress, I'd love to hear it.

homosexuals. Case in point: Omar Mateen, the man responsible for the largest shooting in United States history. Self-haters also tend to make the worst bullies. I was bullied by both a self-hating lesbian, Melissa Cortez, AND a self-hating deaf kid, Red Richy.

People with fetishes, for whom abstaining from such fetishes is dangerous and makes them feel shame and an inability to feel accepted (e.g., homosexuality), it is better for them to be loved and accepted unconditionally, for one cannot just remove the arousal template they were given in the first years of their life[612]. Failure to accept the person seeking acceptance is a failure before God. Like a beggar, they do us a favor by allowing us to perform *tzedekah*. Treating it like an addiction when it is not does more harm than good and is what is meant when we say, "The road to hell is paved with good intentions," which is believed to have come from Saint Bernard of Clairvaux.

Richard Crisp came up with the imagined contact hypothesis, which is essentially imagining better positive social interaction with people with whom we felt prejudiced against (as opposed to toward) and matches what Maxwell Maltz believes in *Psychocybernetics*. This improves attitudes we have toward sexual minorities. Whatever traces of prejudice we have left after using this process can be eliminated by eliminating emotionally charged labels and nouns.

Since "recovery," I have concluded that the definition of an unsuccessful person is someone with addictive behavior(s). If addictive behavior comes from shame, and shame keeps us from success, then everyone who feels unsuccessful or is still aiming for success must feel unworthy of it. Looked at it from that perspective, *very few* people are without shame. Most people have such behaviors (a.k.a. "sinful behavior") and that is why so few people are successful.

Anyone who feels shame can turn anything into addictive behavior. Healthy behavior does not require coping strategies; habits formed from a place of self-acceptance are tools for abundance.

How Far Do You Eliminate Your Old Self?

I was ready for "recovery" when I had squeezed out all the crunchy goodness I could out of sexual pursuits.

At a certain point in my sobriety, I decided to take back a part of my old self.

One thing I kept was my lack of inhibition. My ability to get the party started was valuable because even after I had given up nudity, I was still able to be the first to sing karaoke, or the first to get on the dance floor, thereby giving other people unspoken permission to sing or dance. My lack of inhibition was therefore not a bad thing, just misdirected.

---

[612] Even though, boy, do people try, especially with exorcisms and prison.

AudAx

From knowing my addictive pattern, I also know my gifts. For instance, I know that I love getting to know a variety of new people.

It wasn't until I was in "recovery" for sexual compulsion that I realized I could transform desperate attempts at agape to charity, love of humankind.

I do not like being in a paradigm of "recovery" and am glad to be "recovered" enough to focus on other things.

Ironies of Addiction and Recovery

The ironic thing about addiction is its requirement for dishonesty to act out because in my writings and conversations with acquaintances, I have been told that I am the most honest person people have ever met. Have you noticed the irony of the most honest person people have ever met being told that because she is a compulsive, she must be dishonest? Have you noticed the similarity to the irony of the person with anxious attachment being told that because she is a compulsive, she must have an intimacy disorder?

One unexpected result of going through the recovery process was that I learned that, unlike with other addictions, I made my truest friends when I was drowning in my addictive behavior. Why did I keep them as friends? Because you can never be reminded too many times that you're loved, especially as someone whose life revolved around the "need" to feel loved. The irony here is that the very people who helped foster my addictive behavior were the very people who could save me from my addictive behavior.

Another irony about recovery is that the significant other seeks only for the behavior to stop, with no thought about what's behind the curtain. Recovery, much to the chagrin of the significant other, requires looking behind the curtain to see all the things the recovering person used to deny about the significant other.

Giving Thanks

I feel like I have been so blessed to have had so many wonderful experiences with exquisite food, decadent luxury, and mind-blowing sex that those experiences could last in my memories for a lifetime and that I would have no need for anymore. I have been overly satisfied.

I am thankful that all of the introspection I am going through, all the emotions, all the experiences, are timely for me and others. Everything recent impacts and influences those around me—my boyfriend, my friends, my family—in a positive way and may cause them to reflect on their own life.

The universe truly had my back.

I thank God that I'm a female because whenever I acted out, I didn't have to spend money or do something too illegal. (I've never even paid for porn or pay-per-view.) And I never dehumanized anyone (intentionally). I may have been shallow by preferring appearances or by letting sex come first, but I would never hesitate to pray for anyone I acted out with.

I thank God I never auditioned as a stripper, despite how much I prepared for it. From the stories I heard from men who hit rock bottom, I no longer see how I could have had a fulfilling career if I were surrounded by people who were desperate for affirmation, by people drenched in shame.

I thank God that the Internet wasn't my weakness because there are so many non-sexual things to do on the Internet, and it is a treasure trove of resources. My issues were not the Internet, my issues were unprotected sex and affairs. Unprotected sex is not so much an issue outside of monogamous relationships, and affairs are not an issue in a nonmonogamous one. *The fact that I had mixed the two was enough to consider myself a sexual compulsive.* (For example, if I were monogamous inside a commitment phobic nonmonogamous relationship, or nonmogamous inside a jealous monogamous relationship, that would have been a problem, which it ended up being.)

I might not have always lived a godly and pious life, but I lived a life of allowing myself to return to Him, the Source of all things.

The true value of making addiction recovery into a lifestyle is in making life a conscious experience. In the same way that people make a difference with the environment, they can make a difference with conscious sexuality. Those who feel guilt are missing the point, and those are the ones who will stay in a cycle of pain and suffering until they've had their fill.

I also found that recovery, for lack of a better word, was the most effective way to remove blockages, and for that I am truly grateful for the opportunity to truly live.

Top 10 Negative Feelings For Which I'm Grateful:

1. Becoming who I am and want to be regarding my relationship with my father

2. Food

3. Having a tedious pace at work

4. Knowing my weaknesses (anger) and strength

5. Learning lessons about the ego

6. My increase in salary

7. Recognizing the feeling of obsession

8. Recognizing the need to slow down and maintain

9. Seeing my reflection

10. Seeing red flags sooner and recognizing risk

I am thankful for the experiences I have had, but I am more thankful for change. I am thankful to be young when I was young, but I am even more thankful for having a future. I am thankful for tantra, water, and the opening of the sacral chakra.

Resources

Anything by Patrick Carnes, Pia Mellody, or Melody Beattie

Before I Leave

"Letting go of past glory can be the hardest thing of all, for what is left when those things that make us who we are begin to fade?" (Varcas, 2016)

When one-night stand agreements were broken by a call or text asking for a two-night stand (and I'm not referring to a place to put a lamp near the bed), I realized it was time to stop. When I forgot to consider a stranger's soul and regarded their person as an inconvenience or annoyance, I realized my journey had come to an end. Anyone who does what I have done specifically will get no sympathy from me, and only time will tell what lessons e has learned against a backdrop of high risk (such as dating someone from one's bus; that can get awkward).

At age 30, I was at the point where I could believe in being a one-man woman. If you had told me that when I was in college, I would not have believed it for a minute. At the age of 31, when I lingered in legal single status for too long, I wondered what was wrong with me, but eventually I asked, "What's wrong with men?" There's nothing wrong with men per se, but whatever it is that men are taught is not conducive to a happily married home, and the people who teach them are either his parents or his peers ("parents" includes a womyn). If the men aren't taught what they need, then neither are the wimmin because it's not just that wimmin need men, but that "we are people who need people." At the age of 33, I realized that I had reached the true age of adulthood because that was the age when people realize that their actions have consequences.

I hope that the reader has come away from my past experiences more enlightened, more questioning, and more accepting of self and others.

May this book be seen as a history, a plea not to judge those who differ from you, and even a quest to understand our own spirituality through the greatest vehicle known to man. As is believed in the east, which is where I was born, no life is complete without a thorough knowledge of the sexual energy underlying humankind.

Now that I have accomplished what I set out to accomplish in this book, such continued behavior as this book required no longer serves me. Coitus is highly overrated. The only thing that matters is character, not even what's between your ears.

Whatever you do, sexual or otherwise, do it in alignment with Source. Feel good about it. Anything that brings a smile to someone's face is good. Don't ever do something you don't feel awesome about.

At the age of 34, I am glad that I can now close the book on my 1 Challenge Number.

As I close this chapter of my life, I say goodbye to the past. I have a future, and I have someone waiting in the wings if he'll take me.

Epilogue

Less than a year after my "recovery," I opened up communication with those I thought were relatively safe, or with those whose friendships truly mattered, and discovered that I had inspired them not only to get married, but to be in open marriages. If I could not inspire those I dated to marry, I was at least glad that I inspired other men on the outskirts to do what the men I dated would not do.

Astrological Dating

After I had gotten "sober," the universe decided to bring me (unbeknownst to me until I connected the dots) men whose signs were in their sun around the time that I met them and who only stayed for about a month for various reasons. I dated a Leo when the eclipse was in Leo, I returned to a Scorpio when the sun was in Scorpio, I dated a Pisces between when the Sun and New Moon was in Pisces, and I dated an Aries when the sun was in Aries. The most exciting of all this was when Venus was in Aries square Saturn in Capricorn because the sky reflected my boyfriend's natal chart, and even where a planet wasn't a perfect match to the natal chart, the planet was in the correct element.

Reflections on My Longest Relationship

Out of more than 100 romantic relationships, I only found one man who was a chaser[613]; he was the only one who pursued me. However, the problem with a chaser is that to keep a chaser interested, one has to feign a light interest in him. The way I handled that was to spend more time being interested in others. It was an unsatisfying relationship because, for him, he never won, and, for me, I couldn't put my full self into it without him labeling me as "crazy" or a "nag." It easily devolved into a "hurry up and wait" relationship, perhaps on both sides. I had to hurry up to prove my devotion and wait for him to remember that I existed. But it wasn't just me who felt that way. He had to prove that he loved me and wait for me to actually receive that love if it wasn't in my love language.

Sex as a Common Love and Uniter

In the time succeeding my "recovery," I tried so hard to be normal, to do what normal wimmin do, like listen to dating bullshit. That's normal, right? Because it has nothing to do with sex, or even love. But I have to remind myself that men love me not because I'm normal, but because

---

[613] Older i.P. audAx: Meaning this that men who chase, at least in my life, are as rare as those who experience extreme jealousy. Don't believe everything you're told about the other gender.

I'm like them. Because I have a passion for something that men have a passion for too. Because we share a common love. I might have intercourse rarely now, but I will never be a prude. And those (all those) I have loved before, I will love forever. Even if that love came at a cost. Because if one is love, one cannot be not love.

Appendix A: New Terms (from The Meaning of a Metaphorical Life)

New Terms A-D

Andor- And/or

Circles- Obese people

Culture- Societies compared with other societies

Demise- Death

E- He or she; Him or her (non-gender specific pronoun)

"Why not create a gender neutral pronoun that applies strictly to people? (I do not think that anyone wants to fall under the heading of the neutral pronoun it.) This new neutral might seem strange at first, but, in the end, our language would be stronger and less biased. [...] Not wanting to use the masculine gender and unwilling to refer to a coworker as "it," many turn to the plural, but gender-neutral, pronoun they use as a substitute for a singular noun. These befuddled souls realize that they are still talking about single individuals, so they match their plural pronouns with singular verbs. This will not do. Where is our gender-neutral pronoun?" (Strumpf, 2004, p. 190)

New Terms E-H

Godinterm- adj. This term refers to the time when all positive, ideal traits are exalted in the use of a single term that only slightly hints at the term's proscribed definition in daily use. For example, "human" "civilized," "soul," "pure," "virtue," "beauty," etc. Notice especially when this is used in *The Bible*. Any term using this is synonymous with each other insofar that they all mean "good" to the person using it.

The Great Controller- Money

The Great Divider- Opinions

The Great Lesson- The 20th Century

The Great Warning- World War II

The Greatest Story- Everyone's life

Happiness- Whenever I refer to happiness I refer to what I perceive is the happiness Thelma from Thelma and Louise has when she says, "I feel awake."

New Terms I-L

Knowledge: One either knows something or does not. If, one knows something then one cannot be taught to know something because knowledge by my definition cannot be expressed with words or movement. However, it can be gained through the act of creation, for the C/creator knows H/his creation.

Learn: One can be taught to learn something because learning is adding to the brain's database.

"It's not what you eat, but what you digest, that makes you strong. It's not what you earn, but what you save, that builds your wealth. And it's not what you learn, but what you remember, that makes you wise."—Unknown

New Terms M-P

Memory- Container of oral literature

Memory San Kofa- God

Moment of Moral Weakness-regret

Moment of Recollection- Conversion experience

Ne plus ultra- the highest point capable of being attained; nirvana

Onely- Only

Onyx- Black; Negro; Colored; African-American

Paranoid- The feeling that people are staring at you

Perfect- Applies to everything because everything is perfect

Prostitute- A lover who does not discriminate

Psuche-Soul

Pt- Past, present, and future; was, is, and will be

New Terms Q-T

Rememberers- Historians

Remembrances- History

Society- The system of bias

Soulculture- Individuals

Spacetime- Space and time

Term- Word

Think- The act of organizing words and movements for practical use

Thoughts- Audial or visual forms that must be potentially similar in character with its object without being its object, within the Kantian phenomenal world.

To-day- Today

Tree of discrimination- Tree of knowledge

New Terms U-Z

The Unknown Variable- The Answer

Wilderness- Nature

Wimmin- Women

Womyn- Woman

Appendix B: Spiritual Credentials[614]

Disclaimer: Though I value spiritual knowledge, in no way have my spiritual pursuits been of a compulsive nature; they have not interfered or been a way to escape from challenges I have had.

"Experience God"

You have not lived until a summa cum laude graduate has wooed you.

You have not lived until your private parts have been worshipped and

described in terms of a delicious item on the menu of a five-star restaurant.

You have not lived until your very image and name evokes a strong orgasm or another feeling never before experienced through image and name alone.

You have not lived until you have experienced God.

Discovery Path	Cognitions That Led to the Next Lesson
Law of Attraction	My most common form of communication is through feeling.
Psychic workshops	I also communicate with thought.
John Belldodge	Even when people say opposite things, they are actually intending the same thing. Words are really the least effective communicator. They are most open to misinterpretation, most often misunderstood.

---

[614] Older i.P. audAx: The censored version of this book is the only version of this book. I originally had sexual credentials in the appendices, but I found that to be akin to bragging and, therefore, unhealthy.

Discovery Path	Cognitions That Led to the Next Lesson
Conversations with God/A Course in Miracles	See quotes below.
The Bible, "Parable of the Sower"	Most of my messages are not heeded. Some, because they seem too good to be true. Others, because they seem too difficult to follow. Many, because they are simply misunderstood. Most, because they are not received.
Jay Runon	Do you not see that I could just as easily work through your imagination as anything else?
World Knowledge Organization	"[I]t is you who have invited Me. For I have come to you, in this form, right now, in answer to your call."—Walsch, *Conversations with God*
Synchronicity	"Because some people are willing to actually listen."—Walsch, *Conversations with God*
Lessons for George	"You cannot know God until you've stopped telling yourself that you already know God. You cannot hear God until you stop thinking that you've already heard God. I cannot tell you My Truth until you stop telling Me yours."—Walsch, *Conversations with God*

Discovery Path	Cognitions That Led to the Next Lesson
Angels in forms of butterflies and bats	"And should I come in any other form, to any other people, the first say I did not appear to the second, because I did not look to the second as I did to the first, nor say the same things--so how could it have been Me?"—Walsch, *Conversations with God*
Gospel of Thomas	"For God does not reveal Godself to Godself from or through outward observation, but through inward experience."—*Conversations with God*
World Knowledge Organization	If, then, revelation is requested, it cannot be had, for the act of asking is a statement that it is not there…
Law of Attraction	The correct prayer is therefore never a prayer of supplication, but a prayer of gratitude.
The Bible, "Parable of the Mustard Seed"	"If you have but the faith of a mustard seed, you shall move mountains."—Matthew 17:20 (Unknown version)
A Course in Miracles	"God's is the only Will. When you have recognized this, you have recognized that your will is His."—*A Course in Miracles*, Lesson 74 (Schucman 2007)
Ordo Templi Orientis	"Do what thou wilt shall be the whole of the law."—Aleister Crowley (from "Fais ce que voudras."—Rabelais)
A Course in Miracles	"[T]he ultimate outcome is assured."

Discovery Path	Cognitions That Led to the Next Lesson
A Course in Miracles	Every human thought, and every human action, is based in either love or fear.
Adoption	And where did you get the idea of how much less than magnificent you are? From the only people whose word you would take on everything. From your mother and your father.
Gospel of Thomas	Yet the greatest reminder is not anyone outside you, but the voice within you.
World Knowledge Organization: "If you know something and do not do it, you do not know it."—Unknown	You can know yourself to be generous, but unless you do something which displays generosity, you have nothing but a concept.
Science class	"From the No-thing thus sprang the Everything – a spiritual event entirely consistent, incidentally, with what your scientists call The Big Bang theory."—Walsch, *Conversations with God*
The Emanation of Wellness church	God produced, from pure energy, all that now exists.
Bible discussion: "in the *imagination* of God"	"image and likeness of God"—The Bible
A Course in Miracles: Purpose of communion	Your job on Earth, therefore, is not to learn (because you already know), but to re-member Who You Are.
My antonym theory, which became the wedding ring theory	A thing cannot exist without its opposite.

Discovery Path	Cognitions That Led to the Next Lesson
Predestination/Past life regression	If you conclude from this that past, present, and future exist at one and the same "time," you are right.
A Course in Miracles, Lessons 23, 26, and 135, as well as Chapters 6, 8, 11, and 24: It is impossible to attack or be attacked.	"[T]here are no victims in the universe."—Walsch, *Conversations with God*
"Nothing is either good nor bad, but thinking makes it so."—Shakespeare	"The mistake is not in choosing them [bad things], but in calling them bad."—Walsch, *Conversations with God*
Parable of the Taoist farmer	Envy not success, nor pity failure, for you know not what is success or failure
Parable of the Little Soul (during my trip to Korea in 2010)	"And so the little soul in question was as a candle in the sun."—Neale Donald Walsch, *Conversations with God* and *The Little Soul and the Sun*
The Bible	"Father, Father, why hast Thou forsaken me?"—Matthew 27:46 (Unknown version)
Adoption experience/vision of flashlights on my feet in a dark tunnel	"And forget not Who You Are in the moment of your encirclement by that which you are not."—Walsch, *Parable of the Little Soul* and *The Little Soul and the Sun*
Chad Wastone/George Mireille/Jessica Roostard	You are turning out a new manifestation literally as fast as you can think.

Discovery Path	Cognitions That Led to the Next Lesson
DC/Virginia Earthquake, Hurricane Irene, and Tropical Storm Lee in 2011	"And mass consciousness? Why, that is so powerful it can create events and circumstances of worldwide import and planetary consequences."—Walsch, *Conversations with God*
John Belldodge/Lessons for George	For it is only when they can accept responsibility for all of it that they can achieve the power to change part of it.
George Mireille	So long as you entertain the notion that there is something or someone else out there "doing it" to you, you disempower yourself to do anything about it.
Roche Slim	It is much easier to change what you are doing than to change what another is doing.
Cat Stevens	If you want to feel bad, feel bad.
George Mireille/Roche Slim	"[Hell] is the experience of the worst possible outcome of your choices, decisions, and creations."—Walsch, *Conversations with God*
Church/Spanish: "Sin" means "without"/*A Course in Miracles*: Depression is blasphemy	Yet there is an experience of the soul so unhappy, so incomplete, so less than whole, so separated from God's greatest joy, that to your soul this would be hell.
Karma/intuition over conscience	Consequences are results, natural outcomes.

Discovery Path	Cognitions That Led to the Next Lesson
Lady Gaga's *Born This Way*	"[Y]ou are the one who has decided Who and What You Really Are--And Who You Want to Be."—Esther Hicks, *Ask and It Is Given*
Mom: Living vicariously	This is My ideal: that I should become realized through you.
Shakespeare	"There are more things in Heaven and Earth, Horatio, than are dreamt of in your philosophy."—Shakespeare
World Knowledge Organization: Your Genie Is In You	"There is nothing you cannot be, there is nothing you cannot do. There is nothing you cannot have."—Neale Donald Walsch, *Conversations with God*
The Bible	"And the Lord said, 'Behold, the people are one, and they have all one language; and this is only the beginning of what they will do: and now nothing will be restrained from them, which they have imagined to do."—Genesis 11:6 KJV
Past life regression: I chose my parents	You may, however, select the persons, places, and events…with which to create your experience.
"Nothing is either good nor bad, but thinking makes it so."—Shakespeare	A thing is only right or wrong because you say it is.

Discovery Path	Cognitions That Led to the Next Lesson
Coworker Falafel Herd (same age/ graduated same year/same employment/ functional job)	A lawyer's career would end tomorrow were there no more litigation. A doctor's career would end tomorrow were there no more illness. A philosopher's career would end tomorrow were there no more questions.
Dad/Usman Hassan: "God helps those who helps themselves."—Algernon Sidney	I will do nothing for you that you will not do for your Self.
George Mireille	Not to decide is to decide.
Hana Unity	[L]earn to greet each such incident as a small part of a larger mosaic.
A Course in Miracles/World Knowledge Organization	You cannot fail.
My philosophy	There is no coincidence, and nothing happens "by accident."
World Knowledge Organization: Your Genie Is In You	The First Law is that you can be, do, and have whatever you can imagine.
George Mireille	The Second Law is that you attract what you fear.
My poetry	A thought is forever.
Down the Rabbit Hole	Like energy attracts like energy
Einstein	Einstein came closer than any other human…to discovered, explaining, and functionalizing the creative secret of the universe.

Discovery Path	Cognitions That Led to the Next Lesson
The Bible/Napoleon Hill's Mastermind	"Wherever two or more are gathered in My name [...]"—Matthew 18:20 (Unknown version)
Lynn McTaggart's *The Love Wave*/Bianca Ben-Lassie's The Emanation of Wellness church	"[C]ommunities or congregations often find miracle-producing power in combined thinking."—Unknown
A Course in Miracles	The realm of the relative was created in order that I might experience My Self... This does not make the realm of the relative real.
A Course in Miracles	This book is far from My only tool.
Rose: Help with clairaudience	Listen to the words to the next song you hear.
Dianetics	Engrams=Samskara
The Urantia Book	[Text lost]
Goth-friendly church in 2016	There is a place for me.
Umbanda (Brazilian/Portuguese) in 2016	It is the right time for me to move.
Spiritualist (Mediumship Church)	[Text lost]
Kabbalism (Practical Jewish Mysticism)	Do things that are outside your comfort zone.
Dao (Chinese; not Tao) in 2016	[Text lost]
Moorish Science (Moorish) in 2016	[Text lost]

Discovery Path	Cognitions That Led to the Next Lesson
International Temple of Deliverance (Revivalist Healing Church) in 2016	Healing still exists in churches.
Mega Memory/Dianetics/Maum Meditation (Korean)	The things we remember cause the greatest harm.
Dying to Be Me by Anita Moorjani	Our highest calling is to be our authentic selves.
Landmark Forum	The stories we tell ourselves are attached to events
"It's not what we eat but what we digest that makes us strong; not what we gain but what we save that makes us rich; not what we read but what we remember that makes us learned; and not what we profess but what we practice that gives us integrity."—Francis Bacon Sr.	If our memories are poisoned with stories, then we are not here to learn.

Appendix C: Discussion Questions

What are you really looking for in sex? This is a question everyone should ask themselves.

Works Cited

Alexie, S. (Ed.). (2015). *The Best American Poetry 2015*. New York, New York: Scribner Poetry.

Ali, Drew. *The Holy Koran of the Moorish Holy Temple of Science*. Califa Media, 2014.

Aurelius, M. (1944). *Meditations*. Oxford: Clarendon.

Ba, M. (1981). *So Long a Letter*. Oxford: Heinemann.

Baier, Annette. *Doing and Being: Selected Readings in Moral Philosophy*. Edited by Joram Graf. Haber, Macmillan, 1993. Trust and Anti-Trust

Belanger, M. G. (2005). *The Merriam-Webster Thesaurus* (New ed.). Springfield, Mass.: Merriam-Webster.

Brown, D. (2003). *The Da Vinci Code: A Novel*. New York: Doubleday.

Carnes, Patrick. *Out of the Shadows: Understanding Sexual Addiction*. Hazelden Information & Edu, 2001.

Craddock, Ida. "The Wedding Night by Ida Craddock." *The Wedding Night*, 13 Oct. 2018, www.idacraddock.com/wedding.html.

Crick, M. (1976). *Explorations in Language and Meaning*. New York: John Wiley & Sons.

DeBartolo, A. (1998, June 11). 'Newest' Apes Are Teaching Us About Ourselves. *Chicago Tribune*.

Dever, V. M. (n.d.). *Aquinas on the Practice of Prostitution*. Retrieved January 9, 2015, from Essays in Medieval Studies 13: http://www.illinoismedieval.org/ems/VOL13/13ch4.html

Dil, A. S., & Friedrich, P. (1979). *Language, Context, and the Imagination: Essays*. Stanford, Calif.: Stanford University Press.

Dodson, B. (1996). *Sex for One: The Joy of Selfloving*. New York: Crown Trade Paperbacks.

Ellis, J. (2014). *The Awesome Guide to Life: Get Fit, Get Laid, Get Your Sh*t Together*. New York, NY: HarperCollins Publishers Inc.

Garry, Ann. "Pornography and Respect for Women." *Social Theory and Practice*, 1978, pp. 395–421.

Genis, D. (2014, September 18). *A Gentleman's Guide to Sex in Prison*. Retrieved September 18, 2014, from The Concourse: http://theconcourse.deadspin.com/a-gentlemans-guide-to-sex-in-prison-1634995425

Giese, S. (2014, October 7). *Target's Response To My Calling Out Their Girls' Clothing Problem*. Retrieved October 7, 2014, from Huffington Post: http://www.huffingtonpost.com/stephanie-giese/targets-response-to-my-calling-out-their-girls-clothing-problem_b_5923274.html?1412286243&ncid=fcbklnkushpmg00000037

Gladwell, M. (2005). *Blink: The Power of Thinking Without Thinking*. New York: Little, Brown.

Gottman, J. (1999). *The Seven Principles for Making Marriage Work*. New York: Crown Publisher.

Grover, Lea. "This Is What Sex-Positive Parenting Really Looks Like." *The Huffington Post*, TheHuffingtonPost.com, 8 Nov. 2017, www.huffingtonpost.com/lea-grover/this-is-what-sex-positive-parenting-really-looks-like_b_5516707.html?ncid=fcbklnkushpmg 00000046&ir=Women.

Hicks, Esther. *Ask and It Is Given: An Introduction to the Teachings of Abraham-Hicks.* Hay House Inc, 2011.

Hill, A. A. (1969). *Linguistics Today.* New York: Basic Books, Inc.

Hill, N. (1988). *Think and Grow Rich.* New York: Fawcett Columbine.

Hill, N. (2011). *Outwitting the Devil.* Toronto, Ontario, Canada: Sterling Publisher.

Hillenbrand, L. (2010). *Unbroken: A World War II Story of Survival, Resilience, and Redemption.* New York: Random House.

Hingston, S. (2012, February 20). *The Sorry Lives and Confusing Times of Today's Young Men.* Retrieved December 13, 2014, from http://www.phillymag.com/articles/ the-sorry-lives-and-confusing-times-of-today-s-young-men/3/#fd4fKwzAvQoIL7kg.99

Holland, D. C. (1987). *Cultural Models in Language and Thought.* (N. Quinn, Ed.) Cambridgeshire: Cambridge University Press.

Houghton-Mifflin Company. (2003, November 16). *American-Heritage Dictionary of the English Language,* 4th. Retrieved from http://www.bartleby.com/61/24/L0262400.html

Jameson, J. (2004). *How to Make Love Like a Porn Star: A Cautionary Tale.* New York: ReganBooks.

Larsen, Aaron, et al. *The Art of Argument: an Introduction to the Informal Fallacies.* Classical Academic Press, 2010

Madigan, Timothy L. "The Discarded Lemon: Kant, Prostitution and Respect for Persons." *Philosophy Now: a Magazine of Ideas,* Philosophy Now, 1998, philosophynow.org/issues/21/ The_discarded_Lemon_Kant_prostitution_and_respect_for_persons.

Maltz, Maxwell. *Psychocybernetics: a New Way to Get More Living out of Life.* Wilshire Book Co., 1976.

McCasker, T. (2015, August 13). *The Emerging Fetish of Laying Alien Eggs Inside Yourself.* Retrieved October 22, 2015, from http://www.vice.com/en_au/read/ the-emerging-fetish-of-laying-alien-eggs-inside-yourself

Mellody, Pia, and Lawrence S. Freundlich. *The Intimacy Factor: the Ground Rules for Overcoming the Obstacles to Truth, Respect, and Lasting Love.* HarperSanFrancisco, 2004.

Meretrix, M. (2003, October 26). *In Nomine Babalon: Sacred Whoredom in a Thelemic Context.* Retrieved October 26, 2003, from Beds of Purple - Sex Magick, Sacred Whores, Spiritual Sex, Forums and More - Essays and Rituals: http://www.realm-of-shade.com/meretrix/beds/ essays/babalon.html

Merriam-Webster, Incorporated. (2004, April 7). *Merriam-Webster's Online.* Retrieved from http:// www.m-w.com

Miller, J. (2014, March 5). *How An Appropriate Use of Nakedness Can Promote the Goals of Religion, Spirituality, and Personal Development.* Retrieved March 5, 2014, from Ashtar Command Community: http://www.ashtarcommandcrew.net/profiles/blogs/ how-an-appropriate-use-of-nakedness-can-promote-the-goals-of

Pardes, A. (2014, September 14). *What You Masturbation Style Says About You.* Retrieved October 28, 2014, from Refinery 29: http://www.refinery29.com/masturbation?utm_source=email& utm_medium=editorial&utm_content=everywhere&utm_campaign=140927-masturbation -style#slide

Peters, C. (2004, March/April). Sex in Service of the Marketplace. *The Diogenes Lantern, 4*(2).

Phlias, Sex Terms, and Slang. (2002, December 4). Retrieved from Erophilia: http://www.erophilia. com/HTMLS/PHILIAS.html

"Playing Hard To Get | Dating 'The Rules' Vs 'The Game' | Soulmates | The Soulmates Blog." *The Guardian*, Guardian News and Media, 21 Mar. 2014, soulmates.theguardian.com/ blog/dating-locations/dating/dating-the-rules-vs-the-game#.WuKgMBZMGaM.

Random House. (1991). Love. In *Random House Webster's College Dictionary.* New York: Random House.

Random House. (1997). *Random House Webster's College Dictionary.* New York: Random House.

Redbook. (2014, October). Your Marriage Secrets. *Redbook, 223*(4).

Riley, J., & Rule, D. (2015, January 15). Kink 101. *Metro Weekly: Washington's LGBT Magazine*, p. 25.

Ross, B. (n.d.). *Dead End: Suburban Sprawl and the Rebirth of American Urbanism* (1st ed.). Oxford, England: Oxford University Press.

Ryan, J. (2002, April 2). *#1 Adult Sexual Health Terms Advisor.* Retrieved April 2, 2002, from http:// www.number-one-adult-sexual-health-terms-advisor.com/unusual.htm

Sapir, E. (1970). *Culture, Language, and Personality.* Los Angeles: University of California Press.

Schucman, Helen. *A Course in Miracles: Text, Workbook, Manual For Teachers.* Foundation for Inner Peace, 2007.

"Sexual Assault Prevention and Awareness Center." What Is Consent? | Sexual Assault Prevention and Awareness Center, University of Michigan, 2017, m.sapac.umich.edu/article/49.

Sheff, David. *Clean: Overcoming Addiction and Ending Americas Greatest Tragedy.* Houghton Mifflin Harcourt, 2014.

Silverman, S. (2010). *The Bedwetter: Stories of Courage, Redemption, and Pee.* New York: Harper.

Spalding, Tina Louise. *Jesus: My Autobiography.* Light Technology Publishing, 2015. p171 and p197

St. John, H. (2014, Fall). Nurturing Your Marriage. *The Virginia Home Educator.*

Stewart, J. (2004). *America (The Book): A Citizen's Guide to Democracy Inaction.* New York: Warner Books.

Strumpf, M. (2004). *The Grammar Bible: Everything You Always Wanted to Know About Grammar But Didn't Know Whom to Ask.* New York: Holt.

Tansey, L. (2003). *A Prostitutes Perspective on Feminism.* Retrieved 2003, from Sex Trade Opportunities for Risk Minimization: http://www.escapeprostitution.com/6.0tansey,%20pros%20 persp%20on%feminism.htm

The American Heritage Dictionary. (1992). *The American Heritage Dictionary of the English Language* (3rd ed.). Boston: Houghton Mifflin.

The Urantia Book Fellowship. (2003). *The Urantia Book: A Revelation* (Indexed Version ed.). New York, New York: Uversa.

Tirado, L. (2014). *Hand to Mouth: Living in Bootstrap America.* New York City, New York: G. P. Putnam's Sons.

Ulmer, G. L. (2003). *Internet Invention: From Literacy to Electracy.* New York: Longman.

Walker, Chris. "Reel Life: Netflix's Voyeur Doesn't Capture the Full Story of Gerald Foos." Westword, 21 Dec. 2017.

Walsch, Neale Donald. *The Complete Conversations with God: an Uncommon Dialogue*. Hampton Roads Pub. Co., 2005.

Webster, Inc. (2005). *The Merriam-Webster Dictionary* (New ed.). Springfield, Mass.: Merriam-Webster.

Weiss, B. (1988). *Many Lives, Many Masters*. New York: Simon & Schuster.

Wierzbicka, A. (1997). *Understanding Cultures Through Key Words*. New York: Oxford University Press.

Winthrop, J. (1730). *A Model of Christian Charity*. New England.

Ziglar, Z. (1979). *See You at the Top*. Gretna: Pelican Publishers.

Zilbergeld, B. (1992). *The New Male Sexuality*. New York: Bantam Books.

Index

About the Author

The sexiest author, by definition, is a cross between Barbara Carrellas and Aleister Crowley whose life was made for more than marriage (though it had room to include it). She is the Liz Earls for the second millenium, and the Mark Z. Danielewski for philosophy. Her idols are Jenna Jameson and Jason Ellis. She is a former polyamorous-con-slut-extraordinaire-cum-aspiring-sexologist (pun intended) and religious sex thinker with dreams of being trailer trash (as opposed to a Stepford wife) and being wanted dead or alive.

She is someone who listened to powerful female singers in the '80s and '90s and took third wave feminist ideas, or anti-second wave feminist ideas, and incorporated those into her beliefs (which, according to Abraham-Hicks, is a thought one keeps thinking) and lifestyle. However, in the end, she is a menist, like a feminist, but in support of men, who have more anxiety than women. The fact is that she lives in a patriarchy. Therefore, she believes that the people in power shoulld be the healthiest if we want to have a healthy society.

She is a zelig. The ability to fit in benefits a sexual connoisseur. She was an Asian in a white family and a Goth in a white collar job. If Asian is a culture, then she was as black as she was white. Fitting in is easy. Fitting in gives one more mobility, making it easier to go outside of your usual comfort zone haunts to meet new types of people. Variety is the spice of life. Though her astrological desire for newness can be detrimental in certain circumstances, it was the key to fulfilling her purpose of writing this book.

Lastly, the author was chosen to be a codependent by God, so that she could experience the extremes of human behavior and bring that understanding to the world so that no one else would have to suffer the challenges she faced. She is codependent so you, the reader, don't have to be. She is a lone warrior fighting a giant culture of hatred. She would have either made an excellent counselor or porn star. Where did she end up? In neither profession. She became a writer.

Writing, she defines, is like thinking of cute instant messenger away messages all the time and keeping a record of them. She knows that reality is stranger than fiction and finds nonfiction to be more revolutionizing and controversial than revolution couched in fiction.